The
English
Heritage

The English Heritage

J.H. Plumb

Frederic A. Youngs, Jr.

Henry L. Snyder

E. A. Reitan

David M. Fahey

FORUM PRESS

First Printing January 1978
Second Printing January 1979
Third Printing August 1979
Fourth Printing December 1980

Published simultaneously in Canada.

Printed in the United States of America.

Library of Congress Catalog Card Number: 77-92987

ISBN: 0-88273-350-8

Designed by Jerry Moore and Janet Moody

Maps designed by Norman T. Carpenter, and compiled and drafted by Patrick T. Biggar, John R. Parsons and Mr. Carpenter.

Contents

Maps

Preface

The English Heritage introduces one of the most remarkable national heritages the world has known. We may share that heritage directly because some of our ancestors were English in origin, yet even if our families have no English roots, the English heritage is ours because it exists in so many places and influenced so many societies where English people went. It belongs to whites in North American and Australia, to blacks in Nigeria and Jamaica, and to orientals in Hong Kong and India. The English heritage is itself a fusion of cultures — of Celts, Germans, Vikings, and French—and today is diffused to every continent. The Introduction of this text by Professor J. H. Plumb shows in particular how the English heritage and America are intertwined.

The English Heritage reflects the authors' belief that a brief introductory text best serves both the student and the professor. It sketches for the student the main aspects of England's heritage and introduces briefly the themes which will be developed more fully in class. It is a reference work to which one can return for clarification, a source of auxiliary aids such as maps and illustrations which stimulate and reinforce. Above all, it is the chronological framework into which can be set the information in lectures, discussions, and resources, all of which together are the heart of the course. A brief text allows the professor great flexibility in combining a variety of resources which reflect his or her interests and experience. *The English Heritage* is intended to be less than half a course's reading, a vital part in the total assignments which together will help introduce the diversity of the English heritage.

The English Heritage presents a compact and integrated whole, avoiding the lack of continuity in multi-part texts. Although of necessity politics and government form the chronological framework, great attention is given to English society, to the conditions in which English men and women lived, worked, prayed, studied, and enjoyed life. This balance in treatment justifies the use of the inclusive concept of heritage. There is special attention to the structures of English society, in order to re-create the institutions and attitudes within which English history developed. There are character sketches not only of political leaders, but also of people in many walks of life whose contributions shaped England's social and cultural heritage. Among the special features of *The English Heritage* are frequent studies on London, with sections on Chaucer's London in the middle ages, Shakespeare's London, Johnson's London of the urbane eighteenth century, Victorian London when English power was at its height, and modern, swinging London. Because the story of the English heritage spans over a thousand years, there are special pauses or "stocktakings" to evaluate where England stands at crucial points in its development—in 1485 near the close of the middle ages, in 1660 after the agony of the Civil Wars, in 1783 after the loss of the American colonies brought the "first Empire" to a close, at 1850 when industrialization had altered Victorian England, and in 1977 when Elizabeth II celebrated her Silver Jubilee as Queen.

The great joy of teaching is the sharing of something precious with young people willing to appreciate things of value. *The English Heritage* is thus dedicated to those who would know more of themselves by knowing England's heritage. The authors owe a debt of appreciation to their fellow historians whose comments and criticisms have helped make this a better book, and therefore express gratitude to Roy A. Austensen of Illinois State University, Richard Boyer of the University of Toledo, Robert C. Braddock of Saginaw Valley State College, Lawrence E. Breeze of Southeast Missouri State University, Suzann Buckley of the State University of New York at Plattsburgh, Charles Carlton of North Carolina State University, Valerie Cromwell of the University of Sussex, John F. Glaser of Ripon College, James M. Haas of Southern Illinois University, W. Kent Hackmann of the University of Idaho at Moscow, Thomas F. Hale of Idaho State University, Paul H. Hardacre of Vanderbilt University, Dale Hoak of the College of William and Mary, Daniel W. Hollis, III of Jacksonville State University, Henry G. Horwitz of the University of Iowa, Ray Kelch of San Francisco State University, Donald Lammers of Michigan State University, Arthur Marder of the University of California at Irvine, James I. Miklovich of the University of West Florida, Charles F. Mullett of the University of Missouri-Columbia, Patrick V. O'Dea of St. Bonaventure University, Jerome V. Reel, Jr. of Clemson University, Charles Ritcheson of the University of Southern California, Timothy J. Runyan of Cleveland State University, James Schmiechen of Illinois State University, Lois G. Schwoerer of George Washington University, Beverly A. Smith of the University of Cincinnati, Leo F. Solt of Indiana University, and R. Dean Ware of the University of Massachusetts-Amherst.

Because many will want to find additional information on the personalities and themes developed in *The English Heritage,* there is a section at the end of each chapter, SUGGESTIONS FOR FURTHER READING, which suggests helpful books and articles. There are a number of books which are basic to a fuller understanding of English history which cut across the chronological divisions of the individual chapters and are listed after Chapter 17.

The authors also wish to express their appreciation to the staff of Forum Press for their assistance in the publication of this book. We are especially grateful to Dorothy L. Ilgen for her editorial suggestions and guidance, and to Erby M. Young, Managing Director of Forum Press, who suggested the project and supported the authors throughout its development.

Frederic A. Youngs, Jr.
General Editor

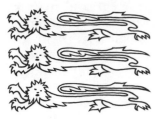

Britain & America
The Cultural
Heritage

J.H. Plumb

When the first English people landed and settled at Jamestown and Plymouth, they brought with them more than their tools, seed, and passionate religious faith. They were English people who accepted most of the institutions of their country as well as its history. History, for the Protestant Briton of King James I's reign, was the unfolding of God's purpose which he interpreted as having a very special role for the English. They were, as they were told in sermons, pamphlets and books such as Foxe's *Book of the Martyrs*, "God's Englishmen," the defenders of the true Protestant faith, an elected nation which had been chosen for a special, "manifest" destiny; indeed, chosen to rule. Theirs was a God-destined future of greatness. This deep belief quickly struck roots in American soil, grew and spread and flourished, and became an instinctive belief for the vast majority of Americans of the eighteenth, nineteenth, and twentieth centuries, breeding a confidence in the future that was only battered by the Great Depression and World War II. And it is impossible to understand America's sense of manifest destiny without understanding the interpretation seventeenth-century English people put on their own past. The roots of America's sense of its own greatness lie in Britain.

As with the belief in manifest destiny, so too the belief in liberty. Liberty was an ideal that seventeenth-century men and women, who emigrated to the New World in hopes of attaining their freedom, had deeply rooted in their heritage. The most fundamental liberties of Americans which are based on English common law were hard won by the English in their long struggle during the Middle Ages with the ever-encroaching feudal monarchy. The results of this medieval struggle for liberty are symbolized by Magna Carta, the jury system, Parliament, and countless other institutions and laws, such as the sheriff, the justice of the peace, and common law — all of which have their American counterparts. Those early seventeenth-century colonists began their search for freedom in the New World in a new society structured on the one they had forsaken.

Strong common roots were further extended in the seventeenth and eighteenth centuries. Quickening commerce, a thickening population in the great Eastern seaports created what was, in effect, an extension of British society. Up to the Revolution, America was a part of British society as much as Yorkshire or the Lowlands of Scotland, and much more so than Ireland or the Scottish Highlands.

Without intending to diminish in any way the unique qualities of much American experience and culture, this author would rather stress the vitality of our common culture which burgeoned during the first centuries of American history. For about a hundred years after the Revolution this commonality of culture was strongest in New England and amongst its educated elite. And the cultural leadership belonged to Britain. After 1870 the English influence on American cultural life was threatened by waves of immigration from other European countries. The cultural bond might easily have been broken at that time but it was not, even though the relationship changed drastically. From 1910 America took the leadership and stimulated not an elitist culture, but a mass culture in Britain. The key to understanding the deep roots of our cultural relationship, now three-and-a-half centuries old, lies in the nature of American society, particularly between 1720-1820, when America was a part of provincial Britain — possessing some individual characteristics but in essence British.

Some of the difficulty of understanding the close and complex involvement of Britain and America stems from the natural propensity of all English travellers after the Revolution to look for, and harp on, the differences between the two countries and to take the similarities for granted. Furthermore, from the early days of the Republic, Americans themselves began to stress their independence, not only of Britain, but also of Europe, and to take pride in what was purely American — a note struck by George Washington himself at his Inauguration. On May 6, 1789, the *Gazette of the United States* reported that "The President of the United States on the day of his inauguration appeared dressed in a complete suit of homespun clothes, but the cloth was so fine a fabric, and so handsomely finished that it was universally mistaken for a foreign manufactured superfine cloth. This fact, the editor hopes, will apologize for his not having mentioned in his last paper a circumstance which would be considered as not only flattering to one manufacturer in particular, but interesting to our countrymen in general." The Vice-President followed the President's example, as did, to the editor's delight, several members of Congress.

There was a growing awareness during this era of the institutions of social life and politics by both American writers and European (mainly English) writers who were determined to look for differences, or to claim as novel to America what indeed was hoary with age in Britain. Between 1785 and 1835 there were about eighty books published in English about America that divide sharply into rosy-tinted propaganda for emigrants to bitter criticism by middle-class writers and journalists, an attitude that was maintained with the ever increasing volume of literature about America that was published throughout the nineteenth century. Francis Trollope, Charles Dickens, even Rupert Brooke, complained contemptuously of tobacco chewing, spitting, meals bolted, overheated houses, absence of ruined abbeys, Elizabethan mansions or a single building of hoary antiquity (a point made more subtly by Matthew Arnold). There was, at times, lukewarm praise for American hospitality, for the acceptance of equality between rich and not so rich, and the absence of true poverty by European standards. Most writers condemned slavery out of hand, ignoring the conditions of the factory system in northern England or the exploitation of their own workers at home. The vast bulk of this literature is as tedious as it is superficial, whether enticing immigrants or disdaining Americans.

There was greater insight shown by Alexis de Tocqueville in his writings on the United States. Although fearful of the long-term effects of democracy which he felt quite wrongly to be a threat to liberty (it was only a threat to liberties, and not much of a threat to these), there were institutions he greatly admired, indeed selected for especial praise. Almost unfailingly these were British by origin — for example, the jury system and the town meeting in New England. The jury system was of Anglo-Saxon origins and a New England town meeting would have been familiar to a moderately well-to-do English peasant of the fifteenth, sixteenth, or seventeenth centuries — similar to his village meeting, which took place in a parish church. England as well as New England had its village democracies. Nevertheless, de Toqueville did illuminate very real differences in American social structure compared with Europe. Even so, some, like equality, he exaggerated; others, such as democracy, had distinct British origins.

Naturally, American historians, philosophers, politicians and commentators looked for, or invented, specially American attributes. In many ways their attitude to England and to Europe was similar to a provincial Englishman's attitude to London. The Old World was corrupted by age and luxury, especially luxury that led to a decay of all standards in politics and morals. And it was a matter of pride to point to the obvious tyrannies of monarchy and aristocracy from which America had freed herself. Much of this is true. As John Adams reiterated almost to the point of boredom, America was a simple, more unsophisticated, and more egalitarian society. But the public and private morality of America, its simple virtues, were grotesquely exaggerated; as John Adams mournfully realized, the primitive provincial style of life could not last.

Americans insisted that they had achieved the first free democratic society and American historians in the nineteenth century, from Jared Sparks to Francis Parkman, believed that America's experience was unique as well as God-destined. By the miracle of the Revolution it had avoided not only the corruptions of England, but also those of Europe; and in so doing had discovered its providential destiny which was to be the bulwark of liberty and freedom and the guardian of the highest public morality. As Washington Irving wrote to John Lothrop Motley, "the American Press [was] — that rising tribunal before which the whole world is to be summoned, its history revised and re-written, and the judgment of past ages cancelled or confirmed" — an arrogant statement as any affirmation of religious bigots. In essence that was its origin. Irving was expressing in secular terms the ideas and hopes for American society which had stirred the hearts and minds of William Bradford or John Winthrop, who believed that God had directed them to create a New Jerusalem on America's shores. And again this was mere repetition of what many a stern English Puritan felt about England itself. Although a millennialist theology might be translated into a manifest destiny for the New England elite, social attitudes reach far deeper than the mystifying magic of words.

From the 1690s, if not before, from Massachusetts to Virginia, social life had been steadily secularized, and secularized in almost precisely the same ways that English life, both metropolitan and provincial, had been. There had been a similar development in politics (not surprisingly if one bears in mind that America was a part of provincial Britain). More Americans and Britons were becoming aware of purely political issues, developing criticism of what they both felt to be political persuasion and pressure. In both societies they were active groups of men bent on radical change. In America they became supporters of the Revolution and won; in England they became the supporters of America and lost.

To understand the true depths of these relationships one must take a close look at the eighteenth-century experience. From the early eighteenth century onwards both England and her American colonies enjoyed a great expansion of commerce. This is the period when the Virginian planters no longer thought of themselves as transients in search of a fortune that was to establish them in affluence in Britain. They began, as Edmund Morgan has shown, to build brick houses, to import British furniture, pottery, and silverware, or to patronize local craftsmen who could imitate with some fidelity British fashions. As Henry Laurens wrote, "The planters are full of money." What was true of Williamsburg or Charlestown was also true of Boston and Newport, of New York and Philadelphia (which, by 1770, was the second largest city in the British Empire); and its prosperous and growing middle class were educated, entertained, housed, clothed and equipped like their counterparts in Birmingham or Bristol. The extraordinary surge in American population between 1700 and 1800 was phenomenal, and this growth both increased the numbers of the middle classes and their purchasing power. This growth was mainly, if not entirely, of British origin, either by natural increase or immigration. The large German element in Pennsylvania was not strong enough to maintain for more than a decade or so a powerful separate culture. Apart from the Negro slaves and, to a lesser extent, the Catholic Irish in New York and Boston, ethnicity was of no great importance to American society before the middle of the nineteenth century, perhaps later.

Philadelphia or Boston, like Bristol or Liverpool in England, developed a prosperous commercial oligarchy who were earnest-minded and concerned very much with cultural self-improvement for themselves and for their children, but not averse to modest ostentation or inexpensive amusement. And much of their taste was formed by London, by its craftsmen, its artists, its writers, and its fashionable men and women; provincial England, stimulated by its own wealth and London's example in the eighteenth century underwent a cultural revolution; America, which was but a more distant province, underwent exactly the same experience.

England witnessed the growth of a provincial newspaper press; so did America. Newspapers were established in Savannah, Charlestown, Williamsburg, Philadelphia, New York, Connecticut, Rhode Island, and Massachusetts. By 1750 twelve newspapers had been published in America; by 1775, forty-eight. They were identical in shape, layout and content to those printed in England. And one of their prime features was to alert their readers to cultural activity — books, music, theatre, scientific lectures, or the arrival of new fashions. The magazine, which played so large a part in England's literary culture, rooted itself more slowly in America, but Americans were not deprived of such reading.

One consignment of books, in April 1775, from Thomas Longman of London to Henry Knox of the London Bookstore in Boston, consisted of fifty London Magazines, sixty Town and Country Magazines, twenty Gentleman's Magazines, twelve Universal Magazines, fifteen Oxford Magazines and, notably, twenty-eight Lady's Magazines. The same consignment contained a parcel of Oliver Goldsmith's *She Stoops to Conquer,* which enjoyed the same public success in America as Goldsmith's *Deserted Village,* both bestsellers in England. In Boston there were, in 1771, ten printers and publishers, eight booksellers and six printers who were also booksellers, which is comparable to an English provincial town of the same size. The British methods of stimulating sales were also used by American booksellers — printed catalogues, book auctions, and circulating libraries. All the side-lines exploited by the English provincial booksellers — patent medicines, prints, musical and artistic materials, printed forms, and sometimes even tea — were used by American booksellers. Most of the developments in the diffusion of printed materials were almost contemporaneous with those in England; at the most rarely more than a decade later.

W. Guthrie, who had spent a part of his early life in America, maintained that "learning was more generally diffused among all ranks of the people than any other part of the globe." A mature illiterate, he said, was a great rarity. Certainly the spread of newspapers, libraries and the like was quite remarkable. By 1790, over thirty thousand copies of newspapers were printed weekly in New England. Before that date Connecticut had over one hundred libraries. And we know that the Charleston Library Society, the first circulating library in the South, opened in 1743, had over 6000 volumes, which compared very favourably with similar libraries in Norwich, England. In these libraries and bookshops, the overwhelming majority of books and pamphlets and prints were English. As in the English provinces, there was a small but steady growth of local publication; during the Revolution there was certainly a surge of pamphlets written by Americans, but even then the situation is more confused than is commonly allowed. There were eighty-four pamphlets which explained the relations between America and Britain between 1764 and 1770; thirty-seven of these were published immediately in Britain, and all the major English pamphlets, as well as newspaper articles, were published in America. After the pamphlet war subsided, the situation was largely that which had preceded the Revolution — whether it was novels, plays, histories, divinity, children's books, geography, or the classics, the Americans, for the most part, read English authors or English translations. Hence, the literary culture was essentially English until long, long after the Revolution. The implications of that situation are vast, too vast to explore here in all their complexity.

Education, so prominent in early American life, once more presents a mirror image of what is happening in England. In both places a purely classical education was felt to be increasingly inadequate to a growing commercial world. Nevertheless, in Boston and in Philadelphia classical education was as deeply entrenched as in Newcastle-upon-Tyne or Bristol. Its supporters were still capable of victories; under the Rev. William Smith, the Boston Latin School swamped the department devoted to English and practical studies in Benjamin Franklin's Academy. Eton, Westminster, Winchester and other public schools in England resisted innovation and stuck limpet-like to the classics. But clerks and navigators were needed, and the new aspiring middle class demanded for their sons and daughters an education that was both practical and genteel, that would lead to a professional career as well as to social polish. This need was satisfied on both sides of the Atlantic in a similar fashion. Enterprising men and women opened schools, provided the subjects required — anything from surveying to modern languages — charged fees, and hoped for a profit. Between 1740-76, over one hundred and twenty-five teachers offered their services in Philadelphia, all of them concerned with "modern" subjects. This compares surprisingly closely with the one hundred schools advertised in the *Northampton Mercury* between 1720-60, or the sixty-three in the *Norwich Mercury* between 1749-59 — all advertising similar subjects. The trend in Leeds, England, was felt in New York: by 1730, it was possible for the industrious apprentice to attend evening school to learn reading and writing and arithmetic. In these schools, the books used were English text books; indeed, more often than not the schoolmasters and mistresses were themselves English immigrants.

Just as in Britain, there was in America a passion for self-improvement, and an insatiable appetite for new knowledge, particularly new scientific knowledge, and the itinerant scientific lecturer, with his electrical machines and complex automated gadgets, was as ubiquitous in the major cities of America as in the provinces of England; electricity, magnetism, and astronomy were the great draws in both countries. Both countries were alert to novelty. The first balloon, decorated with stars and stripes, to rise in Philadelphia was in 1785, the same year that saw a balloon take off from the pleasure gardens in Bury St. Edmunds, Suffolk. The science lectures, the curious new inventions, and the balloons created in both places a sense of wonder and encouraged a belief in the value of modernity — that improvement of man's lot could be achieved by experiment and mechanical ingenuity. This view was previously held by an elite, but was now spreading in both societies like a dye.

If we move from literature, learning, and education to the

decorative arts, whether it be painting or gardening, we discover the same dependence on the maturer culture of Britain. It could be accidental (although that would be highly improbable) that America's first important painters — Benjamin West, John Singleton Copley, Gilbert Stuart, and Charles Willson Peale — were contemporaneous with the great flowering of English art, or that at a lower level the cities of both countries should be flooded with drawing masters during the middle decades of the eighteenth century. And in both countries, there was strong stress on a double social value of artistic training. It made the drawings of mechanics and engineers more exact, hence useful for boys; indeed, advertisements in both countries stress its utility. It also, however, provided a genteel accomplishment for girls.

There was a similar resonance in music; provincial concert halls did not exist in England in 1700, in 1770 they abounded. In 1700 none existed in America, by 1770 all the major cities possessed a room in which musical events took place; and as in England, the favourite composer was Handel. In gardening, too, there was a keen interest in both countries. English botanists were deeply excited by the flora of America and imported large quantities of specimens, many of which were quickly domesticated. Virginia oaks could be bought by the thousands from several nurseries in England in the early eighteenth century. What is less commonly known is that England exported large quantities of vegetable seeds because the skill in developing new and improved varieties had not been developed in America. Although the kidney bean was native to America, improved seeds were being imported into Boston from London in large quantities. On February 28, 1774, Elizabeth Greenleaf was offering fifty-four varieties of vegetable seeds imported from London — peas, beans, carrots, savory, cauliflower, cabbage, lettuce, onion, endive, parsnip, beet, radish, spinach; seven other seedsellers (of whom five were women) were advertising in the Boston press an equally comprehensive list of vegetable seeds at that same time. The Bostonians may have rejected English tea, but they certainly consumed English vegetables!

All this clearly demonstrates that the texture of social life in America before, during, and long after the Revolution was, in all essentials, predominately English. It was, of course, most marked in the middle and lower middle classes of the cities, but in no way confined to them. The most important aspect of this common culture, from literature to garden seeds, was its stress on novelty, on modernity, on the exciting virtues of material things; that a new world of experiment and change, of expanding commerce and social delight was becoming available to more and more people. Here are the roots of America's social ethic which were being successfully transplanted from British soil. The fabric of a common social life that is so closely woven could not be easily torn up and destroyed by a political Revolution; indeed it never has been. America developed to the full much of the social culture of eighteenth-century England, which was partially inhibited in England itself, during the nineteenth century, by the growth of imperial responsibility.

There are yet deeper linkages than these, and ones which, curiously enough, rivet America more closely to some aspects of England of the eighteenth century than present-day England itself. One such linkage is the American Constitution, for the American Constitution can be best understood in the context of English history.

In the seventeenth century, English persons radically opposed to the undefined prerogatives of monarchy, who had the *Magna Carta* very much in their minds, attempted time and time again to obtain a written constitution. *The Agreement of the People* and *The Humble Petition and Advice* were such attempts during the constitutional upheavals of the Civil War and Commonwealth. In 1689, the more radical Whigs, worried by the exploitation by James II of his prerogative rights, attempted once more to obtain a written constitution of *The Bill of Rights.* Fortunately or unfortunately, their attempt was whittled down in committee to a mild condemnation of the King's misdemeanours. The decision to draw up a written constitution for America was not an inspired piece of originality — a new departure in political practice — but one that arose from the long tradition of English constitutional debate.

There was a widespread belief in eighteenth-century England, amongst Tories as well as radicals, that the glaring corruption of eighteenth-century politics was a betrayal both of the inherent virtues of the British constitution and of the ideals of the seventeenth century. The Tories, led by Charles Davenant, Lord Bolingbroke and others, believed that the balance of the constitution had been overturned. The executive had come to dominate the legislature, and worse still, the prerogatives of the crown had been filched by self-interested politicians and exercised in their own and not the national interest. Hence royal prerogatives needed to be restored; that is the burden of Bolingbroke's *Idea of a Patriot King.* The radical Whigs, also, regarded the corruption of the legislature by the executive as the negation of Parliament's independence. Indeed, what the founding fathers set about doing was to create a constitution on British lines purged of its decadence. Considering that many of them had been raised on the literature of the English political opposition, it is not surprising that this was so. Their political assumptions were strengthened by their reverence for Montesquieu, who had absorbed the same mistaken views of the English opposition as to the true, uncorrupted nature of the British constitution.

As the English had done after the execution of Charles I, the Americans abolished monarchy and aristocracy, or so they thought. Aristocracy certainly, but monarchy — not quite. True, the Presidency was not hereditary and the occupation of the office limited in tenure, but the powers were those which many of the Tory opposition in England wished to see restored to the monarchy, as for example, the right to veto. Queen Elizabeth II still, in theory, possesses that right. The royal veto has not been exercised for nearly three hundred years; the practice was moribund by George III's day. The founding fathers, however, endowed the President with this obsolete monarchical prerogative.

Technically, the British monarch had the right to appoint his executive, and, although the Hanoverians were steadily losing that right not only to appoint but even to reject, they retained, even in 1770, vestigial powers, but compared with the power given to the President, their influence was minimal. Similarly both monarch and President were commanders in chief of their countries, but, again, the influence of the monarchy in Britain on all army and naval appointments was rapidly waning by the time of the Revolution. The Queen now exercises no personal power whatever in military affairs. The President's power is still massive. These prerogatives given to the American head of state were not drawn from Ancient Greece or Rome or from the treatises of political philosophy, but from the former practices of British Constitution which many British Tories wished to see re-established. It could be argued that the American President is an *ad hoc* Stuart monarch in civilian clothes.

Similarly, the separation of powers; that the executive, judicature and legislature should be entirely independent of each other, had become a cliché of opposition politics in England long before the birth of any of the founding fathers. Almost every year from 1690, the King's men of business in the House of Commons were denounced, and their exclusion demanded; and from time to time the opposition secured a success and removed some. Likewise the long life of the House of Commons was a matter of constant debate from the Revolution of 1688 to the nineteenth century; hence the proper duration of legislatures was not a matter to which the men who drafted the constitution came with blank and open minds; the debate in England had been largely concerned with the merits of annual Parliaments or triennial ones. And like the Tory opposition in England, the founding fathers came down on the side not only of the total separation of powers, but also of frequency of elections.

Again, when the composition of the senate was debated, there was no reference, as far as this author knows, to the English Parliament. There was great debate about the balance between the North and the

South. Nevertheless, it is hard to believe that the makers of the Constitution were not influenced by British practice. The most prestigious members of the House of Commons were the Knights of the Shire. They were men of great substance in their counties, and usually belonged to families of long standing. They were regarded as the most honest, the most independent and the least corruptible members of the Commons. There were two from each shire — two from tiny Rutland, far smaller than Rhode Island, and two only from England's largest county — Yorkshire, some twenty times larger and more populous than Rutland. The similarity with the composition of the Senate is too close for accident. No other constitution in the world has adopted so idiosyncratic a system. After the reform of 1832, Britain departed from this system and made the county representation correspond, roughly at least, with property and people. (Representation by population was, of course, established by the Constitution.) America has maintained the system so that Alaska or Hawaii have equal voice with New York and California in the Senate, another quaint eighteenth-century heritage.

Again, American historians and politicians often congratulate themselves on their democratic institutions, or on the extent of the suffrage after the Revolution. Leaving on one side the validity of that claim, it is well worthwhile pointing out, however, that the democratic experience of England in the seventeenth and early eighteenth centuries — a time when emigration from Britain was so considerable — was far more profound than is commonly realized. Recent research by Derek Hirst and this author has shown that the electorates of the English county constituencies were vast during this period. The forty-shilling freehold, which was the qualification for the suffrage that, owing to the rapidity of inflation in the sixteenth century, had embraced, as Hirst has shown, almost all adult males with a cottage by 1640. Indeed, the size of the electorate remained a menace to men of property, creating a necessity for the debate of political issues and forcing up costs to such an extent that finally the only way to avoid this difficult electorate was not to hold elections at all. The concept that men of very small property, of a value of no more than forty shillings — quite insignificant by the eighteenth century — was a part of the English tradition, and was transplanted in the seventeenth and early eighteenth centuries in America.

More important are economic ties and development. The greatest revolution in human living since men began to grow food and domesticate animals has been the development of industrialized society. Society was first industrialized in Britain — the growth of the factory system, the invention of a moveable source of energy, the steam engine; the deliberate investment of large and small scale capital in industrial development, whether it be canals or railways or a small factory with steam-driven machinery — all of these factors and many more gave Britain world leadership in industrial growth up to the 1840s. Her machinery, her methods, her capital, and her craftsmen crossed the Atlantic with exceptional rapidity and began the industrial revolution in America. As in so many other ways, America developed and made more sophisticated the techniques and inventions taken from Britain. And this symbiotic relationship has lasted down to modern times. Not only did Britain invent the steam engine and the railway train but also the jet engine, radar, the computer — all of which America has developed and sold back to the world.

In religion, too, the influence of England is exceedingly large, if not paramount; Episcopalians, Presbyterians, Congregationalists, Baptists, all descend directly from either the Church of England or its dissenting sects. Methodism swept America as it swept England in the eighteenth century, and John Wesley and George Whitfield played as significant a role in the religious history of America as they did in their own country. As with political, legal, and economic institutions, the churches with which Britain endowed America are more vigorous than in their country of origin. But there is one vital difference. The founding fathers wisely separated Church and State, a separation which has never taken place in England. This bred in the youthful America a tolerance of belief that took at least another century to achieve in the mother country where the ruling class was so closely identified with Anglicanism.

Yet political institutions and traditions, legal forms and procedures, even the origins of religious beliefs and rituals, important as they are to the common heritage of America and Great Britain, might not have sustained the close bond between the two countries. There were other factors of varying importance. The strongest was the maintenance of a common cultural tradition. The texture of social life of England and America, as has been stressed, was very close between 1700 and 1850. Differences there were, and they increased as the nineteenth century progressed, but a great deal survived, and this is particularly true in the world of scholarship and letters. So long as New England dominated the literary world of America, as it did for most of the nineteenth century, authors of both countries shared a common audience because their educational background and cultural assumptions were so similar. Longfellow and Emerson were as popular in Britain as Tennyson and Carlyle. There was scarcely a writer of any stature in either country who did not have a following in the other; this was particularly true of English authors as American publishers could pirate them at will. But the process was a reverse one, too; Mark Twain had as idolatrous a readership in England as America. And at a lower level of literature, America has played an enormous and vital part in the imagination of young English men and women. They read avidly not only James Fennimore Cooper but also Zane Grey; English children played endlessly at cowboys and Indians. They built covered wagons or wigwams in gardens, hunted imaginary buffalo and day after day scalped the boy next door. The American West was as much a part of every English boy's dream life as it was of the boys in New York or Boston, and it was based entirely on cheap literature, "the Westerns" of the local circulating libraries.

However, this common mass readership might have been endangered in the twentieth century — the vast waves of immigration began to change our common language and rendered Americans far more esoteric to Britons; novelists, poets, writers of every kind began to explore the experience of the South, Middle West and West, or the Jewish world of New York, all deeply foreign to English experience. But the common literary culture was sustained, indeed revived and expanded by technological inventions. From 1910 to 1940 the dream world of America, created in Hollywood, became the dream world of Europe, but most particularly of England where, once talking pictures were introduced, language was no bar. As well as the film, popular American music swept across the Atlantic and flooded Britain. Increasingly, American life-styles in varied ways began to root themselves in the British lower middle and working classes. With television, the process was carried further. Since World War II the flood of cultural influence has, however, partially reversed the direction. When the British television show, Monty Python's Flying Circus, intensely British nonsense, cluttered with British slang, became a huge popular success all over America, the cultural divergence between the two societies could no longer be regarded as an unbridgeable chasm.

And what has happened to mass culture, has, to a very large extent, been matched by a strengthening of common bonds at the highest levels of culture — a revival and strengthening of our mutual involvement. The spread of science, exchange of technology, the growth of scholarship, the proliferation of universities in the second half of the twentieth century, has led to a massive exchange of intellectuals belonging to all subjects and disciplines, unique in the world's history. The Greco-Roman cultural interchange was complex and far-reaching, but not comparable in any way to the Anglo-American experience. And a common language, although fundamental, for language defines so many of our responses as well as the patterns of our thinking, is not the only answer. Equally important is history; the history of a common past. For the best part of two hundred years America was a part of British society in all of its aspects, in some ways far more so than Scotland or Ireland, in spite of obvious provincial differences such as the theocratic nature of New England society or slavery in the South.

From about 1680-1770 England and America developed a social structure, a way of living that was intensely close, sufficiently close for it to persist long after the Revolution itself. True, it steadily weakened; in 1870, America was a far more alien place to most Englishmen than it had been in 1770. Probably the cultural and social strands that bound us together were weakest about the turn of this century, when they began to strengthen again, at first not amongst the elite, but on a mass basis. Naturally this has been all too frequently denounced as shallow, vulgar, strident, plastic, a semi-literate dreamland. No worse, if no better, than the popular culture that both countries enjoyed in the eighteenth century — the fatuous novels like *The History of Cornelia* or *The Adventures of a Guinea,* or the crude cartoons, the boring ballads and tediously sentimental plays. Then, as now, the culture of the sophisticated was not alien to a mass culture, not a separate enterprise, but grew out of it and at times reflected it.

Americans are not merely English with different accents, nor are American political, legal, and social institutions entirely British, somewhat distorted by time and experience. Nevertheless, the uniqueness of America, the distinctive, quintessential nature of itself, has been overstressed in recent decades; and the common roots of much of our social and political experience and more particularly of our intellectual and cultural traditions avoided or ignored. It seems to me that England and America have enjoyed, and still enjoy, a unique historical experience; a mutual heritage of language, institutions, and culture that must, for the foreseeable future, create a special relationship no matter how politicians may seek to define it or evade its implications. These can only be understood in the context of each other's histories.

The
English
Heritage

I
The Earliest Britons

to 1042

When the glaciers of the ice ages receded, Britain was part of the European land mass, but about 8000 B.C. glacial melting raised the level of the sea to form the North Sea and the English Channel and to leave Britain as an island. The sea was no real protection — wave after wave of invaders came from continental Europe so that the story of the creation of the English state is at first an appreciation of what the different invading people contributed to an emerging British culture.

THE EARLIEST BRITONS

The earliest large migration of Europeans across the Channel came around 2750 to 2500 B.C. These settlers are called Windmill Hill people after the name of the archaeological site where the remains of their camps were found. Because the weapons and utensils of their Stone Age culture were not very versatile, they settled on the open unforested plains of the south and east where hunting, the grazing of animals, and some light ploughing were possible. For protection they dug circular ditches around the camps and used the dirt to form stockades. About 1900 B.C. a warlike people whose tools, weapons, and ornaments were

ABOVE 500 FEET
BELOW 500 FEET

0   100
MILES

0   100
KILOMETERS

Berwick

Tweed R.

CHEVIOT HILLS

Newcastle

Carlisle   Durham

SOLWAY FIRTH

LAKE DISTRICT

PENNINE MOUNTAINS

NORTH

SEA

York

HUMBER

IRISH

Mersey R.

Chester

Trent R.

Witham R.

THE WASH

Lincoln

Derby

Nottingham

SEA

CAMBRIAN MOUNTAINS

Shrewsbury

Severn R.

Welland R.

Norwich

Wye R.

Ouse R.

Stour R.

Cambridge

Gloucester

COTSWOLDS

Colchester

Oxford

CHILTERNS

River

Thames

Bath

SALISBURY PLAIN

London

Canterbury

Salisbury

Winchester

DOWNS

Dover

EXMOOR

Exe R.

DARTMOOR

Tamar R.

Exeter

Plymouth

ENGLISH CHANNEL

TOPOGRAPHY OF THE
BRITISH ISLES

made of bronze entered and captured Britain. Called the Beaker people because of the characteristic shape of their drinking vessels, the new wave of invaders became so economically successful from grazing and breeding animals that they were able to undertake trade with lands thousands of miles distant, selling not only agricultural products but also beautifully fashioned ornaments and jewelry.

Some idea of the Beaker people's level of development can be gained from the impressive monuments which they built. At Avebury the largest of the concentric circles of massive stones had a diameter of 1400 feet and included nearly thirty acres. At Stonehenge the inner ring consisted of vertical stones thirty feet high which weighed five tons apiece, joined by equally large stones laid horizontally across them. The whole site included outer concentric rings and was probably a temple for sun worship, but from recent computer-assisted calculations an astronomer has argued that Stonehenge was also an astronomical calendar and clock of great sophistication. The implications of such a theory are far-reaching, suggesting that the monument's builders had the economic abundance and religious commitment needed to dedicate labor and material to a construction project which took many years, the mathematical competence to make alignments and take measurements of celestial movements with amazing accuracy, the engineering skill to move huge stones hundreds of miles from the quarry, and perhaps the political unity which guaranteed the peaceful conditions needed to erect the monument.

From the eighth to the first centuries B.C. there were successive waves of invaders called Celts who used iron in their weapons, tools, and implements. Iron plows could turn the soil and make agriculture more productive, and the Celts worked skillfully with metals to fashion swords, daggers, and shields, and luxury goods such as brooches. Regions began to specialize in different products and trade between them was facilitated by minting coins. The new Britons exported to continental Celts many products such as grain, leather, animals, and highly prized tin, which was mined in the western regions.

The increase in populations from newer migrations caused a severe competition for land. The Celts grew more warlike and aggressive, erecting hillside forts and venerating the warriors as an aristocracy. As a result of continued fighting several more stable kingdoms were formed from the smaller tribal groups. A priestly caste called the Druids conducted sacrifices for many gods, kept the oral traditions and laws, divined the future from omens, and perhaps conducted human sacrifices. About 75 B.C. a particularly fierce group of Celts called the Belgae occupied Britain and they continued to assist their relations who had remained behind in northern Gaul. The latter were threatened by the conquering Roman armies, and because the northern flank of the

Stonehenge.

Roman Empire would be safe only when Gaul was secure and the aid from Britain was stopped, the Roman general Julius Caesar looked toward the British Isles.

ROMAN BRITAIN

The Military Conquest. Caesar attacked in 55 B.C. with two legions, each with six to seven thousand soldiers. The Celts resisted fiercely and after several partly successful engagements the Romans returned to Gaul. Caesar began the attack afresh the following year with five legions and the Romans decisively defeated the Celtic kings of the southeast. The Romans did not intend an occupation and allowed the conquered Celts self-government provided they paid tribute and agreed to live in peace without aiding Rome's enemies. These arrangements lasted nearly a century, allowing the Celts great opportunities for trading within the Roman Empire and a breathing space for political consolidation. These successes made the Celts chafe at their dependent status and so in 43 A.D. the Romans decided to invade and occupy Britain in order to end the military and political dangers which the Celts posed.

This time the invaders skillfully separated the Celtic forces and won decisive victories at the onset. In the next thirty years the Romans moved their control westward and northward into the mountainous regions. They suffered occasional defeats as when Queen Boudicca led her people in rebellion in 60 A.D. and destroyed nearly an entire Roman legion in battle. When in 70 A.D. a previously friendly buffer state in the north turned hostile, the Romans mounted a massive military effort and then erected the town of Eboracum (later called York) to consolidate the hard-won successes.

The Romans succeeded because their army was such a formidable fighting force, a self-sufficient and mobile town on the move which carried the equipment needed to overcome man-made fortresses and to deal with natural barriers by erecting bridges and roads. The soldiers were extensively trained in marching and fighting, and after twenty-one years of well-paid and respected service the state offered them special privileges if they would settle in areas near the frontier to be available if their military talents were ever needed again. The Romans called these fortified places *castra* and the survival of names in variant English forms — Chester, Colchester, Gloucester, Exeter — shows how extensively the Romans organized the conquered country. Three legions were normally stationed in Britain, about a tenth of the Roman Empire's entire fighting force, but the Romans were still unable to conquer all the island. The northern frontier was set soon after the troops in the north suffered a severe defeat in 122 A.D., when the Emperor Hadrian then had a wall built across an eighty-mile narrow stretch to keep out the Picts who occupied what later would become Scotland.

Life in Roman Britain. Secure behind the military shield, the civilian areas of Roman Britain enjoyed the most advanced civilization in the western world in common with the rest of the Empire. "Civilization" refers generally to the social heritage of ideas, attitudes, and style of living which one people passes on to its descendants. For the Romans civilization meant life in cities, and thus Roman Britain was a network of cities linked together by well engineered, straight roads. The cities had wide streets laid out at right angles and enclosed within protective walls. The center was the forum, an open square onto which faced the basilica, the hall for public meetings. There were temples, baths, shops for the highly developed economic life of the town, and homes whose exteriors were often shops but in which the domestic area centered interiorly on open courtyards. The floors of the richer homes were made of tiled mosaics, the walls plastered and colorfully painted, the windows made of glass, and the whole heated by a central heating system which used a system of pipes and water. Underground sewers kept the cities clean and outside the walls there was sometimes an arena

Roman baths, Bath (Bath City Council, Department of Leisure and Tourist Services).

for pageants and sports.

Life within the cities was varied and cultured. Young men and women were tutored in Greek and Roman literature and philosophy and practised oratory. There were theaters for plays, baths for relaxation and gambling. The Emperor was worshipped officially for the sake of political unity but other gods were venerated as well. Christianity came to Britain at first as one of many religions, then in later years finally became the religion of the Empire. The upper ranks of British society were greatly influenced by Roman culture but the vast majority of Britons were completely unaffected. Their lives were centered in the rural settlements, on farming and raising animals. The only important Roman presence in the countryside was on estates known as villas. They differed considerably in size but in general were large-scale farming operations with many workers under a well-to-do and highly romanized owner. Because the villas were self-sufficient they had little impact on the native Britons nearby.

The first decay in Roman life in Britain came when many city dwellers started to move to the countryside to escape the high taxes and public demands of city life. The decline in urban living sapped the cultural vitality of Roman Britain and contributed to a loss of political unity. In the third and fourth centuries many soldiers stationed in Britain were recalled to the continent because of political difficulties in the crumbling Roman Empire. Faced with the prospect of being left defenseless, the British appealed to Rome for assistance — only to be told by the Emperor Honorius in 409 to look after their own safety. The Britons were ill-prepared for fighting because the Roman soldiers had guaranteed the peace for centuries. Thus the British sought the services of German mercenaries to protect their island. Ironically, in time the Germans would be responsible for totally eradicating Roman culture from Britain. Roman ways would indeed have a role in shaping later Britain, but that came only when in later centuries the Christian church reintroduced many Roman practices.

ANGLO-SAXON BRITAIN, 450 TO 870

The Anglo-Saxons. The Angles and Saxons of northern Germany were closely related in language, customs, culture, and especially in their reputation as fierce fighters. Their territories had never been part of the Roman Empire so that they were untouched by Roman civilization and Christianity. Loyalty to the tribe was paramount and military skill was highly praised, but because they were illiterate the details of their gradual conquering of Britain from about 450 to 600 are sparse. Some evidence of their settlements can be gained from archaeological remains and from place names such as *ingas* which survive in Reading and Hastings, and *tun* as in Southampton.

Legend has it that when the Romans left and the Saxons were hired, the mercenaries liked what they saw and began to conquer Britain, coming up the rivers to penetrate deep into the interior. At first the British were able to resist the small bands of invaders and under the leadership of Arthur they stopped the Germans temporarily at Mount Baldon. The legends about Arthur and his Round Table are many, and although his existence and military skill cannot be doubted, the site of the battle and of his kingdom of Camelot, if indeed he was a king, are unknown. By about 600 when the conquest was complete there were nearly a dozen independent Anglo-Saxon kingdoms. In times many of the names of the settlers had become the names of the kingdoms so that the lands of the East Saxons, West Saxons, and South Saxons had become respectively Essex, Wessex, and Sussex, and the East Angles had given their names to East Anglia. A slower advance northward produced several kingdoms, notably Bernicia and Deira which were later unified as Northumbria ("north of the river Humber") and Mercia ("the borderers' area") in the midlands. The old cities were naturally

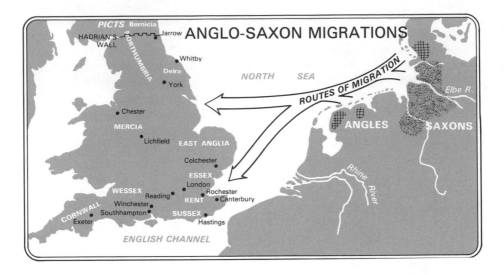

inhabited but the urban Roman style of life was totally foreign to the invaders.

Many of the Romano-Britons had fled northwards and westwards into the mountainous areas to avoid the waves of pagan invaders. By the end of the seventh century the native British people had been forced into three geographically separate kingdoms. In the far southwest was Cornwall which would later be conquered by the Anglo-Saxons. The kingdom of Wales in the west would flourish until well into the Middle Ages. The Scots, who were originally from Ireland, and the Picts created the northern Celtic kingdom known from about 850 as Scotland.

The Conversion of the Anglo-Saxons. There were two distinct missionary efforts to bring Christianity back to Britain, one from the Celts in the north and west and the other sent from Rome. About 575 in Rome a monk had seen several youths from Anglo-Saxon Britain and had been deeply moved by their ignorance of Christ. When he became Pope soon after, Gregory commissioned another monk named Augustine to lead a band of missionaries to Britain, and in 597 they arrived in the extreme southeast corner of the island. Augustine and his companions preached to various kings in the hope that a converted king would allow the evangelization of his kingdom. The first to be won was Ethelbert of Kent, a well disposed ruler whose wife had been raised a Christian in her native Frankland. As the faith was spread the gains were consolidated by the erection of dioceses, geographic areas under the supervision of a bishop, such as Canterbury where Augustine himself settled.

The Celtic missionaries had a distinctly different character. The Roman traditions had been learned by the Celts during Roman rule, and St. Patrick (*c* 389-461) had established the church in Ireland by erecting dioceses which were coterminous with the tribes. But soon after his death the diocesan organization was abandoned and the tribal chiefs established monasteries whose influence was unlimited by geographic borders. When Oswald became King of Northumbria in 633 he opened his realm to the Celtic monks who had been responsible for his earlier conversion.

The Roman and Celtic missionaries also differed in religious customs. A particular problem arose over the different ways of calculating the date of Easter, the central feast of the Christian year. Rome had accepted newer and improved mathematical techniques for measuring cycles upon which the church's liturgical calendar was based, but the Celts who had been isolated from Rome when the Anglo-Saxons invaded had retained the older ways of calculation. This issue was merely one of many which arose from the fundamental question of whether British Christianity would develop in union with the universal church based on Rome or maintain its by now unique features. A Council in Whitby in 663 agreed to follow the Roman ways and to develop monasticism in the diocesan framework. The ecclesiastical unity which resulted made the missionaries' work easier and provided an example for and a stimulus to seek the ideal of political unity instead of the multiplicity of the Anglo-Saxon kingdoms.

The Legacy of the Law. One of the most precious gifts of the invading Germanic tribes was their tradition of an unwritten but binding customary law. As they settled in different parts of Britain their tribal law became the law of the territory they occupied. The laws of the kingdoms were generally similar but there were differences, just as there were differences between the East Saxons and the West Saxons. All the laws sought to provide protection and to ensure a fair way to handle disputes.

The Germanic law had been intended as an alternative to the endless feuds and bloodshed between families seeking revenge for what outsiders had done to their kin. Each person had his own "peace" and it was far more serious to attack someone and break his peace within the privacy of his home than elsewhere. If a crime was committed the law sought to prevent revenge by ordering the guilty to pay money as damages. If the accused had not been caught in the act or if there was no other presumption of guilt, he was allowed to swear an oath asserting his innocence. The value of his oath was based on his rank so that a nobleman's was many times more valuable than any other person's. If his oath was not deemed sufficient to free him from the accusation he could bring in oath-helpers who swore to his trust-worthiness, and the latter were unlikely to support a guilty person because of the penalties for perjury. When guilt had been determined then damages were assessed depending on the extent of the injury and the victim's rank. Thus the damage for the loss of a nose was twice that for a thumb or ear and nearly seven times as much as for a finger. The damages for causing a death, called the wergeld, was of course the highest.

If the procedures of oath-taking had not determined guilt or innocence, and after elaborate safeguards for the rights of all parties, the decision was left to God through one of several types of ordeal. In the ordeal by water, for example, the defendant first prepared himself by prayer, fasting, and the sacraments. Then a priest blessed a body of water such as a small pond. The defendant was thrown into the water and a struggle on his part was taken as a sign of guilt because the purified water would not receive a defiled criminal. If the water received him unstruggling, he was in time brought up and declared innocent.

Toward Political Unity: The Bretwaldas. Not until the tenth century was there political unity in Britain. From about 600 the different Anglo-Saxon kingdoms struggled for political dominance, with warfare the tactic and overlordship the result. The victorious kings who dominated others were called Bretwaldas. The crucial question was the quality of that overlordship: was it to be a recognition as the first among many essentially independent kings, or was it to be so effective politically that the lesser kingdoms under a Bretwalda's control would lose their independence and become absorbed within his own kingdom? To a striking extent the answer depended on the leader's strength of character. A series of able rulers could consolidate their predecessors' gains but a weak successor could lose in a single battle the advances made over many years.

Kent was the first of the dominant kingdoms but when Ethelbert died in 616 Kent's overlordship ended. Northumbria dominated the remainder of the seventh century. Of necessity it was militarily oriented because as the northernmost Anglo-Saxon kingdom it was exposed on its frontiers to the hostile Celts, Welsh, Picts, and Scots. King Edwin (616-32) won Northumbria's independence from the Celts, his successor Oswald reunified the kingdom; a third Bretwalda maintained Northumbria's dominance until late in the century when weak kings gained the throne.

Mercia dominated the eighth century, principally because of the ability of two kings who ruled for a total of eighty years. Ethelbald (716-57) combined military power with a ruthless personality, if a letter by the saintly missionary Boniface which condemned the King's immorality accurately reflects the situation. Offa (757-96) enjoyed the greatest esteem of any Anglo-Saxon king up to that time. His wisdom in government was profound, his reputation on the continent so renowned that the great King of the Franks, Charlemagne, considered marrying one of his sons to Offa's daughter, and his importance to the church sufficient to move the Pope to send a legate to him and even found (temporarily, as it turned out) a third archbishopric at Lichfield in Mercia. Under Mercia's control there was a striking acceleration of the movement toward political unity. The kingdoms of East Anglia, Essex, and neighboring areas were wholly incorporated in Mercia and lost their independence so that the number of competitors for power was significantly reduced. Thus London became a Mercian city and lent its prestige to the kingdom.

The dominant power in the ninth century and later was Wessex. Mercia had attempted to divert the crown in Wessex from Egbert, the proper successor, and placed one of its own claimants on the throne. Egbert fled to Charlemagne's court where in time he absorbed a thorough schooling in statecraft at that most important of European kingdoms while awaiting a promising time to return from exile. In 825 he came back to win a crushing victory over Mercia and in the next several years he became overlord of all southern Britain as well. But the logical advance toward political unity which he represented was interrupted by an external force of great power, the Vikings.

The Vikings. Out of the north swept the fierce Vikings, attacking not only Britain but most of Europe as well. These Scandinavians were well schooled on the seas: the mountain ridges which dominated their homelands had rendered internal travel difficult and forced them to rely on the sea and the extreme climate turned them away from the land to seek a living by fishing or trade, or by the much more lucrative profession of piracy. The long, sleek Viking boats, propelled either by sails or by oars, had such an extended range that they even reached North America.

The Viking raids on Europe began in the eighth century. Their vessels were so swift that they could strike quickly and surprise victims both along the seacoast and even many miles inland along rivers which emptied into the sea. They terrorized the inhabitants of towns, looted extensively in nearby areas, and then withdrew before any help for the hapless victims could arrive. The undefended wealthy monasteries of Britain's eastern seacoast were particularly ripe targets.

Although the name Viking is used generically of all Scandinavians, the Danes concentrated their attacks against Britain and the Norse struck at Ireland. The Danish efforts against Britain continued intermittently for many years, but from 865 onward they abandoned the tactic of strike and withdrawal and began to make permanent settlements in Britain. As the Norse had begun their settlements on Ireland's eastern coast at Dublin, so the Danes settled Britain's eastern shore first. Their roving army quickly reduced the east and then subdued major parts of Mercia. Within a few years the only English kingdom totally free of Danish occupation was Wessex.

ALFRED THE GREAT AND THE CREATION OF ENGLAND

Alfred the Great. The only English king ever to be called "Great" succeeded to Wessex's throne, determined to overcome the Vikings. Alfred (871-99) began to build his military strength, rallying the men of Wessex and forming an alliance with the unoccupied part of Mercia. The combined forces stopped the Danes' second campaign in 875 and in 878 Alfred led his forces to defeat them decisively when they mounted a third attempt. An agreement was made which left eastern Britain to be governed by Danish custom (the area came to be known as the Danelaw) and the west to the Saxons. Alfred then used the twenty remaining years of his life to lead and inspire the kingdom to develop its military and naval strength. The navy was organized to protect the coastline and cut off the Viking lines of communications and on land he consolidated his victories by erecting fortified strongholds to protect the countryside and people. Although the time to begin a sustained campaign to recapture the Danelaw was not yet ripe, he had prepared the military base which his descendants would need.

Alfred was an inspiration to his people culturally as well. If it had not been for his zeal, few writings in English (as the Anglo-Saxon language came to be called) would survive. In addition to the *Anglo-Saxon Chronicle* in which Alfred had a role and legal documents from his government, Alfred translated Pope Gregory's *Pastoral Care* from Latin so that his bishops might be guided in properly shepherding their flocks. To give his people a sense of their heritage he translated the *Ecclesiastical History of the English People* written by the Northumbrian monk Bede. To encourage learning he rendered Boethius' *Consolations of Philosophy* into English, and to stimulate his subjects' piety he had lives of the saints translated. There can be few more appealing pictures than of this King who lamented his own lack of an early education, who then painstakingly worked to learn to read and write, first English and then Latin, and who later gathered around him educated men to instruct others. His encouragement of learning led other Englishmen to study Latin, the international language of scholarship and of the church. Thus horizons to European culture were opened.

The Creation of England. At Alfred's death there were five major and a number of smaller kingdoms in Britain. The two Saxon kingdoms of Wessex and Mercia controlled the southwest and had been united politically by marriages between their royal families. The east was controlled by the Danes, primarily in the Danelaw but also in a few lesser kingdoms in the northeast. There were two Celtic kingdoms, Wales in the far west and Scotland in the north, the latter dating from a union of the Scots and Picts about 850. The most important steps toward political unification were the successive military victories of Alfred's son Edward (899-924) and grandson Athelstan (924-39) which resulted in the conquest of the Danelaw and the minor Danish kingdoms in the north and in the stopping of any Celtic movements southward. By the middle of the tenth century an agreement had been made with Scotland as to territories, the entire area south of the river Tweed to be the one unified kingdom of England.

Thenceforth England was a political unit never to be subdivided. When outside kingdoms threatened to invade, the whole of England was to be the prize. The kings were now the Kings of England, solemnly bound to the realm as was demonstrated by the coronation oath of Edgar in 973. The ceremonies of coronation were traditional and included crowning, anointing, and investing with the royal insignia; the oath was new, the King's sworn promise to govern England well and lawfully, to give justice to his people and protection to the church.

The Powers of Kingship. An Anglo-Saxon king's immediate claim to power had rested on his military ability and thus he was the greater as he conquered or subdued more territory. But once England had been unified, kingship had to be expanded to include non-military tasks as well, and the king's prestige grew accordingly. Because the Germanic kingdoms had been communities which stressed the law, the preeminence of the king developed first in that area.

The king grew to paramount importance in the law in three ways. First, the wergeld on his life was set so high that no one could pay it and thus an offender would be executed. The king, therefore, had a unique form of protection and the crime of taking his life came to be considered a separate legal offense, treason. Second, the king became the normal person to make the decisions about the unclear or undeveloped areas in the customary law. As these decisions were made and pronounced in *dooms,* the king was enhanced as a lawgiver. The dooms began a series of written royal law which at first, however, was of much less importance than the main body of unwritten law.

Third, the kings began to develop a system of separate royal law administered exclusively by royal agents. The kings took the notion of "peace" which was so important in Germanic law and expanded the "king's peace" greatly. It was made to apply to persons other than the king (such as his family and royal officers), to places other than his royal court (churches, fairs, highways), and to times other than the king's ceremonial wearing of his crown (Sundays, feastdays of the church). A small number of offenses were defined as breaking the peace on those occasions and the case was to be heard before a royal officer. The guilty party upon conviction had to pay a fine to the king as well as damages to the injured victim.

The king was advised by a council, a group of his closest advisors called the Witan. He was not bound to take their advice, but it was to his advantage to consult them since he thereby associated the leading men of the realm with royal policies. The Witan had the right to designate the successor to the throne; usually it chose the king's son although this was not always done since an hereditary right to the crown was not yet an unquestioned legal right. In practice the Witan chose the obvious candidate, often passing over a very young son of a deceased king to choose an older relative or someone else who could actively exercise the office.

As non-military administration became more important with an expanded kingdom, two offices within the royal court grew to greater importance. The Chamberlain, who was at first the keeper of the king's bedding and personal effects, began to keep the king's treasure as well and thus received and disbursed royal funds on command. The clergy, who cared for the king's spiritual needs, were often the only literate men in the court and also served by writing the king's orders (the writs) and his grants of privileges and rights (the charters). These documents were cut so that a tongue of parchment hung down from the main writing, to which wax shaped with a mold (the royal seal) was affixed as an authentication.

Local Administration. As Wessex led the unification of the realm the kings needed to assert and assure their control over an increasing number of localities. A system of shires was developed, shire meaning "a share" or part of the whole. When former kingdoms such as Essex or Sussex were deemed small enough for administrative efficiency they became shires in themselves, but larger kingdoms such as Wessex were subdivided into several artificial shires as was done also for the land won back from the Vikings. Eventually over thirty shires were formed.

The king's representative in the shire was at first an ealdorman, but so many new shires were eventually created that it became unwieldy for the king to have to deal with so many of them. Alfred's successors began to group three or four shires under one ealdorman but this increased responsibility made the ealdorman so important that he could even pose a threat to the king's exclusive power, and thus in time the ealdormen were relieved of any administrative responsibility. From the tenth century onward the principal royal officer in the shire was the sheriff (*shire reeve*). He collected the revenues of the king (rentals of land and profits of justice primarily), transmitted royal writs, oversaw the militia of the shire, and assisted in keeping the peace, especially by presiding over the shire court. The shire in turn was subdivided into hundreds or wapentakes, the latter a name which prevailed where the Vikings had had influence. It is not clear whether "hundred" referred to men, to units of land, or to units capable of producing a certain revenue. The constable was in charge of the hundred, below which were tithings ("tenths") which were charged with keeping the peace.

Standing outside this system were the boroughs. The word *burh*, which was the root of "borough," implied a fortified place, often strategically located at the junction of rivers or on hilltops which commanded an area. It was natural that these centers would come to have economic and governmental importance as well and so the boroughs acquired grants of privileges through royal charters, one of the most important of which was exemption from supervision by the sheriffs and constables. The population of boroughs remained generally small, a reflection of the new emphasis on rural life which differed so markedly from when the Romans had dominated Britain.

EARLY ENGLISH SOCIETY

The People of Saxon England. To understand the people who made up early English society first requires putting aside more modern terms such as upper, middle, or lower class because those terms are based primarily on differences in wealth and occupation. Anglo-Saxon society was almost totally agricultural and the distinction was based on degrees of legal and economic freedom. There were three basic grades: slaves who had no freedom at all, ceorls who enjoyed legal but not economic freedom, and a nobility who enjoyed both legal and economic freedom. Persons became slaves when they were captured in battle by men of another kingdom, or were punished for very serious crimes, or when they voluntarily exchanged their freedom for protection or for food during times of acute strife or famine.

The ceorls were husbandmen, tillers of the soil who headed agricultural households and worked in part on their own behalf and in part for their lord. The lowest ranking ceorls spent most of their time in unpaid labor for the lord — in sowing, tending, and harvesting his crops, in minding his animals, and in performing many other menial tasks. They were able to work on their own lands only after completing their legal obligations. The ceorls with the greatest freedom were those who merely paid the lord some rent and did not have to perform personal services. Because their energies could be spent on developing their own lands they could prosper and settle their obligations that much easier. Many ceorls owed a combination of personal and money services. The state of legal freedom but economic unfreedom which English ceorls and men of similar standing on continental Europe had is generally called serfdom.

The nobility of early English society gained their special privileges in the period of the Saxon conquests by their military services to the king. In later centuries they were rewarded also with land and were called *thegns.* Many thegns served the kings as administrators, most notably the ealdormen. As the latter were relieved of administrative duties and replaced by sheriffs in the shires, the Danish title of eorl (later *earl*) was adopted and to its holders it became a more important rank of nobility with preeminence over the others.

Mobility between grades of society was possible. It was to the lord's advantage to make enterprising slaves ceorls, not only because the church encouraged this Christian act but also because the ceorl then became responsible for maintaining himself and yet still owed the lord service. A ceorl might accumulate enough wealth to buy exemptions from the economic services he owed and thus become economically and legally free even though not of noble status. It was also possible to move downward — many were unable to protect themselves from the constant dangers of the Viking invasions or were wiped out by a series of bad harvests and so voluntarily gave up some freedom to a lord in return for protection and the necessities of life. This practice was called commendation and became common in later years so that many people were less free than in the early part of the Middle Ages.

The Countryside. Early English settlements consisted not of single dwellings scattered around the countryside but of villages which were surrounded by the fields which people worked. Some villages were clusters of houses around an open space and others had a single road lined with dwellings through the village. Rarely would there have been any buildings of stone, although some more important churches and the homes of some nobles used stone in construction. The rest of the buildings varied as much as the social standing of the village's families. Prosperous ceorls might live in timbered structures with walls made of mud and wattle, but the poorer ones often lived in hovels, sunken huts covered with straw. The villages usually had a common pasture on which all could graze their animals.

The fields which surrounded the villages were divided, half to be sown while the other half lay fallow to regain its fertility. By the tenth century a system of strip farming had become quite common, perhaps introduced by the Danes. A ceorl would have several strips of land just over twenty yards wide in various parts of the fields, none adjacent but rather separated by the strips of other ceorls. Because oxen were used to pull the plow the strips would be as long as possible so that the team did not have to turn often. When the harvesting was completed in one field the other was immediately sown with wheat and rye, to lie dormant over the winter until germination in the spring, at which time barley and oats were also sown.

Barley was the most important crop and was ground in mills for making bread and also made into malt for brewing beer, the staple drink. Pigs and sheep were raised, but because it was so hard to keep animals alive in the winter because of a lack of fodder, most animals were slaughtered in the autumn and the rest often occupied the houses along with the people. Many areas of Britain were simply not suited for farming and thus animals were grazed in the steep pastures.

Christian Life. The pattern for early Christianity had been set by its rapid spread in earlier periods, and by 700 it had been accepted in all of Britain. Dioceses were created, sometimes coinciding with smaller kingdoms as London did for Essex, sometimes consisting only of part so that Canterbury and Rochester served eastern and western Kent respectively. The Archbishop of Canterbury supervised the southern dioceses and the Archbishop of York the northern. The real importance of Christianity lay in the impact it made on the lives of each individual person, substituting ideals of love, respect, and unselfishness for pagan values. These new virtues were exemplified in the person of Theodore of Tarsus, a Greek who in his service of the universal church came to be Archbishop of Canterbury from 669-90. He actively formed new dioceses and set a personal example of tireless devotion to his flock through teaching, preaching, confirming and ordaining. He convened the clergy to draft codes for morals and penance in order to insure the sound formation of the people in Christian life, and his personal supervision of the higher clergy kept them zealous and dedicated.

The life in monasteries was a jewel of Christian living. Men and women who wished to dedicate themselves to God in lives of worship and contemplation came to monasteries to withdraw from the world's distractions, binding themselves by vows of poverty to be rid of concern for wordly goods, chastity so that family responsibilities did not occupy their time, and obedience so that by losing their own will they might better do God's. In time the monasteries became centers of learning, especially when founders and benefactors presented them with hand-written manuscripts which were so rare in England. Some of the most beautiful examples of copied Bibles were made in northern monasteries such as Jarrow and a particularly beautiful one of the early eighth century from Lindisfarne is an outstanding work of early English art. It was at Jarrow that the monk Bede prepared his *Ecclesiastical History of the English People,* an invaluable source for the history of Anglo-Saxon society which Alfred had translated. The manuscript has a rich and vivid style with unusually advanced descriptions of complex historical events.

The conversion of Britain did not exhaust the missionary vigor of the church. Northumbrians such as Wilfrid and Willibrod brought Christianity to Saxony and neighboring areas which were the original home of the Germanic invaders of Britain. The West Saxon Boniface evangelized down the Rhine in Germany to found Christianity there and to assist in reforming it in nearby Frankland. So famous was the monastery school at York under Alcuin that in 782 he was called by Charlemagne to head the school at his own court at Aachen.

The first Vikings had been pagans whose attacks on monasteries and churches dealt a crippling blow to Christianity. Gradually their conversion, both in England and in Scandinavia, led to a good deal of restoration; but the state of religion in the early eleventh century had not yet recovered to its earlier situation.

ENGLAND IN THE EARLY ELEVENTH CENTURY

For several generations the brilliance and wisdom of Alfred had continued in his descendants, but in the late tenth century there had been a considerable decline in the standards of English society which was personified in great part in King Ethelred the Unready (978-1016). He seemed to reflect the weakness, treachery, and selfishness of the time and his character was blemished by his contemporaries' suspicion that his mother had been implicated in the murder of Ethelred's older brother. When the second wave of Viking invasions began in the early years of his reign he sought to stop the invaders by paying them huge sums of money. England was greatly burdened in raising the thousands and thousands of pounds of precious metals which came to be known as the Danegeld. The new invaders were a professional fighting force whose training and discipline made them a more effective army than western Europe had ever known before. Although this explains in part why Ethelred gave in, his flight in 1013 before another band of raiders, led this time by the Danish king, made many of his subjects esteem him as a coward.

The successful invading Danish king died soon afterward and power passed to his son Canute. Most of the English recognized Canute as their King and when he defeated Ethelred's son Edmund Ironside in battle, and at Edmund's death soon afterward Canute's acceptance was complete. Canute actively ruled a Scandinavian empire made up of the English, Danes, Norwegians, and Swedes. He was a remarkable man who combined the severity and cruelty of the military conquerer with the wisdom which realized that England's government was far superior to the Scandinavian institutions. Unlike earlier invaders he adopted England's government and law and by his military strength he guaranteed the opportunity for its economic growth. He safeguarded the church and appreciated English culture.

After Canute's death in 1035 his two sons who had little ability squandered his legacy and the death of the last of them in 1042 ended one era and began another in the English state. The central problem was who had the right to succeed to the English crown, a problem that would not be finally resolved until 1066. Behind that issue lay a fundamental question — would England continue to maintain its Saxon origins and culture, or be absorbed totally into the Scandinavian Empire, or fall within the influence of its powerful neighbor across the English Channel, Normandy?

SUGGESTIONS FOR FURTHER READING

The earliest times are treated in Jacquetta and Christopher Hawkes, *Prehistoric Britain* (1965). Two useful studies of the Celts are Nora K. Chadwick's *Celtic Britain* (1963) and T. G. E. Powell, *The Celts* (1958). The theory that Stonehenge was a sophisticated astronomical observatory is argued in Gerald S. Hawkins with John S. White, *Stonehenge Decoded* (1965). Geoffrey Ashe and others introduce the vexed question of King Arthur in *The Quest for Arthur's Britain* (1968).

A brief survey of the Roman era in Britain is I. A. Richmond's *Roman Britain* (1955), and in Peter Hunter Blair's *Roman Britain and Early England 55 B.C.-A.D. 871* (1963). The urban style of life is reflected in John Wacher's *The Towns of Roman Britain* (1974).

An excellent survey of the Anglo-Saxon period is Peter Hunter Blair's *An Introduction to Anglo-Saxon England* (1956), while Sir Frank Stenton's *Anglo-Saxon England* (2nd edition, 1947) is a longer classic. The two major contemporary sources have been often edited, such as G. N. Garmonoway, *Anglo-Saxon Chronicle* (1953) and Bede by T. Sherley-Price (revised by R. E. Latham), *A History of the English Church and People* (1955). The best guide to governmental developments is Bryce Lyon, *A Constitutional and Legal History of Medieval England* (1960), and a penetrating discussion of Germanic contributions appears in the early chapters of J. E. A. Jolliffe's *The Constitutional History of Medieval England* (1961).

There are studies of important Anglo-Saxon figures in Eleanor S. Duckett's *Alfred the Great: The King and His England* (1956) and the same author's *Anglo-Saxon Saints and Scholars* (1947), and in L. M. Duckett's *Alfred the Great* (1912). Early agriculture is well treated in H.P.R. Finberg's *The Formation of England 550-1042* (1974). A great emphasis on social and economic matters is in Dorothy Whitelock's *The Beginnings of English Society* (1952), while an illustrated brief guide to early culture is in *Art Treasures in the British Isles* (1969).

2
Anglo-Norman England

1042-1189

King Canute had made England the heart of his Scandinavian empire because he greatly admired its political maturity. His sons reigned only briefly after their father's death and the last of them made the transition of political power easier when he invited his half-brother Edward to return from Normandy. Edward's Norman mother Emma had married Ethelred the Unready, and after his death married Canute. When Edward began to reign (1042-66) he theoretically blended many traditions.

Edward's religious devotion was inspiring to his contemporaries and as "Edward the Confessor" he was canonized soon after his death. Scholars today debate whether his saintly reputation was exaggerated but they agree that the realm was certainly not peaceful. He had spent the first twenty-five years of his life in Normandy and had little appreciation of Englishmen or their values, so that when vacancies arose in the English government or church he filled them with trusted Normans. A resentful native opposition arose which was led by Godwin, Earl of Wessex, by his sons whose earldoms included most of southern England, and by his daughter Edith who was Edward's wife. The quarrels between these mighty English subjects and the King were complicated because Edward had no children, probably as a result of a vow of celibacy which he took just before his marriage.

It seems certain that in either 1051 or 1052 Edward had promised England's crown to his second cousin, William, Duke of Normandy. In later years when Edward withdrew from public life to devote more time to religion and the building of his beloved Westminster Abbey, he allowed his cousin and brother-in-law Harold (a son of Godwin, who had died in 1053) to assume the practical direction of English affairs. Harold was a good fighter whose victories over the Welsh won much admiration. It seemed natural that when Edward died early in 1066 this capable English noble would be chosen King by the Witan. His title was compromised, however, by Edward's promise to William and by an oath which Harold himself made to William, although the terms of the latter are still uncertainly known. Harold's reign as King lasted but nine months. In September 1066 Harold Hardrada, the King of Norway, assisted by the English King's own brother, landed on the northeastern coast of England to re-assert the Scandinavian claim to the crown. King Harold of England marched his forces northward and on September 25 at Stamford Bridge repelled the invasion, killing both his own brother and the Norwegian king in battle. But on September 27, William of Normandy set sail to make good on the promise of Edward the Confessor, so that King Harold of England had to turn his troops and march 250 miles southward to face yet another contender.

THE NORMAN CONQUEST

The Vikings had attacked and permanently conquered Normandy in the ninth and tenth centuries and had gradually fused their culture with the French, but early in the eleventh century Normandy was still a weak and divided Duchy where great nobles were often competitors with the Duke for power. William's resolute leadership dramatically changed that. He was a unique blend of statesman and soldier — a determined, courageous, often brutal fighter who won control within the Duchy and secured its borders against neighboring powers. Then he elaborated on feudal principles to subordinate and harness the abilities of the Norman nobles and to reform the church vigorously according to the principles of the religious revival of the eleventh century, so that the Norman Church served both God and the Duke faithfully. The promise of Edward the Confessor to Duke William gave him the opportunity to expand greatly his area of control.

England Conquered. The battle which Duke William fought against King Harold nine miles inland from Hastings on October 14, 1066, was a dramatic clash between two men who claimed to be England's rightful ruler. Harold's army was drawn up in close order on a hilltop which could only be approached from the south. William sent charge after charge against the English, but neither the Norman soldiers or their rain of arrows could break the English lines. The attackers soon discovered that a feigned retreat could cause some of the impulsive English soldiers to break ranks in pursuit and then the Normans could ambush them piecemeal. This tactic was used repeatedly and then a stray arrow struck and killed King Harold. Leaderless and with dwindling forces, the English retreated and the first stage of the Conquest was complete.

William's political success depended on capturing London, but he advanced on it slowly to let the tales of his brutality toward townspeople who resisted him reach the ears of the Londoners. When his initial demands to them were rejected, he marched his army in a large arc through the areas neighboring London, burning as he went until the Londoners capitulated to avoid the same fate. On Christmas Day, 1066, William was crowned King of England in Westminster Abbey. In the next four years he gained effective control over northern England, at first confirming many English nobles in power if they would support him. William appreciated the more sophisticated practices of English government and wished to emphasize his claim to be heir to the crown by confirming English titles and privileges. But a rebellion of most of the remaining English nobles in 1075 brought this to an end, and after William rewarded the Norman lords who helped him repress the rebellion with the rebels' lands, only a few English nobles remained.

The Feudal System. Although William retained English governmental institutions he did begin gradually to feudalize England. He acted as a lord in granting to vassals land called fiefs (from the Latin *foedum*, the root of the word feudalism) for which the vassals did homage by kneeling before him to swear their fealty, an oath of honor, loyalty, and service. The exact details of the manner and pace with which William imposed feudalism are not known, but it seems that as more and more lands were forfeited to him as the native English lords rebelled, he regranted the lands according to the new system. He also imposed the Norman custom of primogeniture, according to which the eldest son alone inherited his father's lands. William avoided the common continental European practice of granting all land within large areas or provinces to a single nobleman; by granting nobles many scattered fiefs he avoided making them all-powerful in their locality and denied them the means of mounting a concentrated opposition to royal policies.

Under the feudal system a lord kept part of his lands for his own use (as his *demesne*) and granted the remainder to a vassal in return for specified services. The obligations which the vassal owed to the lord were called the *servita debita* and varied considerably. The most common was knight service in which a vassal had to furnish a certain number of men armed and ready for military duty for a set time. Churchmen usually owed prayer and religious services, officers in the king's administration owed their time and talents under the tenure of serjeantry, and occasionally a vassal merely paid a money rent.

Among the vassal's other responsibilities were attending the lord's court, offering him counsel, and paying aids and incidents. Aids were paid when a lord's eldest son was knighted, when his eldest daughter was married, and as a ransom if the lord was captured in battle. The most important incident was the relief, a money payment from a vassal's heir so that the lord would regrant the fief to him. Since a vassal often left minor heirs who were incapable of military or any other service, the lord managed the fief until the heirs came of age under a system known as wardship, and he could arrange the marriages of minor heiresses in order to protect his interests. If a vassal broke the feudal agreement he forfeited the fief to the lord, but if the lord was unfaithful then the vassal was entitled to rise in rebellion.

The elements described to this point were common to any lord-vassal relationship, but as the system was implemented the layers of subordination multiplied. A man who was a king's vassal could himself retain part of his grant as his own demesne and regrant the remainder to other men who became his own vassals. This regranting was called subinfeudation and was quite common in England, doubtless because the possessions of individual lords had been purposely scattered by William. The result was a hierarchial structure of landholding, often schematically described as a pyramid, with the king at the apex and a number of tenants-in-chief holding directly from him, and with as many layers below as further subinfeudation took place. Because it was possible for one vassal to hold fiefs from different lords, the figure of a web can also be used by way of illustration to stress the tangle of interrelated loyalties implicit in feudalism. Because a vassal's loyalties were most immediately dedicated to his own lord, feudalism tended to make minor vassals less concerned with tenants-in-chief or even the king who was far removed above in the pyramid. This diffusion of power and loyalties away from the king who stood at the center of the feudal kingdom can be likened to the centrifugal motion of ripples away from the center of a pond where a stone has been cast. William I attempted to mitigate this diffusion of loyalties by requiring all important men of the kingdom to take an oath of loyalty to him directly.

By means of the feudal system the Norman kings of England were able to weave the aristocracy into the fabric of the English state and bind them to loyal service; approximately two hundred tenants-in-chief

Bodiam Castle, Sussex (Aerofilms, Ltd).

were direct vassals of the king. The common people of England were little touched by the new developments. The fief was the smallest legal unit of feudalism, but since it often coincided with the village which was the social and economic unit, the effect was merely to restate in newer legal terms many rights and duties which had long characterized the obligations of rural agricultural society.

The Normans and the Church. The monasteries had a well established and traditional place in English life before the conquest, and at first only the leadership changed as Norman abbots were appointed. The Normans gradually began to appreciate the fervor of the English monks and as the new abbots introduced the continental reforms which had brought a revitalized spirit to monastic life, the abbeys fused the best of the old and the new. New orders of monks came to England, among them the Cistercians (often popularly called Trappists) who were a particularly austere and fervent order with a preference for settling in remote parts of the country.

The greatest ecclesiastical effect of the conquest was the Norman elaboration of the territorial structure of the church. England had long been divided into geographic dioceses under the direction of bishops, but the Normans rearranged the dioceses for greater efficiency. Later, smaller churches were built throughout the dioceses to serve people in geographic areas known as parishes. This expansion made it imperative to develop further the administrative machinery of the dioceses. Archdeacons were appointed in every diocese to handle administration and legal matters such as cases on marriages and morals; where a diocese included several shires, an archdeacon was usually appointed for each.

There was a special organization for the cathedral church of the diocese, a corporate body called the chapter which was made up of important churchmen called canons. The canons elected one of their number to head the chapter as its dean. In addition to their responsibilities for maintaining the cathedral, the dean and chapter elected a new bishop when a former one died or was moved to a new diocese. This was only a theoretical right because the Norman kings told the deans and chapters whom to elect. The bishops were skilled administrators who had often begun their careers as chaplains in the royal court. Piety and spiritual dedication were important but, in many cases, were neglected in favor of managerial skills so that the zeal encouraged by the reforms and the effectiveness of this well-organized system was at times comprised by the character of some of its leaders. The archdeacons developed a reputation for pressing legal claims down to the last penny so that in later centuries waggish university students were known to debate, half-seriously and half-mockingly, whether it was possible for an archdeacon to save his soul.

THE CONQUERER'S SONS

William the Conquerer and his nobles were forced to divide their time between England and Normandy, at times crushing rebellions of resentful English lords, at other times fighting less successfully to defend the Norman possessions from hostile neighboring French rulers. As William I neared death he adhered to tradition by willing Normandy to his eldest son, Robert, and England to his second son, William. The hard won unity between the two possessions would be destroyed, and the nobility who held lands in both of them feared that if conflicts arose between the brothers they might be forced to choose one and thereby face the loss of possessions in the other's domains.

William Rufus. William II (1087-1100, called "Rufus" by his contemporaries because of his ruddy coloring) was an unappealing ruler who combined all the vices of a soldier with a blasphemy and immorality which scandalized a believing age. Only the code of the camp captured his respect and thus he valued England merely as a source of revenue for battle. When some of his nobles supported rebellions to supplant him with Robert and reunite England and Normandy under one ruler, he responded with a military skill as effective as his father's and with a personal brutality which led him to blind, castrate, and hang the rebels. The governmental officials whom he left in charge in England were ruthlessly efficient and therefore very unpopular. William also took advantage of his brother Robert, an affable and courageous man who was, however, easy-going and irresolute in governing Normandy. When Robert wished to go on a crusade in 1095 he pawned part of his Duchy to William to gain the funds, and William used Robert's absence to gain control of Normandy and to advance its frontiers militarily.

William's personal immorality led him often to refuse to fill vacant bishoprics so that he could appropriate their revenue. When in 1093 he believed that he was dying he decided to make his peace and therefore accepted his councillors' advice in naming Anselm as Archbishop of Canterbury — a man renowned for his personal holiness and as the most outstanding philosopher of the time. When William unexpectedly recovered his health he began to regret the choice. Anselm's behavior was a reproach to the King's and the Archbishop combined a lack of administrative experience with a stubborn streak that further strained his relations with the King. These differences were worsened by the investiture controversy. English feudal custom required a bishop to swear an oath of fealty to the king as did other feudal lords, after which he was invested with his fiefs and the symbols of ecclesiastical office. The Pope objected to the king as a layman seeming to confer a spiritual office. Anselm insisted on the papal position and William resisted lest his control over a feudal lord be reduced. At William's death matters were strained and Anselm was in exile; only in the following reign was a compromise reached which was acceptable to all parties.

Henry I. William's successor was the Conquerer's third son who had been left a large treasure and no kingdom. Henry had played both sides in the struggle between his older brothers and earned the distrust of both so that Robert and William made each other his heir to exclude Henry. When Rufus was on a hunting trip in 1100 he was "accidentally" struck in the neck with an arrow and killed. Henry just happened to be nearby and rode at once to Winchester to seize the English treasury and proclaim himself King of England. William's body lay unclaimed for hours and when several years after he had been buried at Winchester Cathedral the roof fell in over his tomb, it was taken as a certain sign of divine disfavor.

Henry (1100-35) was a capable statesman who immediately bid for the support of important leaders in order to gain their acquiescence in his usurpation. He issued a Charter of Liberties which promised to repudiate William II's abuses in the church and government and kept most of the promises by ruling fairly, so that he was called the "lion of justice." His governmental skill consolidated the achievements of his father and he began new procedures which further enhanced the power and authority of kingship. In 1105-06 he turned on his brother Robert and mounted an English conquest of Normandy, and by defeating his brother in battle he reunited in his person Normandy and England.

Anglo-Norman Government. Most English administrative agencies were more developed than those in Normandy so that the Anglo-Norman kings retained them and expanded them greatly. The Anglo-Saxon writing office which prepared writs and charters acquired the new name of the Chancery and grew in importance as writs became important in law as well as in administration. A council of advisors was retained but was now called by the Latin name *curia regis* rather than the Witan. The greatest Norman contribution to government was feudalism with its contractual ties which bound the aristocracy to serve the monarchy. Now the *curia regis* was to consist exclusively of the king's feudal tenants-in-chief, but since their number neared two hundred most of the day-to-day advice to the King came from the council's members who held the major administrative posts.

Because the kings were often away on the continent to attend to Norman business, William II and subsequent monarchs established the office of Justiciar to direct English affairs during their absence. Later the office was expanded to direct the administration even when the king was in England. William Rufus chose Ranulf Flambard as his Justiciar, a man who worked with such a ruthless efficiency and an ability to make royal rights lucrative that the King had to remove him in order to placate a growing opposition. Under Henry I, Roger, Bishop of Salisbury, held the office, expanding the judicial and administrative powers of government.

It was under Roger's direction also that the first administrative office went "out of court," ceasing to travel with the king and his royal court as they moved throughout England but instead settling down in one central location with a degree of quasi-independence. The Anglo-Saxon kings had entrusted the collection and dispersal of funds to the Chamberlain in the royal household, and before Roger's time the members of the *curia regis* had superintended the sheriffs' accounting for the king's revenue. Roger developed a new office called the Exchequer which took its name from the checkered cloth upon which the sheriffs accounted after the fashion of an abacus. The cloth was marked in vertical columns to represent units of currency such as pounds and hundreds of pounds, and upon it were placed counters to represent the total revenue which the sheriff was expected to produce. Because the sheriffs had been ordered many times during the previous year to make disbursements on the king's behalf, counters were removed from the cloth to symbolize these proper deductions, leaving a total to be paid into the Exchequer as a result of a process which even the illiterate could follow easily. Pegs of wood shaped like modern tent pegs were notched to indicate the sums paid by the sheriff, wider notches for larger sums down to bare nicks for fractions of pounds, and then the wood (called a tally) was split lengthwise. If disputes arose, the sheriff was able to produce his half to match that kept in the Exchequer.

Thus in administration there was a growing number of administrative agencies — the *curia regis,* the Justiciar, the Chancery, the Exchequer, and the royal court in which much was still done. The legal system grew more complex as well. The Anglo-Norman kings retained two existing systems of law, the Anglo-Saxon local courts with their Germanic principles and the system of royal pleas, and added a third by their introduction of feudalism. The feudal system of justice created many courts because each lord was obliged to hold a court for his vassals. A village might spread over several manors, and thus the duty of keeping order and serving other public duties were often assigned to the village — adding another layer of public justice which grew up alongside the private feudal jurisdiction. William I also separated the church's courts from those of his government. Although this merely followed the Norman practice, in time numerous conflicts would arise over the proper jurisdiction which each type might claim.

ANGLO-NORMAN SOCIETY

Feudalism and the Upper Ranks of Society. When William I replaced rebellious English nobles with loyal Norman and French lords he affected nothing less than an aristocratic revolution. The new nobility differed considerably in their outlooks, attitudes, and values. These changes were evident above all else in their use of the French language which had supplanted English in high society, in their military attitudes which led them to mock the "softer" English with their long hair and finer clothes, and their lack of interest in the arts and literature which many English nobles prized.

Because a much smaller number of new nobles replaced the substantially larger group of English aristocrats, the former tended to be richer and of more individual importance and in time came to appreciate the more cultured English ways as had William I. Growth in wealth had an important part in mellowing the Norman attitudes. As men of property, the new nobles began to devote more time to the management of their estates and less to military skills which had first brought them to prominence. At a later time the Norman kings capitalized on this attitude by allowing the nobility to commute the personal knight service which they owed into money payments which sufficed to hire a smaller number of mercenary fighters.

The character of the knights who stood immediately below the nobility changed as well. At first a knight had been little more than a hired soldier, but once he received property through the process of subinfeudation he too wished to spend more time in managing his estates. As the gradual consolidation of the Norman Empire reduced the frequency of combat there were fewer opportunities for military service. Even the nature of warfare tended to change: the beginning of the Crusades to recover the Holy Land from non-Christians provided an idealistic motive for fighting, and the church promoted elaborate rules of chivalry in the twelfth century to mitigate the worst features of battle. Soon it became more profitable to capture a knight, seize his expensive armor and horses, and then hold him for ransom rather than to kill him.

Because military preparedness was a necessity, a new style of architecture came to England. There were few castles from pre-Conquest days but between 1066 and 1100 over eighty were built as strongholds to dominate and control the areas which the Normans conquered. Most of the early castles were of the motte and bailey type where a protective ditch was dug around the limits of some prominence such as a hill, and then a timber fortification was built on top of the dirt from the ditch heaped within the enclosure. As the haste of the period of conquest gave way to more settled times, these early castles were rebuilt in stone. When the style of building was fully developed in later centuries, there were a number of characteristics: castles' exterior walls were smooth with few openings through which an arrow could penetrate, there was but one entrance so that defenses could be concentrated, and the interior was of sufficient size to house a noble family in proper style, although such a damp, cold building with little light penetrating from oustide would hardly be comfortable. These castles were designed to enable a loyal force to hold out for a considerable time until the royal forces could raise a seige.

Domesday Book and the Peasantry. In 1086, probably fearing a Scandinavian invasion and wishing to understand his realm's resources, William I sent commissioners throughout England to survey landholding and wealth. County by county, hundred by hundred, manor by manor, the commissioners recorded who had held the land before the Conquest, who held it in 1086, what obligations were owed, and what other resources there were such as plows and cattle. Men marveled that one could sooner escape the day of doom and judgment than the questions of the King's men, and so the name stuck to the results of the inquiry. *Domesday Book* helped the King be better informed, provided a record of landholding which was invaluable for settling later disputes at law, and showed clearly the extent of the aristocratic revolution. It also showed that the primary implications of the Conquest were restricted to the upper ranks of society and to a very small number of people. Most agricultural workers saw little more than the substitution of a new lord for the old and the requirement to attend the new manorial courts. Otherwise the rhythm of the seasons with the traditional sowing and reaping continued. English was used as a language on the non-aristocratic level, and at first the resentment at the conquerers spawned periodic violence which meant hardship for the common people.

The number of offenses which were considered to be a breach of the king's peace was expanded and reached thirty-seven under Henry I. The Normans had to introduce a murder fine to protect their own. In English law the victim's family prosecuted someone who had murdered one of their kin, but the Normans usually had no family to avenge them and so there was a great temptation for the English to attack the invaders with little fear of retribution. The murder fine set by the Norman leaders was very high and all the inhabitants of a hundred in which a Norman was slain had to contribute if the murderer went undetected.

Religion and Society. The creation of new parishes made the church better able to serve people's spiritual needs but also created a number of problems. Parishes were often created when a wealthy patron donated land and other endowments sufficient to erect a church and support a parish priest. Because the patron reserved the right to nominate the next priest every time the office became vacant, the priest's primary loyalty was often to the patron. The training before a priest's ordination was usually inadequate so that many lacked the spiritual leadership demanded by the office. Since the priest farmed the land which was the parish's endowment he was subject to the same attitudes, trials, and temptations which beset the flock which he was to guide.

In spite of the problems the reforms of the period kindled a great deal of religious zeal, and the stone churches which the Normans erected were the centers of both village and town life. These churches were erected in a style called Romanesque or Norman and are a testimony to the pre-eminence of spiritual aspirations. This was a massive style of construction limited only by the requirement that the walls and columns be strong enough to support the entire weight of the roof, so that the girth of the columns was usually the same as their height. The floor plan was usually of cruciform shape with the altar and choir on the eastern end to catch the rays of the morning sun, the nave to the west forming the remainder of the long part of the cross, and the north and south transepts making the shorter crossbar. The walls were usually constructed in three tiers with windows only at the highest level lest the wall be weakened, and the circular arch was characteristic of the style. The Norman cathedral thus mirrored the strength and even militant attitude which was characteristic of the feudal period.

The clearest enunciation of the spiritual ideal of the time was to be found in the monastic life where men and women withdrew to live according to a rule of prayer and worship. A good example of early monastic fervor which came close to the ideal was the community at Fountains Abbey. A small number of Benedictine monks at St. Mary's Abbey in York had begun to yearn for a more ascetic and less comfortable life than was normal in their wealthy monastery, and so in the winter of 1132-33 they left York to choose a remote site twenty-five miles away where abundant springs suggested the name Fountains. The following year the monks petitioned for adoption into the Cistercian Order, and under the direction of Abbot Richard endured winters of near starvation until at last their reputation for saintly lives brought both recruits and endowments. Within a decade there were probably 500-600 monks so that three times in ten years offspring monasteries were founded from Fountains Abbey.

Assuming that the daily routine at Fountains was similar to that at other Cistercian abbeys, we can picture the grey-clad monks rising in the dormitories about 2 AM to go to the massive church built in the Norman style, where they began the first of an eight-part combination of prayers called the divine office — a blend of psalms, scripture readings, prayers, and hymns which complemented the two daily masses. About two-thirds of the day would have been spent in the church or in reading and prayer in the cloister, to which the monks added periods of manual labor in the fields. The business of the monastery was conducted in the chapter house and the one or occasionally two meatless meals of the day were taken in the refectory. Silence was maintained except for necessary business, and the rhythms of the seasons were seconded by the regular cycle of the liturgical year which represented Christ's life and held it up for the monks' imitation.

It was difficult to maintain such an austere life in full rigor and many monasteries fell short of the ideal. The wealth which abbeys received from admiring benefactors often caused the monks to spend so much time in worldly management that it intruded on their other-worldly ideals, and ambitious building programs plunged some monasteries into debts and eroded the spirit of prayer. Nevertheless the impact and attractiveness of the ideal was great and the zeal of the reformed houses was an inspiration.

The nave of Durham Cathedral (Radio Times Hulton Picture Library).

ENGLAND AND ANJOU

The greatest threats to the English king's Norman possessions came from France which bordered Normandy on the southeast and from Anjou directly southwards. William I and II had resisted their incursions, and Henry I by reuniting England and Normandy had increased his ability to resist. In Henry's reign the French King Louis VI began attempts to expand his territories beyond the areas immediately surrounding Paris and thus saw Anglo-Normandy as the principal obstacle to his plans. Although France was occasionally at war with the Anglo-Normans, Louis VI assisted Anjou and other more immediate foes to attack Normandy. Henry I remained there over half the years of his reign after 1106 to meet the increased threats.

Matilda and Stephen. Henry feared that his realm's capacity to resist would be seriously crippled by the succession to England's crown. He had numerous bastard children who could not legally succeed him and had only two legitimate children, a son and a daughter. In 1120 the son drowned when a ship in which he and a number of equally drunk companions had embarked sank in the English Channel. Henry had no choice but to order his barons to swear to allow his daughter Matilda to become Queen and reign after his death. A woman ruler was a novelty which few lords could anticipate without dread: Matilda was mismatched by a political marriage to Geoffrey, Count of Anjou, a youth fourteen years old and eleven years her junior when Henry I died in 1135, yet the marriage offered Anjou the potential for dominating England. Furthermore Matilda was extremely arrogant, fond of recalling that by her former marriage with the late German Emperor she had been an Empress.

Matilda never made good her claim because Henry's nephew Stephen seized the throne when the old King died. Stephen (1135-54) was a popular man whose accession was greated with relief by most of the nobility. As the grandson of William I through the Conquerer's daughter he was Matilda's cousin. Most nobles acquiesced in the extraordinarily hasty events of the first three weeks during which time he seized the treasury and had himself elected King as had Henry before him. But this initial decisiveness and foresight was deceptive because for the remainder of the reign he was usually incapable of concentrated and sustained effort. Above all else he showed himself "soft" (as a chronicler put it), ever able to be prevailed upon and to make concessions to powerful forces in the vain effort to sustain an effective control over affairs.

Matilda's arrogance and Stephen's inability were a perfect match — Stephen lost effective control of Normandy to Matilda and neither could decisively win in England during the civil wars which lasted from

Knight and his Lady, monumental brass rubbing.

Geoffrey and Matilda's invasions in 1139 until 1148 when they left England for good. Five years later an agreement was made between them which allowed Stephen to remain King as long as he lived, and to be succeeded by Matilda and Geoffrey's son, Henry.

Henry II and the Angevin Empire. Few kings have been as personally compelling as the twenty-one year old man who began to rule as Henry II (1154-89). He was a bundle of energy, always on the move, able to spend the day in strenuous hunting and other sports and then the evening in conducting the business of his realms. He was up earlier than his ministers and retired later than they did — and he was so taken with nervous energy that his stocky body, which was topped with red hair, often trembled with uncontrollable rage and fury. Few could love a man of such intensity but all respected him.

His inheritance was breathtaking: Anjou and other areas in what is now central France from his father, England as a result of the agreement with Stephen, and Normandy from his mother. When he married Eleanor of Aquitaine he assumed effective control over her territories which included most of the southwest of modern France. The total domain, often called the Angevin Empire (Angevin is the adjective derived from Anjou, his patrimony, also called Plantagenet, from devices on the family coat of arms), stretched 900 miles from England's border with Scotland to the Pyrenees which are the modern French border with Spain. Only the strongest of rulers could hope to hold together so many diverse territories, and then only if there was a strong government by which to rule. England alone offered the potential but first Henry II had to restore the powers of the monarchy which Stephen had frittered away. Within the first year of his reign Henry had regained the crown lands which had been alienated, ridded the country of the hated mercenaries who had fought much of the civil wars, and had taken back the royal castles which the barons had occupied and reduced the others which they had erected without authorization as havens for resisting the royal power.

The barons' loyalties were won back by Henry's vigorous re-assertion of his and their feudal rights. Officials wrote down in the *Cartae Baronum* (Charters of the Barons) the exact terms of feudal obligations. Henry reestablished the effectiveness of the royal administration, choosing the exceptionally able Ranulf Glanville to direct the government and to fashion a staff of loyal administrators who oversaw the enforcement of royal policy. The greatest area of his achievements was in the development of royal law, and the greatest difficulty was in his dealings with the church.

Henry II and the Law. William I had retained English law and fused with it important Norman elements such as feudalism. Henry I, the "lion of justice," introduced a number of innovations which gave royal justices great flexibility. It was Henry II's regularization, systemization, and expansion of justice which made all that had gone before into a coherent and efficient whole. The *curia regis* heard important feudal cases and other important matters for the king, and the Exchequer which by now had gone "out of court" heard cases over disputes on royal revenue. The great elaboration was the provision for hearing cases at royal law throughout England's many localities by the itinerant justices.

The name itinerant (from the Latin *iter* meaning journey) was appropriate because the royal justices divided England into circuits composed of several counties in which they travelled several times a year. Their judicial sittings on disputes over property were called assizes (from the French *assis* meaning "seated," or "a sitting"); on criminal matters, gaol delivery because the trials over which they presided cleared the gaol (as the English spell jail) of all suspects whom the sheriff had detained to await trial. Property matters were heard before a jury (from the Latin word *jurati* meaning "men sworn on oath"). Not until the thirteenth century were juries used in criminal matters because men were not ready earlier to decide a neighbor's guilt when that might result in the death penalty, and when God's judgment was able to be ascertained through the ordeal. The origin of the jury was the Norman inquest, the seeking of information from men under oath. William I used it to compile *Domesday Book* and from 1176 onward it was used for general informational surveys of local conditions which were called general eyres. The latter were very unpopular because men resented having to respond under oath to questions which were felt to be mere fishing for information to which the king had no right. In time the informational eyres were dropped, but the jury remained as a regular part of the judicial process.

A plaintiff began a case at royal law by purchasing royal writs. Some writs were jurisdictional, transferring cases from the feudal courts into the royal courts, while others provided means for determining the right to property or the lawful possession of it. The question of the *right* to property was the most important, and so the writ for this was called the Grand Assize (from the French *grand*, meaning large and implying importance). All parties to the suit had to present full documentation and proof about the ownership of the land and the defendant was allowed many delays before the case was heard. Therefore, many plaintiffs decided to purchase writs which without any delay settled the more restricted question of *rightful possession*. These writs were called Petty Assizes (from the French *petit*, meaning small or of lesser importance) and if through their processes a plaintiff was presumed to be entitled to possess the property he was restored to it until the lengthy and final processes of the Grand Assize were completed. For example, he was restored to the property if the jury found him to be the heir apparent at the time of the "death of his ancestor" (hence the writ *mort d'ancestor*) or if he had been "recently dispossessed" by the defendant (writ of *novel disseisin*).

In time the system of writs was expanded to over five hundred separate types. The king gained financially from the sale of the writs and the fees for his justices who heard the cases, but more importantly he gained prestige as the protector of his subjects' rights. By the end of the Middle Ages the local courts in the shires and the feudal courts of the lords heard only the most minor matters and royal justice had become the dominant system. The kings' subjects used the system because it guaranteed them the right to a speedy and relatively inexpensive trial by a jury of their peers, which was felt to be a far superior process than in the feudal courts where the landlords were the judges.

Henry II and the Church. One area of conflict between the kings and the church was the proper relationship between the Papacy and England, but the settlement of the investiture controversy in Henry I's reign had cleared up most of these problems. The second difference was the degree of control which the kings could exert over the church in England, a problem which often concerned the proper spheres of jurisdiction between the separated ecclesiastical and secular courts for an offense such as murder. The church claimed that a spiritual person should be tried in a spiritual court; the monarchs argued that because the church's courts did not inflict the death penalty but only penance and other spiritual punishments, the culprits escaped serious retribution. Many clerics were only in minor orders, the initial stages in the process towards ordination as priests, and thus enjoyed full protection yet were not full members of the clergy. Henry II hoped to solve this problem and all difficulties with the church by appointing as Archbishop of Canterbury his loyal friend and Lord Chancellor Thomas à Becket. Surely together they could compromise the matter.

Becket surprised Henry and everyone else — from a cleric hardly renowned for piety, a carefree, pliant royal servant, Becket became the dedicated ascetic changed by a religious conversion, and devoted to defending every privilege of the church no matter how unimportant. When Henry II drew up in 1164 a codification of royal rights in the church called the Constitutions of Clarendon, matters came to a head. Becket refused to accept the Constitutions and in particular objected to the claim that clerics convicted before spiritual courts of a serious secular crime should be degraded by the church and handed over to the secular arm for execution. The conflict which ranged over the next years combined the personal bitterness of a former friendship gone sour with exaggerated claims of principles on both sides. Late in 1170 matters had gotten so bad that Becket excommunicated several bishops who had cooperated in a plan of Henry's, and in exasperation the King uttered the words "Will no one rid me of this troublesome priest?"

Taking him literally, four of Henry's knights went to Canterbury and murdered Becket in his cathedral. The effects of this act were profound. Although Henry disavowed the literal intention of his words he was made to do public penance for his carelessness. Becket was canonized in 1173 and his shrine at Canterbury became a center of pilgrimage for Europeans. More importantly, the event forced Henry II and the Papacy to come to an agreement: Henry conceded that felonies of clergymen should be tried in spiritual courts while retaining jurisdiction over the lesser misdemeanors of clerics, and that appeals in some cases would be allowed from church courts in England to Rome. But in other matters which related directly to Henry's control over the church, such as nominating bishops and allowing papal orders to come into England only with his permission, Henry retained the ancient rights of English kings. Because both sides had been forced to come to an explicit agreement, England was not to be subject to the same running disputes with the Papacy during the rest of the Middle Ages as were many European kingdoms.

As marked as Henry's achievements were in so many areas, the seeds for undoing much of his work lay in his own family. Rule as he would throughout his lands, he could not rule Queen Eleanor, who was as formidable and cunning as he was, nor his sons, who spent much of their later years plotting against their father to increase their own inheritances. These family struggles were the more serious because they coincided with the accession to France's throne of Philip Augustus (1180-1223) who dreamed of driving the English out of France and who knew how to exploit the greed and rapacity of Henry's children. Henry II's Angevin Empire stood challenged.

SUGGESTIONS FOR FURTHER READING

A good recent study of the childless king who precipitated the crisis over the succession is Frank Barlow's *Edward the Confessor* (1970). David C. Douglas' *William the Conquerer: The Norman Impact upon England* (1964) is an excellent study of how William first developed effective control over Normandy and then used that experience in

England. A special treatment of the fateful year is Alan Lloyd's *The Making of the King 1066* (1966). A fierce debate on whether Saxon England or Normandy contributed more to the Anglo-Norman experience has long raged, and the varying interpretations are ably presented in C. Warren Hollister's *The Impact of the Norman Conquest* (1969).

Bryce Lyon explains feudalism and Anglo-Norman government well in *A Constitutional and Legal History of Medieval England* (1960), and of special interest for its lucid explanations are S. B. Chrimes, *An Introduction to the Administrative History of Medieval England* (1966). The anarchy of the civil wars between Stephen and Matilda is described in R. H. C. Davis, *King Stephen* (1967). A newer study by W. L. Warren, *Henry II* (1973) replaces several older studies of that important monarch.

There are studies of important churchmen in R. W. Southern's *St Anselm and his Biographer: A Study of Monastic Life and Thought* (1963), and in David Knowles' *Thomas Becket* (1971). The intricacies of the church's organization are explained in Felix Makower's *Constitutional History and Constitution of the Church of England* (1895). The best study of early monasticism is David Knowles' *The Monastic Orders in England 943-1216* (1940).

Social and economic topics are admirably treated in Doris Mary Stenton, *English Society in the Early Middle Ages 1066-1307* (1959, first published 1951), and much on the clothing of the era can be gained from the plates of *The Bayeux Tapestry* (edited by F. M. Stenton and others, 1957). Other topics are covered in A. L. Poole, ed., *Medieval England* (2 vols., 1958) and in Sidney Painter, *Medieval Society* (1951).

3

High Medieval England

1189-1327

The thirteenth century was the highpoint of medieval culture in Europe, and England participated fully in its achievements. It was a century of aspirations, characterized by a religious revival led by the friars who called men to a life of simplicity and an imitation of the Lord's poverty, by the building of cathedrals in the new Gothic style which used height, light, and color to lift man's spirit heavenward, and by the flourishing of medieval philosophy which sparked such an interest in scholarship that universities were developed as centers of learning. It was a century of change in many of the workaday aspects of life as well. Although rural life continued its traditional practices and rhythms and agriculture was the way of life for most Englishmen, the countryside came to be dotted with flourishing walled towns whose newly won charters of privileges and new trade organization of the guilds made them ever more important centers for economic growth. As feudal society was broadened by these new styles of life, so the century witnessed also a fuller development of England's own unique system of common law, a supplement to and at times a competitor with feudal justice.

It was in the years 1189-1327 that England became the first

European power to work out a concept of government, the "community of the realm," which significantly broadened participation in government and altered the relationships between king and subject. The king was both sovereign and servant of the kingdom, one with many privileges and also many responsibilities, the ruler *for* as well as *of* England. Should a king not satisfy the norms of good government, he could be restrained by the community — as Edward II learned in 1327. The leaders in the struggle to realize this notion were the great feudal barons of England. They did not have a fixed theoretical goal toward which to work, nor did they attempt to wrest from the king his right to make policy and serve as England's leader. But through conflict and chance, through efforts at times inspired by great idealism and at other times merely by personal selfishness, they sought to define the king's and their own place in English life. In the process were forged many precedents and institutions that were unique in the European experience, and which are at the heart of British government, most notably Magna Carta and the beginnings of Parliament.

RICHARD, JOHN, AND MAGNA CARTA

Richard the Lion Hearted. Henry II, great King and master of many lands that he was, spent his last years in anguish, his sons fighting among themselves and even rising in rebellion against their father, each asserting his right to be the heir to England's crown. Richard, the eldest son, was the best fighter, and even sought the assistance of the King of France, the young Philip Augustus. Wily Philip knew that the expansion of France required winning back French provinces like Normandy now under English control and so played many roles to Richard — confidant, supporter, perhaps even lover — and was rewarded when in a particularly vengeful act of defiance to old Henry, Richard did homage to Philip for all England's French possessions. Should ever a pretext be found to allege Richard or his successor an unfaithful vassal, Philip had the legal authority under the feudal system to declare those fiefs forfeit.

As King Richard I (1189-99), Henry's eldest son became Europe's most formidable fighter, his chivalry and shining sword winning him the title "Lion Hearted" and the fear and respect of many. So consumed was he with fighting that he spent nearly all of his time on the continent in battle and only six months of the ten-year reign in England, which thus became merely his war treasury, with its offices, titles, and lands for sale to finance the costly wars. He was strong enough to prevent English discontent from erupting into a serious domestic rebellion and so Philip Augustus had no opportunity to turn Richard's act of homage into any gain of territory for France. The machinery of government which Richard's father had developed was capable of promoting justice and good government but it was also possible to use its capabilities for sinister purposes. Richard demanded more feudal service from his tenants-in-chief than could be justified by custom, exercised undue influence in the royal courts, and sought to wring every penny out of the system of royal administration. A less firm ruler would reap bitter fruit from his legacy.

King John. When Richard died from an infection of a minor wound, his brother John came to the throne (1199-1216). John was a talented man capable of brilliance, the favorite son of his father and as such pampered and indolent, a man who hardly ever achieved anything because he could not sustain a course of action. His secretiveness, moodiness, and intransigence provoked men to distrust, and he had the uncanny ability to alienate almost everyone. John played right into Philip Augustus' hands. While travelling through France, he fell in love with a young woman, Isabelle, who was legally betrothed to Hugh the Brown, one of John's vassals. When John married her, Hugh sought justice from John's lord, and when John refused to answer Philip's summons to appear at the French court to answer for his actions, the French King declared all of England's French possessions, for which Richard and then John had done homage, to be forfeited.

John's long efforts to win the French territories back by the sword were a series of failures. At the same time, he had run afoul of the most powerful Pope of the era, Innocent III, over the choice of a cleric to be Archbishop of Canterbury. As was traditional, John nominated a candidate, but another candidate was elected by the Dean and Chapter of Canterbury Cathedral. When the case was appealed to Rome, Innocent disallowed both procedures and installed his own choice. Then followed a series of retaliations on both sides, escalating finally to the point at which Innocent excommunicated John, a spiritual censure which denied the King any ministration of the church and forbade all from having any contact with him. John could not withstand such a public reprimand, nor allow his barons the pretext for their continued opposition to the King because of grievances, so he submitted to the Pope and had the excommunication lifted. The barons had come to feel more keenly a sense of outrage at the way in which John continued Richard's abuses and added his own. Not only did he pervert good government, but he was a failure. They agreed that the King should be forced to accept in writing a statement of the proper norms for government, articles which would spell out the proper relationship between the King and his feudal nobility. So on June 15, 1215, John met a delegation of barons on the meadow at Runnymede near Windsor, and put his seal to the document known as Magna Carta.

Magna Carta. Over a third of the sixty-three clauses of the "Great Charter" set out the exact feudal obligations which the King's vassals owed — these included the terms of wardship, the amount of reliefs, and the occasions when feudal aids were to be paid. Another third were directed against abuses in the royal courts, particularly at John's practice of seizing a defendant's property before judgment was given against him, and the remainder of the clauses dealt with a number of other problem areas, including a promise from the King to respect the church's independence. Magna Carta asserted that the King could receive financial assistance over and above what was already due him only if granted by the assent of the "community of the realm," that is, by the approval of his feudal tenants-in-chief. Although this document dealt primarily with the relationships between the King and his feudal barons, and only incidentally with other Englishmen, it was of fundamental importance to everyone. It stated a principle of the most crucial importance, that the King was not above the law but rather was subject to it. John's assent to this document was an acceptance that he and all Englishmen belonged to a community of law, and that the law governed the ruler as well as the ruled.

Within a year John had repudiated Magna Carta, claiming that his assent was coerced and thus that his oath was not binding, and when he died in 1216 England was in the midst of a civil war as a result of his action. But every succeeding monarch reissued Magna Carta and its role as a precedent was assured. Because tradition and custom were so highly esteemed in England, nothing made an argument more effective than to cite historical precedents to support a claim, but a precedent could be made enforceable only if the aggrieved party had the military or political power to insist upon it. Obviously later kings attempted to evade the law and repeat abuses which he or his predecessors had promised to reform, but in time the rule of law would prevail, and Magna Carta would be vindicated as the fundamental precedent.

HENRY III AND PARLIAMENT

Henry III, only nine years old when his father died, became England's first minor ruler (1216-72). The Regent appointed to look after him reissued Magna Carta in the young King's name, and with the occasion for the civil wars caused by John's repudiation of it at an end, peace returned. The barons banded together to preserve the crown and kingdom for Henry, but when he began to rule on his own, they increasingly felt that their trust had been betrayed. Although the King was cultivated, gracious, and most generous in endowing fine new buildings, he was generally provocative in matters of state.

Household Government. The barons particularly resented Henry's reliance on foreign favorites, kinsmen of his French mother and his Queen. He refashioned his council, ignoring the barons who had a feudal right to give him counsel, and appointed instead the non-noble favorites who were bound to him by a special oath of loyalty. The king found it hard to control the day-to-day operation of the government because important administrative bodies had "gone out of court" (page 44), so he shifted many important financial and administrative tasks away from the Exchequer and the Chancery into household departments of his royal court such as the Wardrobe and the Chamber which were in daily attendance upon him. The growing resentment of the barons over the new council and the household government of Henry reached the breaking point in 1258. Henry sought to provide for his second son by accepting an offer of the Pope to make him King of Sicily. But the Pope did not control Sicily — to win the crown for his son, Henry would have to conquer it himself, and pay all the debts the Pope had incurred in his own unsuccessful wars of conquest! The barons who would have to go to war in order to make these ludicrous terms work had had enough.

Remembering how John had been forced to accept Magna Carta in 1215 when the barons acted together, and realizing that they would have to go further now to regain their rightful share in the government of England, the barons framed a series of articles, the Provisions of Oxford, and forced Henry to agree to them in 1258. The provisions bound Henry to embark upon a plan of reform and gave a supervisory control of the royal government to a council of barons. Henry soon rallied enough support to repudiate his acceptance of the baronial council, and because the barons did not have a single leader capable of stiffening their resolve, the King's promise to reform bought him time. When it became clear that he was insincere, and when the brilliant and mercurial Simon de Montfort stepped into the leadership of the baronial party, the barons began a civil war which ended in 1265 with Henry's capture.

The Beginning of Parliament. De Montfort realized that success in achieving governmental reform was possible only if the demand for it was broad-based and not limited to a handful of baronial tenants-in-chief. He called together in 1265 a Parliament composed not merely of the feudal nobility but also of representatives of England's shires and principal towns. The name "parliament" (from the French *parler*) was not new, because it had been used when the king met with his feudal advisors to discuss matters of state. The notion of representation was not new: the system of juries was based on the selection of men to act for their neighbors, and kings early in the thirteenth century had convened representatives of the localities — some who were even elected — to perform certain specific duties. The importance of the Parliament of 1265 was that it fused into one truly national body with general purpose potentialities the heretofore separate elements of feudal advisors and elected representatives. The two representatives from each county were called knights of the shire, and the two from each of the major boroughs were called burgesses. Although these representatives and the feudal barons might divide into smaller groups to discuss certain matters, they met as a unicameral (one house) assembly.

Later in 1265, Henry III's talented son Edward led the royalists against the barons at Evesham where he smashed their armies and killed de Montfort. But the notion of a truly national Parliament which had arisen out of the conflict was much too valuable to be lost, and Parliaments were frequently convened in the remainder of Henry's reign. At this early stage Parliaments were not legislative in character; the King after consultation could pronounce a law or statute in Parliament on his own initiative, as was done in 1267 when many of the reforms sought in the Provisions of Oxford were granted by the King in the Statute of Marlborough. The real development of Parliament as an institution lay in the future, and we shall see later in this chapter how important Henry III's son Edward was in the process.

The Common Law and Juries. The legal system fashioned by Henry I and Henry II came to maturity in the thirteenth century, primarily because as a quicker and more impartial alternative to feudal justice it attracted a greater part of the litigation. The procedures of the system of writs were uniform, the personnel homogenous because the same judges who sat in the royal courts at Westminster went throughout England twice a year on circuits to hear cases locally, and the principles which they followed were the same. This caused the system to be called the common law, based on the principles of *stare decisis,* to "stand in decisions" in earlier cases which were to be the precedents in similar matters later. This "judge-made law" based on the outcome of court cases naturally called forth a large body of legal literature to quote and comment on the precedents and required a learned profession of attorneys to plead in the courts.

In the thirteenth century the jury system was also applied to criminal cases. Previously it had been used only in disputes over property, according to the terms of the writs, and people were reluctant to judge a neighbor's actions in criminal matters where a conviction brought the death penalty. The notion of leaving the determination of guilt to God through the process of the ordeal had been severely compromised by the practice of allowing a defendant to hire a champion to represent him in the ordeal of battle. The church

ENGLAND AND WALES

recognized this and in 1215 ordered priests not to sanction ordeals any longer, significantly hastening the acceptance of juries.

There were two criminal juries, one for each stage of the process. As large a representation as possible was desired when accusations of criminal misdoings were sought, and so the name grand jury was adapted from the French *grand*, meaning large. The grand jury indicted offenders (from the Latin *in*, meaning against, and *dictum*, meaning speaking), or "spoke against" an individual. A smaller jury was used to hear the evidence and determine whether the defendant was guilty or innocent; it was called a petty jury because *petit* in French meant small. It was asked to "truly speak" about guilt or innocence, and thus rendered a verdict (from the Latin *vere* for truly, and *dictum*). At this early stage the size of the petty jury varied greatly, but in time twelve became the accepted number.

NEW ECONOMIC GROWTH

Perhaps 90 percent of England's population worked in agriculture with its traditional attitudes and techniques. But there were new economic developments which formed the prerequisites for a substantial and relatively sophisticated economic growth in the centuries to follow.

The Towns and Trade. The importance of towns was all out of proportion to their size. Only a few such as London, Bristol, and York had as many as 10,000 people, and the average size of the slightly over 100 boroughs at the beginning of the fourteenth century was about 2,000. The towns became important for a variety of reasons, some because they commanded a harbor or the confluence of two rivers or some other prominent geographical feature, some because they were centers of administration such as a shire, or the seat of a diocese with its cathedral, in which latter case alone were they properly called "cities" regardless of size. The countryside and its interests were very near, and townspeople often helped with the harvest or farmed land within or near the town. The heart of a town's prosperity, however, was trade, and when town became *borough*, the seeds of its trading growth were sown.

The transformation was made when a borough was chartered. A charter normally gave a town a degree of political independence from the shire's officers, conferred economic privileges such as markets and fairs, and enabled the burgesses to enjoy legal rights which reflected their different style of life. Some towns were boroughs before 1066 and enjoyed traditional privileges, but the practice of granting written charters coincided with the great financial needs of Richard I and

August Corn Harvest (Radio Times Hulton Picture Library).

especially of King John. A borough paid the king for its charter, and often hoped to improve on the original terms in new grants which would let it enjoy prized privileges such as those enjoyed by London and Bristol. Important lords and bishops also granted charters for boroughs. If a borough prospered, it became a potential source of greater royal income, and kings developed new types of taxation to share in their growth. But a charter was no guarantee of success, and many boroughs languished or even disappeared.

The political structure of the boroughs was rather uniform. If a borough was large enough, it was divided into wards, each of which elected an alderman. The alderman formed the upper and most important of two borough councils, electing one of their members to serve as Mayor for a year's term. The other council was larger, consisting of a number of representatives from each ward. The borough's officers enforced the laws, punished criminals, collected taxes, and kept "foreigners," as non-residents were called, from usurping the prized privileges of the burgesses.

The economic control of the borough rested with the guilds. In smaller boroughs and in the early years of the larger ones, there was only one guild to control all economic activities — the guild merchant. It enforced the rules of the markets, supervised the quality of the products which were traded, and generally directed the town's economic life. If a town flourished, an economic specialization nearly always followed, and in time separate guilds for each of the crafts were organized, such as weavers, tailors, butchers, brewers, and goldsmiths. These guilds established regulations which governed their reception of apprentices, the certification of them afterwards as journeymen (day workers) entitled to exercise the trade and, in due time, as masters. The transition from a single guild merchant to many craft guilds often involved acrimonious disputes as men fought for control of the economic life of the borough, but in time the craft guilds won out and supplanted the guild merchant.

Although in theory the political and economic control of the borough were vested in different bodies, in practice the same men ran both; to this day, the buildings which house the governmental offices of English towns are called Guildhalls. The town's life blood was the weekly or twice-weekly market; "foreigners" were welcome to buy, or to sell at wholesale those specialized products not made in the town, but the borough's success depended in large part on restricting sale at retail to its own burgesses. A fair might be held once or twice a year, specializing in products peculiar to the area. There was entertainment and fun, but its success depended on drawing merchants from throughout England and even the continent.

The Wool and Cloth Trade. England was the greatest wool-producing kingdom in Europe and from the vast numbers of sheep which dotted the hills of northern England came the fleece to make the wool cloth which most northern Europeans wore. Although it was possible merely to ship raw wool abroad, its value was considerably enhanced if it was made first into finished cloth. So many stages were involved in that process that large numbers of persons were employed full-time on estates which specialized in woolen cloth. Farmers everywhere worked at it part-time to supplement their income. In order to make cloth, shearers first removed the fleece from the animals, sending it to carders who combed it so that the wool fibers lay parallel. Spinners fashioned this into thread which weavers wove into cloth. Fullers bleached the cloth, dyers added the desired coloring, and then the cloth was stretched back into shape and trimmed to size. The cloth was sold either at fairs, or special marketing halls in England, or abroad.

In the earlier years the English were distinctly inferior to continental Europeans in making finished cloth and the conduct of the market for the sale of the cloths was dominated by aliens as well. To learn to make cloth better, the English allowed aliens to enter and to teach the trade. By the beginning of the fourteenth century the English had begun to use the capitalistic method of controlling the manufacture of cloth, in which an entrepreneur gathered materials prepared at one stage of the process and delivered them to the next, and so assumed the responsibility of seeing the product through all its complicated preparation. In 1326 the English moved to gain control of the marketing stages as well, forbidding, as before, purchasers from abroad to travel throughout England to the various fairs to buy cloths, and instead allowing them to buy only in a few regulated halls stocked with cloth gathered by English middlemen. With such a small number of set places for purchase, called "staple towns," the government was better able to supervise the trade, collect a new type of tax in the form of customs duties, and enforce the laws which controlled the quality of the products. Customs duties were also collected on the commodities which the English imported: wine from France, spices from Venice and other areas which traded with the far east, and naval stores such as timber and pitch for building ships from Scandinavia. From these modest beginnings would develop an ever increasing volume of trade, until in the eighteenth and nineteenth centuries England would be the greatest trading nation in the world.

Medieval York. Few towns better illustrate the importance of the new municipal government and the wool trade than York in northern England. On the moors and other hilly terrain to the north and west of this city grazed countless sheep, many on the estates of the Cistercian monks who had introduced the raising of sheep into England. York's location on the River Ouse gave it direct access to the North Sea and thus to continental markets. It was important militarily because it lay astride the only lowland route from England to Scotland and administratively as the center of Yorkshire and as the cathedral city of the diocese of York.

As the headquarters of the Roman garrison whose legions protected the northern frontier of Roman Britain (pages 20-22), York had been laid out on neat military lines. The seventy acres within the walls housed barracks and other military buildings which had been built in rectangular fashion at right angles to the river. Medieval York was different in a number of ways. Gone was the neat pattern of streets, to be replaced by wandering lanes at helter-skelter angles, spilling out beyond the old walls to cover an area three times as great, even though the walls were kept as a fortification. The costly buildings were no longer military but ecclesiastical — forty-seven parish churches, several abbeys, and the jewel of the city, York Minster, the Archbishop's cathedral with its captivatingly lovely gothic arches and windows. These churches were aligned not with the river, but so that the morning sun in the east spilled through the windows to illumine the divine services. There was a Guildhall for the borough's officers and separate buildings to house the guilds of the various trades.

York was alive with activity. Food and drink were sold from dawn to dusk in the open market on the broad expanse of the center of town, called the Pavement, on Tuesdays, Thursdays, and Saturdays, while cloth and household needs were sold in another market on Thursdays

Knight and King, west facade, Exeter Cathedral.

and Saturdays. The areas in which the approximately sixty craft guilds were concentrated were revealed in the street names such as Tanner Lane and the Shambles, the latter where the butchers slaughtered animals in the street, letting the blood and offal ooze towards the Ouse. The narrow paved streets allowed little sunlight or breeze to disperse the smells and sounds of trade, and because the upper stories of the houses extended further into the street than those on the ground level, the streets felt even more constricted.

York's burgesses were prospering, and aside from the laborers, the largest guilds were those of the weavers and tailors. The guilds and the religious confraternities of the city sponsored the mystery plays and pageants which provided much color and entertainment. The city's officers policed the markets to supervise quality and proper measures, so that the deceitful merchant suffered the ignominy and appropriate punishment of having to drink his putrid beer in public, or eat the spoiled food he had attempted to pass off. Urban problems and pollution know no bounds of time or place, but they arose in York to greater degrees because the fleece of the sheep and the success of trade brought population, prosperity, and plenty.

HIGH MEDIEVAL CULTURE

The late eleventh and the twelfth centuries were times of an intellectual revival in Europe. Some call it a "renaissance," a "rebirth" because the rediscovery of classical Roman and Greek writings had a major part. By the late twelfth and thirteenth centuries, the attitudes and institutions of this revival had become a mature part of English life.

The Intellectual Revival. The great rediscoveries which sparked the renaissance were in the fields of literature, law, and philosophy. Medieval scholars studied Roman literature to learn how to improve their own writing style and to discover the virtues and ideals which had let Rome dominate the ancient world. The most accomplished English man of letters was John of Salisbury. He studied abroad, and then applied his considerable talents not only as a writer, but also in domestic and diplomatic services for prominent leaders of the English church.

Medieval man was especially intrigued by the study of law and philosophy because he found them highly amenable to synthesis, the drawing together into one coherent and organized system of a tremendous breadth of knowledge. The rediscovery in the eleventh century of the magnificent codification of Roman law made centuries earlier by the Emperor Justinian spurred medieval scholars to adapt this to the church's needs. The study of canon law flourished in England

and helped provide the theoretical underpinnings for Henry II's legal innovations, and for Becket's insistence on the church's privileges in his quarrels with Henry.

Theology was the most important medieval study: it placed God at the center of things, and began with His revealed truths which were the surest knowledge. The contribution of the intellectual revival was to make philosophy the handmaid of theology, to provide the tools of logic which would allow man to deduce useful knowledge from revelation. The Greeks had been the great philosophers of antiquity, but many of their ideas were unknown in the West. The conquest of the East by the Moslems put them into direct contact with Greek thought. Eager Moslem intellectuals translated the works of Plato, Aristotle, and other philosophers into Arabic and incorporated them into Moslem thought. In the twelfth century translations from Arabic into Latin were the key to reopen a study of classical philosophy in western Europe. A Dominican friar at the University of Paris, St. Thomas Aquinas, "baptized" Aristotle, combining pagan philosophy and Christian dogma to produce a stunningly magnificent synthesis of theology. Before long the contents and techniques of this new learning had captured most European schools.

Universities. The broadened content of medieval knowledge demanded better facilities for study. Good teachers drew good students, but it was easy for landlords and civic officials to victimize the students who were in their early teens, and a teacher might collect fees and then not teach. The first reaction was for students themselves to form a guild to protect themselves, and professors formed their own guild to ensure proper qualifications for instruction and protect their interests. In time a single corporate body called a university developed, with specific privileges and responsibilities set out in a charter. The first English university was at Oxford to which many of the English students came when called home from the University of Paris by Henry II in 1167 during his quarrels with Becket. Gradually a center of learning developed, interrupted by quarrels between the townspeople and the often rowdy students, called "town and gown" riots (The students' academic dress was a gown). These difficulties were overcome at the beginning of the thirteenth century by the bishop's supervision and control. A second university grew at Cambridge, but was a good deal smaller than Oxford in its early years.

Oxford and Cambridge were in reality loose confederations of colleges, as the residential centers of instruction were called. A college was a corporation whose members, later called "fellows," were nearly always priests. Many of the students went on to become priests, and the students' day was much like that in a monastery. They arose before dawn for prayer and mass, and returned for prayer at stated intervals during the day. In the usual three years it required to earn a B.A. degree, they studied the seven liberal arts of grammar, rhetoric, logic, arithmetic, geometry, astronomy, and music. Books were rare, so the students took notes during lectures, memorized them, and then formally disputed selected topics — all in Latin, of course.

Although most European universities were similar, Oxford did have some distinguishing features. Bishop Robert Grosseteste who once headed the university was very interested in science, and urged that the normal deductive process of learning be supplemented by observation, the forming of hypotheses, and experimentation. This uncharacteristic process was also advocated by a Franciscan friar very interested in science, Roger Bacon. Another Franciscan, Duns Scotus, was an influential philosophical thinker who differed in some respects from the accepted system of Thomas Aquinas.

The Friars and the Religious Revival. A spiritual revival was sparked by the creation on the continent of new religious communities, the friars. St. Dominic formed an order of preaching friars in Spain to teach true doctrine and combat heresies, and on the Italian peninsula St. Francis of Assisi renounced his well-to-do heritage to embrace "the lady poverty" and teach his followers to imitate the humility and simplicity of the Lord. The Dominican and Franciscan friars did not live withdrawn from men in monasteries, but went among the people, especially in towns, to teach, preach, and instruct by pious example.

Both communities of friars came to England in the 1220s. Because they believed in the importance of education and sound religious instruction they were well prepared, especially when compared with the often inadequate training of the normal parish priest. Their emphasis on education led many to the universities; we have seen how important the Dominicans were at Paris, and the Franciscans at Oxford. The friars often aroused the jealousy of the parish priests, but their emphasis on preaching to the poor and unlettered made a significant impact on English spiritual life.

Gothic Architecture. The piety of the age was also expressed in stone and mortar, in new churches and in extensions built on the older ones. The Romanesque style of the tenth and eleventh centuries tended to be squat and massive because the walls had to support the entire weight of the roof. The Gothic style which developed in the twelfth and later centuries utilized the discovery that the weight of a roof, if concentrated over a center of gravity atop a pointed arch, could be thrust down through slender columns in the walls. Since the walls proper were no longer supporting the roof, they could be considerably lighter and

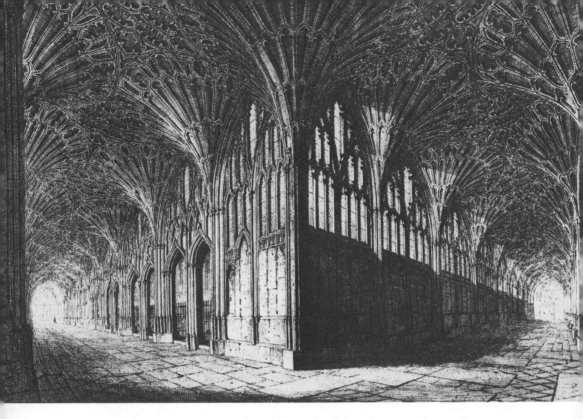

Fan vaulting, Gloucester Cathedral (Dugdale, Monasticon Anglicanum).

include large windows which were usually decorated with stained glass.

The change was immediately apparent when one entered a gothic cathedral: with an interior height reaching and even exceeding 100 feet, the effect was to sweep the eye and, perhaps, the spirit heavenward. The ceilings were beautifully decorated in fan vaulting, as the columns of the walls branched out in fingers along the roof to reach the center of gravity and carry the weight downward. The stained glass windows became textbooks of Bible stories and pious legends to instruct the unlettered faithful. The airy and light effect of Gothic architecture was as refined and reflective of the intellectual outreach of the twelfth century renaissance as the massive Romanesque or Norman style was of the more military emphasis of the eleventh century.

EDWARD I AND EDWARD II

Edward I (1272-1307) was one of the strongest medieval kings, well-schooled by the difficulties of his father's, Henry III's, reign. He was a tall, imposing man who commanded great respect, a talented administrator whose effective use of household government and of Parliament are monuments to his energy and control. Domestic affairs flourished under his leadership, but wars in France, Scotland, and Wales caused no end of difficulty.

Edward I and Parliament. Edward had seen how useful a national Parliament could be. He called as many as two Parliaments a year, and although at first the representatives of the shires and boroughs were called infrequently, his growing need for revenue to finance his wars suggested having present regularly the representatives of his subjects who would pay the parliamentary taxes. In 1295 a Parliament met, which much later was to be called the "Model Parliament," not because its organization became a precedent to be followed invariably thereafter, but because all the categories of membership were present which would be included when the exact composition of Parliament would be fixed in the following century. It must have been a magnificent sight — twenty bishops and seventy abbots in their ecclesiastical robes, fifty earls and barons, representatives of the lower clergy from each diocese, and representatives of the shires and 110 towns, more soberly clad as befitted their common rank.

After the opening prayers and sermon, the King addressed the community of the realm and presented his needs. The burgesses withdrew across the way to Westminster Abbey to deliberate, the King and his inner council moved to a nearby chapel, and the others remained in the Great Hall of Westminster Palace. Over a period of about ten days, these various groups received petitions which protested grievances, considered the grant of taxes, heard judicially cases of great importance, and counseled the King on important matters. This completed, all met together again in the Great Hall to hear the King promulgate as statutes the new laws he granted which were based on some of the petitions, and to thank the assembly for the grant of taxes.

Edward used Parliament very effectively to codify much of the law "Judge-made law" with its reliance on precedents hammered out in numerous trials had been the basis of the common law, but now Edward restated the laws on property, criminal offenses, and other matters succinctly in statutory form. Common law certainly did not disappear — an offence could be punished at common law even if it had not been defined in a statute — but the principle gradually developed that the law could be changed only with Parliament's consent.

A crucial precedent for Parliament's future importance was won in 1297 when Edward was fighting to maintain control of Gascony, the area of southwestern France which was not included in Richard I's homage to the French King and thus still one of England's possessions. So great was Edward's need for funds that Parliament resisted, asking that as a sign of good faith the King reissue many charters of privileges. Included in this Confirmation of Charters of 1297 was Edward's promise not to seek extraordinary funds without the consent of the "community of the realm." Magna Carta in 1215 stated that extraordinary *feudal* income could be granted only with the community's consent, but at the time the "community" meant the feudal barons; the Conformation of Charters set conditions for grants of non-feudal revenues, but now "community" meant Parliament — quite a broadening of the political nation in 82 years. Over future centuries, with much travail and long periods of reversal, these two precedents would give Parliament the control of finances, and eventually of the monarch.

Edward I and Scotland. Scotland had kept its independence by withstanding invasions attempted by the Romans, Anglo-Saxons, and Normans, but its separateness from England was gradually weakened as the Scottish royalty married into the English royal family. In 1173 Henry II had used a minor border clash as the first step in a full-scale battle with the Scots and the defeated Scots King did homage to Henry for Scotland. Later, Henry III had improved relations by marrying his daughter to the King of Scotland, a minor. By 1290 the young Scottish King and all his direct descendants were dead, and the Scots saw no other way out of a complicated disputed succession than to leave the decision to Edward I as overlord. Edward insisted before hearing the case that the claimants and Scotland's leaders take oaths which explicitly reasserted his superior position, and when he kept intervening in Scottish affairs even after choosing a new King of Scotland, Scottish patriotism was awakened.

The Scots began to ignore Edward I, and even to seek an independent alliance with France. In 1296 Edward I ordered deposed the king whom he had chosen and sent him into exile. Robert Bruce, the descendant of the unsuccessful claimant of the same name in the disputed succession case, then had himself crowned King of Scotland and began to rebel against Edward. Edward's military victories won him the title "Hammer of the Scots," but his opponents would not give up, and Edward died in 1307 during still another battle in the tenth year of the struggles.

Wales and Ireland. The Welsh had retained their independence from England longer than the other Celtic kingdoms on the British Isles. The mountains had been an effective barrier against invaders, but because the Welsh leaders were continually bickering among themselves, they were really no threat to England. Llewelyn the Great (died 1240) was the first Welsh leader to succeed in uniting the Welsh against England, but Henry III had defeated him and conferred on his son Edward many Welsh lands to make an English presence felt there. Opposition to England began again in the 1260s, this time led by Llewelyn ap Gruffyd who took the title "Prince of Wales." His early victories especially humiliated Edward whose estates were overrun, and on his father's behalf (and then on his own when he became King), Edward completely defeated the Welsh. The statutes for Wales in 1284 symbolized the English domination, as did Edward I's gift of the title of Prince of Wales to his son, a title to this day born by the heir apparent to the English crown.

England had had far more success at an earlier date in Ireland, which Henry II had conquered with papal approval because of the sad state into which the church had fallen. Two-thirds of the island was under English control and the remainder was the battleground of clan leaders who continually fought among themselves. Under later kings the English system of government and common law was introduced, but the fights of the Scots and Welsh against English control awakened an Irish patriotism which in future centuries caused England no end of trouble.

Edward II. Edward I's son was unworthy of his father's legacy. Indolent, willing to seek any amusement rather than work at government, one who scandalized his subjects because his foreign favorite, Peter de Gaveston, was his lover who monopolized his attention, Edward II brought ruin upon England's military ventures and then upon himself. The Scottish situation was not attended properly, in part because of Edward's vacillation and weakness of character, more importantly because he was protecting Gaveston whom the English barons particularly wanted to remove. English forces in the north lost the military advantage, and Scottish victories such as at Bannockburn in 1314 added to the king's ignominy. He refused to recognize Bruce as King and only a series of truces kept the Scots from occupying even more of northern England.

The barons reacted to Edward by forcing upon him in 1311 a set of Ordinances which committed the King to reform and imposed a baronial council to control government. Edward was able to rally support and repudiate the Ordinances, as John had done with Magna Carta and Henry III with the Provisions of Oxford. But just as Magna Carta had been reissued later, and the Statute of Marlborough granted much the Provisions had sought, so Edward II had to yield in a Statute of York in 1322 many of the reforms sought in the Ordinances. The barons did not stop there, but captured Gaveston and had him executed, sparking the King to further vengeance and obstinancy. Later Edward's wife took a lover, Roger Mortimer, and together they and others of the baronial party who were sick of misgovernment persuaded Parliament to debate how Edward had ignored his promises to govern justly and wisely. Edward was forced to abdicate and allow his minor son to rule as Edward III; within a year Edward II had been murdered in prison to get him out of the way.

SUGGESTIONS FOR FURTHER READING

Henry II's troublesome family is described in Amy Kelly, *Eleanor of Aquitaine and the Four Kings* (1950), and separate studies of her royal sons are James A. Brundage, *Richard Lion Heart* (1974) and Sidney Painter, *The Reign of King John* (1949). A very lengthy treatment of John's son is F. M. Powicke's *King Henry III and the Lord Edward* (2 vols., 1947). L. F. Salzman's *Edward I* (1968) is very brief, and Caroline Bingham's *The Life and Times of Edward II* (1973) is profusely illustrated.

The best study of the Magna Carta is J. C. Holt, *Magna Carta* (1965). Useful for the background to the Parliament of 1265 is Margaret Wade Labarge's *Simon de Montfort* (1962). The organization and powers of the early parliaments have attracted a raft of extremely capable scholars, and so voluminous are the writings that a guide is needed, such as Gerald Bodet's *Early English Parliaments. High Courts, Royal Councils, or Representative Assemblies?* (1968). W. S. Holdsworth, *History of English Law* (7th ed., 16 vols., 1956) treats medieval law, including the development of common law and the origin of juries, in the first three volumes of his work.

H. S. Bennet's *Life on the English Manor* (1937) is a classic; different strata on the social scale are studied in Margaret Wade Labarge's *A Baronial Household of the Thirteenth Century* (1965) and R. H. Hilton, *The English Peasantry in the Later Middle Ages* (1975). Aspects of medieval life and customs are presented in the many separate essays edited by Austin Lane Poole as *Medieval England* (new edition, 2 vols., 1958). Eileen Power's *The Wool Trade in English Medieval History* (1941) is a short introduction. A great amount of historical reconstruction, rarely possible for long lost days, is a result of post World War II aerial photography, reflected in M. W. Beresford and J. K. S. St. Joseph, *Medieval England. An Aerial Survey* (1958).

David Knowles treats the friars in Vol. I of *The Religious Orders in England* (3 vols., 1950), and puts intellectual advances including the medieval renaissance and the origin of universities in an European context in *The Evolution of Medieval Thought* (1962). Doreen Yarwood's *The Architecture of England from Prehistoric Times to the Present Day* (1963) is an excellent brief presentation, and more detail can be found in Hugh Braun, *An Introduction to English Mediaeval Architecture* (1951).

4

Late Medieval England

1327-1529

If England is considered from the aspect of strong political power over these two hundred years, 1327-1529, or of peace and tranquility, or of military success in the wars against the French, then certainly England was in decline. The feudal bonds which had knit society together were unravelling, the Hundred Years' War gained neither territory nor the French crown, and the civil wars of the fifteenth century severely dislocated the political state.

Yet if the intangibles which give a country its unique character are considered, it was a period of transition and not of decline. In the early fourteenth century the leaders of England spoke French and followed French ways. In the early sixteenth century, Englishmen spoke English and attended to domestic business by preference, and distinctly English institutions such as Parliament had an increased importance. The Tudor monarchs who ruled after 1485 even arrested the political decline by reviving royal power and ending the drift of the civil wars. The peace and prosperity which they brought were the preconditions of England's assumption of an important place in European affairs.

THE FOURTEENTH CENTURY:
GROWTH AND DISRUPTION, 1327-1399

Edward III and the Hundred Years' War. Edward III (1327-77) was a warm, cheerful, and inspiring leader, at once a practical man of affairs and an idealist. He had learned from his father's reign how deeply the barons resented their exclusion from the inner circles of power. As a valiant and generous warrior he led his realm to war and thus gave his nobility the sweet taste of victory and the comradeship of a shared mission — no aristocratic rebellion ever scarred his reign. In all of this he set a high moral tone: he made chivalry and pageantry points of policy, and by founding the Order of the Garter as an honorific society he had the means for rewarding men of similar ideals.

The "Hundred Years' War" which Edward began lasted from 1338-1453, but in reality was a series of intermittent campaigns of limited fighting often interrupted by long years of truces. The war was distinctly new in several important aspects. When England fought in the thirteenth century it was to regain territories such as Normandy which John had forfeited to Philip Augustus, but in the fourteenth and fifteenth century the English King fought as a claimant for the crown of France herself. Edward's mother Isabelle was the sister of the childless French King (the last of the House of Capet) who died in 1328. By "inventing" the Salic law which excluded descent through a female, the French denied Edward the crown and instead it passed to a French cousin, Philip VI, the first of the House of Valois.

The tactics of warfare changed also when the English began to use the longbow as a weapon. Before the Norman Conquest the English had relied on the militia of the shires, and after 1066 on the feudal host in which heavily armored knights acted as a mounted calvary. Edward III's bowmen were capable of shooting arrows with a force sufficient to pierce chainmail, so that when the French knights charged the English at Crécy in 1346 the English bowmen slaughtered the flower of the French nobility in a terrible carnage. This success was repeated in 1356 at Poitiers, when the French King himself was captured and held for ransom. It was impossible to convert these individual triumphs into total victory. The cost of sustained warfare was staggering, England lacked the financial resources, and France had a substantially greater area and population. Belatedly the French adopted the new military tactics and thus erased the English advantage, and the capable French leader Bertrand du Guesclin began to wage a war of guerilla tactics which relentlessly destroyed the English forces. By 1377 England's military gains had evaporated and its original holdings in southwestern France had been severely curtailed.

The Growth of Parliamentary Powers. When Edward I promulgated the Confirmation of Charters in 1297 he established the principle that Parliament alone could grant the king extraordinary revenues; Edward's financial needs thus gave Parliament a tremendously increased importance. It was quickly agreed that the consent of the elected representatives of the counties (two knights of each shire) and of the boroughs (two burgesses apiece) was needed to grant taxes. These representatives were present at every one of Edward's nearly annual parliaments, and in 1339 these two classes of members met together to act jointly for the first time; these "men of the commons" were eventually to be the House of Commons. The secular and ecclesiastical lords formed the House of Lords, and the representatives of the lower clergy ceased to attend Parliament but instead met with the bishops in a separate ecclesiastical parliament called Convocation which granted the king taxes on the church's wealth.

At each Parliament many individual petitions were presented to the king. If he decided to provide a remedy for any of the grievances he and his advisors drafted a statute and asked for Parliament's concurrence. Not until the fifteenth century did Parliament gain the initiative to propose legislation and word the bills to specify the remedies, but a step in this direction was taken in 1327 when individual petitions were grouped together into one common petition for the whole realm. This composite was singularly more compelling than the scattered requests, and thus the kings felt a certain moral constraint to provide comprehensive remedies. In 1340 the House of Commons delayed a grant of taxes until the King had first acted on the common petition, and thus the control over the purse became a means to help exact legislation.

The political vacuum late in Edward's reign when he was too old to control his government led to additional gains for Parliament. Edward's third son, John of Gaunt, felt that he could grasp power by replacing the King's councillors with men loyal to himself, but by 1376 the King's eldest son, Edward the Black Prince, led a reaction. In the "Good Parliament" of that year the process of impeachment was used for the first time to remove John of Gaunt's "evil councillors," a process thus initially and henceforth directed at a king's advisors and never at the king himself. Even though John of Gaunt's faction was able to reassert itself a year later, the precedent had been set of Parliament's control of a royal minister.

The Black Death and Agriculture. The plague which destroyed so much of England's population in the first attack in 1348-51 had begun fifteen years earlier in China and had traveled across Europe along the trade routes. The rats on the ships carried the fleas which bore the bubonic plague; the infected persons suffered a grotesque swelling of the glands before death. There are no accurate figures to measure accurately the loss of life. Perhaps 25-40 percent of the entire English population died, nearly half of the clergy, and scores of densely populated settlements such as towns, villages, and monasteries were wiped out — a pattern repeated in much of Europe. Even after the first attack had subsided the plague recurred often in England for three hundred years. The sense of personal tragedy at the horrible toll was profound, the fear evoked by such a visitation was appalling, and the consequences for society were far-reaching and revolutionary. Before 1348 England had been relatively over-populated and many peasants were in effect tied to the soil to render servile labor to their feudal lords on their vast demesnes. This system which was known as "high farming" came to an end with the plague because the ensuing labor scarcity meant that the villeins now had a valuable and avidly sought commodity. They could easily run away from a lord who did not end servile status and another lord who was desperate for help to harvest his crops would hire them, no questions asked.

The immediate reaction of the propertied class was repression, a Statute of Laborers (1351) which attempted to hold wages to pre-plague levels. The agricultural workers felt deeply grieved by the Statute and by novel taxes levied against them as well as the wealthy, and in 1381 many rose in the Peasants' Revolt. The King suppressed the rising, but not before there were many indications of class hostility against the lords. Indeed the lords' style of life was altered as well as the workers' — unable to hire enough men to farm their demesne, the lords leased it out in smaller parcels and thus lived off the rents rather than be directly engaged in supervisory farming as before.

Wycliffe and the Church. The plague had a profound impact on religious life, as men analyzed it in terms of the divine wrath and began to conceptualize God as the God of judgment and retribution rather than of love and popular devotion. The death of so many clergymen necessarily curtailed proper religious instruction so that superstition increased. The prestige of the institutional church was hurt when from 1309-77 the popes were French and resided in Avignon in southern France rather than in Rome. Their stay in France coincided with the Hundred Years' War and strained relations between England and the Papacy. From 1378, for a short time, there were two popes, one at Avignon and one at Rome, each fulminating against the other and thus lowering the church's prestige.

There was no fourteenth century religious revival as their had been in many earlier centuries, and the uncorrected abuses called forth criticism and satire. The Oxford scholar John Wycliffe at first merely

Benedictine monk (Dugdale, Monasticon Anglicanum*).*

criticized these faults, but then moved on to doctrinal heresy. He denied the efficacy of the sacraments as channels of divine grace and rejected Jesus' real presence in the consecrated Eucharist. In turn this led him to denigrate many of the church's roles and to insist that the Scriptures be translated into English to allow personal religious instruction. Wycliff's followers came to be called Lollards, and although he died in 1384 of natural causes, the seeds of doubt which he had sown and which the Lollards nutured in an underground movement had challenged the church's authority.

Richard II and Absolutism. At Edward III's death in 1377 his grandson Richard II (1377-99) was only ten (Richard's father, Edward the Black Prince, had died in 1376). This thoughtful young man had a goal, the restoration of the monarch's powers to the strength of Edward I's reign, and thus he wished to reverse the loss of power wrung from Edward II and the voluntary losses Edward III endured to win taxes to pay for his wars. As a youth Richard gathered about him a "court party" which shared his absolutist goals, but as soon as his domineering uncle John of Gaunt, Duke of Lancaster, went abroad in 1386, Richard was left unprotected and exposed to the barons who abhorred his absolutist views.

In 1386 Parliament impeached Richard's most able minister and imposed a baronial council to reform his government. Richard obtained judicial opinions which supported his views and which denied the propriety of Parliament's actions, but the latter had the power and in 1388 five leading lords "appealed" against Richard's supporters and removed them so thoroughly that it became known as the "Merciless Parliament." His powers temporarily eclipsed, Richard quietly bided his time to rebuild his court party.

By 1397 he was strong enough to pack Parliament with his supporters and this compliant assembly "appealed" against three of the five Lords Appellant and sent the other two into exile, including John of Gaunt's son Henry Bolingbroke. When John died in 1399, Richard refused to allow the normal succession of the Lancastrian lands and titles to Henry, so he returned to England with an army, rallied the lords to his cause, and Parliament debated and then received Richard's abdication when he returned from a campaign in Ireland. Within a year Richard was dead, probably murdered. Although Parliament played a role in the abdications in both 1327 and 1399, the real precipitating causes in both cases was non-parliamentary military might. But in 1327 the normal heir-apparent became King, whereas in 1399 there were cousins with better claims to succeed the childless Richard than Henry IV (as Bolingbroke styled himself). Royal absolutism had been stopped, but tampering with the legal descent of the crown would dictate much of the strife of the fifteenth century.

CHAUCER'S ENGLAND

Chaucer and the Revival of English Letters. Geoffrey Chaucer (*c.* 1343-1400) combined an extraordinarily wide range of personal experiences with a keen eye for detecting the strengths and weakness of men and women, and with a flair for setting down his characterizations in striking prose. He was well acquainted with the world of business because his father and grandfather had been wine merchants in London, and he himself served later as comptroller of customs there. He had served with Edward III's army in France and had even been captured and ransomed, and in later years went abroad on the King's behalf on diplomatic missions. He knew the nobility well and was befriended by the Lancastrians, and was a Justice of the Peace and sat in Parliament.

As one of the first major writers to use and prefer English instead of French, Chaucer allowed his countrymen to experience the richness and suppleness of their native language. One of his greatest gifts was the ability to portray vividly the ideals and prejudices of many different classes and walks of life. In *Troilus and Criseyde* he described the world of the king and court, and in *The Canterbury Tales* he immortalized a monk, a friar, a worldly prioress, and other pilgrims who told stories as they walked to the shrine of St. Thomas à Becket in Canterbury.

Chaucer was the greatest of many writers who wrote in English, but other authors as well increasingly chose to use English rather than Latin. English had long been the language of the towns and byways of rural England where wandering minstrels sang English ballads, versified narratives of heroic deeds such as wars against the French and Scots and recounted episodes of chivalrous romance. Occasionally the ballads reflected social discontent, as in the Robin Hood legends where a man of common stock and uncommon abilities harassed immoral sheriffs and kings. There were other means of popular instruction in English as well. The stained glass windows in churches with their vivid colors had long taught Bible stories to the illiterate flocks; now the church's drama spilled out into the churchyards and towns in the plays called mystery stories. These recreated Bible episodes and pious legends always taught a moral, but sometimes they upset stern officials because the moral lesson was often interspersed with stretches of broad humor which all too accurately portrayed the foibles of sinful man.

Many of the writings on chivalry which were written for the upper classes now were in English. Perhaps the greatest early English heroic poem was *Sir Gawain and the Green Knight*. This epic and many other poems based on the legend of King Arthur seemed to have a special

Geoffrey Chaucer, Ellesmere MSS (Henry E. Huntington Library and Art Gallery).

relevance to a kingdom at war. There were equally as impressive writings on social and religious reform, notable *Piers Plowman* by William Langland, a poor cleric who made his hero a simple man whose sufferings and ideals contrasted favorably with the worldliness and uninspiring lives of many in the church who compromised their Christian principles.

Chaucer's London. The 40,000 Londoners lived in the area of less than a square mile within the city's ancient walls, yet the city was alive with the sights and smells of the nearby countryside. There were signs of the ancient past now abutted by the commercial present, as in the wharves which lined the riverside. Although London was distinctly English, it did house many aliens who were part of the international trading community. The ecclesiastical buildings were the most striking. There were about 100 parish churches within the walls and another 20 in nearby areas, there were numerous abbeys and friaries which housed men and women of almost every religious order in England, and the

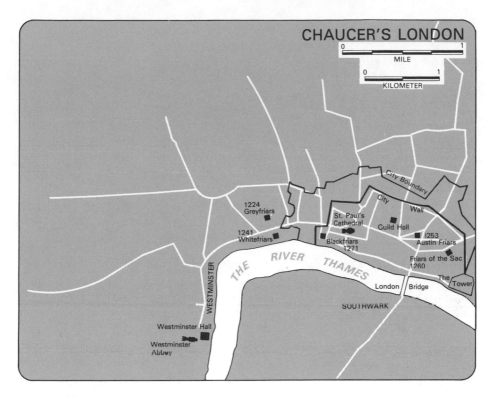

CHAUCER'S LONDON

whole was capped by the inspiring cathedral of St. Paul. This massive building — 560 feet long and nearly 300 feet wide, with an interior height of nearly 200 feet and a spire nearly reaching 500 feet — was much larger than the present cathedral built after the great fire of 1666. London's parishes were not only centers of worship but also served particular craft guilds whose members often worshipped as a group, and housed parish guilds which looked after the poor and cared for widows and orphans. Almost every bishop kept a palace in London, and their sumptuous buildings were concentrated on the main road to nearby Westminster and on the river.

The many buildings dedicated to trade reflected London's position as the commercial hub of England. There were numerous markets to feed London's masses, and names such as Poultry, Ironmonger Lane, Fish Street Hill, and Honey Lane testify to concentrations of tradesmen. Small industry dotted the city, so that workshops and forges were a common sight. Over half of the wool exported from England passed through London and Londoners also dominated cloth export. Foreign merchants such as the German Hanseatic League maintained massive trading complexes in London.

The craft guilds were so important that they dominated the city's government. A man was a citizen of London only if he belonged to a guild and so less than a fourth of the city's residents were eligible to participate in government. Thus a trading oligarchy ruled the city and the greatest had a privileged position — the Mercers and Drapers who dealt in clothing, the Fishmongers and Grocers who provided food, the Vintners who controlled wine, and a handful of other major companies. Power was further concentrated when the major guilds swallowed up smaller but related trades as the Haberdashers did with the Capmakers. London had become so wealthy and important that after 1392 no monarch attempted to tamper with the city's government, but rather courted it for the support and financial assistance his royal government needed.

The city's population also included a number of specialized and important occupations. The king's ministers lived not only in the western suburbs near Westminster but also in eastern London near the military complex in the Tower of London and near the royal mint. Many lawyers lived in and near London because they pleaded cases in the royal courts, and students wishing to enter the profession prepared at the numerous Inns of Court and Inns of Chancery which were centers for legal education. Much of Chaucer's London was glittering — sumptuous pageantry and elaborate processions were frequent; there were many luxury shops which supplied jewels and the newly fashionable embroidered, colored clothing. The homes of the wealthy were larger than ever before and featured handsome furniture and tapestries. But London had the appalling problems common to all English and European cities — poor sanitation, overcrowding, and the threat of the plague and other diseases.

THE FIFTEENTH CENTURY: DISLOCATION AND STRAIN, 1399-1485

The Lancastrians and the War with France. Richard II had tried to deny Henry Bolingbroke his Lancastrian dukedom and lands when John of Gaunt died in 1399, and so Bolingbroke's forces had won for him not only the dukedom but the crown of England as well. Henry IV (1399-1413) was an impressive, thoughtful, skillful man whose youthful vigor was so weakened by failing health that in his last years he neurotically grasped at his last shreds of strength. He needed strength to face many difficulties. Richard II had been childless so that the line of descent through the first of Edward III's sons was closed; Henry was the third son, and his seizure of the crown excluded the

MEDIEVAL ENGLAND
AND FRANCE

0   200
MILES

0   200
KILOMETERS

SCOTLAND

IRELAND

NORTH SEA

York

ENGLAND

Norwich

Cambridge

WALES   Bristol

Oxford

London

FLANDERS

Exeter   Southhampton

HOLY

ROMAN

EMPIRE

DEPENDENT
UPON ENGLAND

Calais

Agincourt

Crecy

ENGLISH CHANNEL

NORMANDY

Paris

UNDER

BRITTANY

MAINE

FRENCH

ANJOU

CONTROL

FULLEST EXTENT OF ENGLISH CONTROL IN FRANCE

POITOU

BAY OF BISCAY

A Q U I T A I N E

Bordeaux

GUYENNE

GASCONY

SPANISH   KINGDOMS

MEDITERRANEAN SEA

second son, Lionel, Duke of Clarence. Not until 1410 did Henry IV put behind him the last of many rebellions raised by Clarence's descendants and their Welsh allies.

Meanwhile the French had seized the initiative in the wars and had even landed raiding parties on the south coast of England. Henry IV's finances were so precarious that resuming a full-scale war was out of the question, but luckily for him two factions of the French royal house, the Burgundians and the Orleanists, began in 1407 to feud among themselves. This gave Henry breathing space which stilled the mounting criticism in Parliament but increased the scheming of his son Henry who was so anxious to press the seeming military advantage that he was willing even to plot with his father's enemies.

Upon his accession Henry V (1413-22) renewed the war immediately. He was an effective and self-confident fighter who insensitively dominated his friends and foes alike. The barons rallied to his side, and the English victory over the French at Agincourt in 1415 was so overwhelming that it evoked memories of Crécy and Poitiers nearly a century earlier. In 1420 Henry sided with the Burgundian faction and together they controlled northern France. Henry and the Duke of Burgundy made an agreement by which Henry would become King of France as soon as the present but insane French King died. It was while Henry was moving southward against the Orleanists that he died of dysentery a few months before the French King died.

It seemed that England was on the verge of its greatest achievements but the reality was just the opposite: under Henry VI (1422-61) the English monarchy reached its lowest point in foreign and domestic affairs. Henry VI became King of France according to the terms of the agreement between his father and the Duke of Burgundy, but the Orleanists under the inspiration of Joan of Arc began a military effort that led to ultimate victory and the expulsion of the English from France. So convinced was the young peasant maiden Joan of the message which she heard from heavenly voices that she conveyed her sense of mission to the head of the Orleanists who was consecrated as Charles VII. As Joan rode in armor with his revitalized forces they swept to victory after victory. Even though the Burgundians captured Joan and delivered her to the English who burned her as a witch, the Duke of Burgundy read the signs of the times and allied himself with the Orleanists. By 1453 when the Hundred Years War ended France was a unified country and England had been left with only one town on the French mainland, Calais.

The domestic legacy of the Lancastrians was nearly as ruinous. Parliament gained many important powers because of the instability and military failures of Henry IV and of the concessions Henry V made to secure funds for his wars. The House of Commons gained in particular when it began to dictate to the King how taxes were to be spent and to examine his accounts to insure that he had complied. Parliament began to frame its own bills rather than to allow the King to dictate the provisions of remedies for grievances.

Henry VI was merely the puppet of his uncles during his long minority, and was so inept as an adult that the government nearly collapsed. He had some personally attractive characteristics such as a love for art and a generosity in founding schools, but his nearly total withdrawal from public affairs led to a breakdown in law and order and internal feuding between the different Lancastrian factions. This vacuum in political leadership coincided with severe economic depressions to make England's prospects grim.

The Yorkists and the Wars of the Roses. Since Henry IV had earlier repressed uprisings by the Duke of Clarence's descendants there had been little further agitation over the Lancastrian usurpation of the crown. Meanwhile a female descendant of the Clarence line had married the Duke of York (a descendant of Edward III's fourth son), and although their offspring bore their father's title they retained the superior theoretical claim of the Clarence line over the Lancastrians.

During the wars with France a Yorkist official had been removed from command and gradually the relations between the two families worsened. In 1455 they fought the first battle in a civil war for the throne which centuries later was dubbed the "Wars of the Roses" because the Yorkists' coat of arms included a white rose and the Lancastrians' (a mistaken assumption) a red rose. The battles were intermittent and restricted for the most part to armies limited in size, but a very large number of the nobles were killed. This and the collapse of government under the inept Henry VI and the bickering of the different Lancastrian factions contributed to a Yorkist victory. In 1461 the mad Henry VI was replaced by the Duke of York who became Edward IV.

Edward IV (1461-83) was a strong, forceful man whose vision of kingship went beyond mere Yorkist dynastic ambitions. He realized that his subjects wanted an end to the civil wars and that England's renewal of the wars with France would squander the fragile kingdom's resources. He restored law and order and won confidence; by reviving household government which placed important financial and administrative powers under his direct supervision in the royal court, he restored the prestige and effectiveness of the monarchy.

Parliament's exclusive right to grant extraordinary revenue had made it nearly indispensable in the Hundred Years' War and gained it many constitutional powers. Edward's refusal to revive the war obviated the need for frequent Parliamentary taxes and allowed him to call Parliament less frequently. The King's greatest potential wealth was his vast holdings of land which now included not only the Plantagenet domains but also the Lancastrian lands added at Henry IV's accession in 1399 and the Yorkist estates added by Edward himself in 1461. By insisting on new techniques of land management he greatly increased the yield from the crown lands and thus reduced further his reliance on parliamentary grants.

Edward IV relied heavily on the abilities and strength of his brother Richard, Duke of Gloucester; realizing that when he died his son would be a minor, Edward stipulated that Richard be regent for the young King. At the death of Edward IV in 1483 the family of Woodville to which Edward IV's wife belonged seized the regency and excluded Richard. Richard in turn argued that the marriage of Edward IV and Elizabeth Woodville had been illegal and thus Edward V (1483) was illegitimate. Richard had himself crowned King, and no one had the strength to resist him.

Richard III (1483-85) placed Edward V and his brother in the Tower of London and nothing was ever heard of them again. There is no proof one way or the other that Richard had any complicity in their disappearance, but his contemporaries believed that he had the young boys murdered and were deeply scandalized. It was the ideal moment for the Lancastrians to strike. The Yorkists had eventually executed Henry VI and his son and so the nearest Lancastrian claimant was Henry Tudor, Earl of Richmond. Henry and Richard met at the Battle of Bosworth Field in 1485, and the victorious Henry placed on his head the crown of the slain Richard III and began to rule as Henry VII.

THE EARLY TUDORS:
CONSOLIDATION AND TRANSITION, 1485-1529

Henry VII. The Battle of Bosworth Field was the end rather than merely the continuation of the Wars of the Roses due to the ability of Henry VII (1485-1509). This tall, reserved, shrewd, calculating, aloof monarch of Welsh extraction was willing to spend long hours supervising every detail of government — consolidating, reviving, strengthening, expanding, searching for means to secure and develop English kingship and his own Tudor line.

Henry was descended from Edward III by tenuous links. John of Gaunt had had a mistress who bore him illegitimate children, and although Henry IV had legitimized his cousins he had forbidden any of that line ever to inherit the crown. The Tudors were descended from this line not directly but only by marriage: Owen Tudor had married Henry V's widow and as a reward for faithful service Henry VI had made one of Owen's sons Earl of Richmond. His son Henry was victorious over Richard III in battle. Thus in spite of the difficulties of descent, Henry VII really ruled by military victory, power, and sagacity. It took Henry ten years to secure the Tudors on the throne. He sought to merge the Lancastrian and Yorkist claims by marrying Elizabeth, the best female Yorkist claimant. He removed the males either by imprisoning them, forcing them into exile, or defeating them in real or imagined plots against himself. Several young boys claimed to be the brother of Edward V, and Henry had to restrain these imposters and the men who attempted to manipulate them.

A precondition to restoring law and order was to deal effectively with the "over mighty subjects" who had led the fighting in the aristocratic Wars of the Roses. In effect many of them kept private armies of retainers, giving them special clothing and badges known as livery to mark them as the lord's own supporters, and "maintaining" them when the retainers were called to account for their lawlessness, sometimes appearing in armor to intimidate juries and local officers who sought to punish their lawbreaking. Henry had laws passed which severely reduced the number of persons a lord could retain. By limiting livery so that a lord had only a few honorific servants and by forbidding maintenance, the King in effect denied to the small number of lords who had survived the Wars of Roses the ability to retain private armies. Henry revived the medieval Court of Star Chamber, a judicial arm of the council which gained its name from the painted roof in its chamber. Because this court was so closely linked with the King, the noblemen did not dare challenge its authority and the "over mighty subject" could be held to account in it.

Henry VII used marriage as the primary element of his foreign policy. He named his eldest son Arthur to evoke memories of that legendary British King, and then married him to Catherine of Aragon, a princess of the Spanish house which was one of Europe's first powers. He married his eldest daughter to the King of Scotland to cement friendly relations with the other independent kingdom on the British Isles. Even after Arthur died, Henry attempted to continue the Spanish alliance by urging his second son, the future Henry VIII, to marry her. Although Henry VII seemed at times ready to forward his foreign policy by war as well as marriage, and even though he sometimes won parliamentary taxes to support the hostilities, he never really fought and thus conserved and augmented his own revenues.

In domestic affairs Henry continued to use household government as Edward IV had done so effectively. Henry greatly increased royal revenues by insisting on the payment of all feudal obligations including some which had long gone uncollected. He vigorously supported foreign trade and took steps, with varying degrees of success, to increase the competitive power of English merchants against foreign traders, increasing customs revenues in the process. By the end of the reign Henry had nearly trebled the ordinary revenue of the crown. He left his son Henry a secure and wealthy kingdom, one which had risen from the internal divisions of civil war to a place of importance and respect in Europe. Henry VII had revived the medieval rights of kingship and made them effective once again.

Henry VIII. The young King (1509-47) was a magnificent specimen — an athlete who excelled in hunting, riding, and tennis, an educated prince with broad intellectual interests and the ability to speak Latin, French, and Spanish as well as English, and a cultured Renaissance man who played musical instruments and composed (he is thought to have written *Greensleeves*). He was also extraordinarily indulgent and vain, a boisterous lover of good times and carousing, a man who had been flattered all his life and had never had to work to achieve fame. He had a flaming and mercurial temper which quickly turned from pettiness into rage and vindictive cruelty.

Although trained in the cultured ways of the Renaissance, Henry applied himself to war, the traditional medieval preoccuptaion of princes. Soon after his accession he had married his brother's widow, Catherine of Aragon, and thus was naturally allied with her nephew Charles, King of Spain. This monarch's domains were unprecedented: he ruled Spain, the Spanish Netherlands (today's Belgium and Holland), the Habsburg dominions (today's Austria, Hungary, and adjacent territories), and the new American territories opened by Christopher Columbus and later explorers; from 1519, as Charles V, he became Holy Roman Emperor. Henry was distinctly the junior partner in Charles' alliances, a King who had little part in the planning, whose battles were minor sideshows, and who had no part in the spoils of victory. Henry won occasional military glory, but his treasury was continually depleted.

Henry VIII was certainly unwilling to attend to the minute details of everyday administration as his father had, and so the burden fell on the willing shoulders of the King's chief minister, Thomas Wolsey. Because Wolsey was not of aristocratic birth, he entered the church where it was possible to rise merely on ability, and after a budding career at Oxford he entered the royal service. Under Henry VIII he became Lord Chancellor and thus took precedence over other ministers and headed the legal system. In the church he was first a bishop, then Archbishop of York, later a Cardinal, and finally at Henry VIII's urging Wolsey was made a Papal Legate. In this last capacity the Pope allowed Wolsey to exercise in England the Pope's own powers, a grant made to allow him to reform the church.

Wolsey was generally unsuccessful as the King's minister. The

Cottages, Longstocks, Hampshire (Radio Times Hulton Picture Library).

aristocratic power elite were offended at his humble origins and resented his ostentatious display of the trappings of power. His arrogance ill-equipped him for the delicate tasks of managing Parliament and for the delegation of responsibilities which was the key to effective administration. In foreign affairs Wolsey substituted a pro-French alliance for friendship with Spain and thus risked England's wool and cloth exports which flowed through the Spanish Netherlands. He did serve well in the law, especially in the Courts of Star Chamber and Chancery where he presided and increased the jurisdiction. His greatest failings were in the church. Although made a Papal Legate to reform its abuses, he was seen by his contemporaries to personify them. His calling required him to be chaste but he had an illegitimate son; to serve his offices faithfully, but he was a pluralist who multiplied office holding and was therefore non-resident in most posts; to administer his posts faithfully and without gain, but instead he accepted bribes for favors.

Renaissance and Reformation Ideas. Early sixteenth-century England was starting to share in the flood of ideas and attitudes from continental Europe. The Renaissance which began in fourteenth-century Italy had been primarily cultural and artistic, but as it spread into northern Europe in the fifteenth century it became more concerned with scholarship and religious reform, notably biblical studies. The development of printing in the mid-fifteenth century provided a tool for propagating Renaissance ideas in a way unparalleled in the western world.

Henry VII had invited Italian humanists to England and during his son's lifetime the most renowned Christian humanist, Erasmus of Rotterdam, lived and worked in England. William Caxton set up the first printing press in England and from 1477 the English press played an important part in the Renaissance. Humanists such as John Colet placed a great emphasis on education as a means for realizing human potential, and his school at St. Paul's was a model. Sir Thomas More wrote *Utopia* to present an ideal city which was a profound contrast with the realities of the time. Soon political theorizing came to have an important role in the English state.

Although the ideas of the Christian humanists were well received, the teachings of the Protestant Reformation were officially suppressed. Martin Luther began his public confrontation with the Catholic church in Germany in 1517 and unleashed a flood of religious controversy and interpretation. Henry VIII wrote an answer to Luther, a book entitled *Assertion of the Seven Sacraments*, and the Pope rewarded his orthodoxy by conferring on the King the title "Defender of the Faith." Wolsey and other governmental ministers worked to suppress Lutheran books, including William Tyndale's English translation of the Bible (1525) which had numerous Lutheran explanatory notes.

In the late 1520s Henry VIII revealed his belief that his marriage with Catherine of Aragon was invalid, and thus began a long series of events leading up to an annulment of his marriage. In the process he borrowed many of the ideas of both the Renaissance and Reformation. Because Cardinal Wolsey was unable to win the annulment which Henry wished, his usefulness was at an end and he fell from power in 1529 — the very year in which the Reformation Parliament began its existence, and out of which would come many of the elements which were central to the transition from the medieval to the early modern English state.

A STOCKTAKING: ENGLAND IN 1529

Politics and Government. In the later Middle Ages a number of limitations on royal power had been imposed. It was clear that the law limited the king, a principle enunciated explicitly in the established convention that law could be changed only by the king acting in Parliament. It was also clear that the king's power tended to diminish in direct correlation to increased expenses in foreign wars, and so wise kings such as Edward IV and Henry VII freed themselves from parliamentary surveillance merely by declining to fight. The forum for holding a king and his ministers accountable was now Parliament, but in the depositions of 1327, 1399, 1461, and 1485 it was military power which made Parliament's role possible.

Yet any monarch who was willing to rule by law, to cooperate with Parliament and include the great feudal lords in the realm's policy and planning, and to avoid costly wars, possessed extraordinarily great powers of government. He controlled policy-making; directed an effectively organized and sophisticated royal administration; provided a system of royal justice which with its writs and jury system protected Englishmen's rights better than did any other European monarch; enjoyed feudal rights; and in general presided over a kingdom protected from continental involvements by the sea. This potential royal power could reach even greater heights when combined with that all-important intangible, success.

Even in local affairs the king's power was great. Borough charters rested on the royal favor, the king's management of trade brought prosperity to merchants and port towns alike, and the office of Justice of the Peace which had been developed from the fourteenth century on enabled the king to have royal officers close to local happenings. Local communities had been delegated important powers of self-government, not only in the institutional sense but in other responsible activities such as juries.

Society and the Economy. The aristocratic upper class had been the dominant group in society throughout the entire Middle Ages. In the early years of feudal England they were the indispensable military arm and the exclusive advisors of the monarchy, men who employed vast numbers of villeins in high farming. The Black Death had made these nobles landlords living from rents; the use of the longbow and the decline of the knights had made the nobles' military service less important although their military leadership was still recognized; and the rise of the House of Commons lessened their political status but did not take away their predominant place in government. The greatest change was the bloodletting of the Wars of the Roses which left only twenty-nine surviving secular nobles.

In early feudal England the knights were immediately below the lords, but their military role had declined and they had become socially allied with the aristocracy but politically allied with the burgesses in the House of Commons. The expansion of professions such as law and the royal administration had begun to create a non-agricultural middle class which was swelled by the merchants who managed England's expanded trade. Life in the cities was structured and sophisticated, temporarily diminished by depressions in the fifteenth century, but reviving in the sixteenth. London had become more than a trading center — octopus-like, its tentacles reached out to take away the economic importance of lesser port towns and to monopolize trade.

Many of the agricultural workers in the lower strata of society had been economically unfree in the early Middle Ages, but nearly all had been freed by the cataclysmic changes from the Black Death. This economic freedom did not, however, guarantee economic success, and most of the peasantry continued to live by subsistence farming, at the mercy of the weather which governed the crops and could in bad times send famine to decimate the countryside.

It seemed to many that late medieval economic life was stagnant and constricted, but by 1529 the first steps to expand the economic horizons had been taken. Henry VII had encouraged John Cabot (a native of Genoa as had been Christopher Columbus) to sail from Bristol to explore America for England. The success of that brave explorer which won for England a claim to these new lands went temporarily unexploited, and the value of the Atlantic was as yet unrealized.

Religion and Culture. Although religion was certainly one of the unchallenged values in English life, the institutional church had suffered greatly and became a less effective force in England. The Black Death had swept away half the clergy and wreaked havoc on the monasteries and friaries which, in earlier centuries, had been the principal repositories of reformed religious ideals and centers of inspiration. The Papacy's prestige had been lowered by the Avignon "captivity," and Lollardy had first rent the doctrinal unity of English Christianity.

From the time of the Conquest, French cultural values had supplanted the English in the upper echelons of society, so that in the cosmopolitan literate society and the intellectual community with its Latin learning, England had been part of a truly pan-European world. The flowering of the English language at the upper as well as the lower levels of society from the fourteenth century had reawakened an ancient heritage, and even in areas such as architecture the later Middle Ages had witnessed a separate, more austere native development. When considered together with the distinct political and governmental institutions, England was well on the way toward an appreciation of uniqueness which was soon to be assiduously cultivated.

SUGGESTIONS FOR FURTHER READING

The politics of the later Middle Ages and the Hundred Years' War can be followed in May McKisak, *The Fourteenth Century, 1307-1399* (1959) and E. F. Jacob, *The Fifteenth Century, 1399-1485* (1961). The constitutional implications are treated in S. B. Chrimes, *English Constitutional Ideas in the Fifteenth Century,* (1936), and in B. Wilkinson, *Constitutional History of England in the Fifteenth Century 1399-1485* (1964), the latter with selected documents and a good bibliography. K. B. McFarlane's *The War of the Roses* (1965) and *The Nobility of Later Medieval England* (1973) show changes in upper society. The Yorkist revival is shown in Charles Ross, *Edward IV* (1974), and P. M. Kendall's, *Richard III* (1956) is also very good. S. B. Chrimes has a good study of the first Tudor king and his government in *Henry VII* (1971) and a more popular essay is Lacey Baldwin Smith's *Henry VIII: The Mask of Royalty* (1971). Also useful are Garrett Mattingly's *Catherine of Aragon* (1941), and a biography of Cardinal Wolsey by Charles W. Ferguson, *Naked to Mine Enemies* (1958).

G. C. Coulton, *Chaucer and His England* (1957) places that versatile man in context, and Basil Cottle's *The Triumph of English 1300-1500* (1969) traces the rise of the vernacular. A good short treatment of London is A. R. Myers, *London in the Age of Chaucer* (1972), and a fuller study is Gwyn A. Williams, *Medieval London. From Commune to Capital* (1963). The commercial importance of that city is shown in Sylvia L. Thrupp, *The Merchant Class of Medieval London (1300-1500)* (1948). An excellent study of another medieval town is Sir Francis Hill's *Medieval Lincoln* (1965). The depopulating effects of the Black Death on so much of England is evident in Maurice Beresford's *The Lost Villages of England* (1954). P. M. Kendall, *The Yorkist Age: Daily Life During the Wars of the Roses* (1962) is a good study of mid-fifteenth century family life. The upheaval in religion is well outlined in K. B. McFarlane's brief *John Wycliffe and the Beginnings of English Nonconformity* (1952), and a good survey of the state of the church's clergy at the end of the medieval period is Peter Heath's *The English Parish Clergy on the Eve of the Reformation* (1969). J. H. Hexter, *More's Utopia: The Biography of an Idea* (1952), treats the earlier part of Sir Thomas More's career.

5

Early Modern England

1529-1588

Winds of change were stirring early sixteenth-century Europe. The flowering of the Renaissance in northern Europe produced new attitudes toward the state as well as new cultural expressions; Christopher Columbus' voyages had opened man's horizons westward; and religious change in Germany and elsewhere brought agony and conflict. During the century many old ways would be shed and new attitudes adopted, so that these years can be seen as a major watershed in European history. The early modern state in England was a time of challenge and problems, and of great achievements.

HENRY VIII AND THE ENGLISH REFORMATION

The religious reformations in Europe led by men like Martin Luther in Germany and John Calvin in Switzerland naturally affected England, but there were to be so many differences in the English Reformation that we must first determine its character before tracing how it came to be. There were two fundamental differences: The English Reformation was not made by religious leaders but instead by the English government, by King and Parliament, and the Reformation did not sweep away all of the old, but retained the organization of the Catholic Church, with bishops and dioceses, parish priests and parish churches, and a vast organization of courts and administrative officers.

Furthermore the English Reformation was made in two stages, the first of a markedly political nature in the 1530s under the guidance of Henry VIII, the second of a distinctly religious character in the reign of his son Edward VI (1547-53). Henry severed the jurisdictional ties which bound the church *in* England to the Pope, and became the Supreme Head on earth of the Church *of* England, as expressed in the Act of Supremacy, yet he insisted that the beliefs, form of worship, and practices of orthodox Catholicism be kept. Only when Edward became King did a religious Reformation begin, and because men cannot be told what to believe, a way had to be found to make England Protestant. This the Act of Uniformity did by commanding the exclusive use of the *Book of Common Prayer* in which the services of worship were distinctly Protestant. The theology of the new church would be learned from its liturgies. The twin pillars of the English Reformation were therefore the Acts of Supremacy and Uniformity.

Henry's Marriage. In 1527 Henry revealed his belief that his marriage with Catherine of Aragon was invalid. Reading literally a biblical text that God would punish anyone who had relations with a brother's wife (Leviticus 18:16) and sadly reflecting that the sons Catherine bore him were stillborn or died soon after birth, Henry wanted an annulment — a decree that a valid marriage had never existed. Henry had obtained a precautionary dispensation from the Pope at the time of his marriage with Catherine, but if Scripture forbade such a union, then no Pope could dispense from the divine law. Would not the Pope free him now by recognizing the situation?

Were Henry's religious scruples sincere? Was he eager for another marriage which might produce a son, so there would be no repetition of the civil war which happened in the twelfth century when Matilda attempted to succeed Henry I? Was he uncontrollably swayed by lust, his passion for Anne Boleyn kindled to flame by her refusal to be his mistress without marriage? Regardless, a speedy resolution of the matter seemed likely, because as a Papal Legate Cardinal Wolsey could exercise many of the Pope's own judicial powers.

They had not reckoned on the proud and stubborn resolve of the devout Catherine of Aragon who refused to allow so many years of her life to be cast aside as sinful and her daughter Mary declared a bastard, or on the Pope's refusal to allow Wolsey to handle the matter completely. Spanish soldiers had captured a great deal of the Italian peninsula and the Pope could hardly afford to antagonize the Spanish king by allowing his aunt to be judged a paramour. Wolsey was only

Henry VIII (National Portrait Gallery).

allowed to hear the evidence, and the Pope's intention to stall indefinitely became clear when many obstacles were raised even in that preliminary stage.

Wolsey's usefulness was clearly at an end, and Henry found an unusual weapon to remove him. The fourteenth-century statue of Praemunire had forbidden appealing to Rome legal suits about the right to nominate men to serve as parish priests, and Henry enlarged and distorted his understanding of the statute to hold that it forbade *any* appeals to the Papacy, arguing that Wolsey's papal legateship made him the worst offender. Wolsey realized that the King's intention to be rid of him was as firm as the law's intention was dubious. He sought a pardon without a trial, retired from his governmental posts, and died a year later of natural causes.

The Break with Rome. The Parliament which first sat in 1529 was so cooperative that Henry kept it in existence for seven years. The legislation which Henry proposed and it passed earned it the title "Reformation Parliament." But from 1529-31 there was no positive plan of action, and although it passed acts to reform minor clerical abuses, the impasse over Henry's marriage remained. From 1532 onward, however, there was a definite plan, and because Thomas Cromwell rose to the position of Henry's chief minister at that time it has been argued that Cromwell was the architect of the political Reformation.

Efficient, calculating, expert in administration, the superb parliamentary manager, the stable counterpart and often bullied foil to the exuberant, emotional and sometimes vindictive King, Cromwell brought purpose and organization to Henry's government. His plan was breathtakingly simple: separate the church from Rome, and make it a department of the English state with the King as its head. The groundwork was laid in 1532 when King and Parliament acted to end the church's legislative independence and stop the flow of funds to the Papacy from England. The church had always made its own rules (called "canons") and now the King gained control over all of them then in force through a commission he appointed which was to determine which canons should continue. Henry gained the right to license all future canons. This was only a potential power, as was the authority to stop funds flowing from the realm. The purpose was still to pressure the Pope.

The need for actions and not threats became obvious in January 1533 when Anne Boleyn was found to be pregnant. Henry secretly married her, but it would not do to have the future heir tainted with illegitimacy, and so in March Parliament passed a law forbidding appeals out of England in matrimonial cases. In May an English court granted the annulment and Henry's marriage to Anne was revealed. Then the Pope excommunicated Henry who had violated an earlier papal ban against his remarriage while the case was in litigation. In turn Henry implemented the legislation of 1532. But to Henry's dismay all of the promise of 1533 was not realized — Anne did not bear Henry a son, but rather a daughter, Elizabeth. The new Queen's days were numbered, and in May 1536 she was executed on charges of adultery which seemed both then and now to have been trumped-up.

The separation of the church from Rome was only a prelude to its total subordination to the English state, a process completed in 1534-35 in a series of statutes. An oath was devised so that men could be tested for their agreement with the new arrangements which were epitomized in the Act of Supremacy of 1534 which recognized Henry's claim as Supreme Head, and provided penalties of treason for those who would not conform. Now Henry was the head of a sovereign national state which owed no allegiance to any foreign power, and of all the subjects of the realm, whether laymen or clergymen.

The Dissolution of the Monasteries and the Aftermath. Parliament had cooperated in the changes in part because of Cromwell's skill as a parliamentary manager, but more importantly because Henry seldom asked for new grants of revenue — a loss he more than made up from the proceeds of the dissolution of the monasteries between 1536-40. He ordered Cromwell as the new Vice-Regent for Spirituals to investigate the spiritual life of the monasteries. Abuses there certainly were, but probably nowhere near the degree pictured in Cromwell's lurid reports which served as the basis for the legislation to abolish the monasteries and friaries. Since they controlled somewhere between a quarter and a third of the land of England, the King was greatly enriched. The monks and nuns were dispensed from their religious vows, a welcome relief for those who had no religious vocation, but a tragedy for the majority. In time Henry and his successors gave or sold at reduced rates most of the newly acquired lands. The purchasers received not only the land but also the priceless social standing which it conferred, and in turn the King associated them in the continuance of the Reformation — were the nation to return to the Catholic Church, the lands would have to be returned.

For most, the severe penalties of the new legislation were an effective deterrent against protest. There were a few outstanding resisters, notably the saintly Bishop John Fisher and Henry's own Chancellor, Sir Thomas More, renowned throughout Europe for his humanism and integrity. He resigned his office rather than give an opinion on the changes of which he certainly disapproved, and was convicted by perjured testimony. The single popular uprising was the Pilgrimage of

Grace in 1536, a futile rebellion in two northern counties. Although the rebels demanded a return to Catholicism, they were also inspired by a number of socio-economic grievances which arose from the decay of traditional feudal values, and Henry was quickly able to put them down and hang the leaders.

A more serious problem was the division in the King's own Council. Cromwell and Archbishop Thomas Cranmer had been strongly influenced by continental Protestantism and wanted religious reform, while the faction led by Thomas Howard, Duke of Norfolk, resented Cromwell's humble social origins and Cranmer's great influence on the King, and wished to maintain traditional Catholic beliefs in the new English Church. Henry had married a third time, gaining at last a son and heir, but losing young Edward's mother Jane Seymour soon after she was delivered. The Cromwell-Cranmer faction urged a fourth marriage to Anne of Cleves, a German whose Protestantism was known. Henry's dislike of her plain appearance helped provide the lever for Norfolk's triumph over Cromwell who was executed in 1540. Henry's fifth wife was Catherine Howard, Norfolk's niece, but her adulteries cost her her head, and Norfolk his seeming ascendancy in Henry's favor. The sixth wife, Catherine Parr, agreed with the more Protestant party. Although Henry was able to master and control both factions, the unity of purpose which marked the earlier years was lost.

Early Modern Government. Cromwell had spent much of the 1530s in reorganizing the royal administration so that it would function for the King without his detailed supervision. In part this recognized that Henry VIII did not care to invest as much time in day-to-day affairs as his father had, in part it reflected Cromwell's vision of the state which looked beyond medieval traditional practices to newer roles of governmental service. In the place of the traditionally large advisory medieval Council, Cromwell substituted a Privy Council of fewer than twenty. The Council's function was not only to advise but also to act as an executive agency to supervise the royal administration. He then developed and himself held the office of Principal Secretary — receiving reports from royal officers and agents, preparing the Privy Council's agenda, and then drafting and issuing the letters and commissions needed to implement conciliar decisions. Of course the King's decision prevailed on important matters, but the Privy Council made lower level decisions. Financial offices were created to handle the new revenues produced by the Reformation, but these were absorbed into the Exchequer in Mary's reign, and did not survive as permanent governmental institutions.

Cromwell's dedication to the management of parliamentary affairs reflected the growing importance of Parliament in English government.

As the Tudor prosperity increased the wealth of the gentry and they came to see the House of Commons as a focus for their political energy, and especially as Henry VIII increasingly made the Commons partners in making the Reformation, the lower house became increasingly important. Thomas Cromwell the commoner sat there, bringing in government bills, attempting to keep the proposals intact as independent-minded M.P.s considered them in the three readings and committee investigations, and keeping relations between the King and the House of Commons harmonious. The King and Parliament were both the beneficiaries of this cooperation, a far cry from the acrimony not uncommon in the middle ages.

THE YEARS OF CRISIS: EDWARD AND MARY

With Parliament's approval, Henry VIII stipulated in his will that his son Edward accede to the throne, and were he to die childless, then Mary, and finally Elizabeth. Henry was under no illusions about the problems in store for the Tudor dynasty: Edward would be a minor at his accession, and should a daughter reign later, there would be unprecedented difficulties. To forstall these problems, Henry ordered that a Council and not an individual should serve as the Regent for his son. But time would prove that this precaution was in vain, and the next decade proved how prophetic his fears were.

Crisis in Government. The provision for a Council was quickly set aside by the nine-year-old King's uncle, Edward Seymour, who as Duke of Somerset directed the government as his nephew's Protector. Somerset was necessarily concerned with sustaining his irregular position, which meant concessions of power to court the House of Commons, and a counter-productive willingness to tolerate dissent in the hope of winning men's minds and assent. Even the most resolute leader would have had difficulty in coping with England's problems, and the Protector was not successful. In 1549 Somerset was swept from his position by a fellow Council member, John Dudley, who as Duke of Northumberland assumed control of the young Edward and a few years later had Somerset executed on trumped-up charges of treason. Northumberland was self-centered and grasping, an impetuous leader whose own faults were magnified by the corruption of those around him. The insecurity of Northumberland's position as a conservative opposition grew led him to side with radical Protestantism which in turn became a test of political loyalty. But because young Edward who had approved of this Protestant emphasis lay dying in 1553 of lung disease, all that had been begun was in jeopardy because the Catholic Mary Tudor was next in the succession. Northumberland's desperate plan was to avert this by proclaiming as Queen a great-niece of Henry VIII, the appealing Protestant Lady Jane Grey, to whom he married his own son. Such blatant self-interest awakened a nearly universal opposition, and within two weeks Mary and the forces of legitimacy had overthrown the plot, so that Lady Jane is not recognized as having ruled.

Mary's reign (1553-58) accelerated the drift in government. To marry an Englishman would be beneath her rank; to marry a reigning monarch would probably make England's policy subordinate to that of her husband's nation. Mary Tudor — the fiercely proud thirty-seven year old daughter of Catherine of Aragon, the woman whose childhood was scarred by the dishonor of her mother, the disinterest of her father, and the legal stigma of judicial bastardy, the ruler who was the focus of all the fears of the Protestant party — had little ability or inclination to face or deal with the problems of government. Her marriage to Philip of Spain, heir to his country's throne, compounded her problems in England. Philip cared not a bit for his wife and her hopeless wish to bear a child, but rather sought Parliament's recognition of the title "King of England" for himself, and England's participation in Spain's wars against France. What he won was a title that was not to survive his wife's life, England as an ally in a war so unsuccessful that it lost its last possession in France, and the hatred and distrust of his wife's subjects. Mary died alone in 1558, leaving a country repulsed by her religious policies, humiliated by the wars, bereft of leadership. Her death probably resulted from a uterine cancer, the first manifestations of which suggested pregnancy and eventually led to ridicule of the pitiful queen when her term was up and she was still childless.

The bitter fruit of both monarchs' lack of leadership was the frequency of rebellion. The religious policies of Edward's government brought uprisings from both Catholics and Protestants, in which keenly felt economic and social grievances had a part. Mary's proposed marriage to Philip produced a multi-county plot, dangerously near London, led by Sir Thomas Wyatt. There were spasmodic eruptions of discontent at other times in lesser degrees, and governmental fears of insurrection at times bordered on paranoia. In Parliament the lack of leadership occasionally meant that private members dared to introduce bills on religion heretofore the exclusive concern of the government, a precedent which when repeated in Elizabeth's reign provoked a constitutional issue.

Crisis in Religion. The death of Henry VIII had removed the principal obstacle to the development of Protestantism in England, and Archbishop Cranmer with Somerset's encouragement had begun gradual reforms. Early in 1549 Parliament enacted the first Act of Uniformity and its *Book of Common Prayer* which was worded with a good bit of ambiguity in order not to alienate the Catholics. But there were unmistakable signs of new changes, particularly when the chantries were suppressed just as the monasteries had been in the previous reign. Reformed Protestantism did not believe in a purgation after death from the bad effects of sin, and thus on theological grounds argued that the chantries in which masses were sung for the dead should be suppressed. The monasteries closed by Henry were usually rural, but the chantries were often in larger centers and their priests often served as schoolmasters, so that the impact of the suppression caused significantly more discontent. Under Northumberland a Second Act of Uniformity and a *Book of Common Prayer* were adopted in 1552 which made a definite break with Catholic teachings on the mass, the real presence of Christ's body in the communion bread, and many other beliefs repugnant to Protestantism. Priests were now allowed to marry and other changes were made, but Edward's early death ended further reform.

Mary's desire to return England to her Catholic religion involved two elements, the repeal in Parliament of the Edwardian Protestant statutes and the reconciliation of England with the Papacy. The first was made palatable to Parliament because Mary wanted a modified Act of Supremacy which would keep state control over the church, but especially because it was made clear that reconciliation would not require returning the lands seized at the dissolution of the monasteries. The legal preliminaries over, the Papal absolution for England was pronounced late in 1554. Mary next tried to uproot Protestantism in England. Most of its leaders left England voluntarily with the Queen's tacit approval to go to European Protestant centers such as Geneva and Frankfurt, but while they drank at the pure springs of reformed Protestantism abroad, their fellow religionists suffered mightily in England. The government had reenacted the harsh medieval laws against heresy which Edward's government had repealed and nearly 300 were martyred for their heresy by burning at the stake, many for radical Protestant views which were equally intolerable to Edwardian Protestants. Most were of lower social ranks, but a few had been notable leaders of the earlier movement, including Thomas Cranmer. It is still not clear if the burnings were at the insistence of the coldly unbending Queen, or of her Spanish advisors whose own country had a reputation for ferocity in dealing with heretics, or of the Queen's English councillors, but such severity was unprecedented in England although very common in Europe. When Catholic Mary was succeeded by the Protestant Elizabeth, the reputation of "Bloody Mary" as a great religious persecutor was assured.

Both the Edwardian and Marian religious settlements were imposed

Death of Thomas Cranmer (Foxe, Acts and Monuments*).*

from above, and neither had time to win a voluntary assent from the ordinary subject. Instead the rapid changes bred confusion and suspicion, and the intolerance of the times which was an English and an European characteristic meant a legacy of enduring bitterness for the young Elizabeth.

Crisis in the Economy. Edward and Mary had no monopoly on economic problems, but two crises which affected the whole century became particularly acute in their reigns. The inflation which was felt throughout all Europe intensified as never before, and in 1552 the wool market, which served England's principal export, collapsed.

Prices had been relatively stable in the fifteenth century, but in the sixteenth century before Edward's accession, prices had risen nearly 50 percent, and in the troubled decade thereafter nearly doubled again. There were many causes: the wars against France and Scotland led to huge governmental deficits, and there was a bloated money supply, primarily the result of the practice of Henry, Edward, and Mary of stretching the value of English coins by mixing base alloys into the pure metal to increase their number (called "debasement"), in part a participation in the European inflation from the flood of precious metals from America via Spain. In an agricultural society where land was the main source of wealth, landlords were faced with the problem of increasing the yield from the land, whether in produce or rents, to keep pace with rising prices. Before 1552 one of the most appealing alternatives was to switch from farming to raising sheep, because the wool produced a higher return than the sale of crops. Some landlords sought to increase their efficiency by forcing small farmers off the strips of land they held, and then consolidating all the holdings into a more efficient, larger farm, while others began to enclose the commons and wastes which had been such a valuable source of supplemental income for the villagers. This process of enclosing was bitterly resented.

The social effects of enclosure wrought a major though gradual change in English life. The aristocrat who traditionally lived lavishly found it increasingly hard to maintain his economic standing when compared to the more industrious smaller landowner whose thrift and efficiency allowed him to buy land (much of it formerly monastic) now on the market. The monarch, as the largest and often the most inefficient holder of lands, was particularly vulnerable to this relative decline. Many small landowners were forced off their holdings through unscrupulous lawsuits and became leaseholders in a subordinate position to a landlord, or perhaps merely wage earners. The gap between rich and poor widened, and to the extent that men forced off the land could not find another job, the number of unemployed and vagabonds rose, intensifying the already serious job of maintaining law and order. The extraordinary rise in English prices meant that the cost of English wool abroad continually rose, and in 1552 reached such a height that it was priced out of competition and the market collapsed. It was nearly thirty years before the exports rose to the pre-1552 level, and of course the unemployment which resulted in England was particularly severe. Governments of the sixteenth century, English and European, had no tools of economic analysis to discover the roots of the problem or to suggest remedies. In vain they attempted to treat the symptoms, to return to the days of stability by ordering that as many men be employed or that as much land be tilled as before.

ELIZABETHAN STABILITY

The heir to the promise and problems of England's crown was another woman, the twenty-five-year-old "reformation child," the daughter of Henry and Anne Boleyn. Elizabeth's lengthy reign (1558-1603) was to be so successful and distinctive in many areas that the "Elizabethan Age" is seen as the springtime of early modern England. The often over-romanticized adulation of the period should not blind us to its serious problems, but the stability and progress which helped characterize the era arose in great part from the remarkable acumen of Elizabeth Tudor.

Queen Elizabeth I (National Portrait Gallery).

The Young Queen. Because she was an astute judge of people, Elizabeth surrounded herself with advisors whose fierce dedication to England's welfare matched hers. The Queen was iron-willed, cold and calculating in dealing with the issues. She often delayed making decisions, and because procrastination was so often the best policy when confronted by seemingly insurmountable problems, her conservatism usually worked well. Yet she was adroit enough to recognize a genuine confrontation brewing, and to realize when it was good politics to yield — more than one unctuous speech to Parliament won back affections recently strained. Elizabeth was remarkably secular-minded in a century of religious passion. France was torn by religious civil wars and the advancement of Catholicism was a principal motive of Spain's foreign policy; in contrast, Elizabeth made her church serve England first, then Protestantism. She chose loyal, cool, and dispassionate men to run the government such as Sir William Cecil, later Lord Burghley, who could see and weigh all sides of an issue. Elizabeth also relied heavily on Sir Robert Dudley, later the Earl of Leicester, and although there was a romantic attraction between them, she kept rein over her heart to use him in government.

These ingredients jelled into effective leadership because of the Queen's immense popularity. Her subjects obeyed her because they loved her, and they loved her because they could see themselves in her. She mirrored their zest for the bawdy and bloody amusements of the day, attending with relish the cock fights, bear baitings, and plays. She reflected their extravagence, wearing ornately jeweled, outrageously ruffed and decorated clothing. Even in personal items which seem so unusual today — the reddish wig she wore, the heavy white make-up caked on her face, the blackened teeth — she was characteristic of the pre-medical age, hiding as did so many subjects the ravages of smallpox, which left people hairless and pockmarked, and the indulgence of an excessive consumption of sweets.

The Elizabethan Settlement. The earliest problem was religion. Elizabeth's intentions were moderate, a return to Henry's national church, and so she sought only a new Act of Supremacy. But the Protestant exiles who returned from the continent were successful in getting passed in Parliament a Protestant Act of Uniformity which revived the *Book of Common Prayer* of 1552. Elizabeth wisely yielded to these pressures but eased tensions by refusing to insist on a zealous enforcement of the new settlement. Another major problem was the Queen's marriage. Should Elizabeth remain unmarried and childless, the crown would most likely go to Mary Stuart, Queen of Scotland, an ardent Catholic cousin of Elizabeth. Elizabeth had assisted militarily the Protestant rebels in Scotland who sought to end that country's traditional alliance with France, and the Protestant leaders soon tired of the scandals surrounding Mary's romances and expelled her from Scotland. Her infant son James was the new Scottish ruler, and Mary Queen of Scots became an unwanted exile in England, the symbol of the dangers of a Catholic succession if Elizabeth did not marry. When the Parliaments in the 1560s tried to insist that Elizabeth marry, she pacified them by making firm promises to handle the matter herself.

These early years also saw steps aimed at restoring confidence in the economy. By calling in the debased coins of earlier reigns and issuing in their place coins of pure metal, the Queen acted to slow inflation and to rebuild the prestige of the English government. The successes of the first decade were particularly apparent in the ease with which two crises were handled. In 1569 two earls from families which had enormous feudal importance in earlier centuries led a rebellion which sought a restoration of Catholicism and which reflected the frustration over the severe socio-economic dislocations felt acutely in northern England. In 1570 the Pope excommunicated Elizabeth, an action involving a theoretical deposition of the Queen and an invitation to other monarchs to invade England to bring it about. But after eleven years of successful rule, Elizabeth was secure in the affections of her subjects, and neither threat could topple her.

Anglican, Puritan, and Papist. Because only the Church of England was legally established, everyone was theoretically an Anglican, the name derived from *Anglicana* which in Latin means "English." Different types of dissent marred the theoretical inclusiveness of the church. A substantial number within it agreed that the Reformation had not gone far enough, that some things still needed to be "purified." These "Puritans" differed over reform: some wished to remove the hierarchial structure from bishops downward, others only to be rid of vestments and other symbols also kept from Catholicism; all agreed that if some element was not in the Bible, it should be discarded. While Puritans were all "against" something, a smaller group within Puritanism known as Presbyterians was "for" a positive alternative, the form of worship developed in John Calvin's Geneva where many Englishmen had lived in Mary's reign. Still other Protestants were so impatient at the un-reformed elements that they wished to disassociate entirely from the Church of England, and were thus called "Separatists." The Catholics who retained a loyalty to the Pope and wanted to return to the universal church were derisively called "Papists."

The threat from Catholicism was slow in developing. Many of the leaders of Mary's church went into exile, but most priests accepted the Elizabethan settlement. The laymen attended the Anglican services to avoid prosecution, so the drift into Anglicanism had begun. In 1574, however, the first of what was to be a steady stream of "missionaries" began to arrive secretly in England. The exiles had established seminaries abroad to train young Englishmen as priests who would reconvert their countrymen. These "seminary priests" were joined in 1580 by English members of the Jesuits, a community which was the most important element in the Catholic Counter-Reformation in Europe. The seminary priests worked silently, but the Jesuits demanded public debates on religion, and taught English Catholics that they could no longer outwardly conform by attending Anglican services.

The most important element in the government's response was to stop the priests: new legislation in the 1580s defined a priest's mere presence in England, with no overt act whatsoever, to be treason. Over 100 priests were to be martyred, suffering by hanging, drawing and quartering — hanged until nearly dead, then cut down and while still alive castrated, arms and legs cut off, entrails cut out and burned, and finally the heart cut out and the head cut off. An unrelenting propaganda campaign branded the Catholics as traitors, drawing on the Pope's excommunication of Elizabeth and the fact that certain English leaders abroad urged Philip to invade England. Yet English Catholics remained loyal to Queen and country in 1588 when Philip attempted an invasion. Finally, the government threatened to ruin financially the Catholic gentry whose example was so influential with their tenants. The penalty for non-attendance at Anglican services was raised to £10 per month (the average agricultural worker earned just over £5 per year). Persecution, propaganda, and financial pressure spelled the end to an effective domestic Catholicism.

Puritanism involved less of a confrontation but more of a sustained threat. A principal reason for its success was that laymen as well as churchmen shared its leadership, so that its pressures for reform were made not only in the church, but also in Parliament. The early efforts at reform were piecemeal, seeking the removal of pre-Reformation religious practices. The reformers believed that the Queen favored further reform and sought to hasten matters by making proposals in the church's Convocation and in Parliament. They were surprised when she refused to let the proposals be discussed in the House of Commons, arguing that as head of the church, its reform was her exclusive right. Some in the Commons recalled contrary precedents for parliamentary initiatives in the two earlier reigns, but Elizabeth refused to let a religious matter became a constitutional issue, and promised to make reforms herself.

In the early 1570s Thomas Cartwright, a professor of divinity at Cambridge, and other Presbyterian leaders began to write and surreptitiously print books urging change. Not only Cartwright but even an Archbishop lectured the Queen on her religious duty to delay no

Queen Elizabeth in Parliament (D'Ewes, Journal).

longer; Elizabeth struck back by ordering the enforcement of religious uniformity against Puritanism. Not unnaturally the movement went underground, and in the 1580s a clandestine Presbyterian organization was established in some parts of England, completely ignoring the Anglican church. Elizabeth triumphed when the new Archbishop of Canterbury, John Whitgift, made his own diocesan tribunal into a nationwide Court of High Commission in which Puritan churchmen were charged, tried, and removed from office and influence. Laymen who wrote books urging reform were branded "seditious," and thus John Stubbs, a Puritan author, had his right hand cut off. The underground was discovered and suppressed, so that by the late 1580s Puritanism was nearly as ineffective as Catholicism.

Meanwhile, three decades of internal growth had enabled Anglicanism to develop and enunciate its principles. The most mature expression was in Richard Hooker's *Laws of Ecclesiastical Polity*, an argument that Anglicanism was a *via media*, a "middle way" between unreformed Catholicism and radical Protestantism. Anglicanism accepted as a valid norm for the church not only the Bible but also the tradition of the first centuries of the church before the great growth of Papal influence — thus it accepted the episcopal form of government, creeds, and practices, but rejected the belief of Puritans and others that man's will was not free.

Conflict with Spain. A state of war between England and Spain existed from 1585-1603. Its causes were longstanding: Elizabeth helped the Protestant Dutch who were fighting for their independence from the Spanish Netherlands; English seamen tried (unsuccessfully) to intercept the treasure ships returning from the New World; English merchants attempted to break the Spanish monopoly on trade with America; and above all, the Catholic King sought the triumph of his cause over the Protestant Queen.

The major campaign of the war was the attempted invasion of England in 1588, when the Spanish Armada, a fleet of about 130 ships, left to rendezvous with soldiers under Spanish command in the Netherlands, then ferry them across for the invasion. The plan was beyond the capabilities of the time: communications were inadequate, there was no deep water in which the Spanish ships could anchor to pick up the soldiers, and the prevailing winds from west to east were likely to prevent the westward attack even if the troops reached the ships. The English seized the initiative by moving upwind, and with the wind at their backs they could harry the Spanish fleet, let the English heavy guns wreak havoc, and then even send unmanned fire ships into the Spanish when the latter moored their ships. Unable to retreat westward, the Spanish had to turn northward and circle Scotland, returning past Ireland. Philip had trusted God to overcome the obstacles his commanders had pointed out; the English knew God to be Protestant, and felt His "Protestant wind" was their best ally.

The war ran on another fifteen years, but the psychological victory had been won. A small nation, prostrate and unimportant after civil wars a century before, had stood off the mightiest nation in the world, the symbol of the Catholic Counter-Reformation. There could have been no greater boost to English self-esteem. The trials of battle had proved that early modern England was of age — flourishing, proud, successful.

THE ELIZABETHAN AGE

Elizabethans knew their time was exciting, adventuresome, alive to new opportunities — a quickening time. But doubtless they would have been as hard pressed to analyze its spirit as we are to describe our own. Perhaps it can best be approached through three of the most important intangibles: a sense of discovery, a richness in expression, and an enjoyment of life.

Discovery. The printed word was often the key to discovering new experiences. Caxton's world of printing a century before emphasized the theological, legal, and philosophical; Elizabethan booksellers also offered practical "how to do it" books on better farming, navigation, correct manners for polite society, planning a garden, interpreting dreams, or being an effective Justice of the Peace. England itself was open to discovery in the pages of William Camden's *Magna Britannia,* and John Stow described the hub of Renaissance England in his *Survey of London.* Freshly printed maps could be bought, often brightly colored by hand, awakening the imagination with sketches of sea monsters, the Indians of the New World, and strange animals in far away lands. Elizabeth's tutor, Roger Ascham, argued for new teaching techniques in The *Scholemaster,* and Sir Thomas Gresham founded a college in London where merchants were taught in English and discovered the world of mathematics, business, and science.

The sea was rediscovered — Elizabethans came to realize that what the Mediterranean had been to the ancient world, the Atlantic would be to the modern, and that their location on it offered exceptional advantages. John Cabot's voyages of discovery had been forgotten by mid-century, but now interest was reawakened, often through the writings of Richard Hakluyt who recounted *The Principal Navigations, Voyages, and Discoveries of the English Nation,* or urged colonization in his *Discourse of Western Planting.* In 1585 Sir Walter Raleigh began a colony at Roanoke Island on what is now the shore of North Carolina.

When the first attempt failed a second was made, but locked among history's secrets is the fate of the first colonists who could not be found three years later when a relief ship arrived.

If the time was not yet ripe for sustained colonization, it was for other sea-related efforts. The navy was completely reorganized, and fighting ships redesigned and armed with heavy guns capable of inflicting damage from a distance. The successes on the sea helped make naval heroes as important as soldiers in the national imagination. The most promising venture, however, was the development of the joint-stock company, a means for pooling the funds of many investors to finance sustained shipping trade with distant areas of the world. By 1588 companies existed to conduct trade with such far-flung places as Russia, the Barbary Coast of North Africa, and the west coast of Africa. Signposts to a later empire were the chartering in 1600 of the East India Company and Hudson's Bay Company in 1670.

Expression. Literature is a mirror of the themes which fascinated the Elizabethan imagination — courtly and human love, violence and savagery, human emotions in turmoil, a search for national identity through the pageantry of past kings, the confident realization of uniquely English values. The exclusive use of English and the predominance of secular themes distinguish this literary outpouring from the medieval.

The most polished literary expression was poetry in its myriad forms: now the simple yet revealing description of everyday life in a folksong, sometimes the intricate multi-part counterpoint of the madrigal, perhaps the stylized organized verse of the romantic sonnet, often the simple romance of the ballad or the haunting melody of songs such as *Greensleeves*. Although the themes might harken back to past times, the manner of composition pointed to the new. Edmund Spenser's narrative *The Fairie Queene* was set in the medieval world of virtue personified, but the imagery was intended for Elizabethan ears hungry for sumptuous description. Sir Philip Sidney served his Queen as a soldier, but unlike most soldiers combined with it a literary career, using his artistry to express the soldier's ideal of chivalry.

The Elizabethan love for drama flourished in a reawakening of the theatre. Unlike medieval times, the themes of late sixteenth-century plays were rarely religious, painting instead the vividness of battle, the humor of the buffoon, and the intricacies of romance. The first English playhouse was built in 1576 by John Burbage just ouside London, and the plays performed in it delighted eager audiences (see pp. 131-32). A more stylized classical drama was emphasized in the universities, but because it was becoming fashionable for the nobility and gentry, and not just potential clergymen, to attend university, more and more persons encountered drama in some form.

The Elizabethans built in stone and brick as well as prose. The huge stately mansions of the nobility and upper gentry were monuments to the peace and prosperity of the era, and symbols of the owner's importance. The new buildings ignored the irregular floorplans, ornate decoration, and gothic features which had prevailed early in the century, adopting instead cleaner classical lines, with symmetrical floorplans in the E- or H-shape and an extravagant use of glass. Lord Burghley had three different mansions, the second largest of which (like many other new homes) was built out from a suppressed monastic building at the east end. The interiors of these homes featured elaborate wood panelling, sculptured plasterwork ceilings, and tapestries hung on the walls to provide color and keep out the cold. The style of entertaining was as ornate as the exterior — Elizabeth and her court of nearly 500 visited Burghley a dozen times, each time costing him huge sums (perhaps £5000) in hospitality. The homes of the middle gentry were often of a distinctive new style called half-timbering, in which the darkened wood color of the beams used in construction was contrasted with white exterior plasterwork in between.

Enjoyment. The brilliant things of the Elizabethan era were thoroughly and gustily although not widely shared, and the degree to which one participated in them depended above all on rank. A multitude of externals bore witness to gentle birth and its privileges: gentlemen could bear arms and amuse themselves at gambling while ordinary men could not; gentlemen wore hats and workers caps, and even within the upper ranks the gradations were apparent from whether one wore cloth-of-gold, or silk, or velvet, or more ordinary cloth in his apparel. The higher the rank, the greater the expected adherence to the principle that work was beneath his dignity. With little other than leisure, there was time to enjoy gentle sports such as hawking and hunting, or go up to London to tend to legal business, or to entertain lavishly. The road to preferment was usually in public service. The unpaid Justice of the Peace demonstrated his status to men below him and his suitability for higher offices to the government above.

The entrée into the ranks of the gentry was the possession of a coat of arms from the College of Heralds. The Elizabethan era provided expanded economic opportunity for the industrious, a market in land spurred by the dissolution of the monasteries and thus the means to acquire the most important status-conferring asset, and a College of Heralds who for a price could search energetically and successfully for the gentle origins of one's ancestors. The enlargement of the ranks of the gentry and their increasing economic importance often cost lesser

Longleat, an Elizabethan stately home.

men dearly. The unemployed victims of enclosure tended to drift into cities, especially London, only to find endemic outbreaks of the plague, squalor, overcrowding, and a distinct loss of amenities. Crime was one possible solution, begging another. Even criminals and vagabonds lived according to rank, from the confidence man at the top down through levels of thievery such as "priggers of prancers" (horsethieves) to beggars — some of whom elicited sympathy with feigned wounds or intentionally maimed children. The pockets of human misery, the stench of sewerless streets, the hand-to-mouth subsistence dependent on the vageries of weather and good crops — all are reminders that although participation in the good things of life had broadened, it was yet very shallow.

SUGGESTIONS FOR FURTHER READING

The best introduction to political events is G. R. Elton, *England Under the Tudors* (2nd edition, 1974). Elton's thesis that Thomas Cromwell inspired the plan for the Reformation, and that his administrative changes mark the watershed between medieval and early modern government, was argued in *The Tudor Revolution in Government* (1953), with elaboration in other works such as *Policy and Police, the Enforcement of the Reformation in the Age of Thomas Cromwell*

(1972) and *Reform and Renewal, Thomas Cromwell and the Common Weal* (1973). Differing or opposing views are found in W. C. Richardson, *Tudor Chamber Administration 1485-1547* (1952), in a series of debates in the journal *Past & Present,* 1963-65, and in other writings such as A. G. R. Smith's brief and useful *The Government of Elizabethan England* (1967). The troubled years of mid-century are the subject of Whitney R. D. Jones, *The Mid-Tudor Crisis 1539-1563* (1973). Useful corrections to established views about Edward VI's reign are in Dale Hoak, *The King's Council in the Reign of Edward VI* (1976) and in M. L. Bush, *The Government Policy of Protector Somerset* (1975). A sympathetic treatment of Mary is in H. F. M. Prescott, *Mary Tudor* (2nd edition, 1972). J.E. Neale's biography *Elizabeth I* (1934) is overly romantic and favorable but still the best; his *Elizabethan House of Commons* (1949) and two volumes of *Elizabeth I and her Parliaments* (1953, 1957) are the principal works on Parliament. The best survey of foreign affairs is in R.B. Wernham, *Before the Armada, The Emergence of the English Nation 1485-1588* (1966).

Religious change in the first half of the sixteenth century is surveyed in A.G. Dickens, *The English Reformation* (1964). Foxe's account of the Marian martyrs has often been edited, as in Marie Gentert King, *Foxe's Book of Martyrs* (1968). The best guide to later religious opposition is Patrick McGrath's *Papists and Puritans under Elizabeth I* (1967). An excellent further study of puritanism is Patrick Collinson's *The Elizabethan Puritan Movement* (1967), and the troubles of Catholics since Elizabeth are recounted in John Bossy, *The English Catholic Community, 1570-1850* (1976).

A broad survey of society is A.L. Rowse's *The England of Elizabeth, The Structure of Society* (1950). The workaday world of rural England is reflected in the essays in John Thirsk, ed., *The Agrarian History of England and Wales*, Vol. IV *1500-1640* (1967). The new awareness of the sea is reflected generally in J.A. Williamson's *The Age of Drake* (3rd edition, 1952), in economic studies such as G.D. Ramsay, *English Overseas Trade in the Century of Emergence* (1957), and in many editions of Richard Hakluyt's writings, such as Irwin R. Blacker, *The Portable Hakluyt's Voyages* (1967). The Renaissance in England is shown in Arthur B. Ferguson's *The Articulate Citizen and the English Renaissance* (1965); intellectual history is well surveyed in Christopher Morris' *Political Thought in England from Tyndale to Hooker* (1954).

6
Conflict & Civil War

1588-1660

The Queen whose England defeated the Spanish Armada in 1588 had yet fifteen years to rule. The war dragged on until 1604, and even though the Spanish never mounted another invasion attempt, the cost of defensive readiness in England drained the crown's resources. Particularly expensive was the cost of conquering Ireland to deny Spain that island from which an invasion of England could be launched. Although Elizabeth's generals conquered the Irish, she left a legacy of glossed-over problems for James Stuart, King of Scotland, to inherit in 1603 along with the English crown. In the nearly seventy-five years from 1588, however, England expanded its horizons and outgrew the narrow constraints in which the early modern state arose. Along with advances and new directions in intellectual and economic matters and in territory came the Civil Wars which wrought an important change in English life.

CONFLICT IN CLAIMS: THE STUART KINGS AND PARLIAMENT

James I. James Stuart had become King of Scotland at the age of nine months when the Protestant Scottish lords banished his Catholic mother, Mary Queen of Scots. Now in 1603 when his cousin Elizabeth I died childless, he trekked southward to assume a second crown and rule England as James I (1603-25). His learned but stern Presbyterian tutors had developed the precocious youth into an accomplished intellectual who was particularly learned in theology. But the Scottish Church claimed a total independence in ecclesiastical matters and as the self-styled voice of God freely interferred in James' government as well. The Scottish lords at first dominated the young King and even later as feudal magnates were often able to resist his authority.

James fought back with reason and with force. In his book *The True Law of Free Monarchies* (1598) he set forth the theory of the divine right of kings, demanding obedience as a religious duty from all men including the clergy. Gradually his military successes allowed him to assert his authority over many of the lords, but his flaws of character became known and compromised his reputation. His homosexual preferences were morally offensive to many and often led him to prefer attractiveness in a governmental minister rather than ability. He could be lazy and indolent, preferring horseraces and hunting to the business of state. His fear of assassination bordered on paranoia and he wore thick clothes to blunt a would-be assassin's knife.

James' Religious Problems. Early in his reign the new King received a petition supposedly signed by many Puritan clergymen which sought specific and some general reforms in the church. James presided over the Hampton Court Conference in 1604 to hear the ministers, and when a spokesman used the word "presbytery" the King's memories of his Scottish experiences provoked him to argue that those who would reform the church's leadership would move on to meddle with the state's, or as he put it succinctly, "no bishop, no king." Thenceforth James insisted on religious conformity and many Puritan ministers were removed from their churches. James' early tolerance for Catholics who attended the Anglican services alarmed many Protestants, and under intense pressure from them he reimposed the full rigor of the penal laws against Catholics. Guy Fawkes planted gunpowder in the basement of Parliament, to be ignited when James opened the session in 1605. The "Gunpowder Plot" was discovered (some argue that it was contrived from within the government to discredit the Catholics) and Fawkes and other Catholic conspirators were executed.

James became increasingly pleased with the Anglican Church which naturally championed the rights of its Supreme Head — the wood of the pulpit and of the Council table came from one tree, as some put it. Under his auspices a new translation of the Bible was begun, the strikingly beautiful King James Version of 1611 which would rank as a masterpiece of the English language. But his intolerance of Puritanism alienated many reformers, and since many of them sat in the House of Commons the relations between King and Parliament increasingly soured.

King and Parliament: Claim and Counterclaim. James often called Parliament into session because he needed taxes to offset the annual deficits and to service the debts from Elizabeth's Spanish and Irish wars. He had none of her talents for conciliation and parliamentary management, and by raising Privy Council members to the ranks of nobility he automatically transferred them from the important House of Commons to the House of Lords. With few adept spokesmen in the lower House, reform-minded Puritans often seized the initiative, acting with an intemperance and unwillingness to compromise that often matched that of the King. Rather than be opposed or lectured by the Commons, James usually dissolved a session before taxes had been granted and thus his financial problems worsened.

The Commons responded by making many theoretical claims which would deny him many rights long exercised by kings. They reacted to his anti-Puritan statements at the Hampton Court Conference by asserting that Parliament's consent was needed to alter religion. In 1610 they attacked impositions, a surcharge on customs rates which James had levied earlier without Parliament's approval but which a court decision had affirmed to be within his rights. By 1610 James was so short of funds that his ministers proposed a Great Contract, offering to give up impositions and other offensive revenues if Parliament would "buy out" his rights with a large lump-sum cash settlement. Not only was the proposal unsuccessful, but the Commons passed a resolution which argued that King-in-Parliament was superior to King-outside-Parliament and thus could review and control royal powers, impositions included. While none of these claims had the force of law, they showed quite clearly the growing estrangement of the two most important parts of the English government.

James also came under fire from a judge, Sir Edward Coke. This brilliant lawyer had been able to condense centuries of legislation and judicial precedent into a four-volume treatise, *The Institutes,* and his reputation was such as to awe and cower opponents. Coke argued against royal absolutism, asserting for instance that the King did not have the right to legislate temporarily in royal proclamations when an urgent need could not wait for Parliament to meet, and that the King could not remove judges from office. Under Elizabeth, Coke had been a champion of royal rights; now in his zeal to champion the law and attack James he used both his learning and the shady practice of inventing precedents when he needed to clinch an argument. Dismissed from his judgeship in 1616, Coke remained in the House of Commons where his learning served to raise occasional opposition into a principled cause.

The Duke of Buckingham and the Spanish War. James's problems were aggravated by his choice of ministers. His affections were dominated by George Villiers whom the doting King made the Duke of Buckingham, and the minister set out to grasp all patronage into his own hands. James also fancied himself the Protestant King who could maintain peace with Catholic rulers. His wife was a Catholic and he sought to marry his surviving son Charles to a Spanish princess. But James's son-in-law Frederick was elected King of Bohemia in 1618 and thus became the head of continental Europe's Protestant forces, the last hope of stopping the military successes of the Catholic Counter-Reformation. In the Thirty Years' War which began in 1618, Frederick badly needed his father-in-law's assistance. James seemed paralyzed by inaction, the pacifist temperamentally unwilling to go to war, financially unable to assist.

In the parliamentary session of 1621 the Commons began to argue for war with Spain and the support of Frederick, but by initiating a debate on foreign policy it was encroaching on the exclusive right of the King. James dissolved the session but just before its end the Commons escalated its theoretical claims in a protestation that Parliament had the right not only to discuss, but even to "treat, reason and bring to conclusion" matters concerning the liberties of Englishmen. In a fit of rage, James tore the page from the Commons' journal. As the tempo of hostilities abroad increased, Buckingham and Prince Charles made a romantically foolish secret trip to Spain to woo the princess, and were ill-treated. In the Parliament of 1624, James allowed a free discussion of foreign policy, and when he died the following year England was at war with Spain and assisting Frederick.

Charles I and Parliament. Charles was at once intensely strong and weak. As a child he had learned late to walk and speak, and felt very insecure faced with his father's learning and wit. Although he overcame these problems during his young adulthood and reign (1625-49) he appreciated neither the sincere passion for individual rights which animated the parliamentarian, nor the intense religious zeal of the Puritan. He needed strong advisors upon which to rely, but if any man deceived him, the King felt no moral constraint to keep his own word.

The war which Charles inherited led him into actions which were so grievous to Parliament that those of his father's reign were as naught. Charles and Buckingham, now responsible for a war which Parliament had urged but was unwilling to finance properly, were at times inept managers, and even in success they were unpopular. A seaborne strike against Spain in late 1625 was a complete fiasco. Troops and ships were unwilling to go for lack of pay, the small force which landed captured not the enemy but casks of wine and were lucky not to have been killed in their drunken stupor. The plague struck them during the homeward voyage. Those who did not die in the ships did so in the streets of Plymouth on their return, a pitiful testament to a mismanaged war. Faced with the lack of adequate war funding, the government began to "borrow" from lenders who knew they would not be repaid, and to imprison without charges those who refused. Decent citizens were ordered to accept into their homes a certain number of soldiers, often the dregs of society, and refusals could lead to a declaration of martial law. In 1628 Parliament framed a Petition of Right, demanding that the King cease these improper measures. Charles agreed, but continued to protect Buckingham whose impeachment Parliament sought. An assassin's knife took Buckingham's life in 1628, but Charles had more problems to face.

When he had first become King, Parliament refused to grant Charles the customs for all his reign as was traditional, but doled them out in periods of years and months. After 1628 Charles began to collect the customs as if they had been granted, and Parliament saw that the Petition of Right was no total protection. The militance of Parliament in 1629 was so great that the King decided quickly to dissolve it. While the royal messenger was barred from entering the Commons, the angered parliamentarians held the Speaker in his chair to prevent the dissolution and then passed three resolutions which branded as a traitor to the state anyone who would support the alterations which Charles had introduced. The infuriated King stated that Parliament would not be called again until it learned its rightful, respectful place in the kingdom.

The King Rules Alone. Without calling a parliament for eleven years of "personal rule" (1629-40), Charles ended the wars and balanced his budget. Two ministers especially made his policies successful. Thomas Wentworth brought efficiency to areas heretofore very difficult to control, first as Lord President in the North and then as Lord Deputy of Ireland, in reward for which he was raised to the peerage as Earl of Strafford. Archbishop William Laud removed Puritan ministers from office and strengthened the Church of England in anti-Puritan and anti-Calvinistic attitudes. The spirit of these achievements frightened some more than the specific details. Strafford and Laud called their insistence on efficiency and compliance with the King's wishes a policy of "thorough," and even though their activities were limited and often far from thorough, the King's opponents feared that any spread of "thoroughness" to other aspects of English life would spell the end of individual rights. Laud placed great emphasis on the continuity of Anglicanism with pre-Reformation Catholicism. The revival of ancient Catholic ceremonies was intended to bring the "beauty of holiness" to Protestantism, not to supplant it with Catholicism, but to the Puritans who emphasized the simple, unadorned preaching of the word it seemed to threaten the Reformation.

What Charles called success his opponents branded as "tyranny"; to them "thorough" was a form of despotism, the "beauty of holiness" nothing but popery. They objected to the King's raising revenue without Parliament's consent by arbitrarily extending the boundaries of royal forests and then fining people within the new limits for unlicensed dwelling, or transferring cases to the Star Chamber so that huge fines could be levied. The greatest problem was Charles's levy of ship money. Monarchs had an undisputed right to ask residents in the coastal shires to contribute money in time of war for the building of new ships which would provide an added and immediate means of defense. Charles began to levy ship money on inland counties as well, and in times of peace. When John Hampden, a prosperous gentleman, refused to pay a small sum levied on him out of principle, he lost the case by a 7-5 verdict, but won a moral victory from the dissent of so many royal judges.

It was religion which brought matters to a head. Charles tried to impose Anglicanism on his kingdom of Scotland, but the General Assembly of the established Presbyterian Church strongly resisted. Charles mounted an ill-conceived and inadequately financed invasion, but his armies fled without fighting when they saw the Scots. The King realized that he could put an effective army in the field only if it were adequately funded, and that required calling a Parliament. The session which began on April 13, 1640, ended the eleven years during which a wide range of issues had become crystallized and the sides polarized.

It was but a short time until the Civil War broke out in 1642, but it was the product of more than disputes in politics and religion. In many ways the King represented an older order in which royal control over most aspects of English life was taken for granted. The years 1588-1640 witnessed many new attitudes and emphases which arose and flourished at variance with or completely ignored the monarchy. The next two sections study these changes and provide a fuller context for the wars and the aftermath.

IDEAS AND THE CHALLENGE TO AUTHORITY

Science and Practical Learning. Medieval thought was characterized by deductive reasoning which used logic to draw particular conclusions from general truths. Sir Francis Bacon, a royal official to James I, wrote

Anatomy lecture, 1581 (The Wellcome Trustees, Wellcome Institute of the History of Medicine).

to urge a reorientation: man should begin with the particular, and by repeated and extensive observation form an hypothesis expressing a general truth, capable of proof by experimentation. Bacon was sure that this scientific method would expand knowledge and produce many practical applications. Obviously the old was not instantly displaced — Oxford and Cambridge continued to teach the traditional curricula in Latin and many were suspicious of change — but the ideas of Bacon and many like-minded Europeans found fertile ground in the English emphasis on the practical. At Gresham College in London the instruction was conducted in English and emphasized scientific matters and applications in the business world, such as in navigation and shipbuilding. When Sir John Napier published his discovery of logarithms in 1614, a professor of astronomy popularized it and provided useful tables.

Scientific reasoning captured the imagination of the learned. In 1628 William Harvey set forth his theory that the blood circulated through the body, a major anatomical discovery. Navigational instruments like the telescope were widely produced, and the emphasis on mathematics awakened an interest in statistics and resulted in reliable and accurate maps. By mid-century many of the upper classes had laboratories in their homes, even if just to be fashionable. An indirect result of the scientific method was to make authority and tradition less important and to emphasize the things of this world. When scientific discoveries proved wrong some of the churchmen's scientific orthodoxy, it impugned their credibility in religious matters as well. The full impact of all of this was felt fully only toward the end of the century, but seeds of disruption had been sown alongside those of scientific advances.

The Social Ethic of Puritanism. Puritanism was important in politics and religion but it also became a social ethic, a set of attitudes which became a lasting part of English society independently of religion. Preaching was all-important to the Puritans, not only stressing religious truths but also inculcating discipline and industriousness. The Puritan was taught that God rewarded His elect with material success in this world as well as with bliss in the next. Labor thus became a social duty and idleness a religious evil. This teaching appealed to artisans and merchants who lived in towns and ports, for whom frugality and hard work were necessary to get ahead. Puritans tended to be distrustful of agricultural society with its periods of inactivity, and resentful of non-productive persons, both of the poor and of the nobility and gentry whose social status exempted them from toil.

Because only Anglicanism was legally allowed in the parish churches of England, the Puritans had to seek other platforms for their views, and sympathetic town officials often endowed lectureships from town funds to provide a forum for preaching. Unwilling to accept the teaching in the parish churches, the Puritans placed great emphasis on Bible reading and spiritual formation in the home, a deemphasis on the Church's role which had social as well as religious consequences.

The profits of the industrious Puritan became capital ready for investing, and the business contacts they formed across England meant the creation of a network of economic interests. The Providence Island Company, for example, was formed to colonize in the West Indies, but most important members of the Puritan opposition in the House of Commons participated in it. This sense of economic cooperation made it possible to shift capital to new areas of the economy, but also had political ramifications in that it helped shape a body of men for whom political cooperation was but one step advanced from economic. This helped form a strong nucleus of opposition to the King's policies.

Capitalism and Trade. Most Englishmen continued to work in agriculture, but although landowners paid greater attention to scientific ways of increasing production, it was in industry and trade that the seeds for England's future economic growth were sown. Increases in the scale of operation were often more important than innovation and invention at this stage, and thus vast supplies of capital for investment were required. In particular it was realized that England's vast coal resources were exceptionally valuable, as the supply of timber for fuel and building dwindled. Seams near the surface had long been mined, but capital was needed for digging deep shafts and for the pumps to clear gasses and water and to help raise the coal. As production grew eight-fold in a century, the coal from centers in the northeast such as Newcastle-upon-Tyne came to be valued as important for England as Peru's silver had been for Spain a century earlier. The iron industry grew apace and the huge increase in the production of iron benefited both older industries such as making cannons and nails, and newer fabricating trades.

Wool and unfinished cloth had been England's principal exports, shipped almost exclusively from London to a few continental markets such as Antwerp, and thus subject to vicissitudes outside England's control. Attempts were made to produce newer types of cloth such as worsteds and to finish cloths before export, but neither succeeded and trading depressions continued into the seventeenth century. The opening of non-European trade revived English commerce. The highly capitalized trading companies traded with the new colonies in America and with parts of Asia and Africa. More ships were needed and a new rivalry was thus created with the Dutch, a powerful maritime nation determined to dominate the seaborne carrying trade.

Capitalists became important in domestic trading also. Middlemen were needed to bring foodstuffs from distant counties to feed London's burgeoning population, and to put out the wool to spinners and weavers and then bring the finished cloth to the market. The increased demand for food encouraged a vast engineering project, the draining of the marshy fens of eastern England. Before the end of the seventeenth century nearly 400,000 acres had been made fit for farming.

The crown supported many of these ventures — the manufacture of gunpowder was important militarily, the new trading companies had royal charters, and Charles I himself invested in draining the fens. But the more common royal attitude was indifference and even hostility. Capitalism was feared because of the new concentrations of wealth it created, for the social unrest which often followed, and because it was often unregulated. The Stuarts sought to control trade as the Tudors had earlier and they often exploited the wealth of the trading companies. The monopolies so freely granted to increase royal revenues often stifled economic development. Although most Englishmen were untouched by the new economic activities, the new economic

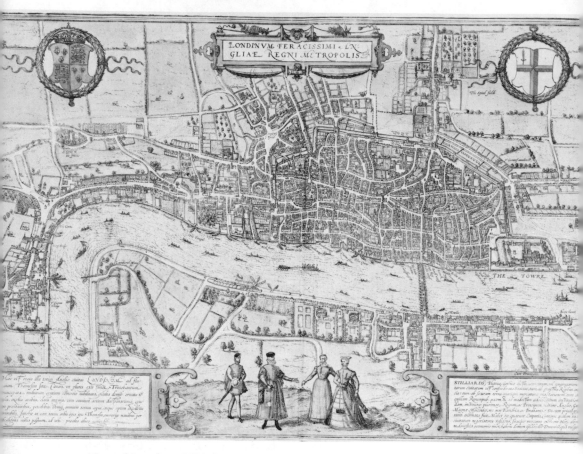

Map of London, 1593 (Henry E. Huntington Library and Art Gallery).

entrepreneur came to resent the crown's attitude. A good deal of the military geography of the coming civil war was determined by the degree to which merchants and traders had welcomed or resisted royal interference in the economy.

EXPANSION AT HOME AND ABROAD

Shakespeare's London. Greater London grew enormously, spilling out beyond the square mile contained within the medieval walls, growing from about 50,000 in 1500 to 200,000 in 1603 and to 400,000 in 1660. It was a glittering Renaissance city for the upper ranks of society, the home of the Court and the hub of the legal world, the center of a social season with plays and amusements. For the merchant it was a place of exceptional opportunity, the largest and most lucrative market in all of Europe, the center of a fast trading world of commerce. London also attracted the less fortunate — the unemployed agricultural workers no longer needed on enclosed fields, the ne'er-do-wells who wished to escape the tedium of country life, and the criminal who saw a golden opportunity. Slums grew quickly, especially when unscrupulous builders subdivided buildings into small, dark tenements. Plague and poverty were as much at home in Renaissance London as opulence and entertainment.

London in 1588 was still a city of half-timbered wooden buildings along winding streets. There had always been much greenery in the city and the countryside was not far away, but there was evidence of growth everywhere. The first expansion was internal, filling up empty spaces and especially tearing down the suppressed monastic buildings to erect dwellings in their place. North of the walls the expansion was limited by poor soil and drainage, but the movement westward and eastward showed two different reasons for growth.

The expansion westward was primarily residential. In 1588 only a thin line of palatial homes for the wealthy lined the mile along the river between London and Westminster, but by 1660 the area was extensively developed. The more opulent homes in the west housed those who wished to be near Westminster and the Court. Some sections were strikingly beautiful and well planned as at Covent Garden where the Duke of Bedford as patron and the builder-architect Inigo Jones as designer laid out a square and surrounding buildings in the classical style. Nearer London's western walls were many slum areas. The expansion eastward was to service the new docks which harbored the royal navy. Also located there were docks of the new trading companies; the East India Company built moorings and warehouses in an area of river frontage which covered ten acres. The relative unattractiveness of this commercial area was worsened when the use of coal spread; soot from London was usually blown eastward over the docks.

London's officials lived in fear of the plague and of social disorder which were always possible in so densely crowded an area. Because many of the offices were Puritans, they were horrified at many Londoners' idleness and at the plays and other profane amusements. The Lord Mayor of London was able to keep theaters outside the city's limits, and thus the most famous playhouse used by Shakespeare's company, the Globe (1599), was built on the south side of the river in a different county. The problem of keeping order in burgeoning London was complicated by the inability and unwillingness to coordinate actions between the officials of London and the different jurisdictions outside the walls but within the metropolitan area.

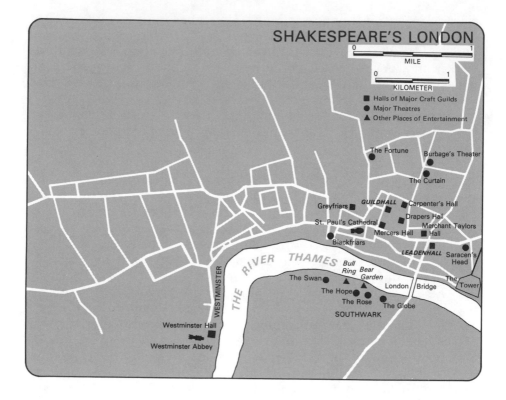

SHAKESPEARE'S LONDON

The Globe's interior was patterned after the arrangement of tiered balconies overlooking a courtyard as plays had traditionally been given in the courtyards of inns. Little scenery was used and women did not act, so that the success of a play depended on the vividness and reality created by the spoken word. Shakespeare gave brilliance to the stage — his polished characterizations and innovative use of language dazzled audiences which ranged from the unlettered penny public to the sophisticated Court, and even to Elizabeth and James. The audiences loved realism so that an actor was expected to be an accomplished acrobat, wearing concealed bladders of red liquid which when pricked by a dueller's sword after a spirited fight would graphically simulate death. Shakespeare made comedy and tragedy alike come alive, and many Englishmen learned the history of their country from the plays he wrote about medieval English kings. The tradition of the theater in which he excelled lasted until the Puritans gained political ascendancy and closed the theaters in 1642.

Colonization. The English colonized near to home, sending Protestant settlers to Ulster in the north of Ireland, and though there were many difficulties in settling in Ireland there were few surprises. The "planting" of colonies in America was considerably more difficult, primarily because the difficulties could not be forseen when the enterprises were launched. Religion motivated some colonizing efforts, the hope of economic profits spurred others, but in every case the impetus was private and not royal. The desire for profit led the London Company to send settlers to Virginia, where the first to arrive in 1607 named their colony Jamestown after the King. Half were gentlemen who in proper English fashion did not intend to work but rather sought to find precious metals or the route to the orient. There was no room in the harsh and hostile new land for such an attitude and not many survived the early years of starvation and Indian massacres; success came only when tobacco cultivation became the colony's economic mainstay.

The landing of religiously motivated "pilgrims" at Plymouth in 1620 was an indirect result of James I's anti-Puritan sentiments. A congregation in Scrooby, Nottinghamshire, left England for Holland to practice their religion freely, then relocated in the New World. They had no legal authority for the move, but as a close-knit community in a relatively unimportant location they were able to practice their religion without interference. Slightly later a great level of maturity in appreciating the difficulties of colonization was manifested by the Massachusetts Bay Company whose settlers first arrived at Boston in 1630. Everyone was equipped to be self-sufficient through early lean years, and the insistence on living in towns gave a degree of success and independence not to be found in England. The settlement in Maryland which began in 1634 had yet a different authority and motivation. Charles I granted Lord Baltimore and his fellow Catholics the territory as a proprietary colony to be held by feudal tenure. As important as these mainland settlements were, the English colonies in the Caribbean islands such as Bermuda and Barbados were more economically beneficial to England.

In each of these instances the actual management of affairs proceeded independently of the King. If abuses arose and the aggrieved petitioned the King, then James or Charles might revoke a concession and nominally take control, but this was more theoretical than actual. The Stuarts had neither a plan for encouraging colonization nor a policy of political management of those which others began. The substantially larger migrations in the 1630s arose from the royal anti-Puritan policies. Only in 1651, when the Commonwealth and not the crown ruled, did an imperial commercial policy begin. The Navigation Act of 1651 required colonists to ship their produce

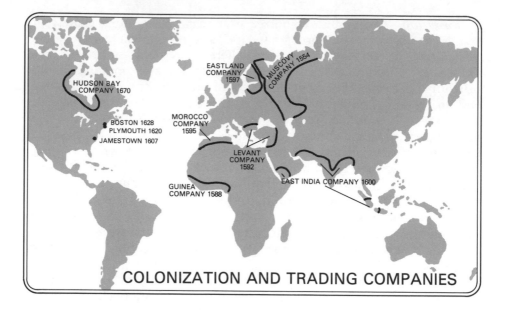

exclusively to England, on English ships manned by English sailors, so that the mother country might monopolize the fruits of its colonies. The full implications of the measure would become clear only later, as subsequent chapters will show.

CONFLICT AT ARMS: THE CIVIL WARS AND CROMWELL

The Long Parliament. Charles called Parliament in April 1640 to demand taxes for fighting the Scots, and as soon as the session opened the able parliamentary leader John Pym rose in the Commons to list years of grievances against the Stuarts and to win approval for debating them first. After three weeks and no grant of taxes, Charles angrily dissolved Parliament (later to be called the Short Parliament), but that summer the Scots invaded and occupied two northern English counties so that Charles had to call a new session in November (the Long Parliament) to meet the crisis. Pym realized that even though two-thirds of the Commons was bent on reform, the proper tactic to keep together the majority was first to focus on removing hated royal officials. Accordingly he sought to remove from office Strafford and Laud, the ministers of "thorough" best able to rally the King's supporters. After months of argument on the proper procedures, both Houses passed a bill in May 1641 which declared the two men traitors and another bill the same month which stated that Parliament could not be dissolved without its own consent.

Then Parliament passed bill after bill to be rid of many institutions and practices which it despised. It abolished the Court of Star Chamber which had coercively enforced questionable royal policies, the Court of High Commission which had stripped Puritans from church offices, and the two regional councils in the North and in Wales. It granted the King customs for two-month renewable periods only, declared ship money illegal, and ended financial expedients such as enlarging the royal forests. It passed a Triennial Act which required Parliament to meet once every three years, so that the King could not once again refuse to call it into session. Charles gave his assent to every bill. People began to wonder why he had allowed his faithful ministers to be executed, his government to be stripped of crucial powers, and Parliament to gain a potential permanence. Late in 1641 Charles began to rally his supporters, claiming that he alone was able to save the Church of England from a minority who would displace it. He requested an army to put down a fresh rebellion in Ireland, and many parliamentarians feared to accede lest an army under royal control would become the instrument to reverse the hard won reforms.

Fears about the King's sincerity were heightened when on January 4, 1642, he burst into the House of Commons to arrest Pym and four other leaders, but they had been forwarned and escaped. Soon Charles left the hostile mobs of London for the more loyal north. Long months proved that an accomodation was not possible, so in August 1642 war broke out between the King and Parliament. Each side justified its actions: Charles claimed to fight to preserve the balance of the constitution and keep the Commons from encroaching all powers; Parliament insisted on a distinction between the office of kingship and the person of the King, asserting that it sought to preserve the office from the unworthy Stuart tyrant.

The Civil Wars. The King's forces, the Royalists, or Cavaliers, advanced in 1642 to the outskirts of London and won a major engagement at Edgehill, but neither then nor in the proposed triple offensive of 1643 were the royal forces able to convert occasional successes into a conclusive victory. In the interim Parliament had to learn to govern the areas under its control. In such a novel situation there was much freedom in discarding traditional but inefficient practices, and gradually Parliament developed effective administrative and taxing procedures.

The war's turning point was Parliament's reorganization of the army made up of Parliamentarians, or Roundheads, in 1644. By passing a Self-Denying Ordinance Parliament excluded its own members from military offices, thus removing men for whom rank and birth and not ability had meant leadership. The result was the creation of the New Model Army which was open to Puritans with real military skills, an innovation as novel for Europe as were striking the new redcoats in which all the soldiers were uniformed. An exception was made for an extremely capable young parliamentarian, Oliver Cromwell, a member of the gentry powerfully motivated by his Puritan faith, a man who kept himself ready to serve God by diligent prayer and self-examination. Cromwell was a major proponent of the role of cavalry in battle and the flair with which he led his mounted soldiers to rout the enemy in disciplined and perfected charges soon made him one of the highest ranking generals and an inspiration for the soldiers. In 1644 the military tide began to shift in Parliament's favor, and at Marston Moor that year and at Naseby in 1645 the royalist forces were soundly defeated.

From the time that Charles surrendered in 1646 the central political issue was the terms of negotiation. Two factions in Parliament were seriously divided by religious and constitutional attitudes. The majority party, the Presbyterians, wished to make the long-delayed religious settlement along the Scottish Calvinistic lines while the Independents wanted to allow a great deal of doctrinal latitude to each individual congregation and to restrict the national church to matters of public policy such as repressing blasphemy. The Presbyterians were constitutionally more moderate, wanting to place no restrictions on the monarch beyond those enacted in the Long Parliament, while the Independents felt that further restraints were absolutely necessary.

The Presbyterians would prevail if it came to a vote, but a powerful force outside Parliament also claimed a role in determining England's political future. Refusing to be disbanded as the parliamentary Presbyterians wished, the Army asserted it had been called "to the defense of our own and the people's just rights and liberties." Its officers prepared a plan of negotiations which strongly supported the parliamentary Independents, and the soldiers through elected spokesmen presented their own scheme based heavily on the philosophy of the Levellers, a radical faction comprised mainly of Londoners of lower social ranks. The Levellers went beyond an insistence on religious equality to demand a "levelling" in economic and political life as well, to be won in great part by allowing all male heads of households to vote.

Meanwhile Charles escaped and the Parliament and army buried their differences, to fight and to defeat him within a year. But when negotiations were resumed, the Presbyterians did not budge from their earlier "moderate" position which the Independents now judged folly in the light of the actions of the "perfidious king." Colonel Pride led an army contingent into Parliament to purge the Presbyterian members,

Royalist portrayal of Charles I as a martyr (The Works of Charles I with his Life and Martyrdom).

and the fifty to sixty Independents remaining immediately set up a court to try the King for his crimes. Charles rose to true nobility in his last days, arguing strongly and persuasively in his own behalf, but his conviction was a foregone conclusion. On January 30, 1649, a few hours after the office of the monarch was abolished, he was beheaded, and then the small remnant of Independents, now called the Rump Parliament, also abolished the House of Lords and the office of bishop. James I's "no bishop, no king" had come true, and thus began an eleven years period called the Interregnum (1649-60), a time of constitutional experimentation to find an alternative to England's traditional form of government.

The Commonwealth. The earliest experiment was the Commonwealth (1649-53) in which the Rump was the legislature and the executive functions were shared by a forty-member Council of State composed of thirty-one parliamentarians and some generals. The psychological wrench of abandoning so many traditional practices was a severe problem. The army was kept busy suppressing royalist uprisings, crushing rebellions in Ireland and Scotland, and the navy in fighting the Dutch in a mercantile war over the supremacy of the sea and the control of colonies. Little progress was made in settling religion, still unsolved since 1642. A diluted form of Presbyterianism was enacted but found little support outside of London. In default of an enforceable plan, all forms of worship were allowed except Anglicanism and Catholicism.

The most important political tension was between the Rump and the Army. The latter wished old grievances settled and insisted that the Rump keep its promise to dissolve itself and call new elections. Cromwell had become the leading general as others died or retired, but he was unwilling to dispense with the Rump lest the last link to the traditional form of representation be broken. When in April 1653 the Rump declared itself permanent, Cromwell finally intervened to dissolve the Rump. He then tried an utterly novel and totally unsuccessful experiment. The Army asked the independent congregations to nominate God-fearing Puritans to enact reforms. The 129 members of the Nominated Assembly proved so radical that it acquired unpleasant nicknames such as the "Assembly of the Saints" and the "Barebones Parliament," the last a word play on its member, Praise-God Barbon or Barebone, whose low social rank seemed to epitomize the perceived danger of entrusting government to others than the well-born elite. Cromwell quickly ended the experiment.

The Protectorate and the End of the Interregnum. Cromwell and the army were ready with another plan, a written constitution called the Instrument of Government. As Lord Protector, Cromwell assumed executive control with sweeping powers such as the right to issue ordinaces which were to have the force of law until Parliament should meet. It was the exercise of these powers that caused unrest. Cromwell realized that the army's power had to be reduced and civilian control extended and this attitude dissatisfied the army, while Parliament was stunned by his use of ordinances to collect money and even settle religious matters. No Stuart king had ever enjoyed such power and independence!

To correct some of these problems, Parliament in 1657 drafted a new written constitution, the Humble Petition and Advice. Cromwell rejected that part of the proposal which offered him the title of King yet accepted most of the rest, including the right to name his successor. But the constitutional dilemma continued and only the extraordinary skills of Oliver Cromwell kept the political state together. When he died on September 3, 1658, and was succeeded by his son Richard, the Interregnum was near collapse.

Richard Cromwell was ineffective — his nickname was "Tumble-Down Dick" — and many of the Army's leaders grew increasingly arbitrary in opposition. The commander in Scotland, General George Monck, took the initiative to end the stalemate by marching his army southward and capitalizing on the public sentiment which called for a permanent solution. First he called back the Rump Parliament, then he added all the others purged in 1648. The restored Long Parliament called for new elections and dissolved itself, and the newly elected body issued an invitation to the son of Charles I to return as King. In May 1660 Charles II arrived back from exile to inaugurate the Restoration — a restoration of the monarchy, of the Church of England, and of traditional government.

A STOCKTAKING: ENGLAND IN 1660

Government. Most of the monarch's powers were restored in 1660. The right to make policy was unimpaired but the Civil Wars which had been fought to end Stuart despotism and to curtail royal rights made for a powerful if only implicit understanding — what Parliament had done to Charles I could be done as well to his son. Charles II realized this, minding his ways "lest I go on my travels again." It would take another crisis, in 1688-89, to prove the new relationship conclusively, but the direction had been set. Some powers were, however, lost forever. To ease his transition into office Charles II confirmed the legislation of the Long Parliament and much of the Interregnum's. Feudal tenures had been abolished and thus the King lost the potentially coercive powers he as feudal lord could wield over landowning Englishmen. The Privy Council had been the heart of the royal administration and its strength rested in part on the enforcement powers which the councillors wielded as judges in the Star Chamber. The abolition of that Court, of the Court of High Commission, and of the Councils in the North and in Wales, was a tremendous loss of power.

The Tudor and Stuart monarchs had heaped endless responsibilities on the Justices of the Peace, but with the end of Star Chamber these all-important local officials were able to realize an unprecedented degree of autonomy. Parliament had learned how much more difficult it was to govern effectively than to protest. Its role in influencing policy was temporarily eclipsed by the fervor greeting the Restoration, but it was now free to debate any topic and was better organized.

Society and the Economy. The size of the aristocracy had grown greatly in the seventeenth century but its importance had diminished. The twin pillars of aristocratic preeminence in the Middle Ages had been military service and the nobility's wealth and influence. Most of

the military responsibilities had been lost in the sixteenth century and
the eclipse of the House of Lords temporarily by the Commons had
diminished their political role. More importantly, the aristocrats' land
ownership was severely curtailed by the Civil Wars. Most had fought for
the King and although those whose estates had been confiscated were
entitled to sue at law for recovery, the nobles who sold their estates for
any reason whatsoever were not able to regain them.

The early modern state had opened up great opportunities for the
gentry. What the dissolution of the monasteries had done to enlarge the
land market of the sixteenth century the confiscation of the nobles'
and bishops' lands had done in the seventeenth. Many of these
newly-landed gentry were in time to rise to the new nobility. The
merchants who formed a non-agricultural middle class along with
professionals such as lawyers had all grown in importance. Success in
any endeavor produced capital ready for investment in myriad new
economic adventures at home and in trade.

The economic restraints imposed by the monarchy were removed.
Gone were regulations governing the quality of manufactures and the
rates of wages; gone were feudal tenures which had disinclined
landowners to invest to improve their crop yield; gone were the royal
monopolies and the Star Chamber which hindered the free marketplace.
The removal of restrictions primarily benefited the well-to-do. The rich
were able to get richer and the poor suffered even more. But many of
the "lesser sort" had been politicized, allowed to speculate freely along
with others in a time of constitutional experimentation, and allowed to
have access to printing presses to propagate sincere reform ideas such as
the Levellers, or the outlandish ideas of religious fanatics. Many of
these movements had been suppressed either in the Interregnum or at
the Restoration, but politics was not likely to remain the closed
precinct of the upper classes alone.

Religion and Ideas. Sixteenth-century religion was based on the premise
that truth was certain and discoverable and that dissent and diversity
were literally intolerable. By 1660 Catholicism was rather effectively
eradicated but Puritanism had temporarily come to supplant
Anglicanism. The varieties of religious dissent had mutliplied and no
longer was it possible to substitute one set of practices and form of
church government for another. Although Anglicanism in the
Restoration would bring an end to the period of practical toleration,
the memory endured. Puritanism had indeed triumphed in many urban
settings as a social ethic. Long after the specific religious teachings had
been lost, the lessons of industriousness and discipline in work
remained to influence many in the middle ranks of society. New
directions in thought emerged, especially the humanism of the

sixteenth century and the scientific inquiry of the seventeenth. The how-to-do-it orientation of many books reflected the practical, this-worldly bent of Englishmen. Many of the old orthodoxies were crumbling as much in the world of religion and ideas as in society and politics; the next quarter century gave a firmer shape to the new.

SUGGESTIONS FOR FURTHER READING

An overview for the entire seventeenth century is Christopher Hill's *The Century of Revolution* (1961). David Harris Willson's *King James VI and I* (1956) is a good biography; a thorough and dispassionate treatment of Charles I is still needed, but a brief, illustrated account is Christopher Hibbert's *Charles I* (1968). A chronological survey of the constitution is J. R. Tanner's *English Constitutional Conflicts of the Seventeenth Century 1603-1689* (1928).

There is a spirited debate on the origins of the Civil Wars, to which a useful guide can be found in Philip A. M. Taylor, *The Origins of the English Civil War. Conspiracy, Crusade, or Class Conflict?* (1960), and in Conrad Russell, *The Origins of the English Civil War* (1973). Narrative histories of the troubled 1630s and 1640s are in C. V. Wedgwood, *The King's Peace, 1637-1641* (1955) and *The King's War, 1641-1647* (1958). The astute maneuvers of the reformers are in J. H. Hexter, *The Reign of King Pym* (1941), while the growth of radicalism is treated by Christopher Hill in *The World Turned Upside Down, Radical Ideas during the English Revolution* (1972).

The military aspect of the wars is in Peter Young and Richard Holmes, *The English Civil War, A Military History of the Three Civil Wars 1642-1651* (1974). Among useful studies of Cromwell are Christopher Hill's *God's Englishman: Oliver Cromwell and the English Revolution* (1970) which stresses ideas, and A. A. Hillary's *Oliver Cromwell and the Challenge to the Monarchy* (1969) which is briefer but with a fuller context. The historiographical debate over Cromwell is introduced in Richard E. Boyer, *Oliver Cromwell and the Puritan Revolt, Failure of a Man or a Faith?* (1966).

Religious issues are briefly introduced by William M. Lamont, *Godly Rule. Politics and Religion, 1603-60* (1969). The literary aspects of puritanism are stressed by William Haller, *The Rise of Puritanism 1570-1643* (1938), the formation of the social ethic in Christopher Hill, *Society and Puritanism in Pre-Revolutionary England* (1964), the instructional side in Paul Seaver's *The Puritan Lectureships, the Politics of Religious Dissent 1560-1662* (1970), and the many sects in George Yule's *The Independents in the English Civil War* (1958).

Useful social surveys are Wallace Notestein, *The English People on the Eve of Colonization 1603-1630* (1954) and David Mathew, *The Age of Charles I* (1951). The political aspects of society are discussed in Perez Zagorin's *The Court and the Country* (1970), and the upper classes in Lawrence Stone's *The Crisis of the Aristocracy 1558-1641* (1965); a provocative study of the less spectacular Englishmen is in Peter Laslett, *The World We Have Lost* (2nd edition, 1971). There is a debate over the political and economic "rise" of the gentry and their role in precipitating the Civil War; a guide to the protagonists with penetrating critiques is in J. H. Hexter's *Reappraisals in History* (1961).

Economic developments are surveyed in Charles Wilson's *England's Apprenticeship 1603-1763* (1965). The broad range of new avenues of thought are studied in Christopher Hill's *The Intellectual Origins of the English Revolution* (1965), and science is emphasized in the European context in Alan G. R. Smith, *Science and Society in the Sixteenth and Seventeenth Centuries* (1972) and in H. Butterfield, *The Origins of Modern Science* (new edition, 1957). Marchette Chute's *Shakespeare of London* (1949) is a brilliant word picture of Renaissance London and a contrast with Stratford-on-Avon. The position that "Shakespeare" was a pseudonym for the Earl of Oxford is argued in Ruth Loyd Miller's enlarged 3rd edition of J. Looney's *"Shakespeare" Identified in Edward de Vere, Seventeenth Earl of Oxford* (2 vols., 1975). The importance of London in politics is studied in Valerie Pearl's *London and the Outbreak of the Puritan Revolution* (1961).

7

Restoration England

1660-1688

When Charles II (1660-85) set foot on English soil at Dover on May 25, 1660, he returned amidst general rejoicing and relief. Charles II appeared to be well-cast for his role. He was dark and swarthy, not handsome; his young, athletic appearance, his stature (he was six feet four inches tall); and his easy manner, sharp wit, and shrewd intelligence made him an instant success. His faults, though evident to his close associates and advisors, took longer to be revealed. Indolent, with little interest for business (though he unquestionably had the ability), insincere and gifted at dissembling (a trait he had been forced to acquire in his struggle for life and throne), an overgreat fondness for pleasure, women, and gambling, he cut the figure of a king but lacked the substance. Perhaps his most important trait, if hardly the most admirable, was an instinct for survival.

THE REESTABLISHMENT OF THE MONARCHY

The Restoration Settlement. Charles left to the Parliament the settling of such vexatious and difficult matters as the arrears of pay of the army, a general pardon, and the forfeited estates of the royalists.

Charles II (Kenneth Spencer Research Library).

Parliament rather than the King thus bore the odium of the disappointed. The Cromwellian army was reduced to a few regiments; the rest of the troops were paid what was owing them and retired from active duties. The Act of Indemnity which forgave all but fifty named individuals was a gracious and healing measure. The land problem was a more complex one and any solution was bound to create opposition. The compromise was sensible if not wholly equitable. Crown lands and those of the church together with confiscated estates were returned to the original owners. Those properties sold by private individuals during the Civil Wars could only be repossessed through court action and then only in the case of abuses of the law not exempted by the Act of Indemnity.

The Political Settlement. The nature of the King's own authority had perhaps the most important long-range considerations. It seemed clear to most people that a return to the old constitution, shorn of the Commonwealth innovations, was the common desire. The Long Parliament, which called for the election of the Convention Parliament, had itself shown the way by resolving that the House of Lords "had and have to be a part of the parliament of England." When the new Parliament assembled the Lords participated fully and equally without any reference to their dissolution in 1649. Their presence and that of a substantial number of royalists insured that the prerogatives of the monarchy would be preserved. The restoration was not complete. The acts passed by the Short Parliament and the Long Parliament until 1642 which had received the assent of the King remained on the statute books, including the acts which had abolished the prerogative courts. As these courts had served to enforce the authority of the Privy Council over county and local government officials, the ability of the central government to influence events at the local level was much curtailed. Indeed, until the great wave of reform legislation in the mid-nineteenth century the Justices of the Peace were relatively free of executive control. The most important changes were left unstated. Parliament had executed one King, now it had restored another to the throne. Though it supported Charles II by restoring the bishops to the upper House, by vesting sole command of all the forces in the King, and by repeal of the Triennial Act of 1641, the fact that these measures were done on the authority of Parliament and King and not the King alone was not lost on the participants. A new constitutional era was inaugurated, one in which authority was balanced between the King and the legislature.

The Financial Settlement. The adequacy of the financial settlement made to support the King's honor and government has long been a subject of debate. The radical innovations enacted by the Long

Parliament in the 1640s had substituted a whole new series of internal taxes to maintain the army and navy and to replace those hereditary sources which had been abolished. These new taxes, especially the excise, an internal tax levied on commodities in general and on liquor in particular, were not popular with the general populace. For some months the Convention Parliament attempted to establish a tax on land to replace the feudal revenues which had been taken from the King. Direct taxes were regarded as an extraordinary rather than a regular source of revenue. When the Commons failed to agree on a land tax, an excise tax on liquor was successfully moved by court members in the Commons. The usefulness of this tax which could be expanded to innumerable other commodities· was evident to the government. The most recent estimate of various taxes voted by the Parliament at the beginning of the reign show that they yielded approximately £980,000 per annum, short of the £1,200,000 which the Parliament projected. Additional taxes voted during the course of the reign brought the average up to £1,170,000 and if the King had managed his affairs wisely they should have sufficed. That they did not is an indictment of the King not the Parliament.

The Religious Settlement. The religious settlement, like so many other aspects of the Restoration, proved to be an interim arrangement. While still in exile, Charles II had promised liberty of conscience to his subjects. During the Commonwealth, Presbyterians and Independents had been introduced into church livings, and both groups had expectations of remaining in an established church. The Anglicans were hardly unanimous in their attitude. That party identified as Laudian or high-church strenuously opposed any relaxation of the forms of the church to please the Presbyterians and showed little sympathy in general for Nonconformists. Others were disposed to define the church broadly so that it would be possible at least to comprehend the Presbyterians. A conference was held in the spring of 1661 to reach an accommodation between the Presbyterians and the Anglicans. Unable to agree among themselves, the Presbyterians who were poorly led and over confident prolonged the proceedings with the consequence that the Cavalier Parliament which met on May 8 took the matter into its own hands. In league with the bishops, the Parliament ruled against an accommodation with the Presbyterians. The Anglicans now employed the same tactics of prohibition and persecution against the Non-conformists that had been used against them in the previous two decades. By the Act of Uniformity nearly a thousand incumbents were purged from the church in 1662 for their refusal to accept the restored church's liturgy and doctrines. The Corporation Act denied Non-conformists the right to hold office even at the local level, though the

Act was never completely implemented. The Five Mile Act of 1665 and the Conventicle Acts of 1664 and 1670 placed penalties on Nonconformist meetings and ministers. An intermittent and not always effective persecution lasted until the Glorious Revolution of 1688, but the disabilities under which the Nonconformists suffered were not removed until the nineteenth century.

The Diplomatic Settlement. Peace was an essential prerequisite to buy time to consolidate and secure the King's government in Britain. The fear of a Puritan insurrection made essential an alliance with a strong continental power who could supply troops in time of need. There were not many choices. Portugal, anxious to obtain allies to confirm her independence of Spain, was the most eager to conclude an alliance with England and offered Charles a bride — Catherine of Braganza — a handsome dowry, and the cities of Bombay and Tangier. Although the offer of Portugal was accepted, the most important link was forged with France. In part Charles was impelled by the ties of family. His French mother lived in retirement in her native country and his sister Henrietta was married to the brother of Louis XIV. The views of Louis XIV on the nature of kingship were congenial to his English counterpart. Above all it was the offer of French gold that persuaded Charles to conclude a treaty for the sale of Dunkirk in 1662.

Restoration England. The social structure of Stuart England was a well-stratified one. One can identify hierarchies both in the cities and in the country; the two are roughly parallel though not identical. The whole was characterized by a very small upper layer with family incomes well above £1,000 pounds a year, and middling groups with incomes ranging from £100 to £1,000 pounds a year. These families controlled the wealth and political power. They and their immediate dependents totalled less than 10 percent of the population. All the rest fell below this level. The principal basis for wealth and political power was property, as in the House of Lords, whose members' titles and affluence reflected landed estates; the House of Commons, the majority of whose members were landowners; the law courts where both the English common law and the litigation arising from it were all based on matters involving real property; the electorate both in cities and in the country, where the franchise was generally based upon a property qualification; or the principal commodities of English commerce, especially wool. The society was firmly tied to the land.

An analysis by the pioneer statistician Gregory King, made at the end of the restoration period, estimates the total population of England at 5,500,000 people. At the head were the nobility, some 160 lay lords and 26 spiritual lords, who were the leaders of the society, both because of their great wealth and their social status. Next in rank were the gentry, also possessing great landed wealth and often holding minor honors, baronets or knights. These were the men who filled the House of Commons and acted as the justices of peace in their counties. Gradations must be recognized within this class. The wealthiest rivaled the loftiest peers in holdings and political power. The lesser gentry were barely distinguishable from the small-freeholders or farmers. Though numbered in the thousands, they still formed a small and discrete class. Their families staffed the professions and the church where places were found for younger sons whose fates were dictated by the English custom of primogeniture, by which the family estates were kept intact to be passed on from eldest son to eldest son. Small freeholders and farmers comprised the largest number in the country, some 300,000 strong, according to King, and nearly six times that when their whole families were counted. They inherited the role of the yeomen of earlier times, though reduced in importance. They were distinguished for their good husbandry and their economic independence. The lowest orders were the cottagers and paupers, who eked out a bare subsistence living by tilling small parcels of soil, grazing on the common, and hiring out as day and seasonal laborers while their families supplemented their income by making thread and by weaving. They numbered more than a million, while the vagrants or paupers at the bottom of the scale comprised only some 30,000 according to the optimistic King. Some 20 percent of the population, essentially this group, received some form of public assistance or relief. Aside from small private charities this was generally provided by the local property holders and organized at the parish level. The professional men and office holders formed another layer, drawn from a middle stratum, whose number were recruited from both the country and the city. King identified four groups, each about 10,000 strong: the clergy, the lawyers, the military and naval officers, and the office-holders. The first and last achieved a slightly higher level of prosperity than the other two.

The leading residents of the cities were the wealthier merchants who controlled the moveable wealth of the kingdom and accounted for much of England's growing prosperity. King counts a mere 2,000 of them plus their families and only 8,000 more among the lesser merchants and traders. They bore a heavy responsibility for developing English trade and laying the basis for that revenue which sustained both the economy in general and the government in particular. Below them one found the shopkeepers and tradesmen, the artisans and craftsmen, approximately 500,000 each in the two groups. The middle and upper classes were sustained by a vast army of more than 300,000 laboring people and outservants, who with their families comprised some 1,275,000.

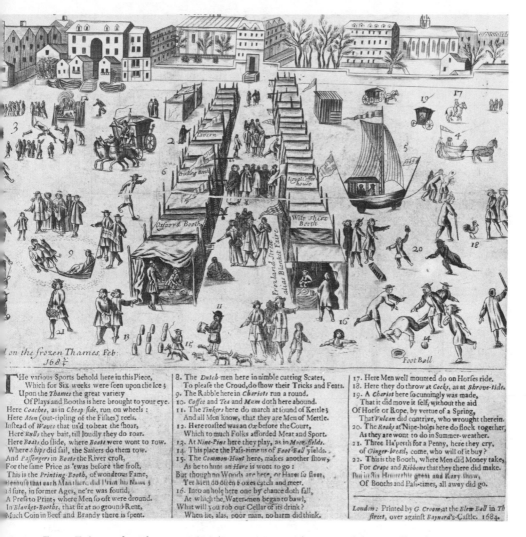

THe various Sports behold here in this Piece,
Which for Six weeks were seen upon the Ice;
Upon the *Thames* the great variety
Of Plays and Booths is here brought to your eye.
Here *Coaches*, as in *Cheap-side*, run on wheels:
Here *Men* (out-tipling of the *Fishes*) reels.
Instead of *Waves* that us'd to beat the Shoar,
Here *Bulls* they bait, till loudly they do roar.
Here *Boats* do slide, where *Boats* were wont to row.
Where *Ships* did sail, the Sailers do them tow.
And *Passengers* in *Boats* the River cross,
For the same Price as 'twas before the frost,
This is the *Printing-Booth*, of wondrous Fame,
Because that each Man there did Print his Name;
And sure, in former Ages, ne're was found,
A Press to Print, where Men so oft were dround.
In *Blanket-Booths*, that sit at no ground Rent,
Much Coin in Beef and Brandy there is spent.

8. The *Dutch*-men here in nimble cutting Scates,
To please the Croud, do show their Tricks and Feats.
9. The Rabble here in *Chariots* run a round.
10. *Coffee* and *Tea* and *Mum* doth here abound.
11. The *Tinkers* here do march at sound of Kettle;
And all Men know, that they are Men of Mettle.
12. Here roasted was an *Ox* before the Court,
Which to much Folks afforded Meat and Sport.
13. At *Nine-Pins* here they play, as in *Moor-fields*.
14. This place the Pass-time us of *Foot-Ball* yields.
15. The *Common-Hunt* here, makes another show,
As he to hunt an *Hare* is wont to go:
But though no Woods are here, or Hares so fleet,
Yet Men do often Foxes catch and meet.
16. Into an hole here one by chance doth fall,
At which the Water-men began to bawl,
What will you rob our Cellar of its drink?
When he, alas, poor man, no harm did think.

17. Here Men well mounted do on Horses ride.
18. Here they do throw at *Cocks*, as at *Shrove-tide*.
19. A *Chariot* here so cunningly was made,
That it did move it self, without the aid
Of Horse or Rope, by vertue of a Spring,
That *Vulcan* did contrive, who wrought therein.
20. The *Rooks* at Nine-holes here do flock together,
As they are wont to do in Summer-weather.
21. Three Ha'peeth for a Penny, here they cry,
of *Ginger-bread*, come, who will of it buy?
22. This is the Booth, where Men did Money take,
For *Crape* and *Ribbons* that they there did make.
But in Six Hours this green and Rary show,
Of Booths and Pass-times, all away did go.

London: Printed by *G. Croom,* at the *Blew-Ball* in Th
street, over against *Baynard's*-Castle. 1684.

Frost Fair on the Thames, 1684 (Pepys Manuscripts, Magdalene College).

London: The Great Plague and Fire, 1665-66. England was visited by
two great natural disasters in the early years of the Restoration. The
great plague struck England in 1665 for the last time. It lasted into the
next year and before it was over some 70,000 had lost their lives out of
460,000 in London alone. The Court and the Parliament fled to Oxford
in hopes of escaping the pestilence. In order to maintain communication with those left behind in the capital and to allay fears throughout
the country the Secretaries of State inaugurated a newspaper, the
Oxford Gazette, to be renamed the *London Gazette* upon the return of
the Court. For a dozen years it was the sole newspaper permitted in the
country, and though rivals began to appear in 1679 the paper itself has
continued down to the present day, a unique publication record.

So much of the old City was swept away that an opportunity for a
London had not recovered from the plague when it was struck by a
second disaster, the Great Fire which destroyed forty percent of the old
City within the walls in the space of four days in September 1666. The
City of London (as distinguished from the surrounding boroughs such
as Westminster which was the seat of government, and Lambeth and
Southwark south of the river) was a maze of wooden buildings and
houses, each story built further out into the narrow street so that the
roofs almost touched those opposite. The City was dank, crowded,
dirty and fetid, and land in it was dear. Merchants and artisans wanted
to live close to their businesses if, indeed, both home and shop were not
on the same premises. Restrictions on new construction outside the
walls tended to retard development in the suburbs and concentrate the
population within the walls. To the west the upper classes were building
their houses; the Earl of Clarendon, the Lord Chancellor, put his up in
Piccadilly shortly before his impeachment in 1667. But in the City
proper and in East London living conditions were poor and crowded,
with a density as high as 40.3 households per acre. Brick and stone were
rarely used in construction until required by proclamation in 1661. The
rapidity with which houses were put up is one testimony to the poor
quality; some houses were built in a night. Frontages were narrow,
as little as eleven or twelve feet, and buildings were deep with the
consequence that there was little light. The average house was a small,
two storied dwelling with a square footage of about 200 in the poorer
parishes, on the average with four to six rooms each. Bed, chairs and
tables were the staple furnishing. After the fire standards improved and
the density of housing declined as some of the people moved out of the
City to avoid the congestion and the high costs.

So much of the old City was swept away that an opportunity for a
whole new start could be made and the heart of the commercial capital
could be laid out on a scale and plan that befitted one of the great
centers of Europe. But the hurry to restore the business and commerce
of the trading center, a necessity doubly important with the losses in

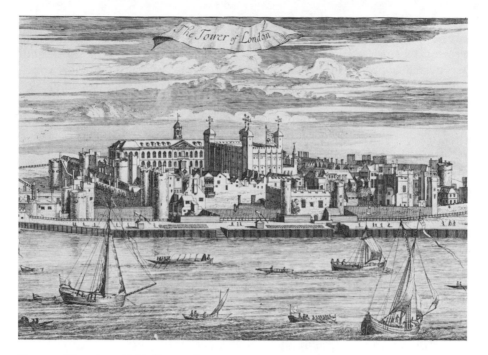

Tower of London, 1720 (Kenneth Spencer Research Library).

revenue suffered because of the plague and the war, and the reluctance to trade building space for broader avenues and parks limited the hands of the planners. The network of streets at least was regularized to some degree, and new building codes reduced the fire hazard for the future. But the main consequence was the opportunity given to Sir Christopher Wren and his assistants and successors to design and build a new cathedral of St. Paul and a series of parish churches that still survive as the great glory of the City of London.

The Royal Society and the New Science. The later seventeenth century was a pivotal time in the intellectual and technological history of Western Europe. England was at the heart of what we now recognize as the scientific revolution. The country was alive with a ferment of ideas, artistic, philosophical, religious, political, and scientific. The Royal Society, founded in 1662, was one focal point for the interchange, discussion, and development of these ideas. A circle of virtuosi, dilettantes, practical men-of-business, wealthy aristocrats, and new professional men was formed, all inquisitive and interested in keeping abreast of the new developments in the natural sciences. Sir Christopher

Wren typified this new breed of men. A student of great brilliance, he shone both as a Latin versifier and a mathematician of distinction. Praised by no less an authority than Sir Isaac Newton as a geometrician, Wren was a professor of astronomy and engaged in scientific experiment and study until he became assistant to the Surveyor-General of Works and devoted the greater part of his life to architecture, a field in which he was largely self-taught. Newton, who joined the Royal Society in 1672, was both the greatest mathematician of his time, and made contributions to mathematics, physics, astronomy, and optics. He was also the Warden and then Master of the Mint from 1696 until his death in 1727. Associated with these two was Robert Boyle who made important contributions in chemical analysis. His work is remembered to this day by the law to which he gave his name on the relation between the volume, density, and pressure of gases.

These scholars were equally at home at the great universities of Oxford and Cambridge and in the salons and offices of London. The fellow of the Royal Society who has given us the most vivid picture of London in the 1660s when it passed through the two great catastrophes was the diarist, Samuel Pepys. As a key civilian official in the navy from the Restoration to the Revolution he was the perfect bureaucrat — industrious, knowledgeable, always protecting the interests of his office and the navy. He illustrates how a young man of ability and connections, though lacking a large fortune, could rise to a position of great responsibility. He lived a rich and varied life. An indefatigable worker, he put in long hours at his office or in attendance on his superiors. As a young man he already had cultivated tastes, was a competent musician, and an ardent book collector. He was also a man of pleasure enjoying the many divertisements of the metropolis, the taverns, women, musicals, and the theatre. London was the center of his life and he rarely left it.

Political Theory and Literature. One of the founders of the Royal Society, Sir William Petty, pioneered in yet another branch of knowledge, political economy. He came to the field after a term as a professor of anatomy and then Physician-General to the army in Ireland. He undertook to make a survey of Ireland for the Commonwealth government in order to map the forfeited estates. He went on to make a complete map of the whole island, a task not finished until 1673. His skill and accuracy set new standards. After the Restoration he wrote a pioneer work on vital statistics and treatises on finance, the growth of the City of London, taxes, the origins of wealth and a host of related topics. The most important political philosopher of the age did not see his *magnum opus* published until after the Revolution. This was John Locke, another physician who joined the entourage of the Earl of

Shaftesbury and employed his pen in defending his patron and his political views. In the early 1680s he wrote his classic *Two Treatises of Government* to refute the *Patriarcha* of Sir Robert Filmer, the latter published posthumously by the Tories in 1680 to support the King's authority. Hounded into exile with Shaftesbury, Locke published his *Treatises* in 1689 as a justification of the Glorious Revolution. Such was the conservatism of his countrymen that his view was not accepted until decades after his death.

The reopening of the theatres in 1660 made possible a rebirth of English drama. The theatre was heavily patronised by the Court, the men of letters establishing that connection with the great aristocrats and politicians which was to reach its fullest flower in Queen Anne's reign. However, the greatest products of English writers were in forms other than drama. John Milton, a vestige of the Commonwealth, blind and out of favor, ennobled the English language with his great epic poems *Paradise Lost* and *Paradise Regained.* Another Puritan, John Bunyan, who found only adversity in the Restoration, wrote *The Pilgrim's Progress* while in prison. The finest literary representative of the Restoration and the poet laureaute to the royal brothers, Charles II and James II, was John Dryden. Though a prolific contributor to the Restoration theatre he is best remembered for his poetry, his translation of Vergil, and his satires. It is not surprising that the prolonged political heats of the Restoration spawned a profusion of polemical works. Dryden's *Absalom and Achitophel*, a satire on the Duke of Monmouth and the Earl of Shaftesbury, is the supreme example and was singularly effective in reducing the Whig cause to ridicule. The full flower of this literary outpouring was to be found in the Augustan Age which followed the Revolution.

ENGLAND, FRANCE, AND THE DUTCH REPUBLIC

Clarendon and the Second Dutch War, 1665-67. The first ministry of the reign was nominally headed by Edward Hyde, raised to the peerage as Earl of Clarendon and made Lord Chancellor. Its record was not a happy one. Clarendon refused to act as a chief minister in the traditional sense by coordinating and supervising the other ministers, and he lacked the suppleness and flexibility to manage the Parliament successfully. He lasted in office until 1667 when he was brought down by the failure of his foreign policy and by discontent arising from the two great natural disasters at home, the plague and the fire of London. Relations with the Dutch, never good since the first Dutch War (1652-54), had steadily deteriorated until war broke out again in 1665. Trading disputes had already led to armed conflict between the two nations in India and Africa. The war finally reached America in 1664 when an expedition from New England seized New Amsterdam and renamed it New York in honor of the King's brother, the Duke of York. The war in Europe opened with an English attack on a Dutch convoy at Bergen the next year. In the European area, the English were able at first to withstand the challenge of the Dutch who were supported by an alliance with France. By 1667, however, their diplomatic isolation told against them. The low estate of the English military and naval power was revealed in that year when a Dutch fleet sailed up the Thames, destroyed half the English navy, and towed away the flag-ship, the *Royal Charles.* The ignominious failure of English diplomacy and arms toppled Clarendon from his post. Made the scapegoat for the disasters, he was impeached by the Parliament and forced into exile to France where he lived until his death in 1674. The King and his other advisors negotiated the two treaties that brought hostilities with the French and the Dutch to an end. By the Treaty of Breda (1667) England regained the islands in the West Indies taken by France, but ceded all rights to Acadia in North America. She kept the Dutch colonies in North America but gave up Guinea and most of her outposts in West Africa except for Cape Coast Castle on the Gold Coast.

The Cabal. The ministers who succeeded Clarendon in the main offices and authority in the cabal, or inner circle, government were as ill-matched a group as one can expect. The fact that the combination of initial letters from their last names — Clifford, Arlington, Buckingham, Ashley, and Lauderdale — spelled *CABAL* was accidental, but the appellation when defined as a small body of persons engaged in private machination or intrigue is not inappropriate. Arlington alone seems to have demonstrated both a consistent and well-considered policy in his field of expertise, foreign affairs. And all the ministers were overshadowed by the King himself, who now undertook the principal direction of affairs of state.

Even as the negotiations for peace at Breda were being concluded, Louis XIV undertook a new diplomatic initiative. Through his ambassador he suggested a defensive league or a joint expedition against the Spanish West Indies. He further implied that if hostilities were to break out again between the Dutch and England, France would no longer intervene on behalf of the Dutch. While negotiations dragged on, Arlington and his supporters sought to achieve the opposite, an alliance with Holland against France. John De Witt, the Grand Pensionary of Holland and chief official in the United Provinces, responded positively to the English overtures. The French seizure of a series of fortresses along the Spanish Netherlands had impressed upon him his nation's vulnerability to French military might and the need for allies. The Triple Alliance (1668) negotiated by Sir William Temple was the consequence, a treaty to which Sweden was also a signatory. In addition to mutual support in case of an attack by a third party, the Protestant powers hoped to lay the foundation for a larger alliance to prevent further French aggression. The alliance met with a positive reception in England. Parliament voted the improvident King a new tax on wine and spirits. More importantly it marked the first stage in the reapproachment with Holland that was ultimately to unite the two great Protestant powers in arms against the ambitions of a Catholic France.

Despite a shared concern by England and Holland over the growth of French power, the Anglo-Dutch rivalry for colonial trade and European markets continued. Charles, chafing from the tedious and irksome necessity of having to persuade a recalcitrant and obstreperous Parliament to give him sorely needed funds, was encouraged to accept a French subsidy. His response to the French overtures was further encouraged in 1669 when his brother and heir, the Duke of York, decided to avow Roman Catholicism. Charles was also inclined to embrace the Roman Catholic faith as one in harmony with his notion of the monarchy and the state. Urged on by his sister Henrietta, by his mother, by Buckingham, and belatedly, by Arlington, Charles broached the terms of a new alliance to France. He would announce his own public conversion to Catholicism and the instigation of war against Holland, if France in turn would provide him with the financial support he so desperately needed.

The Secret Treaty of Dover, 1670. Charles II's financial resources were so depleted that he could not await the results of the inevitably protracted negotiations required for the alliance. He recalled Parliament in October 1669 to seek additional subsidies. Instead of granting him a supply the Commons proceeded to investigate the King's ministers both in England and Ireland and even threatened impeachment. Angrily the King prorogued the Parliament in December; when the members reassembled in February the needed supplies were forthcoming and the threats against his ministers dropped. The King now concluded the secret Treaty of Dover with France on May 22, 1670, in which he subordinated his country to France in order to satisfy his own needs, though in so doing he put his country's very independence and constitution in jeopardy. In order to ally the suspicions of Buckingham and his other Protestant ministers the King openly negotiated a second "bogus" treaty which was identical to the first, except that it omitted the King's avowal of Catholicism. Though the cynicism of the King's designs has left an indelible stain on his record, the treaty made it possible for the English to win commercial advantages over their Dutch rivals in the important trade with France. Even the Parliament seems to have recognized this advantage in the articles made public, for when they were recalled in October they provided an additional subsidy estimated to be worth £800,000 in new taxes for the King's support.

In April 1671, Charles prorogued the Parliament and embarked upon a disastrous course of personal monarchy. Although he did not announce his conversion to Catholicism, he made a bold demonstration in favor of both Roman Catholics and Dissenters on March 15, 1672, when he issued his Declaration of Indulgence, which suspended the execution of all penal laws against noncommunicants of the Church of England. It was an audacious move, a resumption of regal authority that if followed successfully in other areas would have changed the nature of the English constitution. That it did not succeed was because Charles was undone by his own ineptness in the field of finance and by his misadventures in diplomacy. At the beginning of 1672, on January 20, his acute financial distress had resulted in another more desperate gamble, the stop of the Exchequer. Unable to meet his obligations he called a moratorium on all repayments of sums owed by the crown. He consigned his fortunes and those of his government to the long-planned war with Holland which he declared on March 17, two days after the Declaration of Indulgence.

The Third Dutch War, 1672-74. Only success in war could save his plans. But the Dutch siezed the initiative and inflicted a defeat on the English fleet, and the French pushed to the Rhine and into the Dutch Republic itself with nothing to prevent their advance. DeWitt was overthrown and executed by his own people who installed the young William of Orange, Charles II's nephew, in the long vacant Stadholdership of their country as their last hope to preserve their independence from the French. With Charles's gamble having failed and the Protestant strongholds of Europe in mortal danger because of his surrender to France, the King was forced to recall Parliament in circumstances that at best would lead to his humiliation. Meeting in February, 1673 they withheld supplies until the King cancelled the Indulgence. Not content, Parliament passed a Test Act which required office holders to take communion in the Anglican church and disavow the doctrine of transubstantiation, a clause inserted specifically to eliminate Catholics. The Duke of York was forced to resign the admiralty. He was followed into retirement by Clifford, another convert to Catholicism to be replaced by a staunch Protestant, Sir Thomas Osborne, best known by his later title, Earl of Danby. A second disastrous campaign abroad in 1673 only added further to the King's troubles. When Parliament reconvened in winter it criticized the Treaty of Dover, the war, and the Duke of York's recent marriage to a Catholic princess, Mary of Modena. Parliament refused any funds until peace was made. Charles quickly concluded a peace with the Dutch which restored the status quo and he left control of domestic affairs for the most part to Danby for the next four years.

DANBY AND THE EXCLUSION PARLIAMENTS

Danby As Lord High Treasurer. Danby proved equal to his task. He provided a personal direction and control to the ministry that was without parallel in the reign. Assuming the office of Lord High Treasurer from Clifford in 1673, Danby was faced with substantial debts, weak public credit, and mounting war expenses. By maximizing income sources and curbing government expenditures he turned around the Treasury's near insolvency and slowly restored public confidence. He was aided during his ministry by the rise in customs receipts following England's withdrawal from the war on the continent in 1674. As a neutral and active trading nation England enjoyed obvious commercial advantages. She exploited them until anti-French sentiment in Parliament forced Danby to place an embargo on trade with France in 1678. Charles vacillated between his pro-French advisors and Danby, accepting French subsidies in 1675 and 1677 in exchange for prorogations of the Parliament. Danby pressed the King to make common cause against France with his nephew, William of Orange. In November 1677 Charles agreed to the marriage of James's eldest daughter Mary with William, hoping thereby to propitiate Parliament and encourage Louis XIV to make peace with Holland. When Louis resisted, Charles recalled Parliament in 1678 and signed an offensive alliance with Holland. His initiative failed when the Parliament turned against him and Louis came to terms with Holland. Danby's Protestant, anti-French policy enabled him to convince Parliament to grant further subsidies in 1677. But all his efforts were nullified by his inability to curb royal expenditures. A renewed mobilization for a potential war against France in 1678 resulted in a growth once again of the floating debts. On his retirement he bequeathed to his successor a debt more than twice that he had inherited.

When Danby assumed the direction of the King's affairs, he realized that cooperation with Parliament was essential and the grant of additional taxes a necessity. To insure a compliant Commons he began to organize a government party in that house through a careful and judicious use of all the means of persuasion available to him — offices, pensions and bribes. He introduced a new kind of professional management in recruiting and then directing the King's party in the lower house. His analyses of the membership, calculations for critical votes, and records of voting behavior survive in sufficient number to reveal his expertise and assiduity. Danby's efforts resulted in the foundation of what came to be known in 1679 as the Tory party (after the name for Irish Catholic outlaws) and is the beginning of the party system. But party loyalties were uncertain and fickle. The unpopularity of the King's policies and a well-founded suspicion of his intentions were too much for the Lord Treasurer. And the efforts of the opposition led by Shaftesbury, which was given the name of Whig (after truculent Scottish Presbyterians) in 1679 to distinguish them from Danby's Tories, gained an unexpected assist from the exposure of the "Popish Plot" in 1678.

The Popish Plot. This cruel hoax almost precipitated a revolution and kept the country in turmoil for the next three years. The "plot" was discovered by one Titus Oates, a discredited Anglican clergyman, twice an apostate, who revealed a plan by Roman Catholics to murder the King after which James, with French support, would succeed to the throne. When the scheme was disclosed to the King and Council, Charles immediately recognized the bogus nature of Oates's story. But Oates had unwittingly pointed to enough suspicious activities on the part of the English Jesuits and the Duchess of York's secretary, who had been corresponding with French Catholics, that the alarm was raised. The death through misadventure of Sir Edmund Godfrey, the Justice of the Peace before whom Oates had sworn his story, provided further circumstantial evidence to confirm the validity of Oates's discovery.

Shaftesbury and his Whigs made the most of the opportunity. The King and his policies were discredited and thus the opposition-dominated Commons alone possessed popular confidence. Parliament stiffened the Test Act, removed the Catholics from both houses, and attempted to disband the army and replace it with the loyal militia, all while it investigated unceasingly countless wild stories about a Catholic coup centering on the Duke of York. Many innocent Catholics including the Queen herself came under suspicion. More than a few peers, priests, and commoners who were so unlucky as to be incriminated were executed. The King was dangerously isolated and lost almost all power to protect himself. Not the least important consequence of the plot and its aftermath was the impact on the press. The censorship laws were allowed to lapse and the court was powerless to curb the press. Newspapers, pamphlets, tracts, books were published in wild profusion. The role of the press in influencing public opinion and in making the average Englishman aware of the torments his country was undergoing was one of the most important phenomena of these years.

The First Exclusion Parliament. The next two years were dominated by the struggle between the King and the opposition for supremacy and the attempt to exclude the Duke of York from the succession. To appease his enemies Charles ordered his brother into 'exile at Brussels and remodeled his Council by making places for the opposition, including Shaftesbury and the great moderating statesman George Savile, Marquis of Halifax. The closest advisors included the new secretary, Robert Spencer, Earl of Sunderland, who soon earned a reputation for industry and ability as well as deviousness and subservience.

The election in February 1679 of a new Parliament was the first in which the two new parties of Whig and Tory contested for supremacy. The tone of conciliation employed by the King in his welcoming address to the new Parliament failed to appease his auditors. They took up the investigation of the plot again, ignored the King's pardon of Danby, and tried to pass an act of attainder to cut the gordian knot of the pardon granted by the King to stop impeachment proceedings. Danby himself surrendered to the Lords and was incarcerated in the Tower for five years, narrowly escaping with his life. The main thrust of the Commons was to bar the Catholic Duke of York from the succession. Charles responded that he was willing to give his assent to bills guaranteeing the Protestant religion and the laws of property. But he was indissolubly wed to the principle of hereditary succession. After passing a bill to further secure the right of habeas corpus the Commons began work on an exclusion bill and it was only halted by the King's prorogation and then dissolution of Parliament. A sudden and serious illness of the King resulted in the return of James and revealed the precarious state of the realm. If the King had died the Whigs would undoubtedly have precipitated a revolution rather than submit to James's rule. After Charles recovered, James was persuaded to exile himself once more from the court, though now to the more congenial climes of Scotland. There he had the opportunity as High Commissioner to give proof to the fears of his opponents about his rigid and uncompromising attitudes. The *quid pro quo* was the exile of the Duke of Monmouth, the illegitimate son of Charles II who was the hero of the Whigs and the pawn of Shaftesbury. Monmouth was removed from the office of Commander-in-Chief and sent to Holland.

The Second Exclusion Parliament. The King delayed summoning the new Parliament for an entire year while he regained some control over the government, allowing opposition passions to be expended in demonstrations, investigations, and condemnations. The ministry was again remodelled and more compliant officers were appointed drawn from the Tory or King's party. The chiefs were Sunderland and two new treasury commissioners, James's brother-in-law by his first wife,

Lawrence Hyde, and Sidney Godolphin. Rochester (as Hyde later became known) has never received full credit for his achievements at the Treasury. He and his fellow commissioners were able to commit the King to retrenchment in expenditures with such success that a surplus in income was achieved to apply towards the debt. Moreover the new commission, also with Charles's acquiescence, was able for the first time to exercise some control over departmental expenditures, thus establishing a new pattern of government that was to be carefully exploited by their successors. Foreign affairs were also part of Charles's strategy to wrest the initiative back from Parliament. France or its opponents were again the choice. Charles's own principles and his financial need made France the preferred alternative, and still another subsidy treaty was concluded in March 1681. For Charles it meant the promise of financial independence from Parliament; for Louis it meant an investment in monarchy and Catholicism.

When the new Parliament assembled in October 1680, it joined the press wars by ordering its resolutions to be published daily as the *Votes.* A second exclusion bill that not only denied James the succession but also threatened him with the charge of high treason if he returned to England was only defeated in the Lords. Frustrated in this effort the Commons proceeded to address the King to remove Halifax for advising the dissolution of the previous Parliament and then criticized or impeached ministers and judges who supported the King. The King responded to their precipitate action by yet another dissolution in January.

The Third Exclusion Parliament. One last time the King tried to come to terms with Parliament. The location was changed to Oxford where the staunchly Tory and conservative church-dominated atmosphere would encourage a more tractable attitude than the Whig mobs of London and Westminster. The parties were now experienced in election battles and Shaftesbury employed all his energy and experience to secure control of the new lower House. He succeeded all too well. Meeting on March 21, 1681, the Commons devoted the first week to dredging up the old hostilities and platforms. Though Charles had indicated beforehand and in his opening speech a willingness to make major concessions to guarantee that the government would remain in Protestant hands during the reign of his brother, the Commons dismissed his proposals. Even the offer of a regency by the Prince and Princess of Orange and after them the Princess Anne would not satisfy. Shaftesbury made a public offer to Charles to name Monmouth as his successor which the King summarily refused. When the Commons rejected all compromise, Charles dissolved the Parliament on March 28. It was not to meet again in his lifetime.

THE ATTEMPT TO ESTABLISH DESPOTISM IN ENGLAND

The Last Years of Charles II. There followed the last and most ominous phase of Charles' reign. Determined to rule without Parliament and ensure his brother's succession, he was equally determined to bring all elements of government under his control. Diplomats who favored the French alliance were employed in the major English posts abroad. A scrutiny of the lists of Justices of the Peace was followed by a remodelling of local governments throughout the country to obtain Tory officers, and in the event a Parliament had to be called, a more sympathetic membership by control of the electors. The chief weapons of the crown, however, were directed against the Whig leaders. The Rye House plot, revealed in June 1682, was hardly more credible than the Popish Plot, but the Court was able to exploit it with something like the same impact. Two radical Whigs, William Russell and Algernon Sidney, were executed as an example to the others. Shaftesbury was hounded into exile, his party broken. The process of calling in the borough charters was accelerated after London failed to win a stay, and with it the bastions of Whig power in local government were eliminated. When Charles died on February 6, 1685, his authoritarian policy had substantially strengthened his successor's hand.

The Accession of James II. James II (1685-88) was fifty-two years old, an advanced age in the seventeenth century, when he became King. Increasing age had intensified his essential rigidity of thinking, the single-mindedness that characterized his actions. Intolerant of Charles's vices, though he had often shared them, he demonstrated a firmness and sense of moral rectitude that in other individuals would have been admired. But wedded to these were a devotion to Roman Catholicism and a disdain for the hard-won and still vulnerable constitutional guarantees protecting the liberty of the subject and the inviolability of property, all of which boded ill for Englishmen. The new King immediately summoned a Parliament to meet in May. The Parliament which met was the most tractable since 1661, the consequence of the careful remodelling of the corporations under Charles II and Sunderland's assiduity in managing the elections. It confirmed James for life in the taxes he had already begun collecting. Responding to the King's assertions that he required additional income to satisfy the debts of his brother and the obligations of the services, they voted additional duties which gave him a combined income estimated at £1,900,000, almost double that awarded Charles in 1660.

In the midst of the Parliament's deliberations two invasions were mounted to unseat James, one by the Duke of Monmouth in the southwest, another by the Earl of Argyle in Scotland. Both were poorly

James II (Kenneth Spencer Research Library).

managed by their leaders and the disciplined response of the King's troops put a quick end to them. Though able to outmaneuver the ill-trained militia, Monmouth was defeated at Sedgemoor on July 6 where the young John Churchill demonstrated his prowess for the first time with an English army. The manner in which the rebels were treated by the King and his minions was cruel and heartless. In England, Lord Chief Justice George Jeffreys dealt so harshly and punitively with those unlucky enough to be charged with complicity, whether innocent or not, that his court sessions have gone down in history as the "bloody Assizes." Its victims were venerated from the start as martyrs. Jeffreys's disregard for the rights of the accused and the law and its processes gave a clear intimation of the King's lack of regard for the constitution.

When Parliament reassembled in November the King used the failure of the militia in the recent crisis as a basis for requesting still more funds in order to support a standing army, a permanent, professional active military force. The Parliament, stirred by a few old hands, demonstrated once again its unpredictability and resourcefulness by outspoken debates. Several members questioned the use to which the army might be put and warned that the King's introduction of Catholic officers made inadvisable this strengthening which the King sought. The Lords were even more independent and forthright than the Commons in their distrust of royal policies. The King, notoriously sensitive to criticism, prorogued the Parliament even before it concluded action on a bill to provide him with yet another £700,000 which it would undoubtedly have granted. Dissolved in 1687, it never met again during his reign.

James now lost no time in placing Roman Catholics in positions of trust and importance in the army, in the ministry, finally in the church itself. From a few thousand men and officers in 1685 James increased the army to 13,000 in 1686 and more than 53,000 in 1688. The law courts were an early target and James removed four of the judges in the spring of 1686 when they refused to recognize his right to dispense with the test and penal acts. When the King placed Roman Catholics in benefices in the church, the Attorney and Solicitor Generals quickly found themselves out of place when they refused to issue the necessary warrants. In July 1686 James created a panel of ecclesiastical commissioners to act in his name as Supreme Governor of the church in all its concerns. Though not a court — it was not granted the power to impose fines and penalties and its jurisdiction did not extend to laymen — the unconscious parallel to the twice-proscribed early Stuart Court of High Commission was indeed ominous. Exercising its visitorial authorities, it first suspended Bishop Compton of London for refusing to remove a preacher who had offended the King. It then intervened in the affairs of the universities, removing the Vice-Chancellor of

Cambridge from his office as well as his headship of a college for refusing to admit a Benedictine monk to the degree of master of arts. Oxford was even more abused when the King replaced the fellows of Magdalen College with Roman Catholics and then capped this audacity by placing one of his favorite priests in the presidency. James's threats to disturb the quiet possession of property were even more evident in the inquisitorial nature of his administration in Scotland. There opponents were hunted out, tortured, tried, and sentenced to heavy fines, transportation, or death.

Determined not only to restore the Catholics to an active if not predominent role in public life but also to guarantee this restoration after his own reign, James decided in the summer of 1687 to summon another Parliament. Its charge would be to give legislative confirmation to a second Declaration of Indulgence which he intended issuing in 1688. His first Declaration, issued in April 1687, had been grudgingly accepted both in England and in an earlier version promulgated in Scotland. Now a committee directed by Sunderland sent out a questionnaire in October 1687 to the Lord Lieutenants with instructions to obtain replies from their deputies, the Sheriffs, and the Justices of their counties. The questions to be posed were three: Will you, if returned to Parliament, vote for the repeal of the penal laws and the test? Will you support candidates who are in favour of such a measure? Will you live neighborly and friendly with those of a contrary religion? An unexpectedly large number of Lieutenants resigned rather than carry out the instructions. Many loyal Tories who had demonstrated extraordinary forebearance in their acceptance of the King's arbitrary actions were turned into active opponents by these measures.

The second Declaration of Indulgence issued on April 27, 1688, was one of the two immediate causes of the Revolution of 1688. James ordered it to be read from every pulpit for the next two Sundays. Many faithful clergy refused and the primate himself, William Sancroft, Archbishop of Canterbury, together with six of his fellow ecclesiastics petitioned the King not to insist upon his order. The King was outraged by this show of resistance and was determined to set an example by prosecuting the offenders, not by a summons to the High Commission, but rather by a trial for seditious libel in the Court of King's Bench. The trial which began on June 29 was one of the most famous and critical in English history. The judges abandoned their neutral role and risked the King's displeasure (two were subsequently removed) by supporting the defendants. The jury acquitted the defendants who were triumphantly escorted out of the court and back to Lambeth Palace amid great public displays of attention and joy. Even before the trial started the die had already been cast for a rebellion when Queen Mary of Modena gave birth to a son on June 10. With the prospect of a Catholic succession even the most loyal Anglicans now realized that the threat to the liberties of the church could allow for no further delay. The means of their deliverance was at hand: the Prince of Orange.

William of Orange and Revolution. Since assuming the leadership of the Dutch Republic in 1672, William had been watching the conduct of his royal uncles with the closest interest and concern. In the aftermath of the Popish Plot and even before, his small nation had become a refuge for both Scottish and English opponents of the royal brothers. His tacit support of the Monmouth and Argyle invasions in 1685 did not further the cause of family harmony. On every suitable ceremonial occasion he had sent emissaries to James mainly to conduct reconnaissance and to test the loyalty and strength of his English friends. Moreover, William had finally succeeded in constructing an imposing new coalition of European states against France and he wanted to be sure of English support or neutrality. Most important of all, the birth of a son to James in 1688 meant that William's wife Mary was no longer the heir to the English throne. William sent a minister to congratulate his uncle on the birth of a male heir, but the minister's real mission was to secure an invitation for William to come to England. He fulfilled his instructions. On June 30, Edward Russell, cousin to William Russell who was one of the Whig martyrs of 1682, made his way over to Holland with a document signed by himself and six other prominent leaders including Bishop Compton, Danby, and Henry Sidney, brother of the other martyr, Algernon Sidney. William was invited to come to England with his troops to save the English constitution and the Protestant religion.

William had to have the permission of the States General to take away a body of the troops who were the Republic's only defense against a French invasion. Moreover, James, who had finally tumbled to his son-in-law's plans, agreed half-heartedly to accept naval support from Louis to block a Dutch invasion, after rejecting a similar offer of French assistance in June. Fortunately for William, Louis kept the main part of his fleet in the Mediterranean. Still more critical was the French King's decision to concentrate his troops away from the Netherlands to devastate the lower Palatinate as part of a campaign to reduce the Rhineland states to submission.

Meanwhile James, who was urged on by the aged Sancroft and other moderate advisors, began to take tardy steps to regain the support of his countrymen. Early in October he abolished the ecclesiastical commission. He followed this up by restoring the old charters to London and then to the other corporations which had been forced to give them up. Unlike his royal predecessor he could not be brought to renounce his Declarations of Indulgence so that his good faith was still suspect, and he refused to summon a Parliament at this time. Moreover, when he attempted to restore the natural leaders of local government to their posts he found that the majority were unwilling to serve on his terms. This left the government in the hands of men who had been repudiated by their compatriots and thus were without the means to support the King in his troubles.

The imminence of William's descent was known to all, but the intended landing place was a well-guarded secret. James relied upon his fleet under the Protestant Dartmouth to prevent a landing, but the fleet proved a broken reed. Dartmouth's own loyalty is doubtful and the fleet had been subjected to a constant stream of propaganda to support Prince William rather than King James. Whether due to the accident of the winds or to deliberate inaction, Dartmouth's fleet allowed William to land unopposed at Torbay on November 5. Announcing his mission to preserve the liberties and religion of England, he slowly moved towards London gathering supporters along the way. The King desperately sought to make those concessions that done in a timely fashion might have saved his throne. He summoned a new Parliament for January and sent commissioners to treat with the Prince. But the successive desertions of his nephew John Churchill, Viscount Cornbury, who was his most trusted general and long-time advisor; his son-in-law, Prince George of Denmark; and then his Protestant daughter Anne, escorted by Bishop Compton, reduced the King to a state of total despair and helplessness. Having previously arranged for the passage of his son and wife to France, he embarked for France on the night of December 11. Caught by the tide, his ship was boarded by suspicious fishermen who forced the King to return to shore. James was returned to London briefly but his presence was now only an embarrassment and an unwelcome bar to a speedy settlement. He was allowed to slip away again on December 23, never to return to England. The time for decision was now at hand.

SUGGESTIONS FOR FURTHER READING

For the later Stuarts the standard survey is Sir George N. Clark, *The Later Stuarts* (2nd ed., 1955). The fullest treatment is to be found in David Ogg's rich and reflective *England in the Reign of Charles II* (2nd ed., 2 vols., 1956), and *England in the Reigns of James II and William III* (1955). Thomas B. Macaulay, *History of England from the Accession of James the Second* (best edition, ed. C.H. Firth, 6 vols., 1913) is still valuable. Standard biographies include Andrew Browning, *Danby* (3 vols., 1944-51); K.D.H. Haley, *Shaftesbury* (1968) and his

essay *Charles II* (1966); J.P. Kenyon, *Sunderland* (1958);
H.C. Foxcroft, *Halifax* (1946); F.C. Turner, *James II* (1948) and
Maurice Cranston, *Locke* (1957). For studies of particular topics one
may consult Keith G. Feiling, *The Tory Party 1640-1714* (1924),
J.R. Jones, *The First Whigs* (1961), Max Beloff, *Public Order and
Popular Disturbances, 1660-1714* (1938), Godfrey Davies, *Essays on
the Later Stuarts* (1958), Peter Fraser, *The Intelligence of the
Secretaries of State and their Monopoly of Licensed News* (1956),
Clayton Roberts, *The Growth of Responsible Government in Stuart
England* (1966) and J.P. Kenyon, *The Popish Plot* (1972). J.R. Jones,
The Revolution of 1688 (1972) is the best analysis of that celebrated
event. Betty Kemp, *King and Commons 1660-1832* (1957) is a lucid
explanation of the shift in political power.

Charles Wilson, *England's Apprenticeship 1603-1763* (1965) is a
stimulating economic history. C.D. Chandaman has provided a basic
piece of historical revision in his *English Public Revenue 1660-1688*
(1975). Also important is Stephen Baxter, *The Development of the
Treasury, 1660-1702* (1957). Other works of value are Lawrence
Harper, *The English Navigation Laws* (1939), Louis Cullen, *Anglo-Irish
Trade, 1660-1800* (1968), Phyllis Lachs, *The Diplomatic Service of
Charles II and James II* (1964) and John Childs, *The Army of Charles II*
(1976). For the church and the Dissenters see Norman Sykes, *From
Sheldon to Secker 1660-1768* (1959), R.S. Bosher, *The Making of the
Restoration Settlement* (1951), G.R. Cragg, *Puritanism in the Period of
the Great Persecution* (1957) and Douglas Lacey, *Dissent and Parlia-
mentary Politics in England 1661-1689* (1969).

Two classic diaries give an insight into contemporary life: *Samuel
Pepys* (ed. R. Latham and W. Matthews, 11 vols., 1970-) and *John
Evelyn* (ed. Esmond deBeer, 6 vols., 1955). For London see N.G. Brett-
James, *The Growth of Stuart London* (1935), W.G. Bell, *The Great
Plague in London in 1665* (1951) and *The Great Fire of London in
1666* (1951) and T.F. Reddaway, *The Rebuilding of London after the
Great Fire* (1940). Peter Clark and Paul Slacks, eds., *Crisis and Order in
English Towns 1500-1700* (1972) contains three essays on the
post-Restoration period. Gladys Scott Thomson, *Life in a Noble
Household* (1937) and *The Russells in Bloomsbury, 1669-1771* (1940),
David Owen, *English Philanthropy, 1660-1960* (1964), and Joan
Parkes, *Travel in England in the Seventeenth Century* (1925) provide
many insights into English society. Margery Purver, *The Royal Society*
(1967), Richard S. Westfall, *Science and Religion in Seventeenth-
Century England* (1958), Ray Frantz, *The English Traveller and the
Movement of Ideas, 1660-1732* (1967) and David G. James, *The Life of
Reason: Hobbes, Locke, Bolingbroke* (1949) are useful introductions to
intellectual and scientific developments.

8
Revolution
& Succession

1689 - 1714

The Revolution of 1688, the "Glorious Revolution," is one of the great landmarks in English history, yet was no more a revolution than previous accessions except for the manner of James's going. The Revolution was inspired and controlled by the aristocracy and landed gentry to preserve the constitution in its traditional state, so the Revolution settlement itself was conservative and limited in character. There is an European dimension to the Revolution that cannot be disregarded. It could not have occurred without William and his army, and William could not afford to let England remain in the French camp. Furthermore, William III (1689-1702) was by any standard the most effective and most active chief executive of any Stuart sovereign.

THE REVOLUTION OF 1688

But as important as these considerations are for an explanation of *how* the Revolution occurred, we must not lose sight of the fact that the reasons *why* it occurred were wholly domestic and internal. William's new subjects, preoccupied with domestic matters, were loath to heed the European situation or to accept England's critical role in it.

William III (Kenneth Spencer Research Library).

Part of the disillusionment and ultimately the opposition of the Tories to William was the consequence of their realization of William's true motives and interests. The other part of their disillusionment came with the recognition that he was as forceful and domineering as any of his predecessors. The control which this forbidding, cold foreigner soon obtained over the agencies of English government and the commitments he made of English men and English gold to European causes stirred all the traditional hostilities of the aristocracy and gentry to autocratic monarchs. This was the fate of William's ambition and reputation.

The Settlement of the Crown. The question of William's promotion to the kingship of England was never much in doubt, but the matter of securing the Revolution and his rule was far less certain. On the collapse of James's government the peers in and about London had met and taken the government into their hands. Although the country was remarkably quiet, rioting in London and the burning of the chapels and homes of prominent Catholics required speedy action to preserve public order. The lords were soon joined by the surviving members of the Parliaments of Charles II. The assembled leaders requested the Prince to assume the civil administration as he had already assumed control over the remnants of the military forces of the crown. A Convention summoned by the Prince met on January 22, 1689. This body divided essentially on the basis of attitudes towards the succession. Most Tories favored a regency to preserve a semblance of constitutionality and to honor their oaths to James as anointed sovereign. Only the most conservative element favored James's return under carefully controlled limitations. The Whigs were more united in their determination to assert the principles of parliamentary sovereignity by acknowledging a break in the hereditary succession. Most men recognized, albeit reluctantly, that English security was dependent on William's exercise of the executive authority. The question of the legal basis for this exercise was resolved by Mary's refusal to act as Queen Regnant and by William's equally positive assertion that he would not remain in England unless all executive authority was awarded to him for life. The activities of James II's supporters in the other two kingdoms cut short the discussion of constitutional safeguards in the Convention, but before the crown was offered to William and Mary (with all authority vested in William) a Declaration of Rights was passed and accepted by the new sovereigns, and subsequently enacted into law to embody the essence of the Revolution. The monarch was subordinated to the common law, the suspending and dispensing powers of the crown were severely restricted, prerogative courts were declared illegal, and the King was prohibited from levying taxes without parliamentary consent. For the first year and even longer the fate of the Revolution was in doubt. William had only limited financial resources of his own and they were exhausted by the expedition. Although he requested the same revenues that James II had, he was granted the customs for life but the excise for only four years. And these an other revenues were not sufficient to supply the extraordinary requirements of a nation at war.

The Revolution in Scotland and Ireland. Preoccupied with the situation in England and in Ireland, Scotland received little attention from the new King and consequently worked out its own destiny with little interference. The Jacobites, as James's supporters were called, were made up of the Episcopalians in the Scottish Lowlands and the Roman Catholics in the Highlands, and were thus more active and stronger in the northern kingdom than in England. William was only able to send part of the Scottish regiments in Dutch pay to Edinburgh to buttress his supporters. Before they arrived a convention had met and the crown was offered to William and his consort on 11 April. Yet even as the Convention sat, Edinburgh castle was in the hands of Jacobites and forces were raised in behalf of James in Stirling. Fortunately the rebels obtained no reinforcements from abroad. By the end of the summer all the Jacobite troops had capitulated. Because the new government was little beholden to William it was also independent of his influence. The Scots were determined to remove the shackles that James had used to restrain them. The crown-controlled committee which dominated the Scottish Parliament was abolished, and the Episcopal government of the church, a useful instrument for insuring royal control, was dismantled. Scotland now embarked on a collision course with England that was only deflected by the passage of a parliamentary union in 1707.

Ireland was the more immediate problem. The Lord Lieutenant, Tyrconnel, a Roman Catholic, was one of the most able and determined of James's supporters. He and his co-religionists were determined to use this opportunity to secure full control for themselves of their own country. James II came to Ireland in March 1689 planning to use a loyal Ireland as a base for the conquest of England and Scotland. The Irish nationalists refused to submit to his plans, and so James soon found himself in the midst of a war to drive the English and Protestants out of Ireland, a war he pursued with ferocity and determination. With funds provided by the new Parliament, William sailed for Ireland in June 1690. The critical stage of the campaign was soon over, for at the River Boyne William routed James's forces on the last day of the month. The mopping up took another year, but William's attention was now directed to the continent.

The Nine Years' War and the Partition Treaties. The Nine Years' War, King William's War, the War of the League of Augsburg — it is known by all three names — had broken out in the fall of 1688 when Louis XIV laid siege to Phillipsburg and the Dutch took possession of towns on the lower Rhine belonging to the Archbishop of Cologne. William had wasted no time in bringing his new kingdom into the war. Even before James II had left London for France, William had given orders to the English navy to attack French ships. The Nine Years' War is not one of the great European conflicts if measured in terms of notable battles or of major territorial transfers through the treaty which closed it. For England, the war served as a training session. The most seasoned officers in James's army were the Roman Catholics and the remaining cadre of English officers and men were mainly raw, unseasoned troops. This fact, coupled with their dubious loyalty, caused William to employ foreign officers — Dutch, Germans, and Huguenots — in the commands. It was this apprenticeship that permitted the army to perform so well in the next war.

William personally commanded his armies in Europe from 1691 to the end of the war. William was not a great general, but he excelled in terms of organization, discipline, and his care for his troops. The major sieges with one exception were won by the French. In part this was because the King was given inadequate financial support by the Parliament except for 1690 and 1694. The French were always amazed at his ability to regroup his forces after a defeat and his return to the field of battle more determined and stronger than ever. It was this war of attrition that eventually persuaded Louis XIV to agree to a peace. By the treaty of Ryswick that brought the war to an end in 1697, the French King was forced to recognize William as King of England, thus recognizing the Protestant succession and achieving a major war aim of the English.

WILLIAM III, KING AND DIPLOMAT

War Finance — The Bank of England. The extraordinary cost of maintaining both a large army overseas and an expanded navy wrought a revolution in English public finance. The changes that took place in William's reign in this sphere are among the most important consequences of the Revolution of 1688. After a year's delay Parliament granted William the customs for only short terms and not for life. A portion of these were reserved for the support of the King's household and the ordinary functions of government, a new system to be known as the Civil List. The King's recurring need for funds during the war thus required that Parliament be called into session each year. Because of the need for funds to maintain the army and pay off debts, the regular meeting of Parliament was guaranteed. Determined this time to exercise greater control over royal finances Parliament now resorted to the expedient of appropriating funds for specific uses and an accounting was required each year.

The most important impact of the war was the new system developed to raise the enormous sums of money required. Formerly the King had to raise loans on the security of his name alone. Now Parliament, assured of its existence through the system of annual appropriations, undertook itself to guarantee the loans that were required to finance the war. With this kind of security the crown was able to secure funds much more readily and at much lower interest rates. The parliamentary guarantee of the King's credit was the basis for the new system of a national debt, a landmark in public finance. A body of trained civil servants was created to continue to carry the system throughout the violent alternation of party administrations which characterized the quarter century that followed the Revolution. The traditional sources of credit used by the crown proved inadequate to the huge demands placed upon them during the war. To compensate for this deficiency the Bank of England was created, a joint-stock, limited liability corporation authorized by act of Parliament in 1694. With seasoned officials at the Treasury like the veteran Lord Godolphin, the Secretary Henry Guy, and the brilliant young Chancellor of the Exchequer, Charles Montagu, working in collaboration with the predominantly Whig financiers who comprised the Bank's board of directors, England was able to produce the funds needed to sustain her and her allies in the struggle with France. The capture of Namur in 1695 can be directly attributed to the success of the new banking establishment.

The Parties and the Cabinet. William's success in securing his three kingdoms, restoring the strength and credit of the English army and navy, and fighting Louis XIV to a standstill, was not matched in his dealings with the parties and parliament. To begin with, the qualified support for his invasion and succession inclined many politicians to reinsure themselves with the exiled James in case of a Stuart restoration. William's refusal to give his confidence to any of his English ministers and his obvious partiality for his Dutch and other foreign aides created jealousy and resentment. William never really understood or accepted the party structure in England. His first ministries included representatives of all the major party groups as he endeavored to secure broad support for his program while keeping out of the clutches of one particular faction. Initially, he found the Tories most sympathetic to his views on government and the role of monarchy. In the early years of the reign the Whigs' desire to limit the power of the crown was ample reason to keep that party from dominating the ministry. But the setbacks in the land campaign in 1692 convinced the Tories that further expenditures on the army were wasted. William was forced to choose between fighting a war in Flanders with Whig support or pursuing the "blue water policy" — the reliance on the navy and not the army — favored by the Tories. He chose the former. By the end of 1693 the Whigs were in the ascendancy. Their promotion was advocated by Sunderland, who had emerged as the King's political broker or "manager," a practice necessitated by the rise of parties.

One of the most important constitutional innovations of the post-Revolution period was the Cabinet. The Privy Council had declined in authority as the Stuart kings expanded its membership to suit the vanity of the many courtiers who pressed to be included. Its work consequently fell into the hands of standing committees, of which the most important was the committee on foreign affairs. Managed by the senior Secretary of State, it had developed into the principal advisory body of the crown. William III preferred the departmental style of government where he met separately with each minister. Circumstances dictated otherwise. When he went to Ireland in 1690 he left Mary as Regent and instructed her to consult a committee of nine privy councillors who were given the designation of Cabinet Council. Although their authority was strictly circumscribed the precedent was an important one. Continuing to meet during the King's absences, the Cabinet also met with the King from the winter of 1691-92 though less frequently. William's attempt to replace it in 1694 with a smaller, less formal body failed. There were regular meetings in the winter of 1694-95 and the members acted as Lords Justices for him after Mary's death when he was away on the continent. The continuous history of the Cabinet, an informal body unknown to the law, dates from this time.

The Succession in Spain and England. Throughout his reign William III was preoccupied with the problem of the succession to the throne in both Spain and England. Louis XIV showed his concern for his own reasons. The Treaty of Ryswick was concluded in part so both monarchs could turn their attention to the disposition of the Spanish Empire upon the imminent death of the long-suffering Carlos II. Louis and the Austrian emperor, Leopold I, were each sons and husbands of Spanish princesses. The brides of the French kings in each case were senior but had renounced their claims to the Spanish throne both for themselves and their heirs. The other European powers did not want the crown of Spain to go either to the Bourbons or the Habsburgs. Louis and William finally agreed that the throne would go to Leopold's grandson by his first wife, the son of the Elector of Bavaria. The first partition treaty, concluded in 1699, provided for this settlement, but even as the treaty was being signed the young prince died. Louis and

William, both anxious to avoid a major war over Spain, reopened their negotiations. A second partition treaty signed early in 1700 assigned the bulk of the Spanish inheritance to Archduke Charles, Leopold's second son by his third wife.

The death of another young prince, Princess Anne's only surviving child, the Duke of Gloucester, meant that the Protestant succession in England was now in jeopardy. William had long favored vesting the succession in the Electress Sophia of Hanover, granddaughter of James I, and Sophia's heirs. But to do so required the assent of Parliament and a majority of country members had been elected in 1698, many of whom were hostile to the King's continental interests and concerns. The Tory Parliament delivered a series of attacks on the aging King, sending home his Dutch guards and taking back the large grants of Irish land he had made to his favorites. The King seriously considered abdication. But though his health was failing his will remained strong and his ambition constant. These qualities were put to their greatest test at the end of 1700 when Carlos II finally died. He bequeathed the whole of his empire to the younger grandson of Louis XIV, Phillip, Duke of Anjou, and Louis accepted the inheritance in the name of Philip. A new English Parliament elected in the beginning of 1701 was only slightly more Whiggish in composition, but it did confirm the succession of the crown to the Electress Sophia though the Commons included a number of limitations upon the crown which reflected their dislike of William's foreign advisors.

The Legacy of William III. Though the Dutch were cowed into accepting Philip V's accession in Spain, England was not. The Tories found their public stock falling as a result of their vindictive measures, so to restore confidence and regain the King's favour they passed a resolution asking him to take steps to curb the exorbitant power of France. The King responded promptly, appointing John Churchill, Earl of Marlborough, who was the principal advisor to the Princess Anne, as his agent to negotiate a new alliance with the Dutch and the Emperor. Fortunately for William, Louis XIV now entered into measures guaranteed to provoke English hostility. He sent French troops into the Spanish Netherlands to shut off English commerce to the continent and sent other contingents into Milan and its dependencies, thus enraging the Austrian Emperor who claimed that territory for his family. Finally, Louis acknowledged the young son of James II as King of England when the old monarch died in exile in September 1701. Armed with a new grand alliance between England, the Dutch Republic and the Austrian Emperor, William returned to England in the fall of 1701, dissolved the Parliament and began to transfer power once again to the Whigs, the party dedicated to support of his continental policies. Though the election returns gave neither faction a real majority, when the King died on March 8, 1702, after a fall from his horse, he had the satisfaction of knowing that England would honor its commitments. William died respected but unloved. His adopted country had been well schooled in the arts of war, diplomacy, and government, but had not undertaken its tutelage willingly. Now, however, the benefits of William's rule were to be seen, and his successor was able to enjoy the fruits of his labors.

THE EARLY YEARS OF ANNE'S REIGN

The Accession of Queen Anne. The new Queen (1702-14) was hardly a prepossessing figure for the newly emerging power of England. Although Anne was only thirty-five years old, the toll of seventeen pregnancies, chronic ill-health, and the gout had already made her old before her time and rendered her a semi-invalid. After the death of her sister Mary and her father James II she could be accepted as the rightful and legal heir to the throne. A true daughter of the church, her devotion to her people and her country enabled her to draw upon a reserve of affection and loyalty that united at least for a time most of the influential elements in society behind her government.

Anne was a woman who was whole-hearted in her loyalties once they were fixed. She immediately turned over her affairs to her most trusted advisors and friends, a triumvirate remarkable in English history. Sarah, Countess of Marlborough, had been Anne's constant companion and closest friend for a score of years. She was given control of the Queen's entourage and access to her person by the grant of the offices of Mistress of the Robes, Groom of the Stole, and Keeper of the Privy Purse. Her husband, Marlborough, was named Captain-General of the English army in Flanders and Ambassador to the Dutch Republic, with command of the armies of the maritime powers in the Low Countries. The final member of this close-knit circle was another lifelong friend, Sidney, Lord Godolphin. While Marlborough took over the principal direction of foreign affairs and the conduct of the war, Godolphin acted as Prime Minister at home, with sole responsibility for the Treasury and supervision of the executive. He was also the liaison between the ministry, the Queen, and Parliament. If Marlborough as general and diplomat was the architect of England's greatness abroad, it was Godolphin as Prime Minister who made Marlborough's successes possible by the firm support he provided from home.

The Queen's own predilection and the long associations with Marlborough and Godolphin meant that the ministry was initially composed almost entirely of Tories. No eighteenth-century ministry ever lost an election and the new Parliament that was returned in the

Queen Anne (Kenneth Spencer Research Library).

summer of 1702 followed the traditional pattern by containing a Tory majority. Although possessing the complete backing of the Queen, Marlborough and Godolphin had to share power at·first with the principal Tory leaders, Nottingham and Rochester, who returned to office respectively as Secretary of State and Lord Lieutenant of Ireland. Both favored the now traditional Tory "blue water policy" which ran counter to the Williamite policies adopted by Marlborough.

The War of the Spanish Succession — The First Phase. When England entered the war in 1702, campaigns were conducted by the French on three fronts: in Italy, on the Rhine, and in the Spanish Netherlands against the maritime powers. Spain was dynastically linked to France. The Grand Alliance — England, the Netherlands and the Austrian Empire — had only a few German princes in league with them intially. In 1703 Bavaria and Cologne joined France while Savoy and Portugal joined the Grand Alliance. As a condition of her entering the alliance, Portugal insisted that the maritime powers open another front in Spain and endeavor to place the Habsburg candidate on the throne. Savoy brought some reinforcements to the Austrians in Italy but the defection of Bavaria and Cologne laid the Rhineland and southern Germany open to French occupation and made an advance on Vienna a practical reality.

Marlborough had already shown superior tactical ability and generalship in the campaign of 1702. Contrary to the prevailing traditions of the time which favored long and essentially static campaigns devoted mainly to sieges, he preferred to seek out the enemy's army in the field and destroy it, believing thereby that the fortresses would be cut off from re-supply and would fall into his hands. The Dutch, whose political representatives at the field headquarters had to give their consent before their troops could be employed, regarded the army as a defensive weapon, as all that stood between them and a French invasion, and so they were loath to risk it in battle. Determined not to return to the field in 1704 unless he was given greater authority, Marlborough persuaded the Dutch to let him take part of the troops for a daring march up the Rhine to save the Empire. At the Danube Marlborough joined up with the two imperial commanders, including Prince Eugene of Savoy, and together they laid waste to much of upper Bavaria. Marlborough and Eugene dispatched a general of questionable loyalty, and thus freed of his conservative influence, they deliberately provoked a battle with the Franco-Bavarian army. In one of the decisive battles of European history, they defeated the flower of the French army at the little village of Blenheim on the Danube. The victory saved the Empire from French control and

Battle of Blenheim, 1704 (Kenneth Spencer Research Library).

provided Godolphin with the means to fight off the attacks of the parties at home.

The Revolution Church Settlement and Occasional Conformity. After the Revolution of 1688 it was expected that the Dissenters would be rewarded with a relaxation of the laws which were designed to suppress them as a consequence of their refusal to cooperate with James II against the Anglicans. William III, a Calvinist, was fully committed to religious toleration and was even prepared to go further and remodel the church so that it would be acceptable to Presbyterians if not most of the Dissenters. He was frustrated in his efforts because of the means he used to try to force the Tories to consent. They in turn were opposed to concessions both out of conscience and a desire to protect an Anglican monopoly of political offices. A compromise measure, the Toleration Act, was passed though its terms were hardly very generous. It was the refusal of the crown to implement the more punitive measures still in force that really gave the Dissenters a measure of peace. Public office, both in the central government and at the local level, was restricted to communicants of the Church of England. Many Dissenters, however, would take communion in the established church once a year to qualify themselves for office, and then return to their regular worship at their chapels. The high church party, virtually synonymous with the Tories, was outraged at this behavior. After the dismissal of Rochester in 1703 and Nottingham and his colleagues from the ministry in 1704, the Tories seized upon the issue of occasional conformity to try to break the ministry. Two previous bills designed to eradicate this practice had been defeated in the Lords in 1702 and 1703. Now the Tories in the Commons decided to add the provision to a money bill in late 1704, thus forcing its acceptance both by the Lords (who had earlier given up the right to alter money bills), and by the Queen. The motion in the Commons to tack the provision onto a bill was defeated, but only after a most desperate effort by both sides to garner the necessary votes. The man principally responsible for its defeat was the Speaker and new Secretary of State, Robert Harley.

Robert Harley versus the Whigs. Robert Harley was one of the most interesting, important, and yet enigmatic statesmen of the early eighteenth century. Born into a dissenting family, he became the leader of the church party or Tories after starting his political career in Parliament as a country Whig. Elected Speaker in 1701 and again in 1702, he proved to be one of the most successful managers of the Commons in English history. Godolphin and Marlborough came to rely upon him so heavily that by 1704 the three jointly managed affairs, and Harley was persuaded to take high office as a Secretary of State, though he retained the Speakership until the dissolution of the Parliament in 1705. A man of the middle, he was suspicious of the extremists of either party. When Godolphin made an opening to the Whigs in late 1704 to save his majority, Harley was opposed and resisted all efforts to increase the Whig presence in the ministry. In December 1706 the Earl of Sunderland, Marlborough's son-in-law and one of the Whig junto or ruling clique of that party, was made Secretary of State. Harley was unwilling to accept Sunderland as a colleague and now began to undermine Godolphin. In February 1708 he advised the Queen to remove Godolphin and remodel the ministry. Marlborough refused to support this move and without his prestige Harley could not hope to achieve his aims, so that he voluntarily resigned. Just when the Cabinet crisis reached its height, word reached London that the "Old Pretender," Prince James Edward, the son born to James II in 1688, was now on the sea with a French fleet, determined to invade Britain and regain the crown. His landing was thwarted but the threat and excitement tended to reinforce the Whigs so that when parliamentary elections were held later in the spring the Whigs were returned with a solid majority.

John Churchill, Duke of Marlborough (Radio Times Hulton Picture Library).

THE LATER YEARS OF QUEEN ANNE'S REIGN

The War of the Spanish Succession — The Second Phase. After an abortive advance along the Moselle, Marlborough returned to the battlefield in Flanders in 1705 for another year of frustration. Only the successful landing of an allied fleet with Archduke Charles in Catalonia and the capture of Barcelona provided any relief from the dismal dispatches from the other theatres. 1706 proved to be the *annus mirabilis* of the war. Marlborough was able to engage the French in battle at Ramillies, south of Brussels, and the resulting victory put most of Flanders into his hands. The English and their allies won a number of important engagements early in the war but soon the war situation began to deteriorate for the allies. In 1707 the Austrians concluded a truce with the French in Italy, which freed French troops for employment elsewhere. A severe defeat in Spain lost that country for the allies, though the war dragged on there for another four years. In

Sarah Churchill, Duchess of Marlborough (Radio Times Hulton Picture Library).

1708, Marlborough cleared the rest of the Netherlands, but the Battle of Malplaquet in 1709 was so bloody that it sickened the civilians on both sides and the turn of events at home made Marlborough afraid to risk another major engagement. In spite of two further impressive successes against the French, Marlborough was dismissed from all his offices at the end of 1711, defeated not as a general, but as Marlborough the diplomat and the husband.

During the first part of the war Marlborough had held the Grand Alliance together practically single handedly. For several successive years he set out on exhausting trips around the capitals of Europe after the campaign to persuade the allied princes to contribute troops to the armies in the several theatres. In 1706 when the French first sued for peace, he was firm in his refusal to accept anything less than unconditional terms. When peace negotiations were undertaken in earnest in 1709, however, he insisted upon a collaborator, the young Viscount Townshend, and Marlborough left the negotiating to him. It was the same in 1710 when the negotiations were again taken up after Louis XIV's rejection of the preliminaries the previous year. Marlborough's increasing caution and refusal to accept responsibility for anything but his own army was the consequence of political changes at home.

The Decline and Fall of the Godolphin Ministry. The Duchess of Marlborough is often credited with almost complete control over the Queen for the first half of her reign. Yet, in fact, she had lost whatever political influence she possessed even before Anne's accession. The Duchess, a convert to Whig principles, held views which were unpalatable to the Queen. Disagreeing on politics as early as 1702, their relationship became more distant after 1703 when the Duchess went into semi-seclusion following the death of her only surviving son. Though placed in the Queen's bedchamber by her cousin the Duchess, the Queen's dresser, Mrs. Masham, worked to advance the interests and projects of another relation, Robert Harley. The Duchess became increasingly outspoken and strident in forcing her unwanted advice on the Queen. The Queen turned increasingly to Masham and others so that by 1710 all communication between the two former friends had ceased. At the end of 1710 the Duchess was dismissed from all her offices. This estrangement was an important factor in the fall of Marlborough, Godolphin, and the Whigs.

The Godolphin Ministry had fully earned the thanks of the nation by its impressive accomplishments both at home and abroad. Besides maintaining English naval supremacy at sea, a preeminence dramatized by the scuttling of the French fleet at Toulon in 1707, it had made possible the great victories of Marlborough in Flanders and Germany, and subsidized other allied victories in Italy and Spain. One must add to these accomplishments the taking of Gibraltar in 1704 and Port Mahon in 1708. At home the greatest achievement was the passage of the Act of Union in 1707. Precipitated by the Scottish threat to elect a sovereign other than the one to rule England after Anne's death, the English Parliament in 1705 had moved the Queen to appoint commissioners to treat for a union. The Scots were encouraged to participate by the threat of the loss of their privileges in England as subjects of a common sovereign and the promise of full participation in the lucrative colonial trade. The sixty-two commissioners (thirty-one of each nation) chosen by the Queen did their work well. Completing their deliberations in July 1705, they recommended a parliamentary union in which sixteen elected Scottish peers would join the House of Lords and forty-five Scottish members would be added to the 513 members of the English Commons. After a stormy passage in the Scots Parliament the recommendations were accepted without qualification and the union came into being on May 1, 1707.

The increasing and irksome burden of taxation which fell heaviest on the landowners, the jealousy of those excluded from political power, and the growing frustration over the ministry's apparent inability to bring the war to an end, when combined with the estrangement of the Queen, eventually brought down Godolphin and his colleagues. The instrument of the change was an unlikely object, an inflammatory, ultra-conservative Tory parson. The high church clergy were among the most vociferous and influential opponents of the Godolphin ministry and a key element in the strength of the Tories. In order to reduce the clergy to subservience one of the most notorious of their number, Dr. Henry Sacherverell, a fellow of Magdalen College, Oxford, and a popular preacher in London, was impeached by the Commons before the High Court of Parliament in December 1709. This effort to muzzle the Tory churchman backfired on the Whigs. The martyr cleric became a symbol of Whig oppression and tyranny. All those dissatisfied with ministerial policies of every kind now used the parson to demonstrate their true feelings. Emboldened by the reaction and counseled by Harley, the Queen removed her servants one by one so that by the end of the year Harley and the Tories were in control of the executive. An election held in September returned an overwhelming Tory majority.

The End of Anne's Reign. Ignoring Britain's commitments to its allies, Harley opened secret negotiations with the French. By the winter of 1711-12 the preliminaries were sufficiently far advanced that Harley, now raised to the peerage as Earl of Oxford, felt confident enough to dismiss Marlborough and to make public the negotiations. The abandonment of Britain's allies on the battlefield aroused powerful protest both at home and on the continent but Oxford, now assisted by his principal colleague and rival for authority, Henry St. John (created Viscount Bolingbroke in 1713), proceeded to confirm his arrangements with Louis XIV in the Treaty of Utrecht. The gains won by England were the most impressive since the Cromwellian wars and were not to be equalled again in the eighteenth century except by the Treaty of Paris in 1763. In addition to Gibraltar and Minorca, Nova Scotia was ceded to England marking the beginning to a retreat for the French in North America. The fortifications at Dunkirk were to be razed. Important commercial concessions were granted in Spain and the Spanish Empire, and France recognized the Protestant succession in England.

The very success of Oxford in turning out the Whigs and restoring the Tories to power was ultimately his undoing. He found himself the prisoner of the newly-dominant party, unable to play them off against the Whigs and thus retain control; the sickly Queen began to repent the abandonment of her old friends and advisors. With the Queen's health failing, both Oxford and Bolingbroke now looked to the heir to the crown to shore up their positions. But George, Elector of Hanover, loyal to the imperial cause, could never forgive the ministers who betrayed England's allies in the late war. Oxford and Bolingbroke then sought, independently, to ingratiate themselves with the "Old Pretender," the son of the late James II. When he refused unequivocally to change his religion for the crown of England they realized his cause was hopeless. Thus when Queen Anne fell mortally ill at the end of July, the Tories were unprepared to manage the succession. The Whigs, on the other hand, were fully prepared to launch a coup if necessary to secure the Protestant succession and had secretly arranged a takeover of the army if this eventuality proved necessary. It was not, and when Anne died peacefully on the first of August 1714 George I was proclaimed without any challenge.

JOURNALISM AND TRADE:
GROWTH AND CHANGE UNDER THE LATER STUARTS

The Press and the Parties. The fall of the Godolphin ministry, the rapprochement with France, the renewed attack on the Dissenters by the triumphant Tories, which was shown by the passage of the occasional conformity bill in 1711, all inspired political and press battles in England that exceeded even those of the exclusion controversy in their magnitude and ferocity. The party lines had hardened into a clear Whig-Tory split by the beginning of the reign. The successive replacements and then transformation of the ministry had changed its composition from Tory to Whig and back to Tory. The frequent parliamentary elections — 1702, 1705, 1708, 1710, and 1713 — were all fought on strict party lines. Though the parties lacked a formal national organization (that did not emerge until the mid-nineteenth century), the continuity of leadership and principles and the presence of some centralized management, both for elections and control of parliamentary sessions, are clear evidence of the existence of party in Anne's reign. These divisions are particularly well exemplified by the press.

With the lapse of the censorship laws in 1695 a steady increase in publications becomes evident. Newspapers and monthlies began to proliferate and the first daily newspaper, the *Daily Courant,* made its appearance in 1702. In spite of a parliamentary prohibition, accounts of parliamentary debates appeared in annual histories at the turn of the century. The expanded activity of the press in Anne's reign, culminating in the great battles that dominated the last four years, are one of the most important phenomena of modern English history. By 1714 nearly all the features we have come to expect in modern newspapers — the editorial, the news, the advice to the lovelorn, the periodical essay — had all made their appearance. Newspapers began and ended in startling profusion. Press battles, such as those between Defoe's *Review,* Tutchin's *Observator,* and Leslie's *Rehearsal,* were the order of the day. By 1712 between 50,000 and 60,000 individual copies of newspapers were sold in London each week, in spite of a stamp tax imposed by Parliament to curb the Whig press. Nearly all the most celebrated writers of the day were drawn into the press wars. Joseph Addison, Jonathan Swift, Richard Steele, and Daniel Defoe were only the best known and the most active. A polemical tract could inspire literally dozens of answers. The most successful and influential tracts, such as Swift's *Conduct of the Allies* (1711), were sold by the tens of thousands of copies and could swing the opinion of the whole country behind a change in policy. The attacks of Tory writers on Marlborough were sufficient to compromise his reputation for many decades.

The general election of 1710 was fought and won in the press as much as it was on the hustings. Even all the powers and means of a powerful ministry were unable to save the French commerce bill in 1713 thanks to the efforts of the opposition. The electorate represented only a surprisingly high proportion of the adult male population, although in many boroughs the right to return representatives was vested in a very small number of individuals, often under the influence of a local patron. Nevertheless, recent studies of pollbooks have suggested the presence of a swing vote, beyond the control of borough-mongers and responsive to changing public opinion. The success of the Revolution of 1688 and the preservation of English liberties are no better illustrated than in the vigor of its press and the strength of its political parties.

Mercantilism. England's rise to great power status at the end of the wars against Louis XIV was the consequence of English arms backed by English industry and finance. The exploitation of this new eminence was the province of the merchants. The impact of the wars upon England and the other European countries has been hotly debated. The depredations of the French privateers upon English merchant shipping was tremendous. Yet the English gained as well as lost and thousands of French ships were taken as prizes during the same period and incorporated into the English fleet. Though the English merchant marine may have been only marginally larger at the end of the period, and little more than it had been a century ago, the contrast with the situation in France and the Dutch Republic was more important and ultimately decisive. Prior to 1688 Dutch ships carried much of the bulk cargo required by England. The Dutch navy also suffered at the hands of the French and the great burden of war expense took its toll on this small nation; it never recovered from the drain of men, ships, and gold. France, though blessed with far greater resources, both human and material, likewise lost out in the competition with England. England emerged from the war unquestionably the strongest in terms of its fleet.

Some share of this economic success must be attributed to the mercantilist system that was developed in the Commonwealth period and reinforced during the Restoration. Given its classic statement in 1664 in Thomas Mun's *England's Treasure by Foreign Trade,* mercantilism simply stressed the importance of a favorable balance of trade. If England exported more than she imported the consequence would be a steady flow of specie into the country and increased prosperity. The navigation laws, first passed in 1651 and re-enacted 1660-63 restricted the colonial trade and imports generally to English bottoms (ships), thus laying the foundation for the growth of the English merchant marine. As the colonies grew in size and the value of their exports increased, English merchants and the King's tax collectors were the beneficiaries. The colonies, restricted to England as a single trading partner, became a principal market for English goods just as they were an essential source of raw materials. The wars were fought to protect old markets as well as create new ones. When Philip V inherited Spain, he excluded English and Dutch shipping from trading with the Spanish colonies — a trade which was regarded as vital to English prosperity. So too the Levant and Mediterranean trade was assured by the capture of Minorca and Gibraltar and the scuttling of the French fleet at Toulon in 1707.

The demand in unprecedented quantities for supplies for the services, clothing, sail cloth, armaments, and ships gave a stimulus to industry and larger commercial organizations. The lot of the lower classes, whether urban or rural, was not materially altered. But in general it seems that the trading and mercantile community and landowners benefited as well from the war. The unprecedented demand for money sired the Bank of England, encouraged the union of the old and new East India Companies in 1709, created the South Sea Company and thus established a pattern of large-scale increases in capital formation. The more effective mobilization of resources made England's advance to greater power status possible. This was a legacy of William and Anne.

SUGGESTIONS FOR FURTHER READING

In addition to Clark, Ogg, and Macaulay, mentioned in the readings suggested in the previous chapter, one should consult also Henry Horwitz, *Parliament, Policy and Politics in the Reign of William III* (1977) and George M. Trevelyan, *England under Queen Anne* (3 vols., 1932-34). *The Marlborough-Godolphin Correspondence* (ed. H.L. Snyder, 3 vols., 1975) is a basic source. Geoffrey Holmes has contributed a number of important studies to the period including his *Britain after the Glorious Revolution* (1969), *British Politics in the Age of Anne* (1967) and *The Trial of Doctor Sacheverell* (1973). For foreign policy consult Ragnhild Hatton and J.S. Bromley, eds., *William III and Louis XIV: Essays 1680-1720 By and For Mark A. Thomason* (1968); Hatton and M.S. Anderson, eds., *Studies in Diplomatic History* (1970); D.B. Horn, *The British Diplomatic Service, 1689-1789* (1961); Douglas Coombs, *The Conduct of the Dutch-British Opinion and the Dutch Alliance during the War of the Spanish Succession* (1958); Roderick Geikie and Isabel A. Montgomery, *The Dutch Barrier 1705-1719* (1930); and A. David Francis, *The First Peninsular War* (1975) and *The Methuens and Portugal* (1966). Major biographies include Stephen Baxter, *William III* (1966); Henry Horwitz, *Revolution Politics* (1968); Winston S. Churchill, *Marlborough, His Life and Times* (2 vols., 1947); and David Chandler, *Marlborough as Military Commander* (1973). Bishop Burnet's *History of His Own Time,* (edited by M. Routh, 6 vols., 1833) is a rich contemporary source. The country is graphically described in Zacharias Conrad von Uffenbach, *London in 1710* (1934); *The journeys of Celia Fiennes* (edited by C. Morris, 1949); and Daniel Defoe, *Tour thro' the whole island of Great Britain* (best edition, ed. G.D.H. Cole, 2 vols., 1927). Other useful studies include Angus McInnes, *Robert Harley* (1970); H.T. Dickinson, *Bolingbroke* (1970); James O. Richards, *Party Propaganda under Queen Anne* (1972); and William Speck, *Tory and Whig, the Struggle in the Constituencies* (1970). Colorful and helpful are David Green, *Sarah, Duchess of Marlborough* (1967) and *Queen Anne* (1970). G. V. Bennett, *The Tory Crisis and Church and State 1688-1730* (1975) and Norman Sykes, *Church and State in England in the Eighteenth Century* (1934) are fundamental to an understanding of the dilemma of the Anglican church. Scotland and the union are well treated in T.C. Smout, *Scottish Trade on the Eve of the Union* (1963); P. Hume Brown, *The Legislative Union of England and Scotland* (1914); and P.W.J. Riley, *The English Ministers and Scotland, 1707-1727* (1964). For Ireland consult J.G. Simms, *Jacobite Ireland* (1969); J.C. Beckett, *Protestant Dissent in Ireland, 1687-1780* (1948); and F.G. James, *Ireland in the Empire, 1688-1770* (1973). Specialized studies of value are Ian K. Steele, *Politics of Colonial Policy, 1696-1720* (1968); Lois G. Schwoerer, *"No standing armies"* (1974); John Ehrman, *The Navy in the War of William III* (1953); J.H. Owen, *War at Sea under Queen Anne* (1938); and G.H. Jones, *The Mainstream of Jacobitism* (1954). P.M.G. Dickson, *The Financial Revolution in England, A Study in the Development of Public Credit 1688-1756* (1967) is a work of major importance.

9

Augustan England

1714-1754

George I (1714-27), a homely, stout, fifty-three year old German, was hardly the popular image of a king. Though King of Great Britain, he also remained ruler of Hanover; his dominant interest in the latter and lack of concern for the former upset the British who habitually resented foreigners and particularly feared their influence on British foreign policy. George was set in his ways, accustomed to complete mastery over his territories and subjects, and unfamiliar with Parliament and parties. A number of his personal traits also rankled the British. George I dined in public once or twice a week but could discourse only with persons who spoke German or French. He preferred to spend his days quietly in his chamber, giving audiences to his ministers. He took his supper with one or both grotesque German ladies in his household — the tall, spindly, middle-aged Duchess of Kendal, George's morganatic wife, and the fat, rouge-cheeked Countess of Darlington, George's half-sister, who were respectively but irreverently known as the maypole and the elephant. His entourage also included two German advisors and a Hugenot secretary who managed the King's Hanoverian concerns. The most popular members of the family were the Prince and Princess of Wales who spoke excellent English and were as affable as the King was reserved.

George I (Kenneth Spencer Research Library).

THE SETTLING OF THE HANOVERIAN DYNASTY

Even before George's arrival in England there was a shuffling of political leaders in readiness for the new order. Bolingbroke was sacked and the Whigs repossessed all of the great offices of state. The greatest authority was granted to the two Secretaries of State — Charles, Viscount Townshend, and James Stanhope. Townshend took the lead in domestic affairs, especially after his brother-in-law, Robert Walpole, succeeded Halifax at the Treasury in 1716; Stanhope was dominant in foreign affairs.

The Elections of 1715. The new ministers sought to consolidate their political gains by calling for the election of a new Parliament. Proclaiming their loyalty to the Protestant succession and denouncing the Treaty of Utrecht, the Whigs triumphed and were returned with a solid majority of 150 seats. When the Whig leaders proceeded to impeach the former ministers, Bolingbroke, who thought his life was in danger, fled to France and entered the service of James Edward Stuart, the Pretender to the British throne. The vindictiveness of the Whigs, the influence of the foreigners in the King's entourage, and the affront offered even to those Tories who had supported the Hanoverian succession, coupled with the fears of the church, turned popular opinion to the Tories. At the height of this reaction the Earl of Mar slipped away from court to raise the standard of James Edward Stuart in Scotland on September 6, 1715.

The Jacobite Uprising of 1715. The Jacobite Uprising of 1715 was a badly conceived, poorly concerted movement. The Pretender's only hope for success depended upon the support of France. The aged French King, Louis XIV, died, however, on September 1, and the Duke of Orleans who became Regent for the minor successor, Louis XV, adopted a policy of watchful neutrality — disastrous to the Jacobite cause — because the Regent himself was a candidate for the French throne and support from Britain might spell the difference in his ambitions. The Jacobites nevertheless pressed on; they had the initial advantage, for as poorly prepared as they were, the government had even fewer forces at its command. The Jacobites' initial successes were short-lived, however. After an indecisive battle at Sheriffmuir, Mar and the Jacobite forces no longer had the means to undertake another engagement. The belated arrival of the Pretender in January, without reinforcements or supplies, was anticlimactic. He returned to France, leaving his unsuccessful supporters to be hunted down in Scotland.

The Diplomacy of Stanhope. The Jacobite Rebellion only reinforced

Britain's pressing need for allies. James Stanhope moved immediately to rebuild the old alliances. As both envoy and general in Spain in the late war, Stanhope had formed an intimate acquaintance with Archduke Charles who had succeeded his brother as the Austrian Emperor in 1711. This friendship now became the hinge of Britain's foreign policy. In June 1715 Stanhope made a personal trip to Vienna to persuade Emperor Charles to permit the Dutch to maintain fortresses in the Netherlands as a barrier against French aggression. Following a treaty of alliance with the Dutch in February 1716, Britain signed the Treaty of Westminster in June 1716 by which Austria guaranteed the Protestant succession. Stanhope's most remarkable achievement was an alliance with France, so recently England's enemy. The resulting treaty, which provided for a guarantee of the succession of the British and French thrones, was concluded in November and approved by the Dutch in February 1717.

The haste with which the treaty was drafted reflected George I's concern for his Hanoverian dominions. In the Baltic area the Great Northern War (1700-21), which had begun as a conflict between Sweden and Denmark, had now grown to include Russia, Poland, and Prussia. Though Sweden was the aggressor, her defeat by Russia in 1709 put her permanently on the defensive. Prussia, Denmark, Hanover, and Russia all hoped to secure additions to their territories at her expense. George I employed the British fleet in the contest first against Sweden and then later against Russia after the death of Sweden's King Charles XII in 1718. With Stanhope's connivance, British forces were used to secure advantages for Hanover, an action which had adverse political repercussions in England. Finally, Britain regained its favorable commercial position with Spain in a treaty negotiated late in 1715.

The Whig Split and the Triumph of Walpole. The sweep of offices the Whigs enjoyed on George I's accession had still not satisfied all of them. Sunderland was disgruntled as he watched Townshend and Stanhope take charge of offices to which he had pretensions. Townshend and Walpole came to resent the influence of the Hanoverian advisors with whom Stanhope was still influential. This division was exacerbated by the ill-feeling that existed between the King and his heir. When George determined to visit Hanover in 1716 Sunderland used the pretext of a visit to Aix for health reasons as an excuse to follow the King to the Continent. There he heightened the suspicions of the King and Stanhope that Townshend and Walpole were in league with the Prince of Wales. On his return the King dismissed Townshend and Walpole, and others resigned in sympathy. When the King banished the Prince and his wife from his presence soon after, the opposition established itself around the Prince.

Because the Septennial Act (1716) extended the maximum life of a Parliament from three to seven years, it would have seemed that the Whig ministers could be assured of lengthy control of government, yet the split in the Whig party made the survival of the ministry tenuous. The dissident Whigs capitalized on popular fears to charge that English interests were subordinated to Hanoverian goals, and after several legislative defeats Stanhope and Sunderland realized they would have to join forces with Townshend, Walpole and other dissident Whigs. The reunion of all Whig factions was capped by a reconciliation of the King and the Prince and a banishment of the Hanoverian advisors in 1720. This consolidation was timely, for the ministry suddenly found itself faced with a grave crisis.

The late wars had saddled England with a substantial public debt. The South Sea Company, organized by Robert Harley in 1711, managed part of the debt in return for the exclusive trading rights in Spain and the Spanish Empire which had been confirmed at the peace table. Offering lower interest rates, the South Sea Company took over the remaining part of the debt not earlier funded by the chartered companies, making a series of stock offerings to finance this undertaking. To create a demand for the stock issues it paid handsome dividends out of capital — a fraudulent practice — and tendered bribes that may have reached the King himself. The shares rose from £130 to £1050 in the space of a few months, but as the South Sea Bubble burst suddenly, along with other speculative enterprises in the summer of 1720, financial ruin was brought to countless individuals. The crown itself was in danger because the Court was deeply implicated, and only the masterly defense by Walpole in the Commons' investigation saved it. Stanhope, who was free from personal guilt, died suddenly during the investigation. Sunderland had to surrender his office of First Lord of the Treasury to Walpole in 1721 as the price of his acquittal. Sunderland's unexpected death a year later left the field clear to Walpole.

THE AGE OF WALPOLE

Walpole's Political System. In 1721 Walpole was in a position to assert his political leadership. He had emerged from the South Sea Bubble crisis without direct taint of corruption, the champion of the investors, and defender of stability. More, however, was needed. He made himself indispensable to the King by shielding George and his friends from the investigation. Sir Robert made himself master of the King's ministers by driving independent or contrary ones out of office. In 1724, for example, he forced Carteret, Stanhope's successor as Secretary and Sunderland's political heir, to resign and then removed him from

Walpole and the Speaker of the House of Commons (Radio Times Hulton Picture Library).

Westminster by making him Lord Lieutenant of Ireland. And again, when the exiled Bolingbroke engineered his return by a sizeable gift to the Duchess of Kendal, Walpole was able to exclude him from his seat in the House of Lords. In Commons and in the constituencies, Walpole built up his support by a pacific policy abroad and low taxes at home. Even the death of George I in 1727 did little to shake Walpole's grasp because he could count on the support of Queen Caroline, the brilliant consort of George II (1727-60). She and Walpole concerted plans for the government, and it was her job to persuade the King to give his assent. It was not easy for her to subordinate herself to her intellectual inferior, but she handled the part well. Her early death in 1737 was a serious blow to Walpole.

Walpole created a new model for a Prime Minister. He developed the use of patronage to a fine art. By the judicious use of positions in the gift of the crown, whether in the military services, the church, the civil administration or the Court, he built a stable majority in the Commons. Secret service funds were generously disbursed to control votes in the parliament and win elections in the constituencies. In the House of Lords the votes of the sixteen representative peers of Scotland, who were chosen from a government-selected list, and of the bishops ensured him a working majority. Walpole's success rested on a combination of royal support, his ability in finance, his skill in forging parliamentary majorities out of the many interests and factions, and, above all, on his remaining in the House of Commons and resisting the temptation of a peerage and his consequent removal to the upper house.

The Opposition and the Excise Crisis. Walpole utilized a solid core of the Court's supporters for votes in the Commons, but without the votes of independent, landed M.P.'s, he could not forge majorities. Power was concentrated in the hands of the landed gentry and the aristocracy — great landowners, many of whom controlled one or more seats in Parliament and whose collective interest exceeded that of the government. It was important to the landowners that the taxes remain low, even though taxes levied on land were the most reliable sources from which to raise funds. The other principal sources of government revenue were customs duties and the excise, a tax levied on selected commodities — a tax best controlled and least abused, and the most easily enforced. In 1733, Walpole proposed the introduction of an excise tax on wine and tobacco coupled with a lowering of the land tax to one shilling in the pound (a rate of 5 percent). He expected that it would be warmly welcomed by the landed gentry. For once Walpole misstepped. Dr. Johnson reflected a widespread attitude when he described it as "a hateful tax levied upon commodities, and adjudged not by the common judges of property, but wretches hired by those to whom excise is paid." The proposal was ballooned into an issue out of all proportion. Walpole was forced to abandon his scheme, in the greatest defeat of his career.

The main credit for the defeat of the excise went to the resurgent parliamentary opposition. The Tories, discredited and disorganized, had been out of office since 1714. By 1716 they began to join forces with disaffected Whigs. William Pulteney, once considered Walpole's protégé, had not been returned to office in 1720 when the Whig split was healed; soon after he began to concert measures with the Tories. The weeding out of Sunderland's followers and any other Whig who showed signs of independence gradually swelled the ranks of the opposition over the next decade. In 1727 under the inspiration of Bolingbroke, they launched *The Craftsman* which became their principal organ, and developed a program which gave them an aura of respectability. The program basis was the perennial issues of the danger of a standing army and the undue influence of the crown in Parliament by the presence of placemen — political appointees to seats in Parliament — and pensioners. By espousing these sacrosanct themes, the very essence of Whig ideology, Bolingbroke could appeal to the patriotism of the voters. Brilliant writers such as Henry Fielding and Alexander Pope lent their pens. John Gay's *Beggar's Opera* was only the most tuneful of numerous stage works sponsored by the opposition. They bore down so heavily upon the embattled Walpole that he introduced censorship for all theatrical productions — a code of censorship survives even to the present and extends to motion pictures. In spite of these assaults, Walpole was not brought down by domestic issues but rather by his foreign policy, the sphere in which he had the least experience.

British Diplomacy Under Townshend and Walpole. Walpole's policy of stability at home required peace abroad. Townshend, who had returned to the ministry as Lord President in 1720, set out to forge a series of alliances which would forward both Britain's and Hanover's interests. By allying Britain with France and Prussia, he sought a coalition designed at once to build a German coalition against Austria and to prevent Russian domination in the Baltic. By providing new security for Hanover, Townshend was in fact following much the same practice as his predecessor. Spain not only rebuffed Townshend's offer of an alliance but also concluded a treaty with Austria, giving more to the Hapsburgs than it received. Britain then became more belligerent toward Spain, and British trade with the Spanish colonies deteriorated, reflecting how Spain had ignored its obligations under the Treaty of Ultrecht. Walpole became increasingly concerned both for the effect of this hostility on trade and hence revenue. In 1730 Townshend was

EUROPE IN THE
EIGHTEENTH CENTURY

ATLANTIC

NORTH

SEA

SWEDEN

Stockholm

DENMARK-NORWAY

Culloden Moor

Sheriffmuir
Stirling Edinburgh

Copenhagen

Prussia

OCEAN

Boyne R.

Dublin

IRELAND

GREAT
BRITAIN

London
The
Hague

Hanover

Berlin

POLAND

Bristol

Brussels

Cologne

Dresden

Silesia

Silesia to
Prussia 1744

Dunkirk
Oudenaarde
Bouchain

Ramillies
Aix-la-Chapelle
Namur

Prague

HOLY ROMAN EMPIRE

Brest

Paris

Lorraine

Phillipsburg
Ingolstadt

Danube
R.

Lorraine to
France 1735

Blenheim

Munich

Vienna

HUNGARY

FRANCE

Savoy

Milan

Turin

Toulon

Tuscany

Tuscany to
Austria 1737

OTTOMAN

EMPIRE

PORTUGAL

Lisbon

Madrid

SPAIN

Catalonia

Barcelona

Rome

Naples

Naples

Almanza

Minorca

Port Mahon

Sardinia

Minorca to
England 1713-1756

Sardinia to Savoy 1720
Sardinia to Austria 1713

Sicily

Gibraltar

MOROCCO

Naples to Austria 1713-1735
Naples to Spanish Bourbons 1735

Sicily to Savoy 1713
Sicily to Austria 1720
Sicily to Spanish Bourbons 1735

George II (Kenneth Spencer Research Library).

forced to resign and Walpole took over the direction of foreign affairs himself.

Walpole concluded a treaty with Spain which restored the rights of British merchants to trade in Spanish America, promising in return Britain's support for Spanish dynastic ambitions in Italy. In spite of Walpole's show of goodwill, Spain had never really reconciled its basic hostility to England and its resentment of England's predominance in her colonial trade. The grievances over the loss of Gibraltar, border disputes in America, and the regulation of trading concessions were problem enough. But the real bone of contention was the lucrative and flourishing contraband trade carried on by English merchants in Spanish America. The Spanish authorities retaliated by seizing British ships and torturing British seamen. At the same time they refused to acknowledge legitimate British complaints about the long drawn-out commission appointed to settle these matters. The clamor of the public to obtain satisfaction for Spanish atrocities committed against British seamen, the agitation of the merchants for protection, and opposition charges that British honor was at stake finally pushed Walpole into the War of Jenkin's Ear with Spain in 1739.

The Fall of Walpole. In 1740 Emperor Charles VI of Austria died and his daughter and heir, Maria Theresa, succeeded to her father's possessions. Frederick II ("the Great") of Prussia used this opportunity to snatch the province of Silesia from the young Queen, thereby launching the War of the Austrian Succession (1740-48). France, Spain, and Bavaria could not resist the opportunity to join Frederick in his dismemberment of the Habsburg domains, the last wresting the imperial title away from Maria Theresa's husband. Walpole had no choice but to come to the aid of the beleaguered Austria. The spectre of a hostile Prussia to the east of Hanover and threatening French armies on the southwest only added to Walpole's predicament. When George II as Elector of Hanover concluded a convention of neutrality to save Hanover (1741) and cast his ballot as Elector for the French candidate for Emperor, Charles Albert of Bavaria, Walpole's humiliation was complete. The aged (sixty-six) Prime Minister was finally forced to retire in 1742 after an embarrassing reversal in the parliamentary elections of 1742 and a series of defeats in the session that followed. His contemporaries viewed him as having outlasted his usefulness, and considered his disgrace a consequence of his corruption, expediency, and lack of principle. By accepting a peerage he escaped the wrath of the opposition in the Commons.

THE PELHAMS

The New Ministry. When Walpole had sacked Carteret in 1724 he had replaced him with the inoffensive but industrious Duke of Newcastle, a man who had inherited great wealth and unparalleled electoral influence. Newcastle's political apprenticeship began when Walpole made him Carteret's successor as Secretary of State in 1724, and he learned well from Walpole the management of patronage; in time he engrossed control over crown appointments in the church, the colonies, and many other places. Because he and his astute brother but junior colleague, Henry Pelham, had favored the Spanish war and acquiesced in George II's capitulation in Germany, Newcastle did not share his patron's fall. William Pulteney, long Walpole's *bête noire* and now finally restored to office, was nominally the ministry's leader but he committed himself to political oblivion by taking a peerage as Earl of Bath. Moreover, he allowed the Treasury to go to Spencer Compton, who also took refuge in the Lords, as Earl of Wilmington. Carteret, who returned to a secretaryship, proved the one really vigorous new addition to the cabinet, where his skill in languages and intimate knowledge of European affairs made him a royal favorite.

The War of the Austrian Succession and the " '45." So far as England was concerned, the middle years of the War of the Austrian Succession were as much a scene of battle at home as they were abroad. Indeed Britain was hardly more successful in Europe than the King was in promoting Carteret. The war largely favored France and its ally Prussia; England and her allies, especially Austria which was important for supporting Hanover's claims, did win a victory at Dettingen in 1743 on which occasion George II personally took command of the troops. Though the French were the opponents, war was not officially opened between the two countries until 1744. The confusion in motives and goals that characterized this conflict is indicated by the several sets of overlapping belligerencies. They included not only the war with Spain but a separate and parallel conflict in the colonies between France and England known as King George's War. Though the real focus of competition lay in the Americas and beyond, the ostensible struggle was in Europe. The critical role of Hanover obscured the real interests of both parties. Carteret, with his preoccupation with European affairs and his disdain for the business of parliamentary management, was forced to give way completely to the Pelhams in 1745, two years after Henry Pelham had been promoted to First Lord of the Treasury upon the death of Wilmington.

The newly unified ministry faced its most immediate challenge from still another source, for yet another (and final) Jacobite invasion was launched in 1745 by France to neutralize Britain. Led by the Old Pretender's son, "Bonnie" Prince Charlie, the uprising began in Scotland in July, and by September Edinburgh had fallen. But Charles mistepped and pressed into England where his local support soon evaporated. He advanced as far as Derby in December but was then forced by his officers to retreat back to Scotland. The King's favorite son, the Duke of Cumberland, aggressively pursued him and the superior resources of the English government soon told. In April Cumberland routed Charles's army, then he mercilessly hunted down the survivors, earning the epithet "the Butcher."

At about the same time, the King precipitated a crisis in London. In February 1746, the King informed Pelham of his decision to reinstate Carteret, now the Earl of Granville, and the Earl of Bath, to head the ministry. Pelham responded by resigning and the entire cabinet resigned *en bloc* in sympathy. The King was undone because Granville had not heeded Walpole's lesson and had not built a base of support in Parliament. Unable to draft a new Cabinet, he and the King were forced to surrender; Pelham and his colleagues returned on their own terms. Seeking to pull the teeth of the opposition, Pelham constructed his ministry on a "broad bottom" basis including as many factions as possible to gain the widest possible support. The only major group left out of the ministry was the faction around the heir to the throne, the Prince of Wales.

The Conclusion of the War. Pelham's first responsibility was to bring the war to an end. While England had been putting down an internal revolt the war had gone badly for her and her allies on the continent. The French capitalized on early victories and occupied Brussels and the Austrian Netherlands, while Britain's allies of Austria and Sardinia suffered defeat in southern Europe. Only the death of the Emperor Charles VII (Charles Albert of Bavaria) early in 1745 offered any hope for a negotiated settlement by opening the imperial throne once more to a Habsburg candidate, Maria Theresa's husband, Francis of Lorraine. Indeed English success in arms existed only in one theatre, but one prophetically important — North America.

The heavy continental military obligations in the wars against Louis XIV and again in the present war had prevented the commitment of substantial forces against Spain in the western hemisphere. Although early disappointments led the British to abandon campaigns in the West Indies, the war went well in the north when, in June 1745, a small expedition of New England colonists supported by British naval forces had captured Louisburg, the great French fortress on Cape Breton Island, which was the key to control of the St. Lawrence River, the gateway to French Canada. The capture of Louisburg was more of an embarrassment than an asset; it retarded peace efforts, for the French could not rest until it was retaken. The British public on the other hand were so overjoyed at this victory that its retention became obligatory.

In 1747 Pelham suddenly called parliamentary elections to take advantage of his newly-found support. The solid majority he won made it possible for him to risk an unpopular peace settlement. French successes in the Low Countries and elsewhere gave little prospect of military success in Europe, though the naval victories of Anson and Hawke in the New World did reassert British supremacy on the seas. France, too, saw reason to negotiate a peace, not least because of a serious famine and a major fiscal crisis in 1747. The peace of Aix-la-Chapelle which followed in 1748 was essentially a recognition of the exhaustion of the belligerents. British ambitions for Canada were temporarily abandoned as Louisburg was returned to France. Both countries recognized that the surcease was not permanent.

Pelham and Leicester House. For the remaining years of his ministry, Pelham strove to maintain his political strength in Parliament while restoring stability to the King's finances and prosperity to the economy. His first effort was to reduce taxes. He did so by renegotiating the government's debts at lower interest rates and by drastically reducing the size of the fleet and the army. In the political sphere, the coalition of parties Pelham had put together proved effective. The main threat to his regime came from the men who gathered around the King's son, Frederick, the Prince of Wales and heir apparent to the throne, and met at his residence, Leceister House. Ever since he had broken with his father, George II, in 1736 the Prince of Wales had sought to maintain an independent political base. In spite of financial difficulties, he had built up a formidable circle of advisors in the late years of the Walpole regime. Pelham had weaned most of them back in building his coalition ministry in 1746. But the advancing age of the king (who was sixty-three in 1746) made Frederick's succession inevitable and Pelham patiently negotiated through intermediaries to prepare himself for this eventuality. The unexpected death of the Prince in 1751 dramatically altered the situation. A resumption of Walpolean tranquillity characterized England in the early 1750s until another early death — that of Henry Pelham in March 1754 — brought it all to an end. George II was perhaps the most sincere and realistic mourner when he commented, "I shall have no more peace."

THE INTELLECTUAL AND RELIGIOUS MILIEU OF THE HANOVERIANS

The Age of Reason. At the same time that Britain's stature in European affairs grew, she participated fully in another European phenomenon, the Enlightenment. As the old religious controversies subsided and the

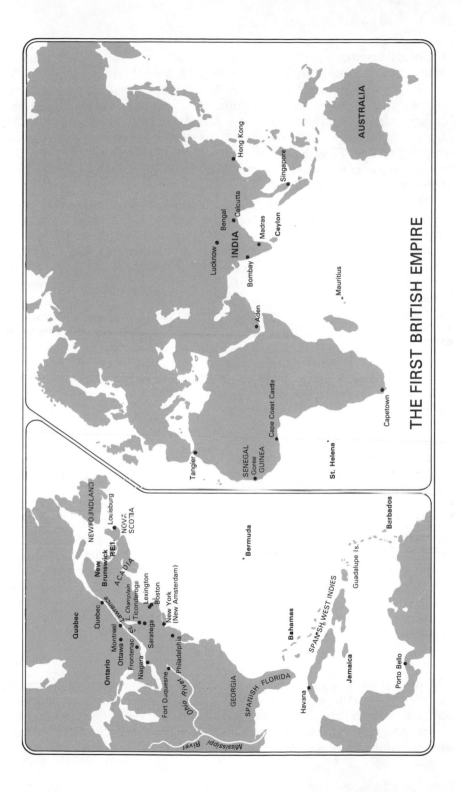

THE FIRST BRITISH EMPIRE

AUSTRALIA

Hong Kong

Singapore

Calcutta
Bengal
INDIA
Lucknow
Madras
Ceylon
Bombay

Mauritius

Aden

Cape Coast Castle

SENEGAL
Goree
GUINEA

Capetown

St. Helena

Tangier

NEWFOUNDLAND
Louisburg
NOVA
SCOTIA

New
Brunswick
P.E.I.
ACADIA

Quebec
Quebec
Montreal
L. Champlain
Ticonderoga
Lexington
Boston
Ottawa
Frontenac
Saratoga
New York
(New Amsterdam)
Ontario
Niagara
Philadelphia
Fort Duquesne
Ohio River
GEORGIA
SPANISH FLORIDA

Bermuda

Bahamas
SPANISH WEST INDIES
Guadalupe Is.
Barbados

Havana
Jamaica
Porto Bello

Mississippi River

ideological contests abated, a new tone and confident spirit characterized the publications of the major British literary figures. The
periodical essay spawned by Joseph Addison and Richard Steele in the
Spectator (1711) had countless imitators well into the middle of the
century when it inspired Johnson's *Rambler* (1750) and *Idler* (1758).
Elegant, devastating satire reached its peak in the mock epics of
Alexander Pope. Elegiac pastoral verse glorified the serenity and natural
beauty of the countryside, a retreat from the glamour and artificiality
of the city.

History as a guide and means of instruction took on a new
importance as a subject for laborious tomes and learned essays. It
reached its peak in the phenomenally popular six-volume history of
England (1763) by the eminent Scottish philosopher David Hume,
which set a standard not to be challenged for a century to come. Hume
also epitomized another aspect of the intellectual life of the Age of
Reason. His several philosophical treatises made all knowledge empirical
and struck at the very foundation of religion. Seeking to create a
system of moral philosophy that would accomplish for the world of
ideas what Newton had accomplished for the world of science, he
stands at the intellectual watershed of the eighteenth century.

The refined elegance of Pope and Hume were not the only models
for eighteenth-century writers. The savage irony of Jonathan Swift in
Gulliver's Travels (1726) attracted a wide audience as did the more
conventional but nonetheless compelling imagination of Daniel Defoe
in *Robinson Crusoe* (1719). Skill in expression was not limited to one
political faction — the dominant Whig propagandists of the Hanoverian
period found their match in the powerful Toryism of the most
celebrated literary figure of the mid-eighteenth century, Samuel
Johnson.

The new quest for knowledge, the growth of a leisured class, the
general increase in prosperity — all resulted in a vast and sustained
increase in the press. Whether practical manuals for farmers or Justices
of the Peace, the newly developed novel aimed at readers of both sexes,
books catering to hobbies and diversions of the most heterogenous
kind, or treatises on topics such as economics, raising fish, or guides for
the grand tour, the emphasis was on novelty and practicality. The most
notable omission was the absence of that emphasis on religion which
had been so characteristic of the preceding century.

The Church in the Early Hanoverian Period. The vehement efforts of
the clergy and the high church party to preserve their monopoly of
political offices and representation in Parliament, their unrelenting
efforts to inhibit and restrict the Dissenters, their churches and schools,
their strenuous support of the Tories, and their equivocal attitude to

the Revolution and the Protestant succession — all were liabilities for the church with the new regime. Only the Whigs' patent weakness both in the Parliament and in the country had prevented them from completing the repeal of the Test and Corporation Acts in 1718 and the reduction of the universities to a place of complete subservience. The opposition of the Anglican archbishop to the proposed statutory repeals condemned him to twenty years of political neglect and isolation. In 1717 Benjamin Hoadley, who had been made a bishop for his services as a political pamphleteer, delivered a famous sermon before the King in which he attacked the very basis of the church's authority by denying its institutional signficance and the role of the priest as intermediary between God and the worshipper. The furor that resulted both in Convocation and the press gave the crown the excuse to prorogue the Convocation which was not permitted to meet again until 1855. The hiatus removed the potential vehicle for badly-needed church reforms.

The pattern and size of the dioceses was woefully uneven, but the income to support the bishops and their offices was even more unequal. In countless parishes the income was insufficient to maintain a clergyman with the consequence that many pulpits lay vacant. Not unfrequently the incumbents were pluralists, holding several benefices at once. In 1704 Queen Anne gave back to the church the fee exacted from each cleric as he entered into his benefice, for use by commissioners to raise the income of the poorest livings. This did something to mitigate the most pressing cases but the essential inequities remained, especially among the bishops whose annual incomes ranged from a low of £450 at Bristol to a high of £7,000 at Canterbury. Many of the duties of the see fell personally on the bishop who was not authorized to employ deputies or suffragans. The requirement for bishops to attend the House of Lords kept most of them absent from their dioceses for much of the year. Some of the bishops either because of infirmity or neglect did not make the return to their dioceses as often or as long as they should. The uneven size of the dioceses created exceptional burdens for some bishops. Lincoln, the largest diocese, had its 1312 parishes — a marked difference from Carlisle which had only 100. Edmund Gibson, Bishop of London and Walpole's ecclesiastical advisor, proposed a number of schemes to correct the worst abuses and to enable the church to carry out its duties. But they all foundered either on the Scylla of ministerial indifference or the Charybdis of lay hostility. Although the civil disabilities of the Dissenters were not removed until 1828 they managed to participate in the political process because a series of indemnity acts relieved them of the statutory penalties. This was the Hanoverian *modus vivendi*, a compromise that satisfied few but was tolerable to most.

Wesley and the Methodist Revival. The church had fallen into such a state of lassitude that it was unable to meet the spiritual needs of the people. Sermons were cold and formal and did little to evoke enthusiasm and religious fervor. The writings of latitudinarian clergymen such as Benjamin Hoadley, the deists, and mystical writers such as the non-juror William Law did little to reinforce a devotion to the established church. Methodism arose within the church to fill this void. The founder and leader was John Wesley. Ordained in the Church of England, a graduate of Oxford, member there of a severe, ascetic society, he went with James Oglethorthe, the founder of Georgia, to that colony in 1735 and on the voyage became acquainted with the Moravians. On his return to England he was deeply influenced by an eminent member of that sect, Peter Böhler, and embraced those tenets which became the foundation of Methodism: the doctrine of justification by faith, the belief that every man existed in a state of damnation until the moment of illumination, and the recognition that Christ had expiated man's sins. Wesley and the band of followers he attracted from the regular clergy preached the new doctrine with fervor and success. Their objective was to create Methodist societies as churches within the church to rekindle religious enthusiasm and commitment among Anglicans. Denied a hearing from the pulpit, the Methodists turned to preaching in fields and any place where they could gain a hearing. In 1739 they created their own chapels, and in 1741 Wesley instituted lay preachers. Those new missionaries were dedicated to saving souls and found an enthusiastic reception among the lower classes, especially in those places where the established church did not reach. In Wales, for example, the great majority of the population joined their chapels.

Though Wesley did his best to keep the societies within the Anglican tradition he finally broke with the Anglican church in 1783 by appointing a bishop to supervise the Methodists in America. In 1784 he began ordaining clergy for Scotland. The Methodists offered the hope of salvation to those whose lot was most unfortunate and miserable. They were responsible for a general revival of religious feeling in England, both within the Church of England where Anglicans were revitalized and reinvigorated, and outside the established church as well.

TOWN AND COUNTRY IN JOHNSON'S ENGLAND

London and Westminster. The jewel of a revitalized Britain was London. When Samuel Johnson, the great lexicographer and pundit and archetype devotee of London first saw the great metropolis in 1737 he must have found much to impress him. The great city of more than a half million people, it was ten times larger than Bristol which was

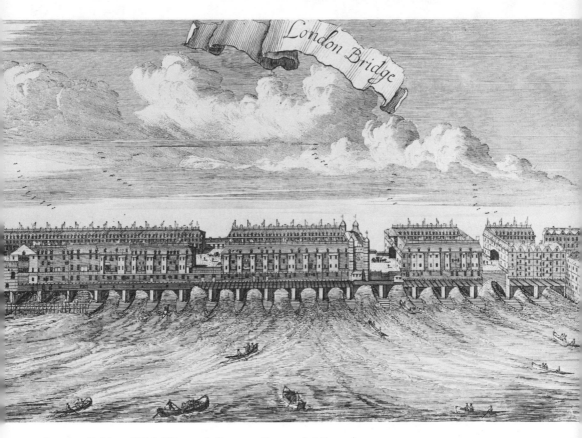

London Bridge, 1720 (Kenneth Spencer Research Library).

England's second largest city. The easternmost part was notable for the bustling Pool of London, the inner harbor which was then the main port for commerce. Rising above it stood the Tower of London, imposing in its Norman splendor, a prominent landmark from the river. If Johnson made his way west from the Tower the next object to command his attention was old London Bridge, located opposite the splendid new cathedral of St. Paul's, Wren's masterpiece which dominated the City skyline. The bridge, the only span across the lower Thames until Westminster bridge was constructed in 1750, had been built over completely. It presented a quaint sight of ramshackle old buildings, of varying heights and style, stuck fast together and hanging perilously over the water, with a bustling traffic crowded into the narrow passage remaining between the houses.

Below the bridge, to the east, scores of tenements, warehouses, and

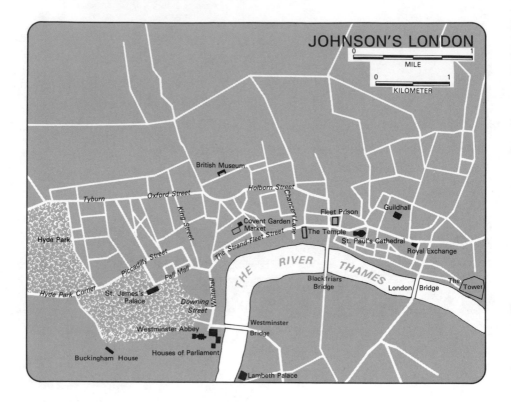

wharves crowded the river's edge. Above the bridge there were most impressive structures to behold. The palaces and great houses of the nobility and wealthy on the north bank extended westward to a bend in the Thames where one found Whitehall Palace and the palace of Westminster, the seat of the Parliament and the law courts. After crossing the bridge Johnson would have made his way through Stocksmarket to St. Paul's Churchyard, past the church "already so black with coal-smoke that it has lost half its elegance," then down Ludgate Hill to the Fleet out of the City at Temple Bar. The streets of London were reckoned by a German writer as "the finest in Europe", full of taverns and pothouses, houses and shops "where the choicest merchandise from the four quarters of the globe is exposed to the sight of the passers-by [and] a stranger might spend whole days, without ever feeling bored, examining these wonderful goods." This was the part of London Johnson especially loved, where he lived, worked, and drank and passed his hours in memorable conversation. The bookshops and printers and the attendant writers were so numerous in this district that one short passage called Grub Street gave its name to a whole genre and period of the English press. North of the Strand the area was filled with fine mansions and was especially marked by Covent Garden, the square laid out by Inigo Jones a century earlier and even in Johnson's time a market for flowers, fruits, and vegetables.

Passing into Charing Cross Johnson could have seen the Admiralty and the famous Banqueting Hall, which was all that remained of old Whitehall palace after it burned in 1698. Ahead lay the palace of Westminster, seat of the Parliament and law courts — a conglomeration of buildings, chapels, houses, meeting halls, and offices, adapted to a multiplicity of uses over many centuries. The most impressive was Westminster Hall which dated to the time of William Rufus, but it was so hedged about with small structures that only the upper portion and roof were exposed to view. Even Westminster Abbey and the parish church of St. Margaret were crowded about, though the lofty towers and the exquisite tracery of Henry VII's chapel were a sight to delight the eye.

Life in London. The appearance of the King's principal London residence, St. James's Palace, was not so attractive; a squat, drab structure which dated from the time of Henry VIII, it was about a quarter of a mile northwest of the Abbey. It was adjacent to the Mall, and a series of parks to the south and west furnished an attractive prospect and a popular place for relaxation and recreation for the inhabitants who lived nearby. The most impressive house in the park was that of the Duke of Buckingham. To the west, at the end of Hyde Park, lay Kensington Palace, acquired by William III in order to escape the damp and fog of the river. Villages and estates generally occupied the land west and north of Westminster and these areas remained predominantly rural into the next century. The streets of the town were of all sorts, some "dirty, narrow, and badly built; others again are wide and straight, bordered with fine houses [and] most of the streets are wonderfully well lighted." This was not so true of the parks, and the public which thronged them on Sundays tried to be back in the town before dark to avoid becoming a target for the highwaymen who frequented the lanes, one of whom at least on one occasion held up the King at pistol point in his own garden.

Beyond the great houses and royal parks, especially in the City, there was squalor, poverty, and filth. Some of those who flocked to London for employment found seasonal work only, serving the needs of the great families when they came into town for the winter season. Much of the year these less fortunate migrants were unemployed and lived by their wits. Robbery and petty thievery were commonplace. Living conditions were wretched; the water was foul because it was taken straight out of the river at the bridge by "a curious machine which turns in either direction, according to the tide, so that it is always in use." The consequence was regular epidemics of cholera and other water-borne diseases until the middle of the nineteenth century. Life expectancy was short. A survey made in 1716 showed that of 1200 children born in a parish, three-fourths were dead within the year. Parish officials consigned the poor to workhouses where conditions were even more abominable. In mid-century another survey revealed that of 2,239 children who passed through the workhouse only 168 were alive at the end of five years. The large criminal class and the ever-present press gangs used to provide recruits for the navy and colonists for the Americas made life so dangerous that the young James Watt who lived in London in 1783 hardly left his house during the entire time of his residence there. Bull-baiting, cock-fighting, and public hangings were the favorite entertainments, beer and gin the standard beverages. The latter was so cheap and unlicensed dram shops so numerous — by 1736, 6,000 to 7,000 in London alone — that consumption arose to unprecedented heights. The city was in literal danger of extinction as the oppressed lower classes drowned their sorrows and forgot their miseries in alcohol.

Country Life. The rest of England was rural. Few towns were greater than 10,000 in population, most much smaller — in reality mere villages and market places. The leading families of provincial towns were professional men and merchants whose scale of living was comfortable rather than ostentatious. Rural (landed) wealth was centered in the aristocracy and gentry whose great country houses rose in stark contrast to the humble, often squalid homes of the rural agricultural laborers and the working poor in the towns. The cottagers who found work were fortunate. Often the only support for a family was that of carding and spinning wool, an employment chiefly reserved for women and children. Until the mid-eighteenth century poor families could eke out a living from the commons, cutting wood, raising geese and perhaps some livestock, taking odd jobs, and poaching. The great series of enclosure acts in the latter part of the century deprived them of these means of subsistence.

The artisan class flourished in the towns. Cabinet makers, shoe-makers, tailors, butchers, cobblers, smiths, and drapers populated the shops. The market towns were specially engaged in serving the local landowners and providing for their amusement and comfort. In the west and the northeast of England the wool trade was their main support. Marked by the absence of paved streets, police, and good water and other amenities, the towns were not improved until the

Needlework panel of a formal garden, 1700 (Montacute House, National Trust).

second half of the century. In the smaller towns, the parish was often the unit of government, with the church responsible for what little education the lower and middle classes received. As roads and communications improved and the nation increased in wealth and population, the county centers began to take on some of the attributes of the metropolis. Newspapers were founded, theaters opened, book-sellers established, and concert assembly rooms erected for the entertainment of local society. But even to the end of the century the scale of towns remained small, their diversions limited.

SUGGESTIONS FOR FURTHER READING

Dorothy Marshall, *Eighteenth Century England* (2nd ed., 1974) and John B. Owen, *The Eighteenth Century* (1973) are reliable surveys. Basil Williams, *The Whig Supremacy 1714-1760* (2nd ed., 1962) provides more detail. The most comprehensive is Wolfgang Michael, *Englische Geschichte im achtzehnten Jahrhundert* (5 vols., 1896-1945) of which the first two volumes have been translated as *England under George I* (1936-39). Still useful and containing essays on many aspects of English life is A. S. Turberville, ed., *Johnson's England* (2 vols., 1933). Many excellent surveys of various aspects of the nation have been published including, Dorothy Marshall, *The English Poor in the Eighteenth Century* (1926), and *English People in the Eighteenth Century* (1956), M. Dorothy George, *London Life in the Eighteenth Century* (1951) and *England in Transition* (1931); T. S. Ashton, *An Economic History of England: the Eighteenth Century* (1959) and *Economic Fluctuations in England, 1700-1800* (1959); Gordon Mingay, *English Landed Society in the Eighteenth Century* (1963) and *The Gentry* (1976); and Edward Hughes, *North Country Life in the Eighteenth Century* (2 vols., 1952-65). Peter D. G. Thomas, *The House of Commons in the Eighteenth Century* (1971) and Sheila Lambert, *Bills and Acts* (1971) report on aspects of parliamentary history.

Political biography is noticeably rich. J. H. Plumb's magisterial *Sir Robert Walpole* (2 vols., 1956) is a good beginning. One should also consult Basil Williams, *Stanhope* (1932) and *Carteret and Newcastle* (1943), Ray Kelch, *Newcastle. A Duke Without Money* (1974), Reed Browning, *The Duke of Newcastle* (1975), Robert Halsband, *Lord Hervey* (1973), and John Wilkes, *A Whig in Power: the Political Career of Henry Pelham* (1964).

Specialized monographs of value include Archibald S. Foord, *His Magesty's Opposition, 1714-1830* (1964), Isaac Kramnick, *Bolingbroke and His Circle* (1968), Robert Robson, *The Attorney in Eighteenth Century England* (1959), Kenneth Ellis, *The Post Office in the Eighteenth Century* (1958), Ralph Davis, *The Rise of the English Shipping Industry in the Seventeenth and Eighteenth Centuries* (1962), W. R. Ward, *The English Land Tax in the Eighteenth Century* (1953) and *Georgian Oxford* (1958), and John B. Owen, *The Rise of the Pelhams* (1957). For intellectual life one may note Basil Willey, *The Eighteenth Century Background* (1957), Gerald R. Cragg, *Reason and Authority in the Eighteenth Century* (1964), A. R. Humphreys, *The Augustan World: Life and Letters in the Eighteenth Century* (1954), and Caroline Robbins, *The Eighteenth Century Commonwealthman* (1959). John M. Beattie, *The English Court in the Reign of George I* (1967) is a definitive study. For a contemporary account of court life one should read John, Lord Hervey, *Some Materials Towards Memoirs of the Reign of King George II* (ed. Romney Sedgwick, 3 vols., 1931), *The Political Journal of Geoge Bubb Dodington* (ed. J. Carswell and L. A. Dralle, 1965), *The Complete Letters of Lady Mary Wortley Montague* (ed. R. Halsband, 3 vols., 1965-67), and Horace Walpole, *Memoirs of the Last Ten Years of the Reign of George the Second* (3 vols., 1847).

10

The Problem
of the Americas

1754-1783

The four decades that followed the Hanoverian succession may be seen in marked contrast to the rest of the century. The country was at peace for most of the period, and the English nation showed ample signs of its new prosperity and international eminence. Great houses in the neo-classical Palladian style sprang up around the country; most of them were based upon landed wealth, frequently increased in not a few cases by advantageous marriages with wealthy merchant or banking families. The scale could be modest though elegant like the Earl of Burlington's superb summer house at Chiswick, the model for Thomas Jefferson's Monticello in Virginia, but the great English Whig grandees could settle for nothing less than palatial residences like the Duke of Newcastle's Claremont, or the Marquis of Rockingham's Wentworth Woodhouse, a mighty edifice with an imposing facade some 800 feet in length.

The interiors of the houses were no less marvellous. Princely libraries were often an important feature; in some cases they were the result of the expertise and interest of the owner, such as the Earl of Sunderland's incomparable collection of incunabula (books printed before 1500) which found its way to the Duke of Marlborough's

Blenheim Palace. Equally important was the vast collection of 14,000 documents, 7,500 volumes of manuscripts, 50,000 books, 41,000 prints and 350,000 pamphlets collected by his political and bibliophile rival, the Earl of Oxford and his son. Sculpture, paintings, and tapestries acquired by the young men of fashion as they made the grand tour on the continent adorned the salons and dining rooms. The tastes and acquisitions of the aristocracy were copied on a grander scale by George III, as evidenced by the 54 paintings and 142 drawings by Canaletto in the royal art collection and his impressive library which was given later by George IV to the British Museum. Exotic birds and rare plants adorned the stately houses while citrus trees blossomed and bore fruit in the orangeries. Britain's increasing traffic with the Orient made Chinese motifs one of the dominant design elements in decorating throughout the century. Chinese wallpaper, furniture, and *objets d'art* were universally admired; porcelain dinnerware specially made in China, often in patterns bearing the family crest or coat of arms, graced the great dining tables. Even when the art of making fine china spread to England in the later eighteenth century the Chinese models were more often than not the basis for the patterns created by English designers.

The manners and fashions of the wealthy were copied at the lower social levels insofar as incomes permitted. The libraries might not contain so many rare books but they were generally stuffed with row after row of devotional works, sermons, and political pamphlets, usually bound up and titled in the same "house" binding. If porcelain could be had only by the greater families, the introduction of a fine cream-colored earthenware by Josiah Wedgwood about 1765 and high grade stoneware by Josiah Spode a little later — both usually decorated in Chinese-style patterns — gave a new refinement and quality to English tables. The engravings of Hogarth and Rowlandson and the mezzotint reproductions of well-known paintings adorned the walls of more modest houses.

Brussells lace, French silk, and Italian velvet were much appreciated in London. Clothing was ornate and full, and increased in sumptuousness with embroidery on the sleeves and coats of the gentlemen and on the dresses of the ladies. By mid-eighteenth century men wore elaborate wigs often tied or knotted at the nape of the neck with the side hair in horizontal roll curls lying one above the other and covering the ears. The lower classes wore wool or linen and the men frequently wore leather breeches. Often they did not possess a change of clothing and wore what they owned until it literally disintegrated. The diet was a heavy one: for the wealthy an exhausting diet of meat dishes and pastries with fruit when in season; for the poor the daily fare was only bread or gruel or soup, with a little meat once or twice a week. The lower classes drank beer or ale and the upper classes drank wine. French claret had been displaced by port and sherry after the Methuen treaties with Portugal in 1703, though French brandy continued to be enjoyed by the wealthy. These tastes and customs were not unique to England. Increasingly they were replicated, with some local modifications, in the English colonies of North America.

THE SEVEN YEARS WAR

The North American Colonies and the Problem of Imperial Defense. In the mid-eighteenth century the rivalry of England and France dominated both Europe and the colonial areas that were under their influence. France possessed important holdings in the Caribbean, Africa, India, and above all, in North America, from Quebec and the St. Lawrence, through the Great Lakes, and down the Mississippi to Louisiana. These possessions and the competition for trade in these areas, in Europe, and in the Spanish colonies brought England and France into frequent conflict. In North America the English colonies were undergoing growing pains. The population of the British colonies grew from 250,000 in 1700 to perhaps one and a half millions in 1750; the settlers penetrated further west, across the Alleghenies into the great river valleys of the Ohio and Mississippi. The French had similar ambitions and though their number was not so great they had visions of linking their two colonies of Quebec and Louisiana and forming a great empire in the mid-North American continent. The expansion of the two empires created friction in Acadia (later Novia Scotia), along the St. Lawrence, around the Great Lakes, along the Ohio, and at isolated points on the Mississippi. Georgia found itself in frequent dispute with Spanish Florida.

The importance of the colonies to the economy and welfare of England and vice versa was mutually acknowledged. North American exports just to England were estimated to be worth over £5,000,000 by the 1740s and employed as many as 3,000 ships, of which half belonged to the colonists. The management of the colonies was the responsibility of the Secretary for the Southern Department and the Board of Trade and Plantations. As Newcastle held the former office for a record thirty years, he had an increasingly preponderant influence and also a considerable knowledge of the situation in the North Americas. He concentrated upon patronage matters, hamstrung the Board, and yet gave little attention to maintaining a tight control over colonial governments. The result was a laissez-faire attitude which had encouraged the growing colonial independence. Newcastle, who had succeeded his brother Henry Pelham at the Treasury in 1754, was not unmindful of the colonists' demands to curb French expansion in America, but was reluctant to engage England so soon in another expensive war. Events in America, however, soon took the initiative out of his hands. In 1753 the French governor of Canada began the construction of a series of forts to control the Ohio River, including Ft. Duquesne at the present day site of Pittsburgh. When in 1754 the French repulsed an attack led by the young colonial officer George Washington, an English response was needed. Two regiments were sent from England under the command of Edward Braddock early in 1755, only to be repulsed again by the French near the same fort. When the French acted to reinforce their troops in Canada the English sent a fleet to intercept the French transports in the spring of 1755. The fleet failed in the attempt but set up ·a blockade of the French Canadian ports. This effort and the expulsion of the French colonists in Acadia were the only accomplishments of the year to balance heavy losses. Nevertheless England had laid down the gauntlet and a formal declaration of war was now only a question of time.

The Diplomatic Revolution and the Advancement of Pitt. In Europe the situation was unstable. Austria, England's traditional ally, still smarted at the loss of Silesia to Prussia and was anxious to obtain satisfaction. England and, even more, Holland were bent on keeping the peace, a goal which was clearly not in harmony with Austrian ambitions. George II feared that if war were to break out Hanover would be caught in a vise between Prussia and France and thus he sought Austria's continuing support to counter this threat. In an effort to garner more allies, England signed a subsidy treaty with Hesse-Cassel in 1755 and a defensive alliance with Russia to counter the threat of Prussia. The Anglo-Russian treaty neutralized Prussia and made that country less useful to France as an ally. Austria meantime had been making tenders to France in order to build up sufficient strength to defeat Prussia. France, whose continental ambitions had waned in the face of her increasing imperial interests, no longer viewed the Habsburgs as rivals but now saw them as potential allies. When Frederick II of Prussia was persuaded to sign the Convention of Westminster with England in January 1756, the allies of both countries, France and Russia, were understandably annoyed. In the case of Russia, it was because Empress Elizabeth had seen the Anglo-Russian treaty as a preliminary to an attack on Prussia. France reacted by acceding to Austria's invitation for a defensive alliance with Austria in May 1756. When the Dutch promised France their neutrality in any conflict, the alliance of England, Austria, and Holland which dated back to William III was at an end.

Hostilities in Europe began in May when the French threatened to cross the Channel and then seized Minorca. This disaster was followed by the loss of Oswego in America which opened the way for further

French advances into the middle of the continent. The attack by Frederick II on Saxony turned the war in Europe into a general conflict, the prospect of which Newcastle and George II had so ardently tried to prevent. The atrocities perpetrated by the French in India in the infamous Black Hole of Calcutta were the last straw. This series of humiliating defeats had precipitated the fall of Newcastle and brought about the formation of a new ministry to prosecute the war under the joint direction of William Pitt and Newcastle in May 1757.

The Seven Years' War. Pitt was not able to influence the conduct of the war (also known as the French and Indian War) in 1757 materially, and the advantage that year lay with France. British attacks on Rochefort in France and the French fortress of Louisbourg in Canada both failed. England's ally, Frederick II, suffered a disastrous defeat at the hands of the Austrians; George II's son, the Duke of Cumberland, surrendered Hanover and its adjoining territories to the French. Everything now hinged on the campaign of 1758. Intent upon America, Pitt was yet persuaded of the necessity for providing some succor for Frederick II in Germany. A major treaty with Prussia was signed in April 1758 under which England subsidized a new army in northern Germany that drove the French out of Hanover and Westphalia. This cover at Prussia's rear enabled Frederick II to withstand the combined onslaughts of the Austrians and Russia while yet retaining possession of Saxony and Silesia. Pitt's main concern was in North America. There he planned a three-pronged attack: on Louisbourg, on Montreal or Quebec from New York and on Fort Duquesne from Philadelphia. Though the second attack miscarried, Bradstreet's attack on Frontenac gave the English the control of Lake Ontario and thus the possession of a ring of French fortresses around Canada.

The great year of the war was 1759. This "year of victories" was the consequence of Pitt's great stress on the revitalization of the navy so that England was able to establish naval superiority in virtually every theatre. This was particularly crucial in Canada because Quebec was weak in foodstuffs and materials, and any lack of resupply rendered the city more vulnerable to attack. A thrust through New York resulted in the taking of Niagara, Ticonderoga, and finally the control of Lake Champlain. An expedition along the St. Lawrence under the dashing General Wolfe ended in the celebrated capture of Quebec in September. Another expedition took Guadeloupe in the West Indies. The taking of Goree in West Africa at the end of 1758 had cut off the main source of slaves for the French islands in the West Indies. In Europe the defeat of French fleets off Gibraltar and Brest averted the threat of a French invasion of England. The year 1760 was anticlimactic, notable only for the capture of Montreal which placed all of French Canada in English

George III (National Portrait Gallery).

hands. In a more distant theatre, India, successes in 1760 capped a series of confrontations with the French dating back to 1756. India was now virtually an English preserve.

KING GEORGE III AND HIS MINISTERS

The Accession of George III. The death of George II in 1760 and the accession of his grandson George III (1760-1820) undercut Pitt's position. The new King placed his confidence in the Earl of Bute, long a member of the entourage of his father and mother. Pitt wanted to continue the war to ensure that England had all the bargaining power she needed at the peace table. He even proposed a pre-emptive attack on Spain in anticipation of her entry into the war on the side of France. But George III and his advisors were anxious to bring the war to an end and public opinion and the Cabinet supported their view. Pitt resigned angrily and though Spain did enter the war as he had guessed, Bute was able to conclude a peace with France and Spain at Paris in November 1762. Though Bute won less than Pitt had demanded, the fruits were still considerable. All of French Canada and the lands west of the North American colonies were granted to England together with the return of Minorca, with its strategic importance in the Mediterranean, Senegal in Africa and four additional islands in the West Indies. From Spain England received Florida, thus securing the southern border of the colonies; England gave up Havana, captured in 1762, in exchange. France was allowed to retain her rich sugar islands in the West Indies and fishing rights off Newfoundland and in the Gulf of St. Lawrence, concessions that were to remain a bone of contention between the two countries until 1904.

The accession of George III, only twenty-two years of age, caused a great change in English politics and introduced a period of turmoil and instability that was to last in some respects down to 1784. George III was the first native-born sovereign since Queen Anne. He gloried in the fact that his heart was truly English. Raised in the circle of Leicester House, long the center of opposition to George II and his ministers, he saw the late King as the prisoner of the Whigs who had dominated the ministries of his two predecessors. He was determined to free the crown from their corrupt influences and to rule without regard for party or clique. In these aims he was encouraged and advised by a Scottish peer, the Earl of Bute, his closest confidant, but unfortunately a man without either the strength or the wisdom to implement his ideas. Pressed by the King, Bute took office and ultimately served for a short time as First Lord of the Treasury. Working to eliminate first Pitt and then Newcastle and their followers, he bought the services of the unscrupulous Henry Fox to shepherd the peace through Parliament.

Finding himself beset on all sides he made a hasty resignation in April 1763, leaving the King alone to face the politicians.

Party Politics in the Mid-Eighteenth Century. The situation with which the young, inexperienced King had to contend in the 1760s was far different than that which in 1714 faced his great-grandfather, George I. The forty-five years of Whig dominance had broken and to a large extent destroyed the old Tory party. The Whigs in turn, contesting with each other for office, had broken up into a series of factions, none of which could be dignified with the title of "party." The majority of the Commons was made up of unaffiliated country gentlemen. Traditionally supporters of the King's government, the gentry were, if anything, more Tory than Whig in sympathy, and refused to be organized into a disciplined party. A smaller group consisted of the civil servants, officers, pensioners and other placeholders whose livelihood depended upon the favor of the King. They could be relied upon to support whatever politicians were in office. The other members were clustered around a few great men, aristocratic grandees of substantial wealth and electoral influence, who led the factions that jostled for the direction of the King's affairs. It was from among these last groupings that the King was forced to choose his ministers. George III found them almost uniformly repugnant.

Although the old parties no longer existed as they had in the early eighteenth century, the names Whig and Tory survived, and many families and individuals identified themselves with one or the other. To a considerable extent the survival of the names had meaning because each stood for an attachment to a certain set of principles. The old Tory loyalties to the crown, church, and established social order were strong. In a similar fashion the association with the city and mercantile interests, the sympathy for the Dissenters, and the support for land campaigns in Europe were regarded as Whig doctrines. With the stigma of Jacobitism finally erased after the failure of the rebellion of 1745 and the end of the Whig supremacy, a new Toryism evolved once again under George III. Some historians saw its origin in the following attracted by the elder Pitt, its formal founding in "the King's friends," or placemen, organized to support the ministry of Lord North, and its full emergence under the younger Pitt.

The Uncertainty of the 1760s. George III had to contend with a situation where old parties were crumbling and new political alignments were emerging. He has often been accused of trying to act as his own chief minister in the manner of the later Stuarts, reversing the trend towards parliamentary government which had been evolving since the death of William III. Most historians now believe that he was faced with a power vacuum; the Whig leadership was old and discredited, and there was no viable, organized party to supplant it and govern the Parliament. George stepped into the breech, but never with the intention of subverting the constitution. He was a man of unimpeachable integrity and dedicated to the interests of his country and his people. He gave every possible support to those ministers who gained his confidence. However, until a new system of political management was created to supplant that employed by Walpole and the Pelhams, the government was too often weak, uncertain, and in confusion.

The King required a prime minister whom he could trust. This minister in turn should be able to lead the Commons, should possess the financial expertise of a Walpole, and should be able to command the allegiance of more than one faction. In the 1760s no one filled these criteria completely.

After the resignation of Bute the King reluctantly gave the leadership of the ministry to George Grenville, an earnest, knowledge-able administrator with considerable expertise in finance, and a man devoted to the Commons. But Grenville was cold and tactless and soon so affronted the King and influential politicians that his removal became imperative. Using his uncle, the Duke of Cumberland, as his political broker the King turned in 1765 to the young Marquis of Rockingham who claimed to inherit the mantle of the Whig party. Rockingham, whose greatest contribution was his promotion of his young Irish secretary, Edmund Burke, lacked the ability and the experience to guide the ministry and manage the Parliament. His following was limited and too many influential leaders were alienated and hostile. The King withheld his full confidence and as soon as he found a convenient excuse, which came in 1766 after the ministry had barely a year in office, he dismissed them.

George had some time earlier become reconciled to Pitt, a man who had been very close to Leicester House in the 1750s. The two had many things in common — both prided themselves on being true patriots, both disdained the pettiness and self-serving of faction, and both believed that government should be above party. Pitt accepted the charge to form a government on his own terms and proceeded to put together a ministry that amazed and confounded his contemporaries. With ministers acting independently of each other, indeed virtually unknown to each other, only a very strong leader could have made a coherent whole of it. Pitt took a peerage as the Earl of Chatham, thereby removing himself from the Commons, the seat of his power. Moreover, his health was broken and he lacked the stamina to direct this curious assemblage. Even worse he fell into a state of profound depression and retired to his country house where he remained incommunicado for more than a year. The young Duke of Grafton

*The Wiremaster and His Puppets (Earl of Bute as the power behind the scenes),
1767 (Kenneth Spencer Research Library).*

gradually assumed nominal control though he was unequal to the task. But out of duty to the King and an obligation to see through certain projects the ministry had initiated — notably a renewal of the East India Company's charter — Grafton somehow held the government together until 1770. In that year his Chancellor of the Exchequer and George's childhood friend, Frederick, Lord North, took command and restored order to the King's government.

The Beginnings of Radical Agitation for Reform. The succession of weak ministries in the 1760s had to contend with unusually agitated times in the body politic. The dislocations caused by the war had to be mended. The war left a heavy burden of debt and a continuing need for imperial protection. Grenville who pursued a severe policy of economy and retrenchment was determined to shift the burden of imperial defense onto the colonists who benefited from it. He first tried to close certain loopholes in the customs duties that enabled the colonists to trade freely with the French West Indies. This alone was sufficient to raise a strong outcry in America. When he imposed a stamp duty on newspapers and legal documents, he provoked active opposition in the colonies — petitions, a refusal to pay debts owing to British merchants, and a general boycott of British goods. Riots occurred in the colonies and colonial leaders even considered joint action in protest. Rockingham, on succeeding Grenville, repealed the stamp tax but reaffirmed Parliament's right to tax the colonies. Charles Townshend, the Chancellor of the Exchequer under Chatham, tried again in 1767 with duties at the ports on glass, lead, paper, paint, and tea. This action provoked further protests across the Atlantic, answered by the suspension of the New York legislature and the employment of troops in Boston.

The claim by the colonists that Parliament had no right to tax them without their consent evoked a sympathetic response in England. Aside from occasional riots in time of stress, the British public was docile and accepting. Harsh laws and brutal punishments were used to impose order on the lower classes. But the unrepresentative character of the Commons, the widespread use of patronage or corruption to lubricate and manage the political machine, and occasional arbitrary actions of the crown began to stir thinking men to champion the cause of reform. In 1763 the thinly veiled attack on the King by John Wilkes in number forty-five of his newspaper, *The North Briton,* so outraged the government that a decision was made to apprehend Wilkes and suppress his paper, on a charge of seditious libel. The Secretaries of State issued a general warrant, an instrument that gave the messengers license to seize any or all persons suspected of a part in the paper, the printing press, and the offending issues themselves. The legality of general warrants was doubtful, though they had been long employed. When Wilkes sued successfully in court, the bench held the instrument illegal, and its future use was condemned by the Commons in 1766.

The government was not yet through with Wilkes. Exposing him as the author of a salacious satire, *An Essay on Women,* it had the strength in the Commons to expel him from the House. Wilkes, already a *cause célèbre*, was now at the center of radical agitation for a decade, first over the issue of general warrants, then his right to sit in the House. He had returned from self-imposed exile in France in 1768 to run for Parliament. Four times new elections were held for his seat and four times the voters of Middlesex, the county around London which felt greatly underrepresented in the Commons, returned him or his proxy by an overwhelming majority. On the fourth occasion, in 1769, the Commons finally voided his candidacy and seated the runner-up. But the government was not rid of Wilkes, whose friends organized the Society of the Supporters of the Bill of Rights to defend his interests. The Ministers and Wilkes's opponents in the Commons were frequently the victims of well-directed mob action. The London populace, in assemblies, petitions, riots, demonstrations, and a host of public displays, continually championed his interests while challenging the crown. In 1770 Wilkes was elected an Alderman of London; the city with rare unanimity was mobilized against the government. Wilkes was then elected Lord Mayor of London in 1774, the year in which he was finally permitted to reenter the Commons. Before this he was involved in still another issue, the unrestricted publication of parliamentary debates in the daily press, a practice long banned by the Commons. John Almon, a printer closely connected with the radicals and Wilkes, successfully challenged the ban of the Commons and won his case with the support of Wilkes and the city officials when the Commons found it wiser to abandon the claim in 1771.

The First Years of Lord North's Ministry, 1770-76. When Lord North accepted the Treasury on January 27, 1770, no one could foresee that he would continue as Prime Minister for a dozen years. The opposition in Parliament was formidable, composed of both the Rockinghamites and Chatham. Through their oratory in the two chambers and their even more effective attacks in the press, the opposition sought to force George III to come to terms with them. Edmund Burke in his *Thoughts on the Present Discontents* (1770) had charged that a secret cabal dominated by Bute possessed the King and hence controlled the ministry. Though a fabrication, Burke and his party seemed to have given some credence to this interpretation in order to explain their own inability to gain acceptance. The government was still on the defensive from the onslaughts of Wilkes and the demands for reform. The final burden was the unrest in the American colonies. North took this all in stride. Though an unprepossessing figure and an over-tolerant and weak Prime Minister, he showed remarkable ability in managing the Commons. With the firm support of the King, the power of the Treasury behind him, and his sure touch with the Parliament, he proved invulnerable to opposition efforts to unseat him. His early years in office were much taken up with financial matters. He proved to be an expert in financial management and genuinely concerned with the reform of the revenue system. Aside from America, the most pressing problem was that of the East India Company.

The supremacy in India gained by the British East India Company at the end of the Seven Years' War brought a new train of problems. The East India Company was a commercial enterprise, organized to earn a profit for its backers and ill-equipped to carry the responsibility of governing non-western people. The enormous power and influence which the Company's managers possessed in India provided unprecedented opportunities for personal gain and, at the same time, for corruption. Mismanagement of the Company's affairs at home and the substantial new financial burdens caused by the assumption of governmental responsibilities in India drained the Company of its profits. The government looked to the Company whose wealth might alleviate the government's pressing financial needs. At the same time the heavy commitments the Company had in the east and their importance to the economy meant that the state might have to insure the integrity of the Company's possessions. This could mean the provision of troops and ships to be used against the French. Temporary settlements in 1767 and 1769 only postponed the day of reckoning while yet acknowledging the government's responsibility and interest. North's Regulating Act of 1773 was a compromise measure intended to introduce some measure of stability and integrity into the Company's operations until the renewal of its charter in 1780. In addition to subjecting the dividend rate to the review of Parliament, a Governor-General and council were appointed to manage the area of Bengal in India. The Treasury or Secretary of State was given the right to review all correspondence from India. That these arrangements did not prove satisfactory was due as much to the persons appointed to serve on the council as the methods employed.

The Trouble with the Colonies. The events that led to rebellion were sometimes small in themselves and often unconnected. But each in turn furthered the breach between the colonies and the mother country; created suspicion on the side of the colonists and provoked English defiance, anger, and then retaliation. The Stamp Act, the closing of the frontiers, the Townshend duties which were taxation by indirect means, and even more insidious, the suspension of the New York and Massachusetts assemblies, the closing of Boston harbor, the firing on the Boston mob — all were seen by the colonists as provocative. The Stamp Act Congress; the circular letter sent by the Massachusetts Assembly; the evasion of customs duties and illegal trade with the French West Indies; the boycott of British goods; and attacks on royal troops — these were equally as offensive to the British. Throughout all this the basic issue became clarified and refined. The colonies were bent upon extirpating all direct English control over their governments and finances though retaining the link of the crown. English political leaders in Parliament were unprepared to surrender English sovereignty to the colonists though they might be sympathetic to their concerns and willing to make conciliatory gestures. Even the Earl of Chatham and the Rockinghamites were opposed to a grant of independence and resisted all such claims until well after the rebellion broke out in 1776. It was North's unhappy lot to precipitate this final rupture.

The East India Company, plagued increasingly with financial troubles, had a surplus of tea. To help it reduce the surplus North proposed to let the Company import the tea directly into the colonies. The colonial merchants now saw their price undercut and the prospect of financial ruin as the Company's direct import would deprive them of their market. In most colonial ports a simple boycott was enough, but in Boston the colonists were more aggressive and, disguised as Indians, stole aboard the ships in the harbor and dumped the offending merchandise in the bay. Once the news of the incident reached England the government responded by passing a bill through the Parliament to close the port of Boston. Subsequent legislation strengthened the control of the crown over the Massachusetts government. The Quebec Act of the same year, which created an appointive rather than elective legislative council for the French-speaking provinces, was regarded as a still more ominous sign or portent of future retaliation, particularly as it was to extend the Canadian system into the Ohio and Illinois territories. Massachusetts responded by calling a General Congress of the British colonies to deal with these threats to their liberties. Even before the Congress met in September in Philadelphia, fighting had begun at Lexington in April 1775. The American rebellion was underway.

THE AMERICAN REVOLUTION AND ITS AFTERMATH

The American Rebellion, 1775-83. England was ill-prepared for the war; the geographical considerations alone made her victory doubtful and the nature of the leadership of the ministry was a further liability. Given these constraints one may ask why England prosecuted war against its colonies. The challenge to the imperial constitution was almost unanimously accepted at home, given the unacceptable alternative — independence for the colonies. The ease with which Britain had fought overseas campaigns in the last war was a misleading example. Now her major European rivals were free of continental operations, had stronger navies, and thus could effectively challenge her in the American theatre and upon the high seas. Lord North was no match for Pitt. Refusing to take full responsibility for the direction of the ministry and the war he left a vacuum that was only partly filled by the King. And Lord George Germain, who as Secretary of State for the American colonies had the prime responsibility for the prosecution of the war, was an experienced and able officer, but he had neither the authority nor genius nor the good fortune of Pitt.

Britain faced war not only in the thirteen colonies but also in India, the West Indies, and Canada. To blockade the whole North American coastline against a skilled and intrepid civilian navy which knew all the innumerable indents and turnings of the coastline was impossible for any navy of that day no matter how large or proficient. But the disorders at home and the weakness of the commanders in America simply compounded the problem. Though the years 1775 and 1776 appeared favorable to the English — Boston was evacuated but New York occupied — 1777 was a disaster, climaxed by the surrender of General Burgoyne at Saratoga. The success of the colonists impelled France, which had supported them covertly since 1776, to conclude a formal alliance with America in 1778. The following year Spain entered the lists against England. The year 1780 crowned the series of diplomatic reverses. Led by Russia, the other nations of Europe declared a state of armed neutrality in which they refused to accept English inspection of neutral cargoes, while Holland joined those ranged in active hostilities against England. The surrender of Cornwallis at Yorktown in 1781 only acknowledged the inevitable outcome of the struggle.

The Impact of the Rebellion In England and Ireland. The demand for parliamentary reform had not died with Wilkes's readmission to the Commons in 1774. The opposition had charged the ministry with handling of the American colonies in an arbitrary and coercive manner, which in turn encouraged complaints of autocratic and corrupt practices in the government in England. The forces of Chatham and Rockingham in the two houses were small and little able to stem the overwhelming support for the ministry and the prosecution of the war against the colonists. But they kept alive the issues, through their contributions in the debates in Parliament, which were duly noted in the daily press. In tracts and journals they influenced an increasing

The Execution by William Hogarth (Radio Times Hulton Picture Library).

number of thoughtful citizens against the government as the tide of war and diplomacy turned against England. The natural turbulence and lawlessness of the London mobs, combined with disaffection and economic misery caused by the war, were sufficient to incite the lower orders to violent attacks on property and on prominent citizens and officials. An outburst of anti-Catholicism which began in Scotland eventually reached the metropolis in June 1780 under the leadership of Lord George Gordon. Catholic chapels were raided, houses burned, the Parliament itself besieged, and Newgate prison demolished, the prisoners let free. Only the personal intervention of the King and the employment of royal troops restored order. With the surrender at Yorktown and the collapse of the government's war effort, even the independent members who were traditionally loyal to the crown turned against the King's ministry. North was forced to resign in June 1782.

One of the contributing factors to the ministry's demise and one of the problems that confronted North's successors was the situation in Ireland. Though that country was composed of an oppressed and destitute Roman Catholic majority, ruled by a tiny but omnipotent Protestant minority, which in turn was subjugated to an indifferent if not hostile English government, Ireland had remained calm and loyal during the great eighteenth-century wars. Its economy had been depressed and to some extent impoverished or strangled by the English who were hostile to any competition from their subject neighbor. Yet the country had experienced a slow but steady recovery since the Revolution of 1688. As transatlantic trade increased Ireland profited from the provisioning trade for the sailing vessels which stopped in route to and from America. Dublin, the seat of government, developed into what remains to this day the finest and most handsome eighteenth-century city in the British Isles.

The government was controlled by the Protestant landed class, many of fairly recent English origin. Supported by an extremely narrow franchise and controlled by the great Protestant landowners, the Irish Parliament dutifully followed the dictates of the ministry in England. By the mid-eighteenth century these "undertakers" were alarmed at how Irish wealth was being used to line English pockets. Even loyal Protestants were suffering at the expense of their English neighbors. Their refusal in the 1760s to submit to further English demands for Irish revenues led to the imposition of a resident English Lord-Lieutenant who ran the government under direct orders from London. It is remarkable that the inhabitants both Protestant and Catholic remained loyal during the American rebellion. When Irish troops were withdrawn to fight in America, the Irish gentry raised volunteer regiments at their own expense to defend their country against possible foreign invasion. The increasing concern about the depredations the country suffered at the hand of England combined with the new-found strength and unity the gentry gained from the volunteer movement led them to demand home rule and the abolition of the several constraints by which the Irish executive and Parliament were bound to the British Parliament and Privy Council. These demands were presented in 1782 just at the moment the English government, beset with difficulties of its own at home and abroad, was least able to resist them.

The Ministries of Shelburne and Fox, 1782-83. Lord North's resignation left George III no choice but to turn to Rockingham and the opposition members whom he disliked intensely and whose efforts to storm the Cabinet he had so long and so strenuously resisted. The government that succeeded was a weak coalition, half controlled by Rockingham and Charles James Fox, the other half by Shelburne and Lord Camden, the heirs of the Earl of Chatham. Initially they had no choice but to act in harmony. The demands of the Irish were met almost without exception and Ireland enjoyed a brief period of almost unhampered political independence, the sole link remaining the crown, but with that the vital power to appoint the executive. The new leaders also moved quickly to pass a series of reform measures that they had long been championing, though the impact was limited. The main features were to prevent government contractors from sitting in the Commons, to disenfranchise thousands of Treasury officers, and to curtail the places available to the King and hence to his ministers for patronage. The early death of Rockingham at age 52 in July 1782 resulted in a competition between the two factions in the ministry for his place. The result was the resignation of Fox and the other Whig leaders and the emergence of Shelburne as Prime Minister.

Shelburne had served in a junior capacity in Chatham's ministry in the 1760s and had many of his mentor's better qualities combined with an equanimity and consistency that the elder statesman regrettably lacked. His attitude to the American colonies was notably liberal and magnanimous and one which served English interests well. The peace settlement which he negotiated gained more for England than she had reason to expect. He decided that the best course was to be conciliatory towards the colonies in hopes of splitting America off from France and ensuring favorable commercial relations between England and America for the future. In this he was eminently successful, aided by English naval victories in the West Indies and at Gibraltar and by the just suspicions of the Americans as to French designs in North America. By the Treaty of Versailles concluded in 1783 the Americans were granted their independence and obtained the lands between the Appalachians and the Mississippi River. France made modest imperial gains and Spain regained Minorca and Florida. Although other minor concessions were made, the British Empire remained essentially intact except for the crucial loss of the thirteen American colonies.

Shelburne had negotiated a peace which was wise and generous, but he fell victim to the political factionalism which divided the Parliament even though he still retained the confidence of the King. The former followers of Rockingham, now led by Charles James Fox, resented the means by which Shelburne had come to power. The followers of North were bitter at the peace settlement which he had made. Furthermore, despite his many good qualities, Shelburne was a man who evoked suspicion and mistrust. In 1783 Fox and North came together in a political coalition which led Shelburne to resign. George III hated Fox and felt betrayed by North. Desperately the King looked for an alternative while Shelburne's Chancellor of the Exchequer, young

Rowlandson's cartoon of Fox and North as "the Right Honourable Catch Singers,"
1783 (Kenneth Spencer Research Library).

William Pitt, son of the Earl of Chatham, headed a caretaker
administration. On March 31 he resigned. George III, left with
no other alternative, was compelled to accept Fox and North as
leaders of a coalition ministry headed nominally by a respected
nobleman, the Duke of Portland. Fox and North completed the peace
settlement and then turned to the explosive question of India. When
Fox's India Bill, presented in the fall of 1783, aroused bitter
controversy, George III seized his opportunity and dismissed the
coalition, naming Pitt to head a minority government. Supported by
the King, Pitt held his ground despite the bitter opposition of the
Fox-North majority in the House of Commons. When Pitt held firm the

independent members of the Commons began to drift back to their usual support of the King and his ministers, until in March 1784, Pitt found a majority of one supporting him. At this point, according to plan, the King dissolved Parliament and called an election in which the full resources of the crown were deployed in support of the young Prime Minister. The result was a stunning electoral victory. Pitt found himself leader of a government with a secure majority, and George III savored the downfall of men who had sought so often to thwart the King's plans.

A STOCKTAKING-ENGLAND IN 1783

The year 1783, which marked the formal close of the war with America and was to usher in the great ministry of the younger Pitt, marked a significant stage in the evolution of England. The decade of the 1780s closed what historians call the "classical age of the constitution." The balance of political power between the monarchy and the Parliament now begins to shift decisively and irrevocably in the direction of the Parliament. Radical agitation — for a more representative House of Commons, an enlarged electorate, freedom of the press, relief for Dissenters and Roman Catholics — entered a new, more violent phase at the end of the decade. Traditional, hierarchal English society headed by the landed aristocracy was soon to be challenged by an urban, industrial and commercial managerial class and a working class. This phenomenon in the social and economic spheres was the consequence of a number of factors discussed at length below. They may be summarized here as increased sophistication and experience in large-scale commercial enterprises; the series of inventions which ushered in the industrial revolution; a rapidly increasing population attended by a shift in concentration from the country to the city; gradual improvements in the field of agriculture.

Though shaken by the loss of the American colonies and by displays of political unrest at home and in Ireland, England was still a remarkably stable and progressive country by any European standard. Though a class-conscious nation, there were still ample opportunities for social mobility given the right combinations of intelligence, perseverance, and good fortune. The signs of prosperity were all around. London above all epitomized this level of enterprise and activity which the country had achieved. It was the intellectual and commercial capital of Europe. A lively press, relatively unfettered by government restraints, was paralleled by a bustling commercial world of manufacturers, bankers, merchants, and traders. Theatres, museums, concert halls, pleasure gardens, stately parks, and well-attended coffee houses and pubs attest to the range of diversions, beloved by Samuel

Supper at Vauxhall by George Cruikshank (Radio Times Hulton Picture Library).

Johnson, who knowingly remarked, "He who is tired of London is tired of life." The erudite and pungent wit of Johnson, the worldly plays of Richard Sheridan, the new economics of Adam Smith, the refined elegance of the portraits by Reynolds and Gainsborough, the technical mastery and revolutionary invention of James Watt, the urbane wisdom of David Hume, and the brilliant prose of Edmund Burke are evidence for a creativity which made England a leader among nations.

With the loss of the American colonies England had lost one empire. But based upon what remained to her in Canada, the Caribbean, Africa, India, and the Far East, she was to build a larger and even greater empire. Her fleet was already supreme on the seas of the world. The long duel for markets and colonies with France had ended in victory for England in 1763, and even the setback suffered in 1783 did not force her from her dominant position. In the long familiar world of small professional armies and pressed navies, England had consistently stood up to the challenge of her European rivals. In the next decade she was to face a new and graver challenge, for which the limited engagements in America might be said to have set some precedent. But this was all ahead. The mood in 1783 was one of satisfaction, complacency, and pride. A relaxed, but conscientious attention to reform and improvement in all spheres without sacrificing the essential nature and constitution of the nation was the goal of the best intentioned and most enlightened leaders in the intellectual, political, and economic circles of the nation. What these leaders could not know was that the country was on the brink of the greatest challenge, economically, diplomatically, and politically, that the country had yet known. This challenge was that of the Industrial Revolution and the Napoleonic wars.

SUGGESTIONS FOR FURTHER READING

In addition to the general works noted in the preceding chapter the reader should consult J. Steven Watson, *The Reign of George III* (1960) and Asa Briggs, *The Age of Improvement* (1959). The imposing *chef d'oeuvre* of Lawrence H. Gipson, *The British Empire before the American Revolution* in 15 volumes is an invaluable reference work for the British Isles and the other colonial possessions as well as the Americas. Volume XIX contains a massive *Bibliographical Guide*, volume XV, *A Guide to Manuscripts*. The most influential of twentieth-century historians was Sir Lewis Namier. In addition to his seminal *Structure of Politics at the Accession of George III* (2nd ed.,

1957), which should be read with John Brewer, *Party Ideology and Popular Politics at the Accession of George III* (1976) and Namier's essays reprinted in *Crossroads of Power* (1962), he began a survey of the period 1760-82. He only completed the first volume, *England in the Age of the American Revolution* (2nd ed., 1961), which bears the subtitle *Government and Parliament under the Duke of Newcastle.* His students have continued it: John Brooke, *The Chatham Administration* (1956), Bernard Donoughue, *British Politics and the American Revolution. The Path to War 1773-75* (1964) and Ian Christie, *The End of North's Ministry* (1958). This may be filled in with Herbert Butterfield, *George III, Lord North and the People, 1779-1780* (1949), and followed with John Cannon, *The Fox-North Coalition* (1971). Excellent works on politics abound for this period. Richard Pares, *King George III and the Politicians* (1953) is indispensable. Also valuable are Ian Christie, *Wilkes, Wyvill and Reform* (1962), George Rude, *Wilkes and Liberty* (1962), Lucy Sutherland, *The East India Company in Eighteenth Century Politics* (1952), Erich Eyck, *Pitt versus Fox: Father and Son, 1735-1806* (1950). There are many excellent biographies to choose from, among them John Brooke, *King George III* (1972), Stanley Ayling, *George III* (1972) and *The Elder Pitt* (1976), Namier and Brooke, *Charles Townshend* (1964), John Derry, *Charles James Fox* (1972), John Norris, *Shelburne and Reform* (1963). Ida McAlpine and Richard Hunter in *George III and the Mad Business* (1969) suggest that the King suffered from a rare hereditary disease while Herbert Butterfield in *George III and the Historians* (1957) surveys changing historical interpretation about the King. The American revolt has been covered exhaustively. From the standpoint of England one should note Gipson's summary, *The Coming of the Revolution* (1954), P.D.G. Thomas, *British Politics and the Stamp Act Crisis* (1975), Charles Ritcheson, *British Politics and the American Revolution* (1954), Piers Mackesy, *The War for America* (1965), Ian Christie, *Crisis of Empire* (1966) and (with Benjamin Labaree), *Empire or Independence 1760-1776* (1976).

Some specialized monographs of interest are John Derry, *The Regency Crisis and the Whigs* (1963), J.E.D. Binney, *British Public Finance and Administration* (1958), and John Brooke and Sir Lewis Namier, *The House of Commons 1754-1790* (3 vols., 1964). Edmund Burke has yet to receive a definitive biography but one may read with profit Philip Magnus, *Edmund Burke* (1939), Carl Cone, *Burke and the Nature of Politics* (2 vols., 1957), Alfred Cobban, *Edmund Burke and the Revolt against the Eighteenth Century* (1929) and Charles Parkin, *The Moral Basis of Burke's Political Thought* (1956).

II
The
Revolutionary Age

1783-1815

In the year 1783 George III had been King for twenty-three years. He was a conscientious, hard-working ruler, who had learned from bitter experience how to use the powers vested in him. His efforts to strengthen the personal role of the monarch he regarded as restoring the practices of the past. In 1782 George III suffered a severe political blow when Parliament turned against the American War and compelled him to accept a ministry headed by his political enemies and pledged to American independence. In December, 1783 George III reasserted his royal powers by dismissing the Fox-North coalition and appointing as Prime Minister the twenty-four-year-old William Pitt, son of the elder William Pitt, Earl of Chatham. The King completed the discomfiture of his political opponents in the spring of 1784 when he used the power of the crown to call a new election, in which the Pitt ministry won a decisive victory. The King who had been humiliated in 1782 had, it appeared, restored the royal power in the appointment of ministers.

GEORGE III AND WILLIAM PITT

George III demonstrated in 1783-84 the decisive role that a determined monarch could play in eighteenth-century politics, but

William Pitt, the Younger (National Portrait Gallery).

those exciting events marked the high point of the personal power of the King. George III had placed Pitt in office, but he was also dependent upon Pitt who was the only alternative to the King's political opponents. Furthermore, Pitt was enormously competent, and the King was willing to allow him to deal with the economic and administrative problems which dominated the post-war period. In 1787-88 George III suffered an attack of mental illness which lasted for about four months. Thereafter he was concerned about his health and reduced his involvement in public business. When war broke out with France in 1793 the King gained stature as a symbol of national unity, but the needs of war thrust more responsibility upon Pitt and his cabinet. In 1801 a political crisis in which Pitt resigned was followed by another of the King's mental breakdowns. Although the King recovered, he was now advanced in years and his political involvement had to be further curtailed. By 1811 his sanity was permanently lost, and when he died in 1820 he was little more than a memory. The long reign of the King who had taken the throne determined to restore the royal power proved to be the reign in which the British monarchy was irretrievably set in the direction of the figurehead monarchy of today.

William Pitt and Charles James Fox. Throughout the eighteenth century, British government worked best when the King had the services of a strong, capable Prime Minister who could lead the Cabinet, supervise finance and administration, and win parliamentary support for his policies. William Pitt was such a man. From the beginning of his ministry he showed himself to be a masterful person despite his youth, and he never ceased to be the dominant figure in his ministry, even as he drew other powerful leaders to his side. He was a superb administrator, using his post as First Lord of the Treasury to extend Treasury supervision into many facets of government. In the House of Commons, where oratory could have a powerful effect, Pitt was inferior to none. He was responsive to new ideas, quick to see how they could be applied to the improvement of government, and also sensitive to humanitarian concerns, such as prison reform and abolition of the slave trade. His ministry, however, depended upon a conservative King and a body of supporters in Parliament who were content to leave well enough alone. Thus his achievements fell short of his aspirations.

One of the important features of eighteenth-century politics was the development of a "loyal opposition." The opposition led by Lord Rockingham had eventually brought about the downfall of North's ministry and the end of the American Revolution. When Rockingham died in 1782, his place was taken by Charles James Fox. It was Fox who was dismissed by George III in December 1783 when young William Pitt was installed in power. For the remainder of their lives, Pitt and Fox were political rivals. Like Pitt, Fox was a superb orator and debater, and in his few brief periods in office he showed himself to be a capable administrator. Pitt relied upon the King for support, and Fox turned to the Prince of Wales, who characteristically opposed the King and his ministers. Fox became the leader of those who called themselves Whigs. The key principle of Fox's politics was his concern for the independence of Parliament and the rights of individuals, which he believed were threatened by the tendency of the crown to draw power to itself. He supported parliamentary reform, reduction of royal patronage, freedom of the press, religious toleration, and abolition of the slave trade. By taking his stand in opposition to royal power, Fox condemned himself to political frustration, but he won a place in the hearts of his contemporaries as a powerful defender of liberty.

Pitt and Reform. It was Pitt's task to restore confidence and unity to a nation torn by partisan strife and shaken by defeat in the American Revolution. He did so with remarkable success. His major achievements were in finance and trade. Britain emerged from the war in desperate financial straits, and Pitt, as First Lord of the Treasury, was primarily responsible for restoring the finances of the government. It was in this area that Pitt's rationality, efficiency, and openness to new ideas were most effectively displayed. He improved financial management by refinancing the national debt, consolidating and simplifying the revenues, reducing smuggling and other evasions of taxes, and improving the management and audit of public money. Another important concern was to improve the revenue by encouraging trade through a series of trade treaties with other nations. Pitt's goal was a surplus of revenue over expenditure, which could be used to begin reduction of the national debt. In 1786 he announced that the necessary surplus had been achieved and could be expected to increase each year. He proposed a sinking fund to be earmarked for debt reduction. Although Pitt's surplus was soon to be consumed by new wars, Pitt's sinking fund had an important psychological effect for it demonstrated that Britain was again financially strong.

Pitt also took the lead in the movement for reform of Parliament. In the previous decade complaints had frequently been made that the House of Commons was dominated by the crown and was failing to represent the views of the public. The influence of the crown was thought to be derived from small boroughs, while the growing electorates of the shires and populous towns were underrepresented. In 1785 Pitt proposed a moderate measure of reform which would disfranchise 36 small boroughs (with compensation) and distribute the seats to London and the larger counties. George III disapproved of tinkering with the ancient constitution, and many of Pitt's supporters were reluctant to support any proposal to change the distribution of seats, no matter how moderate or justifiable. The measure was soundly defeated, and Pitt's effort at parliamentary reform was ended. Fox and his friends raised the issue in 1793 and again in 1797, but without success. Rejection of parliamentary reform in small installments meant that a great crisis was likely to take place eventually. For the moment, however, the political class was content to leave things as they were.

Another problem was Ireland, which had received legislative independence in 1782. Pitt sought to counteract the weakening of British political control by strengthening the economic ties which bound Britain and Ireland together. In 1785 he presented his Irish Commercial Resolutions, in which he proposed to institute free trade between Britain and Ireland in exchange for an Irish contribution to the cost of the navy. Again a statesmanlike policy failed. British economic interests which feared Irish competition mounted a powerful lobby against Pitt's proposals, and the Irish resented Pitt's insistence on support for the navy. The result was another defeat. In the case of Ireland, as in parliamentary reform, Pitt found that problems which had flared in time of war had subsided with the return to peace.

Pitt and the Empire. When Pitt came to power in December 1783, the British Empire had been rocked by the loss of the American colonies. One of his major concerns was to restore British trade, shipping, and seapower, which were thought to depend on Empire. The immediate problem facing the young minister was restoration of commercial relations between Britain and her former American colonies. Pitt's mentor, Lord Shelburne, had favored a generous arrangement which would concede to the Americans some of the benefits of the former imperial connection, but strong feeling developed in Parliament and the nation that the Americans, having chosen to leave the Empire, should no longer enjoy its advantages. When Pitt came into office Orders in Council had already been issued which declared that American ships would be considered as foreign ships and thus subject to the restrictions of the Navigation Acts. Pitt continued this policy which was not modified until 1795. Otherwise, overtures were made to establish good relations with the new American states, and in 1785 John Adams was received as the first American ambassador to the Court of St. James.

Relations with the American states had an important bearing upon the British West Indies, for the American states were an important market for West Indian products and supplied the West Indies with grain, fish, barrel staves, and other necessities. The new trade regulations meant that this trade could not legally be conducted in American ships. The West India interest in London protested this policy vigorously, but to no effect. The British government expected that the

Canadian colonies could supply food and timber products, and that imperial trade would benefit if West Indian products went directly to Britain. Despite their cries of alarm, the British West Indies continued to be profitable. When war broke out with France in 1793 the British government looked favorably upon easier trade relations between the West Indies and the United States, and in 1795 Jay's Treaty gave American ships increased access to the West Indian trade.

Pitt faced serious problems in dealing with the Canadian colonies which had been profoundly affected by the American Revolution. Prior to the war, Canada consisted principally of the French settlements along the St. Lawrence River. The American Revolution led to a large influx of Loyalists into Canada, who demanded a representative assembly and English law, but the French inhabitants preferred to preserve their traditional laws and customs. Pitt's solution was the Canada Act of 1791, which divided Canada into two parts. Quebec (Lower Canada), which was primarily French, preserved French land tenure and the rights of the Roman Catholic Church. Ontario (Upper Canada) had English land tenure and law. Both colonies had assemblies, but there was one Royal Governor for both and his power was dominant. Nova Scotia, New Brunswick, and Prince Edward Island were already separate colonies. Thus the Pitt ministry provided a system of government for the Canadian colonies which proved workable for the next half century.

Pitt's major imperial problem was the extent of the powers of the British East India Company in India, a bone of contention in Britain for the previous two decades. When the East India Company acquired authority over the great province of Bengal, the Company became involved in government and war, while its commercial activities fell upon evil days. Two other problems also emerged: the influence exercised by the East India Company upon British domestic politics, and notorious abuses of power by the Company in dealing with the native inhabitants of India. When Pitt took office the demand in Britain for legislation regulating the Company was overwhelming; the only question was the form it would take. Pitt's India Act of 1784 (amended in 1786) provided a compromise solution. The Company continued to govern its territories in India, but a Board of Control in London and a strong Governor General in India established public authority over the Company. The first Governor General was Lord Cornwallis, who atoned for his defeat at Yorktown by introducing a new standard of rectitude and efficiency into the government of India.

The Pitt ministry extended the Empire into a new area when it began British settlement in Australia. One of the common sentences passed upon convicted felons was transportation, ordinarily to America. With American independence, however, Britain lacked a good place to dispose of convicts, and for several years the government technically met the requirement of transportation by confining the convicts to derelict ships (hulks) anchored in the Thames. The Pitt ministry proposed to relieve the situation by settling the convicts in Australia which had been discovered by Captain Cook in 1770. The first shipload of convicts arrived in 1788, and Sydney was established as a penal colony, governed by a military commander and garrison. After considerable hardship, discharged soldiers and freed convicts began to settle the region and the new colony took root.

THE BEGINNINGS OF INDUSTRIALISM

Economic Growth. The eighteenth century was a period of remarkable economic growth in Britain. These economic changes were so far-reaching in their effects that historians have called them "The Industrial Revolution." There are many reasons why Britain became the first industrial nation. The government of Britain combined political stability, individual freedom, and security of property in a mix conducive to enterprise and investment. Britain's institutions of banking and credit were well developed, and her far-flung trade and Empire provided capital, raw materials, and markets for industry. Strong domestic demand, fuelled by wealth derived from trade and agriculture, stimulated new methods for increased production of goods. The availability of coal, iron, and waterpower was an important factor. A growing population provided labor for factories and mines; a prosperous agriculture produced the food and fibre needed to sustain an industrial economy. Thus in the later half of the eighteenth century a unique set of circumstances, brought together by a generation of unusual inventiveness and enterprise, made Britain the leader in a movement which has transformed the world — the Industrial Revolution.

Iron, Steam, Coal. One important feature of the early industrial age was the manufacture of cheaper and more abundant iron. Prior to the eighteenth century iron was smelted with charcoal, which made it necessary to locate most iron works in forests to obtain fuel. In the eighteenth century a family of iron makers located in the Severn Valley, the Darbys, developed a method of smelting iron with coal by first converting the coal to coke. The most striking of the new industrial ironmasters of Britain was John Wilkinson, who built an ironworks across the river from the Darbys. His cannon boring machine greatly improved the range and accuracy of his cannon, and could also be adapted to make cylinders for steam engines. He promoted iron products in a variety of ways: he built iron barges, installed an iron pulpit in the local church, and was buried in an iron coffin. Wilkinson was a strong willed, hard driving individual of the kind who could take advantage of new processes and transform iron making from small family enterprise to large-scale industry. As a result of these new processes iron production in Britain more than doubled from 1760 to 1788, and quadrupled again in the next seventeen years. One of the leading features of modern industrial society had begun in the green valley of the Severn River.

Another feature of industrialism was the development of a vital new source of power — the steam engine. Engines powered by steam had been in use since the later seventeenth century, but they were highly inefficient and were used mainly to pump water out of coal mines. In the 1760s a Scottish instrument maker, James Watt, began developing a more efficient type of steam engine and also invented a device to convert steam power to a rotary motion. In 1774 Watt went into partnership with Matthew Boulton, a Birmingham businessman, to manufacture steam engines. Watt's engines were first used for coal mines, smelting, and forges, and were later adapted to textile manufactures, rail transport, and ships.

Iron smelting and the steam engine made necessary a larger supply of coal. Britain possessed abundant coal, much of it near the surface, and coal had been an important product since Tudor times. Until the industrial age coal was used principally for home heating, and in the eighteenth century the coal trade from Newcastle to London was extensive. The steam engine created a new demand for coal and made it possible to supply that demand by providing power to raise coal and pump water out of mines. By 1800 coal mines were being opened up in Scotland, Wales, and the west of England. In the 1830s the railroad created a new demand for coal, and also lowered the cost of bringing coal to markets, thus making coal more practical as a source of energy for industry.

Textiles. In some respects the textile industry was the spearhead of British industrial growth. Textile manufacture was old in England; ever since the later Middle Ages woolen textiles had been one of England's most important products. For centuries woolen cloth manufacture was a cottage industry — artisans and their families working in their own homes scattered throughout the towns, villages, and countryside. In the later eighteenth century a revolution took place in the manufacture of textiles, as machines were developed which were too large and expensive to be owned and operated by the workers in their homes. This revolution first took place in the process of spinning thread, where Richard Arkwright became the leader in development of the factory system. Arkwright came from humble beginnings, and got his start in

THE INDUSTRIAL REVOLUTION

Carron
Edinburgh
Glasgow
Prestonpans
R. Clyde

0 ——— 100
MILES
0 ——— 100
KILOMETERS

NORTHUMBER
LAND
R. Tyne
Newcastle

R. Tees
Darlington   Stockton

NORTH SEA

Backbarrow

YORKSHIRE

Leeds & Liverpool   Canal
Halifax   Leeds
Bolton   Bury   Aire & Calder Canal   Hull
Liverpool   Worsley   WEST RIDING   R. Don   HUMBER
Mersey   Manchester   Styal
Runcorn   Sheffield
Bridgewater Canal   DERBY SHIRE
STAFFORD   R. Derwent   R. Trent
R. Dee   Crewe
Ellesmere Canal   Etruria
Gd. Trunk Canal   SHIRE
Nottingham   Holkham

Coalbrookdale   Leicester   R. Welland   Norwich
Birmingham   Coventry
Stourport   Peterborough   EAST
R. Wye   ANGLIA
Hereford   R. Severn   R. Avon   Grand Junction Canal   R. Ouse
Tewkesbury   & Oxford Canal

Swansea   WEST
Thames & Severn Canal
Cardiff   Bristol   London
COUNTRY   R. Thames

Canterbury
THE WEALD

Exeter   Fareham   Brighton
CORNWALL   Portsmouth
Plymouth

ENGLISH CHANNEL

textile manufacture by developing a spinning machine driven by water power. Although his role as an inventor is dubious, there can be no question of his ability as an organizer of production. He built his first factory along an isolated river in Derbyshire and brought in pauper children to tend his machines, housing them in a dormitory near the factory. Arkwright was one of the first textile manufacturers to use steam power, thus freeing himself from the need to locate his mills in labor-short areas where water power was available. Arkwright's genius as an organizer and manager enabled him to apply new inventions, such as the steam engine, to industrial uses. Arkwright drove himself and his employees hard. Like Wilkinson, he may be seen as typical of the new industrialists whose imagination and determination were transforming the production of goods in Britain.

Arkwright was engaged in spinning cotton, and it was in the cotton textile industry that the new methods were most rapidly developed. In the United States, Eli Whitney's invention of the cotton gin greatly increased the supply of raw cotton, and the application of steam power to cotton spinning made possible larger factories in locations not dependent upon water power. The introduction of the power loom after 1815 brought the factory system to the weaving of cloth, but with disastrous effects upon the hand weavers, who had increased in numbers due to the abundance of cheap yarn. Although figures for productivity in the industry are sketchy at best, it is estimated that the value of manufactured cotton cloth increased from £4 million in 1783 to £15 million twenty years later. The value of cotton manufactures doubled again in the next twenty years, by which time cotton manufacture had passed the woolen textile industry, which was slower to change. The dramatic changes in the textile industry are, perhaps, the best justification for the term "Industrial Revolution."

Pottery. Another old industry which was transformed by new industrial processes was the manufacture of pottery. Josiah Wedgwood, a Staffordshire potter, introduced the factory system in the manufacture of earthenware, not only to increase productivity but also to improve the quality and uniformity of his products. Wedgwood's superior product was due to excellent design, carefully controlled processes, and high skill resulting from the division of labor. His basic patterns could be afforded by the middle class, and when decorated by his superb artists they were fit for the crowned heads and aristocracy of Europe. He built a model town near the factory to house his employees, although not all of them appreciated the discipline and efforts at self-improvement which went with it. Since he needed reliable transportation to bring in clay and coal and to take out his products, he was an active investor in canals. When Pitt's Irish Commercial

Iron Bridge, Coalbrookdale.

Resolutions (1785) threatened his industry with cheaper Irish products, he actively opposed them. A man of cultivated tastes and generous impulses, Wedgwood was a pioneer who presented the more attractive face of industrialism.

Transportation. Changes in the production of goods would have had limited effect without improvements in transportation. By the mid-eighteenth century turnpike roads had greatly improved the movement of people and goods by coach or wagon, and the growing size, speed, and reliability of ships contributed to the growth of trade. With her many rivers, England has made important use of water transportation from the earliest times. In the later eighteenth century canal building greatly improved water transportation, especially in the new industrial areas of the north and west of England. A remarkable nobleman, the Duke of Bridgewater, led the building of canals. Bridgewater wanted to exploit the coal on his estates near Manchester; his answer was to build a canal to carry the coal to the Mersey River. In this task he benefited from the services of a talented engineer, James Brindley, who designed a complex canal which included tunnels, aqueducts, and levees to bring coal barges to their destination. In 1776 he finished his second canal, which gave access to the River Mersey and Liverpool. Bridgewater's canals were successful and encouraged a canal building boom which provided cheap transportation for coal, clay, bricks, farm products, and other bulky items necessary in an industrial society.

Agriculture. The increase of British population and industry would not have been possible without an increased supply of food made possible by the growing productivity of agriculture. During the eighteenth century improving landlords and farmers adopted new agricultural methods: new rotations of crops, the use of clover and turnips to provide more winter fodder for cattle, improved breeds of animals, and new agricultural implements and machinery. By the later eighteenth century, the new methods of agriculture led to an extensive movement for enclosure of the open fields. In 1760 probably half the arable land was still farmed in large open fields going back to medieval times. The new methods, however, could not be introduced under the old communal system, and progressive landlords sought to enclose the open fields into small individual fields divided by fences or hedges. Enclosure usually required an act of Parliament and the agreement of the holders of three-fourths of the land. Commissioners were appointed to determine individual rights to the land and divide the land into equitable shares. The principal benefits, however, went to those with the largest amount of land, for those with small landholdings found it difficult to survive without the communal life of the former system. Villagers who did not have rights to land, but who had rights in the common pastures and woodlands, also found themselves at a disadvantage. While enclosure generally increased the productivity of agriculture and provided a necessary base for industrial growth, it was a disadvantage to many of the rural poor.

Industrialism and Society. All elements of British society shared, to some extent, in the process of industrialization. Government provided internal stability, security of property, and the enforcement of contracts. The cost of government was high, especially during the long wars with France, and contributed significantly to distortions in the economy, but despite these burdens the British economy grew phenomenally during the wartime period. The aristocracy and gentry were the dominant political class and took a substantial share of the national wealth for themselves. Much of this wealth they spent on stately homes and comfortable living, but they also contributed to economic growth. As landlords they played an important part in agricultural improvement, and their investments in trade, manufacturing, mining, canals, and turnpike roads were significant. The farmers, including many small freeholders, were directly responsible for the pace of agricultural advance, encouraged by rising prices during the wartime period.

Professional men, such as lawyers, physicians, and the clergy, were increasing in numbers and prosperity, and they were often found organizing banks and canal companies, as well as providing capital for industry as silent partners. Wealthy merchants also invested in industry, although they were more likely to follow the traditional pattern and invest in land for the social prestige which land could bring. Despite the contributions of the leaders of pre-industrial Britain, much of the capital for industry seems to have been derived from the profits of industry itself. The new industrialists were hard-working men who lived modestly. They saved their money and put it back into the business. Their sons or grandsons might join the leisured class, but the early industrialists pulled themselves up by their own efforts, and their success or failure depended primarily upon their own abilities and resources.

Finally, one must look at the contribution of the working class, whose quick hands and strong backs were the basis for the Industrial Revolution. In the pre-industrial age many workers had combined agricultural work and handicraft industries, and a clear separation was not felt between industrial and agricultural workers. The factory system, however, drew workers from the land into new industrial towns at the same time as enclosures were depriving workers of rights they had formerly possessed in the common lands of the agricultural villages. Those workers who remained in agriculture became a distinct social class, dependent upon the farmers for their wages and deprived by industrial competition of the handicrafts which had for generations supplemented the income of rural workers. Lacking prospects for employment in the villages, others left the land for the factory towns, where they swelled the population which was already growing due to the large families of the factory workers. A rapidly growing population seeking employment in industry was an essential factor in the Industrial Revolution, and created a new social class, the industrial working class, which became increasingly conscious of its needs and grievances.

The standard of living of the urban working class in the early industrial age is one of those questions which evoke conflicting opinions. Although historians disagree on this point, there can be no doubt of the sense of injury felt by industrial workers, and especially by craftsmen in long-established industries. The competition of factory-made goods destroyed the value of their skills, and machines which could be tended by children took away the dignity formerly possessed by skilled labor. The Luddite riots of 1811 and 1812 were an early example of the tensions emerging in the new industrial age. The Luddites were framework knitters who made the long knitted stockings used by gentlemen in the eighteenth century. They found their position seriously eroded for a variety of reasons: extreme fluctuations in costs and markets due to wartime conditions, changing styles which reduced

Factory scene, 1840 (Radio Times Hulton Picture Library).

the demand for their product, and new machinery which produced cheaper stockings. They identified themselves as followers of a mythical "King Lud" and protested in the traditional manner, by issuing manifestos and breaking the new machines for making stockings. The Luddites were not a depressed industrial proletariat; they were from the aristocracy of labor, proud of their status and skill. Their expressions of outrage were not purely economic. They were a response to the loss of personal dignity and security which their craft and parliamentary regulation had formerly guaranteed. It was among such persons that protest against the new industrial system was most likely to be found.

Lurking over all was the sense of insecurity found in the depersonalized wage relationship of the new industrial system. The working people of England had always labored long and hard, but in turn they expected to be protected by their employers against short-term fluctuations in prices, wages, and employment, and to be provided for by the parish if afflicted by long-term hardship arising from unemployment, disability, or old age. Many factory owners in the new industries, however, felt little responsibility for their workers. The concentration of industrial growth in certain areas, and the distress resulting from war, inflation, poor crops, and economic fluctuations, contributed to a breakdown of the old system of poor relief. The propertied classes who paid the rates (local taxes) for poor relief complained of an excessive burden, and the poor complained that they were not provided for as required by law. Sometimes the poor reacted with riots and destructiveness; sometimes they read Tom Paine and agitated for political power; sometimes they formed labor unions, in defiance of the Combination Acts. Much of the time they suffered in silence, but they grew increasingly conscious of their grievances. The revolution in production which had created the new industries had also produced a new social force — the industrial working class — which was thereafter an important factor in British life.

BRITAIN AND THE FRENCH REVOLUTION

The French Revolution. In 1789 the French crown was bankrupt. In desperation, King Louis XVI called, for the first time since 1614, the ancient parliament of France, the Estates-General. The impecunious King looked to the estates of the realm — the clergy (First Estate), the nobility (Second Estate), and the people (Third Estate) — to come to his aid. When the Estates-General met, the businessmen and lawyers who forged forward as leaders of the Third Estate, joined by some of the nobility and clergy, demanded that the Estates-General be transformed into a National Assembly which would draw up a new constitution for France. The King yielded, and great excitement spread through France. The French Revolution had begun.

At first the aspirations of the National Assembly were well received in Britain. British political ideas had been widely disseminated in France through the works of Locke and by French writers such as Voltaire and Montesquieu. The British felt a sense of pride that the haughty French had seen fit to follow their example. When Fox heard that the people of Paris had seized the Bastille, the hated symbol of arbitrary power, he declared: "How much the greatest event that has happened in the world and how much the best." Pitt was less enthusiastic about the new political currents in France, but was relieved to think that internal difficulties would make France less a problem to British foreign policy. British reformers were encouraged by the ferment in France. The Revolution Society, formed to celebrate the centennial of the Glorious Revolution of 1688-89, praised the French for following the same course and looked for a revival of the reforming spirit at home.

The initial reaction in Britain soon turned to horror, as the moderate leaders of the National Assembly were supplanted by radicals determined to overthrow the monarchy and the other forms of privilege in France and establish a democratic republic. The domestic upheaval in France was complicated by foreign intervention, as Austria and Prussia came to the aid of the French King. In 1793 the radical revolutionaries seized power, executed the King and Queen, introduced mass conscription, and suppressed dissent with the guillotine. The revolutionary armies repulsed the Austrians and Prussians, and then burst into the Netherlands, the Rhineland, and northern Italy. Soon deposed princes, nobles, and churchmen were arriving in Britain as refugees, telling tales of atrocities and bewailing their loss of property and status. George III, the Pitt ministry, the aristocracy and gentry, the church, and most of the propertied middle class were shocked at the wreckage and were disturbed by the thought that British radicals might attempt a similar upheaval. British dislike of France as the national enemy was heightened by the view of France as the center of a revolution which, given an opportunity, would also destroy the balance of social relationships in Britain.

Conservatives and Radicals. The war with revolutionary France was, in one sense, a return to the long-standing conflict between Britain and France in Europe and on the seas, but it had a new dimension — a conflict of ideologies. Revolutionary France was dedicated to the triumph of reason over tradition, secularism over religion, equality over privilege, and patriotic fervor over the cosmopolitan culture of eighteenth-century Europe. The dominant effect of the French Revolution in Britain was a strong reaction, not only against French power, but against French ideals and, by extension, against most forms of domestic discontent. The chief spokesman of the reaction against French ideology was Edmund Burke, whose *Reflections on the Revolution in France* (1790) first sounded the alarm. Burke had spent most of his political career in opposition, first as the chief parliamentary spokesman for the Marquis of Rockingham and then as a follower of Fox. In 1790, however, Burke came forward as a defender of the *status quo*, arguing that the developments in France were not simply an attack on abuses but a revolution which would destroy the fundamental basis of society, leading eventually to conflict, chaos, and despotism. When Fox expressed sympathy with the French, Burke broke openly with his colleague and gave his support to Pitt. Burke's writings against the French Revolution supplied a conservative philosophy which was in accord with the instinctive reactions of most of the British public.

Replies to Burke were not long in coming. Tom Paine, whose *Common Sense* (1776) had encouraged the American colonists to seek independence, responded with *The Rights of Man* (1791). Paine's ideas were the conventional radicalism of the eighteenth century, but he possessed the gift of stating his views in a direct, pungent manner, which struck home to the ordinary man. He ridiculed Burke's high-flown reverence for institutions based on the injustices of the past, and urged that they be replaced by institutions which would protect the rights and dignity of all men. The ideals of the French Revolution were expounded in more moderate form by William Godwin. Godwin was a doctrinaire rationalist, whose *Political Justice* (1793) held forth the prospect of human progress to perfection as a result of the triumph of reason over tradition and ignorance. Godwin was not a revolutionary who sought to destroy the past by force, but the results he anticipated from the march of reason were every bit as revolutionary as those urged by Paine. In 1792 Mary Wollstonecraft, a remarkable young woman, who later married Godwin, penned her own reply to Burke, *A Vindication of the Rights of Woman*, in which she urged equality for women, especially in education and careers, which would enable them to develop their full potential as persons.

Britain at War. The political and ideological conflict engendered by the French Revolution was intensified by war. In 1793 France, already at war with Austria and Prussia, declared war on Britain, Spain, and the Dutch. By this time the British had come to believe that war was inevitable and necessary, and Pitt changed from the minister of peace and moderate reform to the leader of a European coalition against French power and French revolutionary ideals. Pitt's strategy was to rely principally upon British seapower, using it in areas such as the

Baltic, the Mediterranean, and the Caribbean which he regarded as vital to British trade. The land war he preferred to leave to allies subsidized by British gold. In 1797 a brilliant young French officer, Napoleon Bonaparte, won a startling victory over the Austrians in northern Italy, and in 1798 he invaded Egypt. At this point British seapower struck a heavy blow, as a bold naval officer, Horatio Nelson, destroyed the French fleet at the Battle of the Nile and trapped the French army in Egypt. Napoleon escaped and returned to France, where in 1799 he seized power with the title of First Consul.

By 1800 both sides were ready for peace. Napoleon had again defeated a coalition of European powers and was consolidating his control of France. Britain still ruled the seas, but was desperate for relief from the costs and strains of war. High food prices and economic dislocations caused widespread distress. In 1797 mutinies broke out in the navy, and in 1798 revolt flared in Ireland. The Peace of Amiens (1802) was an uneasy truce, but nonetheless welcome to both Britain and France.

Political Consolidation. In the meantime, the need for resistance to France led to a consolidation of political forces behind the Pitt ministry. George III gained new popularity as the symbol of national unity against France, and became more firm than ever in his defense of traditional institutions. In 1793-94 the largest part of the Whigs, led by the Duke of Portland, gave their support to Pitt. Fox was left the ineffectual leader of a small band of opposition Whigs, who were no longer a threat to the ministry or taken seriously by the public. In 1797 Fox's friend, Charles Grey, moved proposals for parliamentary reform, which were overwhelmingly defeated. The Pitt ministry possessed what appeared to be unshakeable control of the government.

The triumph of conservatism in government was matched by public opinion. In general, Burke's point of view triumphed: the French Revolution was seen as a destructive force which must be contained in Europe, lest it infect Britain. Criticism of existing institutions was stigmatized as disloyalty. Although Pitt was more moderate than many of his followers, political pressures led the Pitt ministry to take strong measures to suppress discontent. In 1794 the Habeas Corpus Act was suspended to permit imprisonment without trial of those persons suspected of political agitation. In 1795 the Treasonable Practices Act defined treason to include words as well as actions. The Seditious Meetings Act, passed the same year, prohibited meetings of more than fifty people without license from the local magistrates. Food riots and naval mutinies led to further repressive measures in 1799: radical societies were dissolved, and the Combination Acts prohibited the formation of unions by workingmen to bargain with employers. The unity of the nation in the face of revolutionary France was primarily a matter of national feeling, but it was strongly reinforced by the use of the power of the state to suppress criticism and organized expressions of dissent.

Ireland. The problem of political control was most marked in Ireland where indigenous discontent was inflamed by French agitators and the prospect of French assistance. Although the Irish were divided by deep social and religious differences, they shared a common resentment of British power, and it was this feeling which Theobald Wolfe Tone used as the basis for an organization called "The United Irishmen," formed to fight for independence from Britain. By 1798 Britain's struggle against France had created the opportunity that Irish patriots were seeking, and the United Irishmen rose in a desperate insurrection. The uprising was doomed from the start: most of the leaders had been seized before it began; Protestant and Catholic malcontents had different ends in view; poorly armed artisans and peasants were no match for the Irish militia; and Wolfe Tone arrived from France with French aid too late to be of use. At this point Pitt decided that the political unity of the British Isles was essential, a project which could succeed only if the Irish were given a fair share in their government. He sent Lord Cornwallis, his favorite troubleshooter, to pacify Ireland, and proposed an Act of Union, similar to that which had successfully joined England and Scotland in 1707. The Irish Parliament would be abolished and the Irish would send members to the British Parliament at Westminster — a group of elected peers and bishops, and 100 members of the House of Commons. The formation of the United Kingdom would, of course, give the Irish free trade with Britain and the Empire, and Pitt planned also to relieve the grievances of Irish Catholics by giving them full political rights. The Anglo-Irish leadership class was totally dependent upon British power in the face of French intrigues and domestic insurrection. With the inducement of generous bribes, they were persuaded to agree to the Act of Union, and the new Parliament of the United Kingdom first met in 1801.

An important corollary to Pitt's Act of Union was his proposal for Catholic Emancipation — admission of Catholics to Parliament and political offices. Pitt recognized that the United Kingdom could not succeed without the support of the Irish Catholic population, but he did not allow fully for the resistance such a proposal would encounter in Britain. George III declared his unalterable opposition to the idea, which he saw as fatal to the position of the Church of England, and then he collapsed in another bout of mental illness. Pitt faced strong opposition in his Cabinet, in the House of Lords, and among many of his followers in the House of Commons. Realizing that he had

overreached himself, he abandoned Catholic Emancipation and resigned, being replaced by Henry Addington.

Pitt's resignation, and the Peace of Amiens which followed, marked
a brief breathing space in the long struggle between Britain and
revolutionary France. Napoleon needed time to consolidate his power,
which he had accomplished by 1804, when he assumed the title of
Emperor. By that time he was ready for a renewal of war. After the
Peace of Amiens he began building up an army and fleet, ostensibly for
an invasion of Britain, and in 1803 the Addington ministry, upset by
Napoleon's restless inability to adhere to the agreements he had made,
again declared war. In 1804 Addington was replaced by Pitt, who
returned to office to form one more coalition against Napoleon. Pitt
was in ill health and had lost some of his former supporters, but his
name and ability could still rally the nation. In 1806 he died, to be
followed by a coalition ministry ("Ministry of All Talents") in which
Fox played an important part until his death a few months later. Once
again Britain was at war with France, but this time without the two
leaders who had held the center of the political stage for almost
twenty-five years.

BRITAIN AND NAPOLEON

The dominant fact of British history from 1804 to 1814 was the
long struggle against Napoleonic France. When Pitt returned to power
in 1804 he persuaded Austria and Russia to join with Britain in another
coalition which would be supported by British money and seapower.
Napoleon reacted suddenly. Abandoning his plans for an invasion of
Britain (or perhaps they were a ruse), he marched quickly against the
Austrians and Russians whom he defeated at Ulm and Austerlitz in
1805. The next year he defeated the Prussians at Jena, and in 1807 he
made a favorable peace with the Tsar of Russia. In 1808 he occupied
Spain. Napoleon had defeated the major powers of Europe and was
busy reorganizing the smaller states of Germany and Italy. As in 1940,
when Hitler's armies dominated Europe, Britain stood alone.

Napoleon's dominance on the continent was offset by Britain's
growing industrial power and by her command of the seas. In 1805 a
British fleet under Nelson defeated a combined French-Spanish fleet off
the coast of Spain near Cape Trafalgar. Thereafter France could not
threaten Britain by sea, and British seapower could be used to destroy
French shipping, blockade the Napoleonic Empire, support allies,
encourage insurrections, and capture colonies. Since the conflict
between British seapower and French power on land had created a
stand-off, the two antagonists turned to economic warfare. Napoleon
scornfully dismissed the British as "a nation of shopkeepers" and tried

Battle of Trafalgar by Stanfield (Radio Times Hulton Picture Library).

to destroy the British economy by depriving Britain of her European markets. His "Continental System" was an attempt to close the Napoleonic Empire to British goods. The British, in turn, reacted with the Orders in Council which established a blockade of Napoleonic Europe. The British blockade affected neutral nations especially, and, along with impressment, contributed to the outbreak of the War of 1812 between Britain and the United States. Neither policy was entirely successful, although each nation imposed a considerable hardship on the other. Britain found new markets for her manufactured goods overseas and maintained some of her European customers through smuggling. Even Napoleon needed some British goods, and permitted their entry through a system of licenses. The economic warfare had some effect, but the eventual decision was to be made on the field of battle.

Seeking an opportunity to engage Napoleon on land, the British turned to Portugal and Spain where French occupation had encountered strong national resistance. In 1808 Arthur Wellesley, later the Duke of Wellington, was sent to Portugal to expel the French and begin the process of driving them out of the Iberian Peninsula. Wellington was thoroughly patrician, a firm, dignified, and stern disciplinarian, a master of careful, systematic warfare. Faced by a hostile population and Wellington's methodical progress, the French slowly gave way. Wellington's Peninsular Campaign was a secondary factor in the eventual defeat of Napoleon, but it gave the British the sense that they had found a way to get at "Boney" and a commander who could make the most of it.

Tory Control of Britain. In the meantime, the deaths of Pitt and Fox, and the long struggle against Napoleon, led to the emergence of new political leaders and a new party alignment in Britain. The name Tories was revived for the conservatives who had previously followed Pitt. The Tories were strong supporters of the monarchy, the church, and the *status quo* in social relationships. They adopted as their watchword Burke's veneration for traditional institutions, without his keen eye for the abuses to which any long-established ruling class is liable. But Pitt had not depended upon Tories alone; it was, after all, the Tories who had abandoned him on the issue of Catholic Emancipation, leading to his resignation in 1801. Pitt had also been supported by a strong contingent of Whigs led by the Duke of Portland. The Portland Whigs continued their cooperation with the Tory government, but they still maintained some of the old Whig tradition of resistance to royal power and support for religious toleration. The opposition Whigs, formerly followers of Fox, were now led by Charles Grey. They continued in their belief that parliamentary government, religious toleration, and individual liberties were threatened by the power and influence of the crown, swollen by the needs of war. And then there was in the House of Commons a small group of radicals who continued to press for familiar radical goals such as a more representative House of Commons and the reduction of political corruption. A large number of independent members who usually supported the Tories were also to be found in the House of Commons. In 1812 Lord Liverpool became leader of a reorganized Tory ministry, holding that position until incapacitated by a stroke in 1827. Liverpool was a poised, confident, capable aristocrat whose father had risen from humble beginnings to a position of great influence under Pitt. Addington (now Lord Sidmouth) became Home Secretary, thus assuring the Tories that domestic agitators and dissidents would be dealt with firmly.

Liverpool had the capacity to attract and utilize young men of talent who came forward as Tories because the Tories offered the only opportunity to hold office. One of Lord Liverpool's younger ministers was Lord Castlereagh, a handsome, intense Irish nobleman, who refused an English peerage so he could continue to sit in the House of

THE NAPOLEONIC WARS

Commons representing his Irish constituency. Castlereagh became Foreign Secretary under Liverpool, serving with distinction in that post until his death in 1822. Another brilliant young Tory was George Canning, whose intellect and oratorical ability made him a powerful force in the House of Commons. Liverpool admired Canning and wished to use him in his ministry, but Castlereagh and Canning were bitter personal enemies, and this fact, more than anything else, made it impossible to bring Canning into office. The third of the capable young Tories, with a long career of public service before him, was Robert Peel, the son of a prosperous Lancashire textile manufacturer. Peel made his mark as a protégé of Liverpool, first in the War Office, and then, when Liverpool became Prime Minister, as Chief Secretary in Ireland. The ability of Liverpool and the talented younger Tories, combined with the conservatism of the country, gave the Tories a grip on power which meant that parliamentary reform, Catholic Emancipation, and other controversial issues would be postponed indefinitely.

Victory and Peace. As the Liverpool ministry settled into place, the tide of battle began to turn in Europe. Napoleon over-reached himself in 1812 when he sent a powerful force against Russia. He defeated the Russians in battle and occupied Moscow, but he could not obtain a formal surrender from the Tsar. Defeated by the Russian army and by the Russian winter, Napoleon's soldiers were left to straggle back as best they could while their commander desperately tried to recruit another army. The Russians, Austrians, and Prussians all joined the war — the first time that all three powers had been included in one coalition. Britain served as paymaster to the coalition, and British gold flowed as never before. Nationalist uprisings against the French took place in Germany and Italy, and in Spain Wellington, supported by Spanish hatred of the French, continued his methodical advance. In 1813 Napoleon was decisively defeated at Leipzig, in eastern Germany, while Wellington crossed the Pyrenees Mountains and entered the south of France. In 1814 Napoleon surrendered, and was exiled to the little Mediterranean island of Elba.

As the victorious allies advanced, they began to think of the peace settlement. Castlereagh, the British Foreign Secretary, was determined that the allies should act together in the peace negotiations and in the post-war period. He was also concerned that France be brought back into the community of nations and thus he advocated a peace which would stabilize the French government, check French expansion, and be acceptable to most Frenchmen. The settlement made with France was along the lines advocated by Castlereagh: the Bourbon monarchy was restored in the person of Louis XVIII, brother of the executed Louis XVI; the borders of France were restored as of 1792; Britain restored most of the captured French colonies; the allies abandoned claims for indemnities; France, at British urging, agreed to abolish the slave trade. Considering the turmoil which France had brought to Europe in the previous twenty-five years, the peace with France was an enlightened one. And Castlereagh's role in the settlement had given Britain a role in European diplomacy which she had not previously possessed or desired.

The peace with France had gone easily, in comparison with the problems and great power rivalries which complicated a settlement of Germany, Italy, and eastern Europe. Thus the decision was made to call a general conference at Vienna, which met in September 1814. The Austrian Emperor provided lavish entertainment for a brilliant assemblage, but the important decisions were made by representatives of the four major powers, led by the Austrian Chancellor, Metternich. When disputes arose concerning Poland and Saxony, Talleyrand, the astute representative of France, was able to obtain an important voice for his country. The conference was interrupted in March 1815, when Napoleon escaped from Elba, landed in France, and rallied his veterans to his standard. The Duke of Wellington was put in command of a mixed army of British, Dutch, and German soldiers, which defeated Napoleon at the Battle of Waterloo (June 1815). Napoleon was then sent off to the island of St. Helena, an obscure British possession in the South Atlantic, where he spent his remaining years under British guardianship. The great struggle which had dominated British history for more than twenty years was finally ended.

Shortly before the defeat of Napoleon at Waterloo, the Congress of Vienna completed a settlement for the territories which had been conquered by France. Each of the major powers had its own dynastic or territorial ambitions, but in general they were determined to restore the European balance of power and prevent a renewal of revolutionary outbreaks. A strong buffer was placed to the north of France by the union of Holland and Belgium in the Kingdom of the Netherlands, while Austria was made dominant in northern Italy by control of Lombardy and Venetia. The Bourbon monarchy was restored in Spain, but the Spanish colonists in the New World continued the struggle for independence which had begun during the Napoleonic period. Germany and Italy continued to be divided among small or medium-sized states, although no attempt was made to restore all the petty states of the pre-revolutionary period. Britain was rewarded with colonies and naval bases. British power in the Mediterranean was confirmed by the retention of Gibraltar, the acquisition of Malta, and a protectorate over the Greek islands. The Cape Colony in South Africa, the island of Mauritius in the Indian Ocean, and Ceylon provided bases on the route to India. Britain also strengthened her possessions in the West Indies and Central America. Britain's policies regarding search and seizure on the high seas were left unchallenged, although these had been a cause of great complaint among neutral nations and a major factor in the War of 1812 with the United States. In short, the Vienna settlement confirmed the naval and imperial supremacy which Britain had gained during the Napoleonic wars.

The dynastic and territorial provisions of the Vienna settlement appeared to be a return to the balance of power diplomacy of pre-revolutionary Europe, but Castlereagh took Britain a step further by committing Britain to cooperation with the major European states for the purpose of preserving peace. In the eighteenth century Britain had been involved in European alliances for specific purposes: to maintain the balance of power, to protect the Netherlands or Hanover, and to have a continental ally in the struggle with France and Spain for colonies and seapower. Many of these reasons still applied, but in the glow of the joint effort by which Napoleon had been destroyed, Castlereagh advocated a British commitment to Europe which was more general. Metternich agreed with the concept, and the result was a

Quadruple Alliance, expanded to include France in 1818, which was designed to keep the major powers in harmony. But "the Concert of Europe" as it was called, meant different things to Metternich and to Castlereagh. Metternich looked for cooperation among the crowned heads of Europe to put down revolutionary movements. Such a policy was less acceptable in Britain. The British already possessed constitutional government, representative institutions, civil liberties, religious toleration, and national unity. They could not, in good conscience, set themselves against movements on the continent which sought those same ideals. This was the dilemma which destroyed Castlereagh's foreign policy and, indeed, Castlereagh himself.

BRITISH SOCIETY IN A REVOLUTIONARY AGE

Stability and Change. The remarkable feature of British society in this age of political, economic, and intellectual change was its stability. To some extent social stability was artificial — a defensive posture adopted by a ruling class using the powers of government to bolster its position. But for the most part, the stability of British society was genuine. The traditional institutions and social relationships of Britain were accepted by the bulk of its population as good, to be defended against French ideologues or domestic radicals. A long period of war imposed new social stresses but also contributed to the sense of national unity which saw Britain through to victory.

But in this age of conservatism, new ideas were taking root in Britain which were, in their own way, as revolutionary as the political and diplomatic upheavals taking place abroad. In France, dissatisfaction with existing institutions had created an ideology of revolution; in Britain, where existing institutions were more satisfactory, the goal was not revolution but reform. One approach to institutional change was philosophical or analytical, examining institutions rationally in terms of their function. The principal exponent of this approach was Jeremy Bentham, whose *Introduction to the Principles of Morals and Legislation* was published in 1789. Bentham believed that institutions should be judged by their utility — by their contribution to human happiness. He ridiculed Burke's mystical appeal to the accumulated wisdom of the past as nonsense designed to perpetuate privileges for which there was no reasonable justification. Bentham was especially interested in law and prisons, both of which were admirably designed to inflict vengeance but which had little effect on crime. In his view the Poor Law ran counter to human nature, and thus was not a rational method to deal with poverty. By 1809, when he wrote his *Plan for Parliamentary Reform* (published in 1817), Bentham was convinced that other necessary reforms would not take place until Parliament itself was reformed to remove the unrepresentative franchises and distribution of seats which made the House of Commons unresponsive to the nation. Bentham was not himself a politician and did not sit in Parliament. His great contribution was to present an intellectual defense of reform, based upon reason and utility.

The rationalistic approach to reform advocated by Bentham and his followers was matched by reform movements based upon religious and humanitarian considerations. In 1777 John Howard, a man of independent means dedicated to prison reform, published a landmark work, *The State of Prisons in England and Wales.* At that time prisons were rarely used as places to serve sentences. They were used to hold accused persons until their trial, or for debtors who were imprisoned until their debts were paid. The prisons were a source of income to the jailers, who charged excessive fees while keeping their prisoners in the most wretched conditions. Sometimes debtors would pay their debts, but be held indefinitely because they could not afford to pay the jailers' fees. Conditions were even more intolerable on the congested, disease-ridden hulks in which prisoners sentenced to transportation were confined. Howard campaigned ceaselessly for the improvement of prisons and obtained some legislation which was largely ineffective. In 1807 Sir Samuel Romilly, then Solicitor-General, succeeded in obtaining passage of a Bankruptcy Act which provided a legal process by which debtors could settle their debts and be freed. The next year Romilly began a crusade to reduce the number of capital punishments — for even such minor crimes as shoplifting by children were punishable by death. Romilly was opposed by the full majesty of judges and lawyers, who thought in terms of punishments and fees; but Romilly's lifetime of dedicated labor began to bear fruit after his death.

Religion. The Church of England was part of the established apparatus of power and privilege, and as such felt threatened by the secularism of the French Revolution and the scoffing of Tom Paine. Archbishops and bishops were appointed and promoted by the crown and they sat in the House of Lords, thus they had to be politicians as well as spiritual leaders. The church regarded the Test and Corporation Acts, which limited political offices to Anglicans, as the essential basis for its established position. The churchmen were strongly supported in this view by the King, the Tories, and most of the political class. The efforts of Nonconformists (non-Anglican Protestants) to obtain some relaxation of these laws failed repeatedly, and the controversy concerning political rights for Catholics (Catholic Emancipation) brought the downfall of Pitt and continued to be one of the most divisive issues in politics.

While the church was struggling to preserve its political and legal privileges, it was being criticized from within for its lack of spiritual vitality. A group known as "Evangelicals" worked to bring about a revival of traditional Christian concepts of personal salvation and holiness, and to imbue churchmen with a more dedicated approach to their calling. The most prominent of the Evangelicals was William Wilberforce, M.P. for Yorkshire, a personal friend of Pitt and other political leaders. As a young man Wilberforce experienced a "conversion" which made his Christian faith the center of his life. He joined with other Evangelicals in the encouragement of Bible reading, prayer, and good works. Wilberforce looked to the political and social leaders of the nation to support his cause, and in his book, *A Practical View of the Prevailing Religious System of Professed Christians in the Higher and Middle Classes* (1797), he criticized nominal Christianity and urged a revival of religious and moral commitment.

Wilberforce and the Evangelicals devoted themselves to many good causes, but the most important was the abolition of the slave trade, in which they were supported by many humanitarians who did not share their religious convictions. Wilberforce agreed to take the lead in Parliament, and in 1788 a parliamentary committee was formed to take evidence. In 1792 Wilberforce, drawing upon evidence from the committee report, moved for abolition of the slave trade. His motion was supported by both Pitt and Fox, but neither wished to divide his supporters on the issue and Wilberforce's motion failed. Wilberforce continued to make an annual motion against the slave trade, but the measure was not passed until Fox put the government behind it in the "Talents" ministry of 1806-07. The efforts of Wilberforce and others also bore fruit in an anti-slave trade clause in the Treaty of Vienna (1815), and eventually in the abolition of slavery itself.

Poverty. Public attention to the problem of poverty focused on the Poor Law, for the local authorities were confronted with an extent of poverty which the existing law had never been intended to handle. The Elizabethan Poor Law was based on the assumption of a stable society, where people spent their lives in one locality, where prices and wages varied little from year to year, and where the community (i.e., the parish) was responsible for providing a minimum subsistence for all its members. Such assumptions were invalidated by violent fluctuations of prices, wages, and employment in this revolutionary age. The problem was not just a matter of providing for the unemployed, although fluctuations in employment frequently placed large numbers of able-bodied workers into this category. Even employed workers were compelled to seek poor relief, for as prices rose, wages based on traditional wage rates were inadequate to support the workers and their families. The employers who dominated the process by which wages were set strongly resisted increases in wages. Workers could not leave their parishes in search of better-paying work elsewhere, for to do so would forfeit their rightful claim to poor relief. The Poor Law authorities attempted to meet their responsibilities by supplementing wages with relief payments (the Speenhamland system). As a result, employers were enabled to keep wages low, for the ratepayers (local taxpayers) subsidized their workers, while employed workers became dependent upon poor relief. The public was confused by the arguments among those who viewed poverty as the result of personal faults, those who advocated a free market in labor which would require both employers and workers to respond to economic fluctuations, and those who felt a sense of community responsibility for the poor. From any of these perspectives, the Poor Law was inadequate.

One observer of the problem, an Anglican clergyman named Thomas Malthus, believed that there was nothing that public policy could do about poverty. In 1798 Malthus published his *Essay on the Principle of Population* (revised in 1803), in which he argued that population would always increase faster than food supply, and thus poverty, famine, war and vice were inevitable. Malthus' main concern was to refute the views of William Godwin, who anticipated the steady advance of mankind to perfection, but the main influence of his book was in discussions of poverty and the Poor Law. In Malthus' view, humanitarianism and the Poor Law only made the population problem worse, for they permitted the poor to have more children than they could provide for. The "dismal science" of Malthus appalled philanthropists and humanitarians, but its "tough-minded" realism had a powerful influence upon the social thought of the age.

A more typical reaction to these problems was presented by a journalist of genius, William Cobbett. A tough, John Bull patriot, Cobbett was angered by the fiscal demands of government and the luxury of the upper classes at a time when an inflated currency and rising prices were destroying the livings and self-respect of British working class. Cobbett deplored the effects of industrialism in destroying the simple life and cottage industries of the old England he knew and loved. Cobbett excoriated the great politicians, aristocrats, bankers, and government contractors who profited from public expenditures while the cost fell on those who toiled in fields and factories. He was a patriot who looked back, regretfully, to an England that would be no more, and who expressed, in angry but powerful words, the sense of loss felt by humble people.

SUGGESTIONS FOR FURTHER READING

General works are R. K. Webb, *Modern England: From the Eighteenth Century to the Present* (1968); J. Steven Watson, *The Reign of George III, 1760-1815* (1960); and Asa Briggs, *The Age of Improvement, 1783-1867* (1959). There are many good biographies of prominent persons. Among the most useful are John Brooke, *King George III* (1972); Stanley Ayling, *George the Third* (1972); Roger Fulford, *George the Fourth* (1949); John Ehrman, *The Younger Pitt: The Years of Acclaim* (1969); Derek Jarrett, *Pitt the Younger* (1974); John W. Derry, *Charles James Fox* (1972); Philip Ziegler, *Addington: A Life of Henry Addington, First Viscount Sidmouth* (1965); C. J. Bartlett, *Castlereagh* (1966); John W. Derry, *Castlereagh* (1976); P. J. V. Rolo, *George Canning: Three Biographical Studies* (1965); Chester New, *The Life of Henry Brougham to 1830* (1967); and Elizabeth Longford, *Wellington* (2 vols., 1969-72). The negotiations which led to the peace settlement in 1814-15 can be followed in J. G. Lockhart, *The Peacemakers, 1814-15* (1968) and Charles K. Webster, *The Foreign Policy of Castlereagh, 1812-1815* (1963, first pub. 1931).

The Industrial Revolution has produced a voluminous literature, but perhaps the best works for the beginning student are T. S. Ashton, *The Industrial Revolution, 1760-1830* (1948); Phyllis Deane, *The First Industrial Revolution* (1965); and M. W. Flinn, *The Origins of the Industrial Revolution* (1966). The agricultural changes which were so important a factor in economic change are reviewed in Gordon Mingay and J. D. Chambers, *The Agricultural Revolution, 1750-1880* (1966). Good coverage of the effects of industrialism on ordinary people can be found in G. D. H. Cole and Raymond Postgate, *The British Common People, 1746-1946* (1947) and an enormously learned and stimulating book, E. P. Thompson, *The Making of the English Working Class* (1964). For a broad interpretation of the social changes of this period see Harold Perkin, *The Origins of Modern English Society, 1780-1880* (1969).

12
Conservatism & Reform

1815-1850

In 1815 Britain was compelled to face the profound changes which had taken place in the previous quarter of a century. Britain's involvement in the European wars had led to a commitment to share in the task of preserving the peace. Her political institutions had held the nation together until victory was won, but now her leaders were required to deal with the sense of alienation which had grown up between those who shared in the political process and those who did not. The growth of industrialism had created new economic problems and social needs. Faced with this challenge, the British did not become revolutionary; their instinctive reaction was to cling to that which was time-tested and familiar. Yet new problems could not be dealt with without new ideas, and by 1815 a variety of new ideas had become available. The result was a period of intense political, economic, and social stress, culminating in the great Reform Bill of 1832.

POSTWAR BRITAIN, 1815-22

Britain faced these challenges with a political system which had withstood the challenge of Napoleon, but which was ill-equipped to deal with the problems of peace. King George III was aged and insane, living out his last years (he died in 1820) in Windsor Castle. His son and heir, George, the Regent for his father, who had once been a bright, lively, charming man-about-town, had now become a fat, peevish, middle-aged voluptuary. His youthful attachment to Charles James Fox and the Whigs was forgotten, and as Regent he continued the Tories in office. The Regency possessed none of the dignity or mystique of monarchy, and the Regent petulantly surrendered to his ministers those remnants of royal power which his father had struggled to preserve. He was separated from his wife, Princess Caroline, a coarse, eccentric woman who lived in Italy accompanied by a disreputable entourage. Their daughter Charlotte, heir to the throne, died in 1817, leaving the succession to the Regent's brother. As he had all his life, George spent freely on himself, his palaces, and the entertainment of his friends. In a period when difficult economic adjustments had to be made, he was not the kind of person who would strengthen public attachment to the principle of monarchy.

The Tory ministry of Lord Liverpool, which had seen Britain through to victory, was unready to grapple with the adjustment to peace. Liverpool was a capable, fair-minded man, but cautious in action and temperamentally unwilling to offer a strong lead. As Foreign Secretary, Castlereagh was hard-working and capable, and willing to take decisions which would involve Britain in serious peacetime commitments to Europe. Lord Sidmouth (Henry Addington) was Home Secretary, a man frightened by dissidents and determined to hold the line against those who threatened the existing order of things. The Cabinet was overwhelmingly aristocratic and quite unsuited by education and experience to cope with the political and economic discontents which were suddenly unleashed when the war ended. The Tory party, which was the backbone of the ministry's support in Parliament, was conservative in outlook, dominated by landed interests, and opposed to reforms of Parliament or the church which would threaten its grip on power. The Tories were supported by the independent gentlemen in the House of Commons, who shared their conservative social views but who sometimes suspected that the Tory leaders and placemen were primarily interested in power for its own sake. The Whigs were led nominally by Charles Grey, once the protégé of Fox, who in 1797 had proposed parliamentary reform; long exclusion from office had reduced their numbers and weakened their morale. To some extent their hopes for the future rested upon able, aggressive middle-class Whigs such as the energetic lawyer and publicist, Henry Brougham. These middle-class Whigs had adopted some of the reform ideas of Bentham and the radicals, criticizing especially the waste and inefficiency of government. A small band of radicals kept alive the demand for reform of the House of Commons. In the later years of the war a spirit of restlessness and dissatisfaction had been evident in many sectors of the public. In 1815 the Liverpool ministry found that victory abroad had unleashed pent-up demands at home.

Foreign Policy. More than twenty years of war had convinced the Tories that stability at home required peace abroad. For this reason the Liverpool ministry, led by Lord Castlereagh, the Foreign Secretary, was willing to make an unprecedented commitment to European peace. In 1814 Britain had joined with Austria, Prussia, and Russia in an alliance to complete the defeat of Napoleon and keep the major powers working together in the peace settlement. At the Congress of Vienna the Austrian Chancellor, Metternich, advocated great power cooperation to preserve peace and stability ("The Concert of Europe"), a concept which Castlereagh strongly supported. The entrance of France into the alliance in 1818 was welcomed by Castlereagh as a further stabilizing force. The principal problem which the "Concert of Europe" offered to Britain was Metternich's determination to preserve monarchy and the existing social order throughout Europe. In 1820 revolutions broke out in Spain and several Italian states. Metternich reacted by calling a congress of the allied powers, which agreed to Austrian intervention in Italy to suppress the revolts. In 1822 another congress met to consider the revolution in Spain, and in 1823 the French sent an army to restore the despotic King of Spain to his throne. Intimations were raised that something might be done to restore Spanish·control over the former Spanish colonies in Latin America.

Castlereagh protested strenuously against these actions, especially the French intervention in Spain. He held that the "Concert of Europe" had been formed to prevent general war, and not to intervene in the internal affairs of the European states. Furthermore, the revolutionists were demanding constitutional government, representative institutions, and civil liberties — rights which the British already possessed and could not justifiably deny to others. Any attempt to restore Spanish control over the former colonies would threaten Britain's access to trade in Latin America. By 1822, when he committed suicide, Castlereagh realized that Britain's domestic institutions and overseas interests made it impossible to cooperate in any meaningful way with autocratic states such as Austria, Prussia, and Russia.

Castlereagh was succeeded at the Foreign Office by George Canning, a brilliant, individualistic, and highly nationalistic man whose boldness and independence stood in contrast to Castlereagh's painstaking diplomacy and search for cooperation among the European powers. Canning could not stop French intervention in Spain, but British seapower could and did block any attempt to restore Spanish authority over the former Spanish colonies in Latin America. The infant United States, acting independently, took a similar position in the Monroe Doctrine.

The most difficult problem which faced Canning was a revolution which broke out in Greece in 1821, as the Greeks sought independence from the Turks. Metternich viewed the Greek revolt as another uprising which should be suppressed in the interests of stability. The Russians, however, prepared to aid the Greeks because they saw an opportunity to gain territory and influence in the Balkans. They had a special reason for helping the Greeks, since both Russians and Greeks were eastern Orthodox in religion. Canning was faced with a dilemma: he was opposed to Russian intervention which might introduce Russian power into the Mediterranean, but he could not in good conscience support the Moslem Turks against the Christian Greeks, especially when the Greeks, fighting for freedom against an oppressive regime, evoked in the British public memories of ancient Greek democracy. The colorful romantic poet, Lord Byron, further dramatized the Greek cause in 1824, when he died in Greece trying to aid the rebels.

Canning's approach to the Greek problem was to bring about Greek independence without leading to a breakup of the Turkish Empire or an extension of Russian influence in the area. He decided his goal could be achieved only by direct British involvement. Britain, France, and Russia joined to force a settlement upon the Turks, destroying the combined Turkish-Egyptian fleet at the Battle of Navarino (1827). The next year the Russians invaded the Balkans and in 1829 the Turks were compelled to sign a peace agreeing to Greek independence. By that time Canning was dead and Metternich's concept of a "Concert of Europe" had broken down badly. Castlereagh's involvement of Britain as a continuing force in the European balance of power had come to a close.

Domestic Dissension. In dealing with domestic problems, the Liverpool ministry showed that its definition of liberty was a narrow one. The adjustment to peace brought a number of severe economic problems. Public finance was in disarray; wartime inflation needed to be curbed; trade and manufactures were depressed by the withdrawal of wartime stimuli and the appearance of new competition from European rivals; and thousands of discharged soldiers and sailors swelled the ranks of the unemployed. Economic problems were made even more volatile by a giant backlog of pent-up political discontent. The Liverpool ministry, led by the Home Secretary, Lord Sidmouth, saw no alternative to repression. The opposition Whigs were equally upset by the spectre of social revolution. Local government authorities in the shires and towns and especially in the sprawling London metropolitan area were overwhelmed by a mass of poverty and distress, and were frightened by the ready resort to violence. It seemed as if Britain, having withstood the challenge of the French Revolution and Napoleon, might fall into internal strife herself.

The immediate problems facing the Liverpool ministry in 1815 were economic. In 1815 landlords and farmers were confronted by a severe drop in the price of agricultural produce which had been driven to unusually high levels by wartime demand. The Tory Party was above all the party of the landed interest, and faced with acute agricultural distress, the Liverpool ministry responded with a Corn Law intended to keep the price of wheat high by imposing a tariff on imports. This action satisfied landlords and farmers but aroused a torrent of protest from industrialists and urban workers who complained that the policy kept food prices high at their expense. The money supply was also an important factor in the adjustment to peace. During the war the Bank of England had suspended payments in gold for its banknotes; thereafter the money supply was based on paper currency. Because the Bank had been judicious in its issue of banknotes, money inflation had not become serious until the last years of the war. With the end of the war, financiers, merchants, and economists advocated a return to money backed by gold, and this step was taken by the Liverpool ministry in the Bank Act of 1819. The immediate result was deflationary, accentuating the postwar depression, although probably beneficial in the long run. Those who suffered from business setbacks and unemployment accused the government of being more responsive to the wishes of landlords and financiers than to the needs of the nation.

Economic dislocations contributed to political discontent, and a radical movement arose with an agenda for reform which found support in both the middle class and the working class. Although radicalism included a wide variety of subjects, the key issues were those which affected the distribution of political power — Catholic Emancipation and parliamentary reform. In Parliament itself the aristocratic Whig leaders favored Catholic Emancipation but were dubious about many other radical proposals, especially changes in parliamentary representation and the franchise. The Whig party, however, attracted a number of middle-class reformers, the most articulate of whom was Henry Brougham, a talented Scot. Brougham's brilliant intellect and restless energy were devoted to a variety of radical causes: reform of the law and prisons, free trade, abolition of slavery, public education, the Poor Law, and parliamentary reform. Joseph Hume, another Scot, was one of the most cogent parliamentary spokesmen for radicalism. His most notable parliamentary achievement was repeal of the Combination Acts in 1824, thus legalizing trade unions.

Outside of Parliament radicalism drew its ideas and support

primarily from the growing middle class. The ideas of Jeremy Bentham were expounded by "Philosophic Radicals" such as James Mill who wrote extensively on a wide range of subjects. The main contribution of Philosophic Radicalism was to develop the habit of rational analysis of political and social institutions in terms of their costs and benefits to society. Seen in this light, the ancient institutions which Burke had idealized as the product of some mysterious collective wisdom began to appear more and more as unwarranted sources of power and income for a privileged minority. Closely related to the rational analysis of the Benthamites was the new economics of a group known collectively as "the Classical Economists," who derived their ideas principally from Adam Smith. The outstanding figure among the classical economists was David Ricardo, who was highly critical of political attempts to control economic development through trade restrictions, the Corn Laws, and the Poor Laws. The economics of Smith and Ricardo placed economic policy in an entirely new light. Gone was the concept of a stable community in which each element of society had its proper status and proper reward. In its place was "the invisible hand" of the market, governing rents, profits, wages, and interest rates, and shaping the lives of individuals and nations. By destroying the older economic views, the classical economists were leaving the field open to aggressive middle-class bankers, merchants, and industrialists who were confident they could succeed in a free market and were prepared to work themselves and their employees hard to do so.

Radicalism also found support among the growing working class of the towns who were increasingly conscious of the effects of political decisions upon their lives. Francis Place, a London tailor, was a master at organizing the artisans and shopkeepers of London and Westminster. Largely self-educated, Place became a friend of Bentham, Romilly, and other reformers. He worked closely with Hume in the repeal of the Combination Acts in 1824. Place was himself an employer and was not an advocate of mass democracy, yet he believed that the well-established workingman was entitled to a voice in the political process. A similar radical movement developed in Birmingham, where the metal trades were organized in many small units and relations between masters and men were close. In Manchester, however, working class discontent took a different direction, for Manchester was the center of the textile industry, where the factory system had created strong antagonism between employers and factory workers. Yorkshire was different again, for there the emergence of the industrial system had left pockets of poverty in the old handicraft industries, such as the hand weavers who struggled in vain to compete against the products of power looms. Despite these variations, three common themes can be seen running through working class protest: the dignity of work was debased by the new industrial system; the wealth produced by labor was unfairly distributed; and the structure of authority was weighted against those who worked. The workers, feeling ignored by the aristocracy and gentry and oppressed by middle-class employers, developed a sense of alienation which has continued to the present.

Repression of Dissent. The reaction of the Liverpool ministry to radical agitation was repression. Drawn from a long-established political and social elite, it was difficult for the ministry, members of Parliament, and local magistrates to accept a challenge to their authority from persons whom they saw as far beneath them in the social scale. The rise of radical agitation in 1815 and 1816 led the government in 1817 to strengthen the powers of the local magistrates. In 1818 public expressions of discontent diminished, but in 1819 another economic depression provoked a new round of protests and mass meetings. Powerful orators such as Henry Hunt traversed the nation, demanding a redistribution of parliamentary seats and a broadening of the franchise. The most striking confrontation took place in Manchester where a great crowd assembled peacefully in St. Peter's Fields to listen to Hunt and other radical speakers. The Manchester magistrates, fearful of a riot, panicked and sent in the militia, assisted by soldiers, to arrest the speakers and disperse the crowd. In the melee which followed 11 persons were killed and over 400 wounded. The government was disturbed by the overreaction of the Manchester magistrates, but felt compelled to support their actions. The dissidents, in mocking reference to the Battle of Waterloo, referred to this "victory" of sabre-wielding soldiers over unarmed citizens as "Peterloo." When Hunt was brought to London for trial he was hailed as a hero. The government responded with the "Six Acts" which further restricted public meetings and the dissemination of inflammatory literature, and placed heavier duties on newspapers. It appeared that more confrontations were imminent.

At this point an extraneous event drew public attention and served as an outlet for popular discontent. In 1820 George III died and his son, the Regent, became King as George IV (1820-30). To the dismay of George IV and the Liverpool ministry, the new King's estranged wife, Caroline, decided to return to Britain and claim her place as Queen. George IV was determined not to accept her and demanded that his ministers obtain a divorce by act of Parliament. The public, however, supported Queen Caroline as a means of showing their detestation for the King and his ministers. The Whigs and radicals, seeing a good popular issue, came to the defense of the Queen. The result was a parliamentary and public hubbub which thoroughly embarrassed the ministry and gave popular discontent an outlet.

Conveniently for George IV and the ministry, Queen Caroline died in 1821. By that time the worst problems of the postwar period had begun to ease. But the affair of Queen Caroline revealed the resentments, hostilities, and sense of alienation which had flourished in the previous six years.

TORY REFORM, 1822-29

Tory Liberalism. By 1822 the worst of the postwar adjustment was over, the economy was improving, political tensions were declining, and the Liverpool ministry was ready to take a more liberal direction in its policies. The death of Castlereagh in 1822 made necessary a reorganization of the ministry, which enabled Lord Liverpool to bring forward Tories who were more progressive in their attitudes. George Canning replaced Castlereagh as Foreign Secretary, Robert Peel became Home Secretary, and William Huskisson entered the Cabinet as President of the Board of Trade. It was agreed that the Tory ministry would continue to stand fast against parliamentary reform and Catholic Emancipation. On matters of foreign policy, economic policy, and social reform, however, the ministry took new directions which have been labelled "Tory Liberalism".

Domestic Reforms of Peel. Although conservative where the distribution of political power was concerned, the Tories showed themselves willing to respond to new social needs. The Tories were heirs of a long tradition of upper-class responsibility for the welfare of the lower orders of society, and as a party identified with the landed interest, they were not unwilling to use the power of government to interfere with urban or industrial elites. The key figure in giving the Tory Party a concern for social reform was Robert Peel, Home Secretary. Son of a Lancashire cotton manufacturer, Peel had been prepared at Harrow and Oxford for a political career. He was a man of great personal integrity and strength of character: he was conservative in that he did not act hastily, and he was liberal in that he was willing to respond to needs that were clearly demonstrated. Peel became the recognized leader of those Tories who realized that an elite could hold power only if that power was used for the welfare of all. Thus he helped define a conservative philosophy rooted in the works of a devoted Whig, Edmund Burke.

At the Home Office Peel was primarily concerned with police, law, and prisons, problems which had become acute as the result of industrialization and urbanization. He took up the cause of penal reform for which Romilly had worked and led in obtaining legislation which greatly reduced the number of crimes which carried the death penalty. He also responded to the work of prison reformers and legislation was passed to improve the conditions of prisons. Peel's most notable achievement was the establishment of the London metropolitan police. The government needed trained policemen to control riots because calling in the army often made matters worse. Members of Parliament and visitors to London, as well as the inhabitants, favored a police force, for they were victimized by London's huge criminal class. Headquartered at Scotland Yard in Westminster, the London "bobbies" (named after Robert Peel) soon gained respect and provided a model for other cities.

Huskisson and Trade. The Tories also took steps toward a more liberal commercial policy, signaled by the appointment of William Huskisson to the Board of Trade. Picking up the legacy of Pitt, Huskisson led in a broad reduction and simplification of the customs duties, thereby improving the revenue. The Navigation Acts which protected British shipping at the expense of trade were modified to permit freer trade between the colonial Empire and Europe. Huskisson also took a liberal attitude toward another major obstacle to trade, the Corn Laws, but this was a subject which was sacrosanct to Tories. The Tories were prepared to be liberal with the economic privileges of others, but not with the tariff protection given the landed interest.

The Emergence of a Crisis. In 1827 Lord Liverpool suffered a severe stroke, and it became necessary to reconstitute the ministry. The Tory Party by this time had become deeply divided. The Duke of Wellington spoke for the conservative Tories, while George Canning was the recognized leader of those committed to the "liberal Toryism" which had emerged from 1822-27. King George IV, recognizing Canning's ability, experience, and wide popularity, called upon him to form a ministry. Wellington and Peel, uneasy with Canning's support of Catholic Emancipation, refused to join the ministry, but some of the Whigs gave him their support. Later in the year Canning died, worn out by strain and overwork. After further dissensions Wellington, with Peel as his principal spokesman in the House of Commons, formed a ministry controlled by the conservative Tories, but many of the Canningites refused to support Wellington. Thus the Tory Party, which had controlled British government since the days of William Pitt, began to fall apart. It appeared that a new political alignment was emerging which was likely to bring out into the open those constitutional issues which Lord Liverpool had shelved — parliamentary reform and the privileges of the Church of England.

Wellington and Peel were immediately confronted with the church question. The Test and Corporation Acts were regarded by the church as essential to its privileged position, for in principle they permitted only Anglicans to hold office under the crown or in local government. The application of the acts to Protestant Nonconformists was riddled with exceptions, but the exclusion of Catholics was of some importance in Britain and regarded as vital in Ireland. In 1828 Wellington and Peel were confronted with a demand from Protestant Nonconformists for relief from the Test and Corporation Acts. Needing the support of Nonconformity in the struggle against Catholic Emancipation, they yielded, and the acts were repealed insofar as they applied to Protestants. In so doing, they found they had opened the floodgates.

While Wellington and Peel were wrestling with the problem of Protestant Nonconformity, a crisis blew up in Ireland. Daniel O'Connell, a Catholic, came forward as candidate for Parliament in an Irish by-election and won with a strong majority, although he was legally ineligible to sit in Parliament. Wellington and Peel were now confronted with the possibility of civil war in Ireland on the question of Catholic Emancipation. Again they felt they had no choice but to give way, and in 1829 they declared themselves in favor of Catholic Emancipation. George IV was enraged and the Church of England was aghast. The Tory party split wide open: Wellington fought a duel with one of the highly influential Tories; Peel was defeated in his constituency; and the country squires, so long supporters of the Tories, felt betrayed. Catholic Emancipation was passed by a combination of ministers, placemen, liberal Tories, Whigs, and radicals. At that critical moment, matters were further complicated by the death of the King, which made a new election necessary at a time of political ferment. A great crisis was at hand.

THE REFORM BILL CRISIS, 1830-32

Background of Reform. For two decades the question of parliamentary reform had been overshadowed by other issues. Ever since the 1780s complaints had been made of the unrepresentative character of the House of Commons: the dominance of the House by ministers, placemen, and other forms of "the influence of the Crown"; the small boroughs controlled by aristocratic patrons or men of great wealth; the "decayed" towns which still sent two members to Parliament while new industrial towns were unrepresented; the manipulation of elections by interest groups; and the disorder which accompanied voting in many constituencies. Despite these complaints, the House of Commons had been accepted as broadly representative of, and responsive to, the national interest and the proper concerns of private interests. By 1830 this sense of confidence had broken down. Conservative Tories had seen Tory ministers use their powers to pass Catholic Emancipation.

Industrial leaders resented the control of the House of Commons by the landed interest who used their disproportionate weight to maintain the Corn Laws. The working class had come to think of the House of Commons as a bastion of privilege which protected the interests of landlords or mill owners while leaving them at the mercy of economic forces. Humanitarians found that the House was the defender of atrocious criminal punishments and slavery. And the Whig politicians seemed to be excluded indefinitely from power. Rather suddenly the election of 1830 brought these various forces together, and parliamentary reform became the overriding issue of the day.

The new King and his ministers little suspected the storm that was brewing. King William IV (1830-37) was a bluff, straightforward man, without strong political opinions, apart from his desire to preserve what was left of monarchical power and the general dislike of change characteristic of the Hanoverians. Wellington and Peel continued in office. Stung by Tory charges that they had betrayed the church, they were more determined than ever to hold the line. In the election of 1830 the aristocratic Whig leaders bided their time. The cause of parliamentary reform was put forward by a number of middle-class advocates such as William Cobbett, the journalist, who attacked the reign of privilege; Francis Place and other London radicals, who stirred up popular demonstrations; and Thomas Attwood, a Birmingham banker, who organized the Birmingham Political Union to agitate for parliamentary reform. In Yorkshire Henry Brougham, the Whig reformer, campaigned brilliantly on the issue. A revolution in France in July expelled a reactionary King and thus stimulated English reformers, but it does not seem to have had much effect upon the election. In the south of England agricultural laborers rioted, burning haystacks and destroying threshing machines. Although concerns of the laborers were economic, their actions added to the sense of emergency. When Parliament met in November 1830, Wellington made clear his determination to oppose any kind of parliamentary reform, and on the first important vote of the session the ministry was defeated by a combination of Whigs, liberal Tories, radicals, and disgruntled country gentlemen. Wellington and Peel resigned, and William IV asked Earl Grey, leader of the Whigs, to form a government. The door to reform was ajar.

The Reform Bill Crisis. Earl Grey was sixty-six years old in 1830 — a poised, confident aristocrat who had entered the House of Commons in 1786 as a follower of Charles James Fox. In 1797 he had presented an unsuccessful proposal for parliamentary reform; when he took office in 1830 his commitment to parliamentary reform was clear but unspecified. The leading spokesman for the ministry in the House of

Earl Grey (National Portrait Gallery).

Commons was Lord John Russell, a younger son of the Duke of Bedford who had been an advocate of parliamentary reform for more than a decade. It was Russell who led in drawing up the Reform Bill and piloting it through the House of Commons. The bill which Russell presented in March 1831 was more drastic than had been expected. The bill preserved the principle of separate county and borough constituencies, but extended the franchise to those persons whose property was thought sufficient to guarantee a responsible use of the vote. The county franchise for freeholders remained the same (property worth 40 shillings per year), but tenants with secure or long-term tenancies worth £10 per year would receive the right to vote as would tenants with short-term leases (amended to include tenants-at-will) worth £50 per year. These provisions would greatly increase the number of county voters, but the landlord-tenant relationship was such that the new franchise would clearly strengthen the influence of the aristocracy and gentry in the counties. In the boroughs the bill made two important changes through a redistribution of seats and the establishment of a uniform borough franchise. In its final form, the bill disfranchised 56 small boroughs and took one seat from 30 others, thus making available 143 seats for redistribution to populous counties and large towns such as Manchester, Birmingham, and Leeds. The borough franchise which had varied widely was made uniform: the owner or tenant of property with an annual rental of £10 per year and who met other qualifications — such as payment of rates (local taxes) — received the vote. In some boroughs the bill extended the franchise, and in others it reduced the number of voters. Similar bills for Scotland and Ireland accompanied the main bill.

The struggle for passage of the Reform Bill was a great national crisis. Although historians may dispute the intentions of the reformers and the effects of the bill, there can be no doubt that those who lived through the events of 1831-32 felt that decisions of fundamental importance to Britain were being made. In March 1831 the bill was approved by the House of Commons by one vote, but when it appeared that it might be whittled away by amendments, Grey persuaded the reluctant William IV to call a new election. The election of 1831 was a national referendum on the bill, supporters demanding "the bill, the whole bill, and nothing but the bill". The advocates of reform won a clear victory and in the new House of Commons the bill passed, 367-231. Then in October, the House of Lords rejected the bill. Russell introduced the bill again in December; it passed the Commons without difficulty, but in April 1832 the bill was blocked in the House of Lords by an amendment which the ministry refused to accept. Grey asked William IV to create enough new peers favorable to the bill to pass it, and when the King refused the Whig ministry resigned. Wellington tried

Noble Lords Opposing the Torrent of Reform (Radio Times Hulton Picture Library).

to form a government, but by this time public opinion had gained such irresistible force that he was forced to withdraw. Grey and the Whigs returned to power, now fortified by the King's promise to create peers if needed to pass the bill. Faced with defeat, Wellington and other Tory peers agreed not to vote against the bill and it was passed in the House of Lords on June 4. Three days later the royal approval was given, although William IV refused to perform the ceremony personally, sending commissioners instead.

The passage of the Reform Bill of 1832 was a great triumph of public opinion and the House of Commons over the King and the House of Lords. Throughout the crisis William IV had shown his distaste for the bill, but when faced with what appeared to be a dangerous situation he twice used the royal power with great effect — calling an election in 1831, and agreeing to create peers in 1832. The aristocracy were also forced to yield. After the election of 1831, Wellington and the Tories were helpless in the House of Commons; they made the House of Lords the last defense against a bill which they saw as a serious blow to aristocratic power. Faced with the King's promise to create new peers, backed up by a majority in the House of Commons and a determined public opinion, the Lords had no choice but to give way.

Throughout the two-year crisis Grey and the Whig ministers

remained remarkably cool, balancing a strong determination to preserve order with the need to gain the maximum political advantage from legitimate political agitation. One must not forget that it was the unreformed House of Commons which passed the bill and the unreformed electorate which produced the majority needed to do so. But the British people were the real heroes of the Reform Bill crisis. Middle-class and working-class leaders shared in a masterful organization and manipulation of public feeling. The political issues involved were thoroughly aired in books, periodicals, pamphlets, and other publications. The amount of violence was minimal but enough to have a salutary effect, and the public remained united in its determination to have the bill despite strong differences of opinion concerning many of its features. By their determination and steadiness during a two-year crisis the British public demonstrated that they were indeed ready for a constitutional change which broadened the base of political power.

EXPANSION AND HARD TIMES

The Railway Age. By the time of the Great Reform Bill, industrialization in Britain had proceeded from initiation to extension. Population growth and urbanization continued: the population of Britain grew from 16 million in 1831 to more than 20 million in 1851, and by that year over half the population lived in centers defined as urban. By 1830 the factory system was well established in the cotton textile industry, and by 1850 the new industrial system dominated textile manufacture in both cottons and woolens. The growth of industry placed great new demands on the iron and coal industries, but until the 1850s the expansion in these industries was more a matter of increases in scale than technological breakthroughs. Perhaps Britain's most important industrial advance from 1830-50 was in engineering and the production of machinery. British engineers and skilled workmen led the world in designing and building steam engines, locomotives, steamships, factories, roads, bridges, docks, and cranes. The British were without rivals in using machine tools to make interchangeable parts manufactured with high precision. Many of these engineers, inventors, and machinists were men from humble families who found opportunities in an expanding economy which needed their talents.

The most characteristic feature of industrial expansion from 1830-50 was the building of the railways. For more than two decades inventors had been working to develop a steam locomotive, and rails had long been in use for coal carts, but it was George Stephenson, son of a Northumberland coal mine engineer, who first put the two together successfully. He served as engineer for the Stockton and Darlington Railway, opened in 1825. His greatest triumph was the

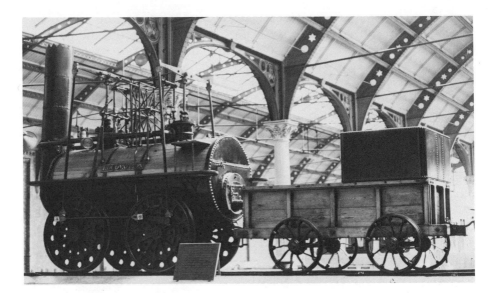

Stephenson's Locomotion Number One.

Liverpool and Manchester Railway which, when opened in 1830, demonstrated the superiority of his steam locomotive over stationary steam engines. Stephenson directed the construction of the thirty-one-mile railway — using cuts, bridges, and viaducts to produce a roadbed with gentle grades. Stephenson and his son Robert, also a railway engineer, became leaders in a railway boom. By 1850 the railway provided Britain with 5,000 miles of track and greatly stimulated related industries, such as coal, iron, and engineering. Surprisingly, although the railway companies had expected that their principal business would be carrying freight, they found that most of their revenues came from passenger traffic, which also required building stations, waiting rooms, and buffets. The economic effects of railway building are obvious; the social and psychological effects of fast, cheap travel can only be conjectured.

Industrial Distress. The progress of British industry was much affected by periodic fluctuations, and the business cycle began to appear as the bane of industrial capitalism. An early speculative boom took place in 1825, followed by a collapse complicated by poor harvests. By 1835 an upswing was taking place, which was aborted by the panic of 1837. By 1840 a full-scale depression was in being which reached its low point in 1842. From 1844-46 the railway boom stimulated the economy, followed by an economic breakdown again in 1846. By 1850 economic recovery had begun, which continued with few setbacks to 1873. One of the results of economic fluctuations was unemployment and distress among the industrial working class. The classical economists, who followed the principles of Smith and Ricardo, held that economic fluctuations were the unavoidable consequence of economic laws and served a useful purpose in redirecting economic activity into the most profitable channels. Others were not so certain, for humanitarians were unwilling to accept the subordination of individuals to the remorseless laws of economics.

Despite the influence of laissez-faire ideas, humanitarian currents and a sense of social responsibility led Parliament and the public to consider regulation of employment in factories. In 1832 Michael Sadler, a Tory M.P. from Yorkshire, led a parliamentary committee which investigated child labor in the factories and issued a remarkable report. Although Sadler lost his seat in Parliament in 1833, the Factory Act of that year responded to the abuses revealed in his report by prohibiting employment of children under nine, and limiting the hours of work of children from ages nine to eighteen. Sadler's place as the conscience of Britain was taken by Lord Ashley, later Earl of Shaftesbury, whose investigation into the labor of women and children in the coal mines shocked the nation and led to the Mines Act of 1842. For many years Shaftesbury worked for legislation to limit the employment of children to ten hours per day, which would also have the practical effect of a ten-hour day for adult workers. Finally in 1847 such legislation was passed. Although Parliament was willing to regulate the labor of women and children, there was still strong reluctance to interfere with the labor of adult males who were considered to be free agents, responsible for making their own contracts with employers.

POLITICS AND REFORM, 1833-41

Whig Reform. The Great Reform Bill was justified by its supporters, not as an end in itself, but as the means to other reforms. The Parliament which met in 1833, the first elected under the new system, was, however, not much different in its leadership and membership from former parliaments. The Whig leaders, Earl Grey and Lord John Russell, had won a great political and popular triumph and were not eager to assume new challenges. Although they had suffered a great defeat, the Tories realized that unity was essential to block a flood of unwelcome legislation. They continued to look to Robert Peel for leadership, because his staunch opposition to the Reform Bill had restored some of the confidence he had lost by giving way on Catholic Emancipation. Many of the gentry and other independent members of the House of Commons, whose strength had been enhanced by the Reform Bill, were primarily concerned to get the country back to tranquillity. The small number of reformers, usually called Radicals, were enormously heartened by their achievement in the Reform Bill crisis, and were aware of the value of public agitation in the achievement of parliamentary goals. Their energy and conviction enabled them to push through Parliament some important legislation before the reform spirit evaporated.

Earl Grey, who had earned his niche in history, retired from office in 1834. After several months of Whig floundering, King William IV called upon Peel to form a government. Peel huried back from a trip in Italy, only to find it necessary to resign a few months later. Once again a British monarch had learned that his theoretical right to appoint his own ministers was severely limited by parliamentary politics. The King turned again to the Whigs, and Lord Melbourne, a genial, easy-going aristocrat, became leader of a Whig ministry which lasted until 1841. Despite these political changes, some important reforms were made in the first two years. The Factory Act of 1833 regulated the employment of children in factories and established an important precedent by providing for inspectors to enforce the act. In the same year slavery was abolished, legislation which primarily affected the British West Indies and the Cape Colony on the southern tip of Africa. Thus the Great Reform Bill had made possible humanitarian legislation which had been long overdue.

The major concern of Radicals, however, was not humanitarianism but governmental efficiency. Two major themes, to some extent contradictory, may be seen in the reform agitation of the period. One approach was Benthamite, emphasizing legislation designed to encourage individual actions which were seen as socially desirable. The other was derived from the classical economists who assumed that individual self-interest would lead to socially desirable actions if governmental interference was removed. In each case, the socially desirable outcomes were similarly defined — productivity, economical use of resources, self-discipline, individual responsibility. The Municipal Corporations Act (1835) was clearly Benthamite, applying to the incorporated towns the general principles of the Reform Bill. A uniform structure of municipal government was established, consisting of mayor, aldermen, and councilors, and the franchise was extended to all resident householders who paid rates. Perhaps the most important feature of the act was the authorization to impose rates for public improvements. As a result, municipal corporations began some improvements in streets, sewers, water supplies, police, and other local facilities, although major advances of this kind did not come until the 1870s and after.

A more controversial example of the Benthamite approach to reform was the Poor Law of 1834 which established central control of poor relief under a Poor Law Commission with extensive powers to set up local administrative units, to inspect local poor relief administration, and to prescribe standards for poor relief. The policies of the Poor Law Commission were Benthamite rather than humanitarian: the poor were encouraged to fend for themselves by making poor relief less attractive than the worst-paid employment, and employers were required to pay market wages by taking away the subsidy involved in relief payments to the employed. The key to the new system was the elimination of "outdoor relief," by requiring all indigent persons to live in the poorhouse. The implementation of the new system of poor relief fell far short of what was intended, and local opposition to the poorhouses was intense. But the Poor Law of 1834 did introduce an element of uniformity and rigor which had been lacking under the old system, without abandoning the principle of public responsibility for mainte-nance of the poor.

Queen Victoria. In 1837 King William IV died, to be succeeded by his niece, Victoria, a sprightly eighteen-year-old girl. Like her pre-decessors, Queen Victoria (1837-1901) tried to preserve some of the vestiges of royal power, as in 1839, when her stubborn insistence on keeping the Whig ladies of her bedchamber led Sir Robert Peel, leader of the Conservatives, to refuse to form a ministry. By that time, however, direct royal authority did not extend much beyond such clearly personal matters, and Lord Melbourne, who served as her friendly advisor and father-confessor, instructed her fully on the limitations of the constitutional monarchy of Britain. In 1840 an important new influence entered Victoria's life when she married Prince Albert of Saxe-Coburg-Gotha, a handsome, dignified, capable German, whose serious purpose made him the most "Victorian" of her subjects. For Albert a new role was devised, that of Prince Consort, and the exclusive responsibility of Victoria to exercise the royal power was never questioned. Yet she had great confidence in Albert's judgment, and relied heavily upon his advice. Under Victoria and Albert the monarchy regained the respect it had lost under her two predecessors.

Political Pressure Groups. By 1837 the reforming spirit of the ministry, never very strong, had subsided as Lord Melbourne presided urbanely over the quarrelling coalition of Whigs, Radicals, and Irish who supported his government. In the meantime, new political issues had arisen, stimulated by the severe depression which began in 1837 and reached its depth in 1842. One of these issues was political democracy, frustrated in the Great Reform Bill, and now brought into prominence by a working-class movement called Chartism. The goals of the Chartists were stated in The People's Charter: universal manhood

Queen Victoria and Albert, Prince Consort (Radio Times Hulton Picture Library).

suffrage, equal electoral districts, annual elections for Parliament, vote by secret ballot, the abolition of property qualifications for Parliament, and the payment of salaries for members of Parliament. The last two would make it possible for workingmen to sit in Parliament, and the first four would create a House of Commons which was democratically elected and subject to annual review.

The Chartists relied upon agitation through speeches, newspapers, pamphlets, and mass meetings to create the kind of working-class support which had been so important in the passage of the Reform Bill. The Charter was presented to the House of Commons in 1839, 1842, and 1848, each time supported by public demonstrations. But Chartism was too narrowly based to succeed. Support for the movement was found almost exclusively among the urban working class. The movement lacked capable leaders and was torn between those who advocated violence and those who preferred orderly agitation through normal political channels. As the economy improved the appeal of the movement waned, and workingmen found they could promote their interests more effectively through trade unions. Eventually, however, all but one of the Chartist goals (annual parliaments) were achieved.

The depression also aggravated the growing conflict between the rising forces of industrialism and the established position of agriculture. The conflict was expressed in terms of free trade, advocated by industrialists, against protectionism, as found in the Corn Laws which the landed interest regarded as vital to its prosperity. In 1839 the Anti-Corn Law League was formed, led by Richard Cobden and John Bright, and supported primarily by middle-class businessmen. For the next seven years the League carried out a highly effective campaign of agitation and propaganda. The issue was an inflammatory one, pitting town against country and drawing upon strong anti-aristocratic feeling. Although suspicious of an organization dominated by factory owners, many workers were attracted by the promise of "cheap food." The issue was inflated out of all proportion to economic realities, but was another example of the strong sense of injustice produced by economic distress. Chartism and the Anti-Corn Law League expressed the feelings of important segments of the British public to whose needs the reformed Parliament was still insufficiently responsive.

THE MINISTRY OF ROBERT PEEL, 1841-46

Political Parties. During these years of economic fluctuation, political controversy, and social discontent, the dominant political figure, in office or out, was Sir Robert Peel. During his brief tenure of office in 1834-35 Peel found that the shattered fragments of the Tory Party were insufficient to support a Tory ministry, despite gains in the election which he called early in 1835. Peel then set to work to build a broader base of support, relying on his Tory nucleus but seeking to attract others who believed reform had gone far enough. In the election of 1835 Peel proclaimed a political philosophy which was both conservative and constructive — the preservation of existing institutions and values by timely reform where needed, and the redress of grievances where a strong case had been made. He addressed his appeal to "that class which is much less interested in the contentions of party, than in the maintenance of order and the cause of good government." In contrast to Peel's statement of principles, the Whig ministry of Lord Melbourne was a loose coalition of disparate groups, without coherent goals. By 1841 Melbourne had lost his parliamentary support and called an election, in which Peel and the Conservatives won a clear majority.

Peel and Reform. As Prime Minister from 1841-46, Peel brought to the office a degree of integrity and competence which marked him as one of the major political figures of the nineteenth century. His concerns were not narrowly partisan, nor was he the advocate of special interests; his purposes were truly national, on the assumption that competent conservatism was what the nation wanted. He was a master of public finance, and in his budgets he removed many of the customs and excise duties which hampered industrial growth and the flow of trade. By 1846 the only important tariffs remaining were the Corn Laws which were sacrosanct to the Tories. The Railway Act of 1844 introduced some regulation of this important new industry. Other important legislation of Peel's ministry strengthened the role of the Bank of England in controlling the money supply and simplified the process of forming business corporations. In short, the Peel ministry was conservative in constitutional matters but responsive to the new needs of a rapidly expanding industrial nation.

Despite his masterful leadership and unquestioned competence, Peel met his downfall when the two issues least susceptible to rational solution converged in a single crisis — Ireland and the Corn Laws. In 1845 a potato blight struck Ireland, and that unhappy land, almost totally dependent upon the potato for subsistence, was devastated. Neither the British government nor private charities were able to cope with the situation, and in the next several years a million Irish emigrated, primarily to Britain or America, and another half million died. Confronted with a disaster of this dimension, Peel could no longer support the tax on food embodied in the Corn Laws, especially when faced with mass agitation by the Anti-Corn Law League. Despite his personal pledges to preserve the Corn Laws, and the insistence of the landed interest that the Corn Laws were vital to British agriculture, Peel bowed to what he considered pressing necessity. In 1846 he introduced proposals for sweeping tariff reform, including repeal of the Corn Laws. In so doing he split his party; with the protectionist Tories (led by the young Benjamin Disraeli) voting against him, the Corn Laws were repealed with the support of Whigs and Radicals. Peel never held office again.

The resignation of Peel and his death in 1850 removed from British politics its most thoughtful and competent leader. But the time was passing when Britain needed leaders of the stature of Liverpool, Castlereagh, Canning, Grey, and Peel. The postwar adjustment had been made and the worst problems of the early industrial age had been resolved. Britain had dealt with these challenges in a helter-skelter, confused manner, but the decisions dictated by logic had been made and accepted. Britain was now entering a period of political calm, when the energies of the nation could be permitted to follow their own courses. Waiting in the wings were Peel's most talented pupil, William Gladstone, and his most ambitious rival, Benjamin Disraeli. Eventually their time would come.

SUGGESTIONS FOR FURTHER READING

Books cited in the previous chapter which are still useful are Webb, *Modern England,* and Briggs, *Age of Improvement,* to which can be added E. L. Woodward, *The Age of Reform, 1815-1870* (2nd ed., 1962). Biographies previously cited which continue to be useful are Fulford, *George the Fourth;* Ziegler, *Addington;* Bartlett, *Castlereagh;* Derry, *Castlereagh;* Rolo, *Canning;* New, *Brougham;* and Longford, *Wellington.* Charles K. Webster continues his magisterial survey of foreign policy in *The Foreign Policy of Castlereagh, 1815-1822* (2nd ed., 1963, first pub. 1934). The period of postwar conflict can be seen in Donald Read, *Peerloo: The "Massacre" and its Background* (1958) and the renewal of confidence in W. R. Brock, *Lord Liverpool and Liberal Toryism, 1820 to 1827* (2nd ed., 1967). A good introduction to the reform crisis is George Woodbridge, *The Reform Bill of 1832* (1970). Philip Ziegler, *King William IV* (1971) and George M. Trevelyan, *Lord Grey of the Reform Bill* (repr. 1970, first pub. 1920) are good biographies of men prominent in the crisis. Good biographies are also available for leading political figures of the post-reform period. Elizabeth Longford, *Queen Victoria: Born to Succeed* (1965) and Cecil Woodham Smith, *Queen Victoria: From her Birth to the Death of the Prince Consort* (1972) deal with the personal traits of the Queen. David Cecil's *Melbourne* (1954) is not only good history but a beautifully written work. The key political figure of the period, Sir Robert Peel, has been thoroughly studied in the works of Norman Gash: *Mr. Secretary Peel: The Life of Sir Robert Peel to 1830* (1961), *Sir Robert Peel: The Life of Sir Robert Peel after 1830* (1972), *Reaction and Reconstruction in English Politics, 1832-1852* (1965), and *Politics in the Age of Peel: A Study in the Technique of Parliamentary Representation, 1830-1850* (1953).

The continuing economic development of the period is reviewed in two good general works, J. D. Chambers, *The Workshop of the World: British Economic History from 1820 to 1880* (1961) and S. G. Checkland, *The Rise of Industrial Society in England, 1815-1885* (1964). Mingay and Chambers, *Agricultural Revolution,* continues to be useful. Perkin, *Origins of Modern English Society,* and Cole and Postgate, *British Common People* also apply to this period. An overview of social history is provided in J. F. C. Harrison, *The Early Victorians, 1832-1851* ((1971). Geoffrey Best, *Shaftesbury* (1964) is a valuable biography. The extra-parliamentary agitation of the period is covered in Norman McCord, *The Anti-Corn Law League, 1838-1846* (1958) and J. T. Ward, *Chartism* (1973). For the Irish problem see J. C. Beckett, *The Making of Modern Ireland, 1603-1923* (3rd ed., 1966), Lawrence J. McCaffrey, *The Irish Question, 1800-1922* (1968), and Cecil Woodham Smith, *The Great Hunger: Ireland, 1845-1849* (1962).

13
Mid-Victorian Britain

1850 - 1886

In his work, *The English Constitution* (1867), Walter Bagehot, a perceptive journalist, described the British constitution as combining "a simple, efficient part" and "historical, complex, august, theatrical parts." At the time Bagehot wrote, the monarchy was the most important of the "theatrical" parts of the British government. In 1867 Queen Victoria was in semi-seclusion, mourning the Prince Consort, Albert, who had died in 1861. Victoria still met with her ministers and read the dispatches, exercising the accepted function of the monarch — "the right to be consulted, the right to encourage and the right to warn," as Bagehot put it. Earlier, with Albert at her side, she had carried out the role of the monarch in a manner which won the approval and allegiance of her people. The high point of the royal family was reached in 1851, when Victoria and Albert presided proudly over the Great Exhibition, housed in the glittering Crystal Palace and displaying the industrial, technological, and cultural achievements of Britain. When Albert died Victoria entered a prolonged period of mourning, until encouraged to return to public view by a shrewd Conservative Prime Minister, Benjamin Disraeli, who realized the magic of monarchy identified by Bagehot in 1867.

POLITICS, FOREIGN POLICY, AND THE EMPIRE

Bagehot's "simple, efficient part" of the British constitution was the Cabinet, comprised of political leaders who were compatible enough to work together with some degree of harmony and who were supported by a majority in the House of Commons. At first glance, a two-party system seemed to function in the ebb and flow of Cabinets, as Cabinets which were predominantly Whig, led by Lord John Russell, Lord Aberdeen, or Lord Palmerston, alternated with Tory Cabinets led by Lord Derby and Benjamin Disraeli. In reality, however, the situation was a good deal more complex. Although the names "Whig" and "Tory" were still used, by the middle of the century the terms "Conservative" and "Liberal" were becoming more familiar. For more than thirty years Lord John Russell, hero of the Reform Bill crisis, had served as leader of the Whigs, but Lord Palmerston, the most popular politician of his day, was counted as a Whig and he was led by no one. Under Robert Peel the Tories had maintained some degree of unity from 1834 to 1846, but Peel's action in the repeal of the Corn Laws had shattered the Tories. A group of Peelites, led by Lord Aberdeen and William Gladstone, followed Peel until his death in 1850, and thereafter found themselves working with some of the more progressive Whigs. Those Tories who had rejected Peel were led by Lord Derby and the brilliant young politician, novelist and dandy — Benjamin Disraeli. In this confused party situation, Cabinets were loose coalitions of political leaders, using personal or party groups as the core of their parliamentary support, but needing additional support from the many independent members of the House of Commons.

The Foreign Policy of Palmerston. The unstructured politics of the mid-Victorian period were possible because, to a considerable degree, a broad consensus existed within the nation and the political class. As domestic conflicts diminished, foreign policy became the major source of political contention. In foreign policy the major figure was Lord Palmerston who served as Foreign Secretary or as Prime Minister for twenty-four of the thirty-five years from 1830 until his death in 1865. Jaunty, confident, ebullient, Palmerston communicated the John Bull patriotism of the British, who were proud of their nation: "a political, a commercial, and constitutional country," as Palmerston put it, which had reconciled individual freedom and the rule of law.

Although Palmerston gave a highly personal touch to British foreign policy, the national interests of Britain were generally recognized and accepted. As an island nation, it was important to Britain to preserve her naval and maritime supremacy and keep open the links with her Empire. Ever since Canning, Britain had avoided close commitments to Europe, yet it was very much to Britain's interest to preserve the balance of power in Europe and to protect the Netherlands and Belgium from dominance by a great power. The British public felt strong sympathy with liberal and national movements on the continent, yet practical realities made it unlikely that Britain could do much more than issue encouraging pronouncements and provide a refuge for exiles. The *bête noir* of Victorian Britain was Russia, that vast, autocratic, expanding state which lurked on the verges of what the Victorians called the civilized world, threatening Britain's interests in the Baltic, the Balkan peninsula, the eastern Mediterranean, the Middle East, India, and the Far East. Britain was most likely to be stung into action when Russia threatened the Ottoman Empire, Britain's decaying bulwark against Russian expansion into the Mediterranean and the Middle East. It was this foreign policy, consistently recognized but inconsistently applied, which occasioned most of the political crises of the period.

Palmerston's approach to foreign policy was seen in 1848-49 when a series of revolutions rocked Europe. He was ready enough with pronouncements but short on action, which made him equally unpopular with threatened governments and disappointed revolutionaries. The reality of the situation was that Britain, secure in her strong government, expanding economy, and invincible fleet, could afford the luxury of such a foreign policy. Palmerston, despite his bluster, had not shed British blood or spent a significant amount of British money. Palmerston's bravado was again demonstrated in 1850 in a petty incident, the Don Pacifico affair. Don Pacifico was a Portuguese

Jew, who claimed British citizenship on the grounds that he had been born in Gibraltar. His house in Athens had been attacked by a mob, and Don Pacifico called upon the British government to help him collect damages. Palmerston came vigorously to the aid of Don Pacifico, acting in such an independent manner that he humiliated the Greeks and thoroughly offended France and Russia who were also concerned, as well as Queen Victoria, who was furious. When his political enemies attacked his conduct of foreign policy, Palmerston replied with a resounding speech in which he boldly proclaimed the British government's support of its citizens, anywhere in the world: "As the Roman, in days of old," Palmerston concluded, "held himself free from indignity, when he could say *Civis Romanus sum;* so also a British subject, in whatever land he may be, shall feel confident that the watchful eye and strong arm of England, will protect him against injustice and wrong." The House of Commons and the British public loved it; the Queen, the politicians, and the diplomats had no choice but to give way.

The less successful side of mid-Victorian foreign policy was seen in the Crimean War (1854-56). In 1853 Russia and the Ottoman Empire entered into one of their periodic conflicts resulting from Russian ambitions in the Balkan peninsula and the Black Sea area. Although the prime minister, Lord Aberdeen, wanted to avoid war, hostility toward Russia in the press and public sentiment forced the government to come to the aid of the Ottoman Empire. The British were joined by France, whose Emperor Napoleon III was eager to play an important role in European affairs, and by the Italian state of Sardinia. The war was fought in the Crimea, on the north shore of the Black Sea, and consisted primarily of a costly siege of the Russian fortress of Sevastopol. The allied generals managed the war with gross ineptitude, which was reported in full detail by war correspondents who accompanied the troops. The British public, which had initially supported the war, was appalled and infuriated by reports of needless deaths and hardships. The redeeming feature of the war was the dedicated work of Florence Nightingale, a resourceful young woman, whose care of the wounded helped establish nursing as a profession for middle-class women. To still the public outcry, Palmerston was made Prime Minister in 1855, and some prestige was salvaged when Sevastopol fell. The death of the Russian Tsar also contributed to peace, which was made in 1856. The result was that Russian expansion in the area was checked, although the problem remained to fester for another twenty years.

The moralistic streak in Palmerstonian foreign policy influenced Britain in dealing with two major conflicts, the War for Italian Unification (1859-61) and the American Civil War (1860-65).

Palmerston and the British public sympathized with the aspirations of Italian patriots for national unity, even though achievement of that goal would require war against the Austrian Empire which controlled the north Italian provinces of Lombardy and Venetia. In 1859 the King of Sardinia, aided by Napoleon III of France, provoked a war with the Austrians, which soon led to uprisings in other parts of Italy. Palmerston and Lord John Russell openly displayed their sympathy with the Italians, and British support contributed to the Sardinian victory which, by 1861, had brought most of Italy under the Sardinian crown. The issue was less clear for Britain in the American Civil War. The initial British view was that the Confederate states, like the Italians, had a right to independence if they wanted it; furthermore, the southern states were major suppliers of cotton to British industry. Palmerston's government at first took a high tone with the Lincoln administration, especially on the issue of the freedom of the seas. When the Civil War became a war against slavery, however, a more compelling moral issue replaced that of southern independence. Despite hardships in Britain due to the Union blockade of southern cotton, Confederate hopes for British aid were disappointed.

The British Overseas. Britain's overseas interests continued to be of the greatest importance, although the value of political control of colonies was diminished by the policy of free trade. Thousands of emigrants left the British Isles every year to seek new homes and opportunities in the United States, Canada, the Australian colonies, New Zealand, and the Cape Colony and Natal in southern Africa. British bankers and merchants pursued their business throughout the world and the British merchant marine and whalers plied the seven seas. The principal value of British trade in the industrial era was in the sale of manufactured goods and the importation of basic commodities such as cotton, wool, tea, foodstuffs, fertilizers, jute, whale oil, palm oil, and tropical woods. In the age of free trade, the British government had little to do with the activities of its nationals abroad. The British navy patrolled the seas from its bases at Nova Scotia, Bermuda, Gibraltar, Malta, the Falkland Islands, Mauritius, Aden, Ceylon, Bombay, Singapore, and Hong Kong. The British consular service offered some help to nationals abroad, and the Post Office extended its overseas services. Otherwise, the British government preferred to let well enough alone, except in instances such as the Opium War with China (1839-42), which opened that great empire to trade with Western nations.

The trend in those colonies where the British had settled in large numbers was toward greater self-government. In 1837 uprisings in Quebec (Lower Canada) and Ontario (Upper Canada) led the Melbourne government to send Lord Durham, a radical Whig nobleman, to visit the Canadian colonies and make recommendations. The *Durham Report* (1839) proposed unification of the two Canadas with "responsible government," i.e., vesting the executive powers in a cabinet with the support of the majority of the assembly. The first of Durham's recommendations was adopted in 1840, although responsible government was not granted until 1847. In the next few years responsible government was extended to the Australian colonies (1855) and New Zealand (1856). In southern Africa, the Cape Colony and Natal offered special problems, both in their relations with the black peoples and with the Boers. The Boers were settlers of Dutch extraction who in the 1830s and 1840s had migrated into the interior and established two frontier republics, the Orange Free State and the Transvaal. British claims in this area led to friction between the Cape Colony and the Boer republics, but from 1852-54 the independence of the Boer republics was confirmed. In 1872 the Cape Colony and Natal received responsible government.

The most striking example of the extension of self-government within the empire was the British North America Act (1867) which formed the present federation of Canada. The economic advantages to be gained by union were considerable, and the lessons to be drawn from the American Civil War were fresh in mind when the proposal was made to join the two Canadas and the maritime provinces (Nova Scotia, New Brunswick, Prince Edward Island) in a federal union. The government of Canada established under the act preserved the Governor-General as the link with the Empire, and continued the imperial relationship in such matters as foreign policy and defense. The federal government, located in Ottawa, followed the cabinet model, with ministers responsible to the Parliament. The federal government possessed power in all matters not specifically delegated to the provinces. Provincial governments were constituted on a similar pattern and provision was made for the addition of new provinces as settlement proceeded. Thus the principles of self-government developed in the Mother Country were extended to her offshoots in various parts of the world.

India with its complex political structure, its ancient and diverse culture, and its great value, was a special case. Pitt's India Act had entrusted the government of the British territories in India to the British East India Company, under the supervision of a Governor-General in India and a Board of Control in London. In 1833 the Company ceased to engage in trade and became exclusively a governing body. The Company developed its own civil service and an army with British officers and Indian soldiers called *sepoys*. From time to time wars broke out with Indian princes which led to extensions of the Company's territories, but the Company never ruled more than two-thirds of India with the rest continuing under native princes dominated in varying degrees by the British. In 1857 a great crisis broke out in India when the sepoys in some regiments mutinied, and for a time it appeared that the authority of the small cadre of British officials and military officers might collapse. After hard fighting, which included the dramatic rescue of a British garrison in Lucknow, the Sepoy Mutiny was suppressed by the British authorities using other Indian regiments. The result of the Mutiny, however, was the dissolution of the East India Company and the establishment of direct British rule of India through a Secretary of State. The civil service and army were continued as before, and British investment in railroads and industries was encouraged, but the new regime, while showing greater respect for Indian customs and beliefs, also contributed to a growing gulf between the British authorities and the Indian population.

The Reform Bill of 1867. In 1867, the year of Bagehot's *The English Constitution,* the casual, unstructured character of mid-Victorian politics began to change as new issues and new leaders emerged. The Whig Prime Minister, Lord Palmerston, who had been a central figure in British politics and foreign policy for thirty-five years, died in 1865, leaving a vacuum in political leadership. Palmerston was succeeded as Prime Minister by Lord John Russell but the most vigorous member of the Cabinet was William Gladstone, a former follower of Peel, who had distinguished himself as a financial reformer. In 1866 Russell and Gladstone came forward with a bill for reform of the House of Commons which called for a moderate extension of the franchise. Parliamentary reform, which had been in abeyance since the Reform Bill of 1832, suddenly gained enormous public popularity, and the politicians discovered they had aroused a sleeping giant.

The result was a series of debates of great intensity and bitterness as old political alignments were shattered. Russell and Gladstone, abandoned by the more conservative Whigs, resigned, and were replaced by a Tory ministry led by Lord Derby and Benjamin Disraeli. Popular support for reform, as demonstrated in mass meetings and demonstrations, persuaded Derby and Disraeli to bring forward their own bill, hoping to win support from the working class. In the ensuing debates Gladstone and the Radicals succeeded in amending Disraeli's bill to make it much more liberal. The bill as eventually passed extended the franchise to urban workingmen, with a modest redistribution of seats to industrial areas. The electorate was almost doubled and although many adult males were still excluded from the vote (as were all women), the issue — clearly seen and debated — was a democratically chosen Parliament, as opposed to a Parliament which represented position, wealth, and education. The dangers as well as the advantages of democracy were thoroughly aired, and when the bill was passed Lord

Derby admitted that Britain had taken "a leap in the dark."

A STOCKTAKING: MID-VICTORIAN SOCIETY

The Idea of Progress. By 1850 Britain had entered a period of comparative political stability, economic growth, and social harmony. The British were proud of their achievements and compared their lives favorably with the despotisms, revolutions, and wars of Europe. Despite great problems of poverty, ignorance, and crime, the general attitude of the mid-Victorians was optimistic. The key concept of the age was "Progress" — belief that the present was better than the past and confidence that the future would be better than the present. To some extent the Victorian concept of Progress was materialistic, supported by statistics showing the increase of population, trade, industrial and agricultural production, and national wealth. But it was also idealistic, for the Victorians took pride in the advancement of scholarship, science, and technology; the material achievements of the age were valued as contributing to the spiritual and moral improvement of the nation. In view of the enormous social problems of the day, this mid-Victorian confidence may be derided as complacency, hypocrisy, or humbug. But the Victorian confidence may also be seen as the spirit of a people at their peak — proud of their achievements and ready for whatever the future might bring.

One example of the Victorian belief in Progress was Thomas Babington Macaulay's *History of England* which began appearing in 1848. Macaulay's work dealt primarily with the Glorious Revolution of 1688-89 and its aftermath, but he took the opportunity to remark upon the advances — intellectual, material, spiritual — which had been made since that time. Macaulay was a staunch Whig and proud of those features which he associated with Whiggism — constitutional and parliamentary government, economic individualism, intellectual and religious freedom, and national pride. The other notable symbol of Progress was the Great Exhibition of 1851, presented in the Crystal Palace, an astounding pre-fabricated structure of iron and glass. Prince Albert was the guiding spirit of the Exhibition; its purpose was to display the industrial, technological, scientific, and artistic achievements of the age. Although the Great Exhibition drew displays from all over the world, most of the exhibitors were British and it served as a showcase for Britain's industrial leadership. Cheap railway excursions brought thousands of visitors from all over Britain, to observe and take pride in "their" achievements.

The Landed Class. Considering the cries of alarm raised by the repeal of the Corn Laws, it is ironic to find that the years from 1850-70 were the

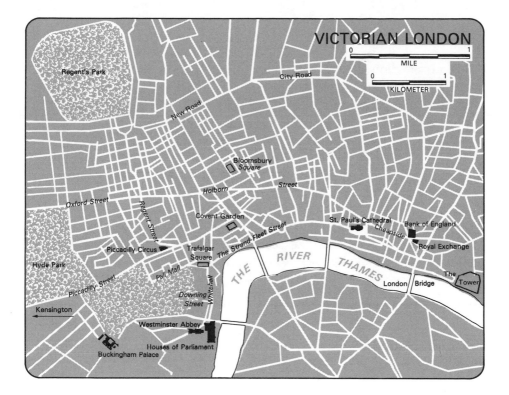

golden age of British agriculture. New methods increased productivity, a growing home market sustained prices, and the effects of foreign competition had not yet been felt. In addition to the profits of agriculture, landowners also benefited from the growing value of urban properties or mineral rights. Great aristocrats such as the Duke of Bedford collected enormous incomes, lightly taxed, from both urban and agricultural properties. Aristocrats dominated the royal court and the glittering social functions related to it, and they entertained lavishly in their comfortable London townhouses or their splendid country estates. Members of noble families were liberally sprinkled throughout the Cabinets and the diplomatic service. The House of Lords was their special preserve, and although most decisions of importance were made in the House of Commons, the House of Lords could delay, alter, or reject controversial legislation, and the Lords also exerted great power as the supreme court of law. The country gentry also prospered and maintained their domination of the government and society of the shires. The life of the landed gentleman continued to exert its fascination, and the aristocracy and gentry were strengthened by the influx of ability and wealth from men successful in government, business, or the professions. The legal arrangements which guaranteed the transmission of the estate to one heir (usually the eldest son) continued; younger sons were provided for by careers in the law, in the church, in business, or in the Empire. Long-established traditions of deference, and the continuing opportunity for successful business and professional men to enter the ranks of the gentry, meant that the landed class remained surprisingly powerful and influential.

Urbanization. The most notable feature of mid-Victorian society was the transformation of Britain into an urban nation. The census of 1851 showed that, for the first time, the number of urban inhabitants exceeded those living in rural areas, and the proportion of the population living in an urban setting continued to grow. The greatest urban center of all was London, the name commonly applied to the metropolitan area which included the City of London, Westminster, and the urban sprawl into the counties of Middlesex and Surrey. London grew because it served a variety of functions, all of which were growing. London was the capital of a dynamic nation and the heart of the world's greatest Empire; London was one of the world's busiest seaports; it was the hub of international finance, insurance, and commodity trading; it was an important manufacturing city, principally of small factories and shops; it was a center of communications, publications, fashion, entertainment, and polite society. London attracted many foreigners who came to visit or to settle, including notable political refugees such as the Austrian Chancellor Metternich, the French Emperor Napoleon III, the Italian leader, Mazzini, and a stream of lesser exiles, publicists, and agitators, among them an obscure German named Karl Marx.

The central position of London in British life was not a new development, but the most striking new feature of Victorian Britain was the rise of provincial cities, whose rapid growth was a counterbalance to the dominance of London. Although London was the largest seaport, other seaports attracted a rapidly increasing trade. Bristol, for centuries the principal western port, continued to be important although it was eclipsed by the rise of Liverpool and Glasgow, both of which served large industrial areas. On the east coast Newcastle and Hull flourished as ports, with special interests in ship-building and fisheries respectively. Old, well-established cities such as Norwich and Nottingham had for centuries served as market towns with domestic industries and now added new industries while preserving much of their pre-industrial character. The most notable provincial cities, however, were those whose growth was the result of the Industrial Revolution.

St. Pancras Station, London.

Manchester, center of the cotton textile industry, was dominated by an elite of landlords, bankers, and businessmen. Birmingham was famous for the metal trades conducted in small shops where masters and men often worked closely together. In Birmingham one found a broad base of political interest and civic responsibility. In Yorkshire, Leeds was the center of an important industrial complex, and another cluster of industries grew up in Scotland, in the valley of the Clyde, with Glasgow as its principal city. These cities were less influenced by the traditions of the past, and were more inclined to seek rational justifications for political institutions or public policy. The political leader who could gain the allegiance of the provincial cities would unlock a powerful new force, especially after the passage of the Reform Bill of 1867.

THE MARCH OF MIND

Political and Social Thought. When the Victorians spoke of Progress, they meant not only the improvement of political institutions and material well being, but the "March of Mind" — the increasing ability of man to understand his world, control it for his benefit, and govern his personal and corporate conduct according to reasoned principles. The most intractable problem faced by Victorian thinkers was the problem of poverty, for the remarkable achievements of the time had also created vast areas of privation, ignorance, immorality, vice, and crime. Although a bewildering variety of answers was available, the question was usually the same: how could "two nations" — the comfortable and the deprived — be justified, reconciled, and eventually brought together in a community of mutual well being?

In the mid-Victorian period the rigorous doctrines of Utilitarianism and the classical economists were softened by a growing sense of humanity. John Stuart Mill, son of James Mill, demonstrated the change which was taking place. A child prodigy, John Stuart Mill was educated by his father in rigid Utilitarian doctrines, and in young manhood he found his emotions touched by Romantic poetry. He lived up to his father's expectations, writing extensively on political and economic questions, but he also recognized that strict logic must be bent to allow for human considerations. In his later years he continued to support the economics of laissez-faire as applied to production, but he conceded that some interference with economic laws was needed to secure a more equitable distribution of the wealth produced by industrial society. In his famous *Autobiography* which was published in the last year of his life (1873), Mill wrote:

> The social problem of the future we considered to be, how to unite the greatest individual liberty of action, with a common ownership of the globe, and an equal participation of all in the benefits of combined labor.

Bluegate Fields by Gustav Doré (Radio Times Hulton Picture Library).

In short, Mill had become what he and his contemporaries called "a socialist."

The most usual mid-Victorian answer to the problem of poverty was to trust in man's ability to master his destiny through the translation of knowledge into practical uses. The Victorians made popular heroes of great engineers who had demonstrated by their achievements man's ability to understand Nature and divert natural forces to his own purposes. Samuel Smiles, a prolific writer, gained popularity with his *Life of George Stephenson* (1857) and his *Lives of the Engineers* (1861-62). In Smiles's view, the successes of the engineers grew out of their knowledge, character, and resourcefulness, qualities which he extolled in *Self Help* (1859) and other works praising moral character, self-reliance, and hard work. Smiles's confidence that moral and technological advances could build a better world was shared by many, although his cheery optimism seemed scarcely warranted. The foremost poet of the day, Alfred, Lord Tennyson, shared some of this confidence in Progress and technology, but was acutely sensitive to the deep-seated flaws in mankind and the losses, as well as gains, which came with change. In *Locksley Hall* (1842) Tennyson

> . . . dipped into the future, far as human eye could see,
> Saw the vision of the world, and all the wonders that
>   would be;
> Saw the heavens fill with commerce, argosies of magic
>   sails,
> Pilots of the purple twilight, dropping down with costly
>   bales.

Tennyson foresaw savage war as well as peaceful commerce and felt deep doubts about the industrial civilization developing around him. Nevertheless, he was optimistic. He was proud to be part of his dynamic new world. He looked forward to a time when "the war drums throbbed no longer, and the battle flags were furled,/In the Parliament of man, the Federation of the world."

In 1859 this generation of hopefulness and generous feelings received a severe blow. For several decades philosophers and scientists had been considering the effects of natural processes over time. Charles Lyell's *Principles of Geology* (1833) explained geology as the result of gradual changes taking place over millenia, as mountains were thrust up and worn down, or as rivers cut valleys and built deltas. Lyell's account left little for the hand of God who, according to the Victorian understanding of the Scriptures, had created the land and seas, mountains and valleys in the year 4004 B.C. The idea of evolution was already in the air when Charles Darwin applied it to living things in his *Origin of Species by Natural Selection* (1859). The key to Darwin's book was his doctrine of natural selection which held that the world of nature was a struggle for existence in which life forms with small advantages were able to survive and pass these advantages on to their offspring, while other life forms, less well equipped, fell by the wayside. In 1871 Darwin applied his evolutionary doctrine to the origin of man. Darwin's concept changed God from a beneficent Providence to a creator who left his universe to struggle for survival; Nature was found to be "red in tooth and claw." Man himself was seen to be a product of struggle, rising gradually to supremacy over the prostrate bodies of his rivals. The mild-mannered biologist with the bold thoughts had introduced a jarring note into the optimism and good feeling of his age.

The concept of evolution gave a new turn to discussions of the social problems of the age. The churches supported the traditional scriptural doctrines of God as creator, governor, and sustainer of all things, including the loving God who provided the means of redemption and fulfillment for all His children, in this world and in the world to come. Advocates of science, such as the brilliant biologist and controversialist, Thomas Henry Huxley, rejected traditional religious explanations, contending that human intelligence had found the key to understanding life and had liberated man from supernatural explanations and hopes. In Huxley's view, the doctrine of evolution was invigorating to man, for while it left man to make himself through his own efforts, his previous achievements gave him reason to believe that he could make further progress up the evolutionary ladder. Herbert Spencer, a philosopher more popular in the United States than in Britain, formulated a philosophy of "Social Darwinism," in which he offered the view that human societies evolved in a manner similar to biological evolution, moving from simpler to more complex forms through the principle of natural selection. In his view, social evolution was to the advantage of mankind, and should not be checked or distorted by legislation or ill-considered humanitarianism. The "tender-minded" sympathies of Mill, Dickens, and Tennyson were challenged by a new "tough-minded" realism which accepted conflict as a necessary part of all existence. Thus the "March of Mind" continued, but in directions little contemplated by an earlier generation.

GLADSTONE AND DISRAELI

Gladstone and the Liberal Pary. Bagehot's analysis of the British constitution was published in 1867, the year which brought a new element into British politics — the beginnings of political democracy. Like the Reform Bill of 1832, the long-range implications and side-effects of the Reform Bill of 1867 were more important than the immediate changes. Cabinets and Parliaments continued to be comprised of the same kind of people, and the two most prominent political leaders, Gladstone and Disraeli, had been in politics for a long time. Yet both of these leaders forged to the front because they were able to understand, accept, and take advantage of new political circumstances. The new political scene was that of emerging democracy: leaders, parties, and platforms with national appeal and national constituencies.

Although Disraeli had proposed the legislation which became the Reform Bill of 1867, the expanded electorate turned in 1868 to Gladstone and those who had joined with him in giving the bill its dominant features. Gladstone was a man of great intellect, energy, administrative ability, and moral fervor. He was unquestionably the dominant figure in his ministry and the principal spokesman for the ministry in Parliament and the nation. Gladstone advocated caution in foreign policy, avoiding involvements in such dangerous situations as the Franco-Prussian War (1870-71) and taking a conciliatory approach to Russian repudiation of restrictions on Russian naval power in the Black Sea. He sought good relations with the United States, agreeing to a generous settlement of American claims for damages done by the *Alabama,* a Confederate warship built in Britain. Thus Gladstone minimized external involvements to concentrate on domestic reform.

Gladstone's major concern was to obtain economy and efficiency in government by removing privilege and waste. The introduction of the secret ballot (1872) was a major contribution to purity in elections. Open competitive examinations were introduced for the civil service and the army was extensively reformed, including the abolition of the purchase of commissions. A major undertaking was the revision of the tangled jurisdictions of the ancient courts of common law. The Forster Education Act (1870) sought to provide elementary education for every child by increased government grants to existing schools, primarily operated by religious denominations, and by instituting local school boards to provide schools maintained by the rates (local taxes) where existing schools were insufficient. One of Gladstone's major concerns was to remove the grievances of Ireland. His most important step in this ministry was the disestablishment of the Anglican Church in Ireland. Gladstone dominated his ministry in administration, Parliament, and public debate, and gave to the office of Prime Minister a degree of national leadership which looked forward to the twentieth-century concept of that office.

Gladstone was also important in the emergence of the Liberal Party, a new kind of political party which supported its parliamentary contingent with party organizations in the constituencies. Although many of the leaders of the Liberal Party had worked together for some time, the Reform Bill crisis of 1866-67, the election of 1868, and the reforms of Gladstone's first ministry had welded them together. On the local level, Liberal associations and clubs organized the voters and fought elections. The Liberal Party appealed to business and professional men, clerks, shopkeepers, and skilled workmen, with a strong leavening of Nonconformity. The goals of the Liberal Party were defined by Gladstone's first ministry: a conciliatory foreign policy, the reduction of imperial commitments, economy in government, institutional reform, free trade, individual responsibility, and removal of Irish grievances. By 1874 those policies had created opponents and brought rankling discontents; the public had become restless with other aspects of Liberalism, such as the temperance movement which worked to limit access to liquor through licensing pubs. In the election of 1874 Disraeli and the Conservative Party won a decisive victory on a platform of saving the country from Gladstone's weak foreign policy and his restless urge to reform.

Disraeli and the Conservative Party. The Conservative Party was, to some extent, the successor of the Tories as the Liberal Party was of the Whigs, but both of these parties were different in important respects from their predecessors. As leader of the Conservative Party, Disraeli's achievement was to develop a party which capitalized on the British desire for continuity and tradition, while giving the party a mildly progressive program. The Conservatives also developed a network of local party organizations linked together by the Conservative Central Office and the National Union. Disraeli's ministry (1874-80) avoided political and administrative reform of the Gladstonian type, but brought forward measures of social reform designed to win Conservative support in the working class. Another Factory Act (1878) codified and extended earlier legislation dealing with working conditions in factories, and the Public Health Act (1875) established a sanitary code. The Artisans' Dwelling Act (1875) was the first important attempt by government to improve the wretched housing of the poor. The Merchant Shipping Act (1878) was passed to improve the safety and health of British seamen. Trade unions, which had been legalized under Gladstone, were given the right to picket. As a conservative, Disraeli sought to preserve the institutions of the past by making them serve national purposes. He persuaded Queen Victoria to abandon her seclusion, and in 1876 she was given the grandiloquent title, Empress of India. Disraeli showed deference to the House of Lords and the Church of England and made clear his determination to preserve British authority in Ireland. The Conservative Party built by Disraeli was still dominated by the aristocracy and gentry, but he succeeded in winning a broad base of support among businessmen, urban workers, and people in small towns and villages. Like Gladstone, Disraeli was a superb

Benjamin Disraeli (National Portrait Gallery).

speaker and publicist. The age of democratic leaders and parties was emerging.

Disraeli's Foreign and Imperial Policy. Disraeli gained attention for himself and flattered national patriotism by activity abroad. The defeat of France in the Franco-Prussian War (1870-71) and the unification of Germany and Italy changed the European balance of power and introduced a period of great power rivalries which eventually became threatening to Britain. Disraeli could do little to affect the European balance of power, but he could strengthen Britain's role in the world by attention to her overseas interests. In 1875 he scored a major success when he purchased 44 percent of the stock of the Suez Canal Company, thus gaining Britain a voice in the management of that vital waterway to the East. In 1877 a threat arose in the eastern Mediterranean when another war broke out between Russia and the moribund Ottoman Empire. The Russians had made extensive gains in the Balkans when Disraeli intervened to maintain the historic British policy. In addition to various warlike gestures, Disraeli was active at the Congress of Berlin (1878) called by the German chancellor, Otto von Bismarck, to resolve the problem. The Congress was a great success for Disraeli, who succeeded in obtaining modifications of Russia's Balkan gains; Disraeli also gained the island of Cyprus as a British base to guard the eastern Mediterranean and the Suez Canal.

Another aspect of Disraeli's policy was to promote the Empire as part of national greatness. The jewel of the Empire was India, and in 1876 he dramatized his imperialism with a magnificent ceremony in which Queen Victoria was crowned Empress of India. Russia was seen as the principal threat to British power in India, and in 1878 the British fear of Russian expansion led to an ill-advised expedition into Afghanistan which was still causing trouble when Disraeli left office. Disraeli also tried to resolve the problems of southern Africa. Conflict was endemic on the borders of the British colonies and the two Boer republics of the interior. In the 1870s these problems were aggravated by the discovery of diamonds in disputed territory. In 1877 Disraeli's government, seeking to unify the area, annexed the Orange Free State and the Transvaal. Two years later, with the Boers still smouldering as a result of this action, war broke out with the fierce Zulus. Disraeli left the problem of Boer resistance and the Zulu War to his successor. By the end of his ministry, Disraeli had found that the flowers of Empire came with dangerous thorns.

Gladstone Again. In the meantime Gladstone had taken his attack on Disraeli's policies to the people. As the Liberal candidate for Parliament from the Scottish county of Midlothian, Gladstone delivered a series of

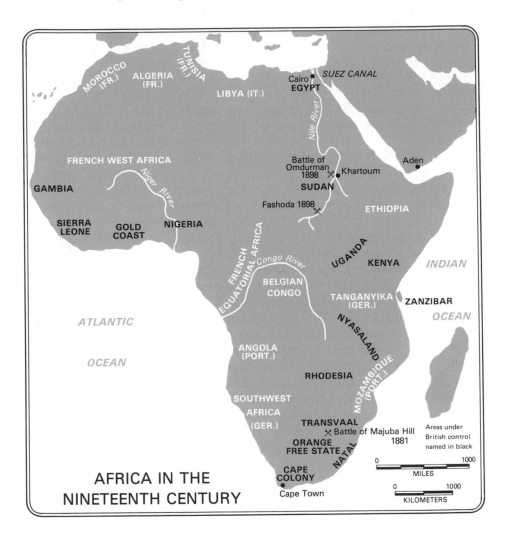

AFRICA IN THE
NINETEENTH CENTURY

powerful speeches which were reported throughout the nation. Gladstone attacked Disraeli's opportunism and manipulation, holding before
the British public the ideal of a foreign policy based on moral principles
and international law. His words fell on responsive ears, for by that
time Disraeli's showy foreign policy, dangerous imperial ventures, and
lackluster domestic reforms had begun to pall. The election of 1880
gave a new mandate to Gladstone and the Liberals. Much to the dismay
of Queen Victoria, who disliked his appeals to public opinion,
Gladstone returned to office as leader of a Liberal ministry.

Gladstone soon found that the problems of the new decade did not lend themselves to clear solutions, especially those growing out of the imperial rivalries of the great powers. Gladstone had severely criticized Disraeli's involvements in Afghanistan and the Boer republics, and was able to pull out of Afghanistan while maintaining appearances. The Boer republics offered a more difficult problem because influential elements in the Liberal Party were reluctant to bring British control to an end. When Gladstone temporized, the Boers of the Transvaal, led by Paul Kruger, rose in revolt and defeated a British detachment at Majuba Hill (1881). Faced with a difficult and costly war, Gladstone agreed to independence for the Transvaal, but under circumstances which appeared to be a response to defeat. Gladstone also found that the rising tide of imperialism drew him into unwanted involvements in Egypt and the Sudan. In 1882 disorders broke out in Egypt and foreign involvement appeared inevitable. Since Egypt was important to the safety of the Suez Canal, Gladstone proposed joint intervention with France. When the French refused, Gladstone sent a British force to restore order. Gladstone was left with a protectorate he did not want, but at that point saw no alternative but to bring solvency and good government to Egypt through British rule. The problem was further complicated by an uprising in the Sudan led by a religious fanatic known as the Mahdi. Gladstone had no desire to become involved in the Sudan, but did agree to send a British detachment under General Charles Gordon to evacuate the Egyptian garrisons there. Gordon, a strong-minded individualist with his own opinions of what should be done, tried to form a counterforce to check the Mahdi, and found himself trapped in Khartoum. After considerable discussion and delay, Gladstone sent an expedition to rescue Gordon which arrived too late — Gordon and his men had been massacred two days earlier by the forces of the Mahdi. The entire episode was seen as a national humiliation, and cast a cloud over Gladstone's second ministry.

Gladstone's major domestic problem was Ireland where economic grievances joined with Irish nationalism to make the island ungovernable. Gladstone's policy was to reconcile Ireland to the Union by redress of economic grievances, but he found that the Irish, led by Charles Stewart Parnell, wanted both land reform and self-government, or Home Rule. Parnell's methods were to encourage violence in Ireland and to use the Irish members of the House of Commons to disrupt the proceedings of Parliament. Gladstone offered both a carrot and a stick. The stick was a Coercion Bill which gave the authorities sweeping powers to seize and detain persons suspected of violence. The carrot was an Irish Land Act (1881) which gave the Irish peasants the three F's: fair rent, fixed tenure, free sale. Parnell would settle for nothing less than Home Rule and violence continued, although the murder of the new British secretary in Dublin's Phoenix Park shocked both the British and Irish into some restraint. But the growing power of Parnell, both in Ireland and as leader of the Irish Nationalists in the House of Commons, made some resolution of the Irish problem essential.

Faced with a stalemate in his domestic reforms, dissension in his cabinet, and open resistance in Ireland, Gladstone's solution to the problem of governing the British Isles was another installment of democracy. In 1884 and 1885 he pushed through Parliament a two-part electoral reform bill. The Reform Bill of 1884 removed the last important exception to universal manhood suffrage by enfranchising the agricultural workers, and a companion measure in 1885 ended the distinction between county and borough constituencies, establishing single-member districts. In so doing, Gladstone further alienated some of his supporters, and his problems were complicated by public dismay aroused by the debacle of Gordon at Khartoum. With his parliamentary support in doubt, Gladstone resigned, and the Conservatives, now led by Lord Salisbury, formed a caretaker government until an election could be held.

In the election of 1885 Gladstone and the Liberals lost ground, but were still the largest party in the House of Commons; the Irish Nationalists, now firmly in the grip of Parnell, held the balance. Gladstone stood quietly by, hoping that Salisbury and the Conservatives would take the plunge for Home Rule, as Disraeli had done for parliamentary reform in 1867. Gladstone's cunning was unmasked when his support for Home Rule was revealed by his son. Parnell then gave his support to Gladstone, and when Salisbury resigned early in 1886, Gladstone organized a ministry committed to Home Rule. Gladstone's Home Rule Bill would have continued the supreme authority of the United Kingdom in matters of foreign policy and defense while establishing in Ireland a separate Irish executive and parliament to deal with domestic matters. Gladstone's bill shattered the Liberal Party, for an influential group of Liberals, led by Joseph Chamberlain, opposed Home Rule. In June 1886, the Home Rule Bill was defeated in the House of Commons, and when Gladstone appealed to the nation by calling another election the Liberal Party suffered a stinging rebuff. Gladstone resigned and Salisbury formed a Conservative government which, with one brief exception, governed Britain until 1905. Gladstone had gambled and lost, and the Liberal Party which he led was no longer the dominant force in British politics.

By 1886 the assurance and stability of the mid-Victorian period was passing. Britain had entered into the age of political democracy, and social democracy was not far behind. Prime ministers and cabinets now held office because they were able, through political parties, to win public support. The diplomatic position of Britain was also changed, by the rise of international alliances, militarism, and imperial rivalries. The British economy was struggling in what is called "the Great Depression" (1873-96): new industrial nations offered unaccustomed competition and agriculture was depressed by foodstuffs brought from abroad by railroads and steamships. Finally, the optimism and confidence of the mid-Victorian period was slipping. Comfort and pleasure replaced the striving of the mid-Victorians as the glories of the Victorian noontide passed into the glow of a pleasant afternoon. The dangers and bitter fruits of the twentieth century were approaching.

SUGGESTIONS FOR FURTHER READING

General works previously cited which continue to be useful are Webb, *Modern England;* Briggs, *Age of Improvement*; and Woodward, *Age of Reform*, to which can be added R. C. K. Ensor, *England, 1870-1914* (1936). Mid-Victorian Britain has evoked a number of interpretive works which attempt to capture the spirit of the age. The most important of these are G. M. Young, *Victorian England: Portrait of an Age* (2nd ed., 1953); George Kitson Clark, *The Making of Victorian England* (1962) and *An Expanding Society: Britain, 1830-1900* (1967); W. L. Burn, *The Age of Equipoise: A Study of the Mid-Victorian Generation* (1964); and Geoffrey Best, *Mid-Victorian Britain, 1851-1875* (1971). James B. Conacher, ed., provides introductions, documents, and modern views of the reform bills in *The Emergence of British Parliamentary Democracy in the Nineteenth Century: The Passing of the Reform Acts of 1832, 1867, and 1884-5* (1971). The foreign policy of Palmerston is covered in Jasper Ridley, *Lord Palmerston* (1970) and Charles K. Webster, *The Foreign Policy of Palmerston, 1830-41* (2 vols., 1951). Cecil Woodham-Smith, *Florence Nightingale, 1820-1910* (1951), tells the story of a remarkable woman.

Previously cited works in economic history which are of value for the mid-Victorian period are Chambers, *Workshop of the World;* Checkland, *Rise of Industrial Society*; and Mingay and Chambers, *Agricultural Revolution.* F. M. L. Thompson, *English Landed Society in the Nineteenth Century* (1963) records the continuing importance of the landed interest, as does Walter Arnstein, "The Survival of the Victorian Aristocracy," in *The Rich, The Well-Born, and the Powerful* ed. F. C. Jaher (1973). The growth of cities is presented in Asa Briggs, *Victorian Cities* (1964) and a profusely illustrated work edited by H. J. Dyos and Michael Wolff, *The Victorian City: Images and Realities*

(2 vols., 1973). London may be followed in Francis Sheppard, *London, 1808-1870: The Infernal Wen* (1971). For social history Perkin, *Origins of Modern English Society* and Cole and Postgate, *British Common People* continue to be valuable. W. J. Reader, *Professional Men: The Rise of the Professional Classes in Nineteenth Century England* (1966) deals with an element of society which increased notably in numbers and importance.

Crucial to understanding mid-Victorian Britain are the lives of its two most eminent statesmen. Biographies are Philip Magnus, *Gladstone: A Biography* (1957) and Robert Blake, *Disraeli* (1967). H. J. Hanham, *Elections and Party Management: Politics in the Time of Disraeli and Gladstone* (1959) traces the changing structure of political parties and organization. For the problem of Ireland, Beckett, *Making of Modern Ireland* and McCaffrey, *Irish Question* continue to provide good guides.

14

Democracy
& Imperialism

1886-1914

When Queen Victoria died in 1901, there was a strong feeling that one age had passed and another was beginning. An observer of the British scene in 1901 would be most likely to notice the continuities with the past: the prestige of the British monarchy was secure; cabinet government and the two-party system were well established; and the franchise had been extended to a large section of the working class. British industry, despite some setbacks and rising competition, still led the world. Britain was the center of finance and trade, the pound sterling was the acceptable medium of exchange around the globe, the sun never set on the British Empire, and Britannia ruled the waves. Victorian Britain in the last fifteen years of the nineteenth century preserved the momentum of the mid-Victorian years. Yet there were many changes in the wind which, from our perspective a century later, can be seen as anticipations of modern Britain.

POLITICAL LEADERS AND PARTIES, 1886-1902

Lord Salisbury and the Conservative Party. If Queen Victoria was the symbolic grandmother to the age, Lord Salisbury (Robert Cecil) was its father figure. Salisbury was a strong and thoughtful aristocrat whose goal was to maintain stability and resolve the tensions generated by the previous twenty years of political conflict and constitutional change. With the exception of a three-year period of Liberal rule (1892-95), Salisbury served as Prime minister from 1886-1902. In matters of domestic and Irish politics, he relied heavily on his nephew, Arthur Balfour, a cool, polished intellectual who had abandoned philosophy for a career in politics. Under Salisbury the Conservative Party took on a new character, preserving its base in the aristocracy and landed gentry but adding an increasing number of wealthy business and professional men. Salisbury also had the support of the Liberal Unionists who had followed Joseph Chamberlain in the break from Gladstone over Home Rule. While supporting Salisbury's foreign and imperial policies, the Liberal Unionists gave the government a thrust toward social legislation which was lacking in Salisbury's more conservative followers.

The dominance of the Conservative Party under Salisbury was, to some extent, a result of the Liberal split in 1886, but was also in accord with the mood of the country. Salisbury was interested primarily in foreign affairs and imperial rivalries, and these occupied much of the attention of the public. The Conservatives were widely supported in their determination to preserve the union of Britain and Ireland. The Conservative policy was to alleviate Irish discontent through the promotion of land ownership by the peasants ("killing Home Rule with kindness"), and this policy had some effect. The Salisbury ministry continued to demonstrate concern for social problems, which Disraeli had made part of his Conservative program. Legislation passed under Salisbury did not break new ground, but included another factory act (1891), the abolition of fees for elementary education (1891), workmen's compensation (1897); later legislation in 1902 reorganized the school system and provided for the further development of secondary education. Encouraged by Chamberlain's Liberal Unionists, the Salisbury ministry sponsored the Local Government Act of 1888 which established elected county councils and a similar form of government for sixty-one urban centers (county boroughs) and the London metropolitan area (London County Council).

The Liberal Party. In the meantime the Liberal Party, split by Gladstone's commitment to Home Rule and consigned to opposition, also began to develop a new character. Normally a major political party in such circumstances would seek new leadership, but such a development was forestalled by the amazing intellectual and physical vitality of Gladstone and by the loss of Chamberlain. The departure of the Liberal Unionists left the Liberal Party with a decidedly more radical stamp — a radicalism different from that of the mid-Victorian period. The new

Liberals no longer saw state action as undesirable state interference. They did not aim at equality, but rather at what has been called the ladder and the net — an opportunity for individual advancement with minimal standards guaranteed for everyone. Liberalism kept its Non-conformist and libertarian flavor and maintained a strong sense of moral crusade against privilege, waste, and abuse of power.

In 1891 Gladstone accepted the need to appease the Radicals, the Nonconformists, and the Celtic fringe of Wales and Scotland. He adopted as party policy the Newcastle Program which had originated as resolutions passed by the National Liberal Federation, an organization of constituency activists. The Newcastle Program included the promise of disestablishment of the Churches of Wales and Scotland, municipal control over water and other services for London, land reform, free elementary education, and a popular referendum to allow localities to prohibit the sale of alcoholic drink. Irish Home Rule continued to head the party program.

In 1892 Gladstone and the Liberals, supported by the Irish Nationalists, returned to power. In his last ministry Gladstone attempted to achieve some of the social goals of the Liberal Party, but Parliament, and probably the majority of the nation, was unreceptive. Ireland was again Gladstone's major concern, and Ireland again proved to be his downfall. In 1893 Gladstone succeeded in getting a Home Rule Bill through the House of Commons, only to have it defeated in the House of Lords. Shortly thereafter Gladstone resigned, to be succeeded by Lord Rosebery, a spokesman for the moderate wing of the Liberal Party. In 1895 Rosebery resigned and a new election returned power to Salisbury and the Conservatives, supported by Chamberlain and the Liberal Unionists. But Gladstone's last ministry had contributed to the new direction taken by the Liberal Party. Throughout his long political career Gladstone had given to British politics intellectual power, moral fervor, and a rare ability to recognize and respond to new needs. It was these qualities which helped to mould a new Liberal Party, which won a sweeping national mandate in 1906.

THE CONDITION OF THE PEOPLE

Agriculture and the Landed Interest. Late Victorian Britain was a wealthy land, enjoying the fruits of Britain's industrial leadership. Yet contemporaries worried a good deal about what they called the "Great Depression," which historians normally date as extending from 1873-96. This "Great Depression" was not a dramatic economic collapse like that which began with the stock market crash of 1929 and extended until World War II. Rather it was a general decline of prices, profits, investment, and interest rates, with effects which varied from one industry to another. Agriculture was the hardest hit, for a dramatic fall in farm prices resulted from opening up new agricultural areas in the American Middle West, the prairie provinces of Canada, the pampas of Argentina, and the interior of Australia. Development of cheap means of transportation (railroad, steamship, refrigerator ship) for bulky agricultural products made it possible to bring these products to market in the industrial centers. Britain's free trade ("cheap food") policy meant that British agriculture was totally unprotected. To some extent British agriculture was able to adjust by turning away from wheat and wool to producing fresh dairy products, meat, fruits and vegetables for urban markets, but such changes also required changes in land tenancy.

Despite the decline of agricultural rents, laments for the landed aristocracy and gentry would be premature. By the late Victorian period much of the wealth of the aristocracy had been invested in gilt-edged securities or well-established industries, and with the fall of prices the purchasing power of fixed-income investments was increasing. The growth of population and cities also meant that urban land or land suitable for urban growth increased greatly in value. By the long-established process of social osmosis, successful businessmen and professional men or their heirs were drawn into the upper class, bringing with them their investments. These were the comfortable people, parodied by Oscar Wilde and gleefully dissected by George Bernard Shaw. When they thought about it, they too felt anxieties. But they had many amenities to cushion their darker moments.

Industry. British industry was not affected to the same degree as agriculture, but clearly it was not keeping pace with industrial growth in rising industrial nations such as Germany and the United States. In 1900, for example, both the United States and Germany passed Britain in the production of steel. Other industries where Britain had formerly held unchallenged supremacy, such as textiles, ship-building, and engineering, were also meeting stiff competition, as was the coal industry. British investors, finding profits in domestic industries declining, were attracted to investments overseas which promised higher returns.

Why this decline in industrial competitiveness? Many reasons can be cited: Britain's factories and machines were old, and British industry did not keep pace with technological improvements; the growing power of trade unions inhibited technological change; the export of capital drained Britain of resources needed to remain competitive; and Britain's free trade policy injured the economy when her major competitors were protecting their home markets with protective tariffs. Although

Britain developed new industries producing consumer goods, the old basic industries upon which her industrial leadership had been based — iron and steel, textiles, ship-building and coal — were losing ground to newer and more progressive producers in Germany, the United States, and elsewhere.

The Middle Class. The deflationary trend which was the dominant feature of the "Great Depression" appears to have been advantageous to the middle class whose numbers and influence increased notably. The growth of the government bureaucracy, of large scale business firms, of retailing, publishing, and service occupations resulted in an increase of salaried persons, while the rising purchasing power of money made it possible to maintain a middle-class life with modest investments. Although the term middle class is difficult to define, Englishmen in the late Victorian period had a reasonably clear idea of what they meant by the term. To some extent, the term middle class referred to income: below a certain income it would be difficult to maintain a middle-class style of life; above a certain income the life of the gentleman beckoned, with its powerful attraction to the Englishman. The middle class can also be defined in terms of work: the middle class man applied himself to a business or profession, and he ordinarily wore a suit and white shirt to his place of employment. But the Victorian middle class was best identified by life-style: the husband went regularly to work; the wife stayed home to manage the house; there was some domestic help; the parents gave careful attention to the nurture, education, discipline, and manners of the children; and emphasis was given to family activities such as church-going, visits to relatives, parlor games, and seaside holidays. Although the middle class advocated economy in government, they were civic minded and willing to support local improvements such as town halls, libraries, and hospitals. They were quickly aroused by social issues such as education, poor relief, and the evils of drink and prostitution.

Questioning of Values. The opulence of the aristocracy and the comfort of the middle class were accompanied by nagging anxieties about matters formerly considered to be certain. The most fundamental of these was the conflict between science and religion. Already weakened by the ideas of Darwin and Huxley, the authority of traditional Christianity was further eroded by Biblical criticism which undermined faith in the divine inspiration of the Bible. The naturalistic view of religion was strengthened by James Frazer's *The Golden Bough* (1890), an anthropological study of primitive religion which showed the extent to which Christianity shared motifs common to early paganism. Perhaps the most telling demonstration of the waning influence of Christianity was the decline of church attendance and the increasing use of Sundays for recreation.

The decline of religious beliefs and hopes was replaced, to some extent, by a new value system which looked to society instead of God to fulfill the lives of men. Although Victorian beliefs faded, the Victorian conscience remained, stung by the disparity between the lives of the comfortable classes and the poverty of a large portion of the population. John Ruskin, an art historian turned social commentator, strenuously denied that most of the population should be condemned to privation in the interests of economic growth, and appealed to the sense of community and fair play so deeply ingrained in the British public. George Gissing, a journalist, gave middle-class readers an insider's view of London life in a series of realistic novels, the best known of which is *Grub Street* (1891). Somewhat later a detailed picture of life in the pottery manufacturing district was presented in the novels of Arnold Bennett. In the theatre, Oscar Wilde made a name for himself by spoofing conventional Victorian attitudes, while another Irishman, George Bernard Shaw, used the stage to criticize Victorian social values in plays such as *Arms and the Man* (the romantic view of war), *Mrs. Warren's Profession* (prostitution and the economic system which encouraged it), and *Major Barbara* (capitalism and war). In short, the characteristic Victorian beliefs in Progress, competitive capitalism, economic growth, and laissez-faire were being seriously questioned by some of the most thoughtful and persuasive writers of the time.

The Status of Women. Another aspect of the questioning of traditional middle-class values was the changing status of women. Middle-class women were not expected to be employed outside the home, and the cheapness of domestic servants, combined with middle-class concepts of status, removed from middle-class wives many of the traditional responsibilities of homemakers. Often they lived empty, dependent lives as elegant decorations, symbolic of the material success of the head of the household. Appropriately, women's fashions displayed remarkable impracticality and extravagance which were characterized by numerous petticoats, huge bustles, or trailing skirts. A still more disabling fashion was tightly laced corsets which reduced many women to suffocation in pursuit of a twenty-inch waist. To attain independence, middle-class women needed decently paid jobs which could not be obtained without education and a change in the attitude of employers. Improvements in secondary education and the establishment of women's colleges opened up new opportunities for women. Teaching and nursing were the most common careers open to middle-class women. In 1891 there were more than 53,000 women

Victorian working-class housing, Newcastle-upon-Tyne.

nurses and over 146,000 women teachers. By the end of the century 40 percent of those employed in the telegraph and telephone service were women.

Women of the upper and middle classes also began to seek legal and political rights. In 1891, in the Jackson decision, the courts ruled that a husband could not coercively retain his wife in his home. In 1883 Parliament gave wives the right to sell or dispose of their property as they wished, and in 1893 a wife's property or contracts became her own legal responsibility. In 1897 a women's suffrage bill made some progress in Parliament, and in the same year a number of women's suffrage organizations joined in the National Union of Women's Suffrage Societies. The very conventional woman who reigned over the kingdom, Queen Victoria, vehemently opposed the notion of rights for women with no sense of the paradox of her position.

The Working Class. One of the puzzles of the "Great Depression" is its effect upon the British working class. In general, it appears that the industrial worker with steady employment was substantially better off: his wages did not fall as much as prices, and thus his purchasing power was increased. Factory acts improved the conditions and safety of industrial employment. The working week was still long, but Saturday afternoons and Sundays off were almost universal. Better housing was available; civic services, such as streets, water, sewers, parks, and

London flowergirl (Radio Times Hulton Picture Library).

libraries were improved; elementary education was provided; opportunities for entertainment and recreation were extended. These advances were seen in the extent to which the "respectable" working class adopted middle-class values, for men in the upper levels of the working class such as shop foremen or skilled machinists were able to keep their wives at home, enjoy a neat house and hot meals, relax with friends, relatives, and neighbors in the evenings or on Sundays, attend church or chapel, and read a daily newspaper. For such members of the working class the most dreaded hazard of all was the workhouse, usually as the result of old age, sickness, disability, or unemployment, for they had little to live upon except their weekly wage.

For those workers who were unskilled or whose employment was insecure, poverty of the most extreme kind was the normal existence. The sweated workers — those who were paid piece wages — were especially badly off, for they lacked even those modest supports which factory workers had gained from the factory acts or their trade unions. Then there was the great mass of wretched people, especially in large cities, who had no steady means of support and lived a hand-to-mouth existence based primarily upon crime, vice, begging, or casual labor. In 1890 William Booth, the founder of the Salvation Army, published a book with wide impact, *In Darkest England and the Way Out,* which told of the lives of these people. The next year Charles Booth (no relation to William Booth) published the first of seventeen volumes entitled *The Life and Labour of the People of London,* supporting with copious detail his conclusion that approximately one-third of the population of London lived in degrading poverty, insecurity, and ugliness. In York, Seebohm Rowntree, a member of a wealthy family of chocolate manufacturers, found similar conditions. The Victorian conscience was shocked and no longer willing to accept the premise of earlier generations that such poverty was an unavoidable concomitant of an advanced economy.

Working-Class Movements. One important factor in changing the conditions of working-class life was the growth of trade unions. The organization of skilled workers had proceeded steadily in the 1850s and 1860s, and in 1872 trade union membership numbered about 400,000. In the 1880s the focus of unionism turned to the "operatives" — workers with some skill, such as railway workers and miners, but who were not trained through the apprenticeship system as in the craft unions. By the end of the decade the "new unionism" was organizing unskilled workers with irregular or piece-work employment. Their plight was dramatized by a series of spectacular strikes: the women matchworkers of London (1888), the London gasworkers (1888), the London dock strike of 1889. Earlier a group of craft unions had formed the Trades Union Congress to bring about cooperation between unions both in political activities and in collective bargaining. By 1900 the trade union movement had grown to almost 2,000,000 members. Women workers remained largely unorganized, as did most piece workers. Hostility to trade unions was strong among employers who attributed some of their competitive problems to union demands and restrictions. The middle class in general disapproved of the conflict which erupted sporadically during organizing efforts and strikes. In 1901 there was widespread satisfaction when the courts, in a celebrated case, held the unions responsible for damages resulting from a strike at the Taff Vale railway in Wales. Nevertheless, when Queen Victoria died, trade unions had already become an important part of British life.

The working class was also able to make its influence felt through political action. Political democracy meant that the two major parties had to compete for the working-class vote, and both parties supported the process by which government accepted increasing responsibility for public health, safety, and poor relief. In the 1880s the ideas of Karl Marx began to have some influence in Britain, and in 1881 H. M. Hyndman organized the Social Democratic Federation, a Marxist political party appealing to the workers. Although the S.D.F. failed to get any of its candidates elected to Parliament, it had some influence in London and contributed to "the new unionism." The Fabian Society, founded in 1884, was a small body of middle-class intellectuals dedicated to democratic socialism. Leaders of the group were Sidney Webb, Beatrice Potter (later Mrs. Webb), and the playwright, George Bernard Shaw. Their goal was to replace private ownership of major industries with public ownership, but they advocated the use of democratic processes to achieve their purpose and relied upon books and pamphlets to spread their ideas. Keir Hardie, a Scottish coal miner, was a leader in founding the Independent Labour Party, which in the 1890s succeeded in electing a handful of members of Parliament on a vaguely socialistic platform. In 1900 various trade unions and Socialist groups formed the Labour Representation Committee to elect labor candidates to Parliament. This group soon turned to association with the Liberal Party as the most practical means of exerting political influence. Through trade unions and political action, the British working class began to make its presence felt. But British workers were not revolutionary; they preferred to work through existing institutions.

FOREIGN POLICY AND EMPIRE, 1886-1902

Foreign Policy of Salisbury. While gradual changes were taking place in Victorian society, a disturbing change had taken place in Britain's external relationships. Salisbury was already an experienced diplomat when he became Prime Minister, and during his thirteen years at the helm, foreign and imperial affairs remained his major concern. He was uneasy as he observed the rise of international tensions, militarism, and alliances. The unification of Germany in 1871 had created in central Europe a powerful new state with a strong military tradition. The German Chancellor, Bismarck, was primarily concerned to consolidate his gains, but the growing power of Germany was also seen as threatening by France, still bitter from her defeat in the Franco-Prussian War. In 1881 Bismarck attempted to check the intrigues of France by forming an alliance among Germany, Austria, and Russia, but this goal was frustrated by the rivalry between Austria and Russia for influence in the Balkans. Forced to choose between the two, Germany strengthened her ties with Austria, and France and Russia responded with an alliance in 1894 which aroused German fears of "encirclement." Thus Europe was divided into two camps, each heavily armed, and each suspicious of the other.

Salisbury wished to preserve Britain's freedom of action as much as possible, but he did not wish to be without friends in such a menacing situation. Salisbury's major efforts in Europe consisted of a series of overtures to Germany which he hoped would reduce German anxieties and permit a relaxation of European tensions, but these overtures were unsuccessful. Salisbury took special pains to eliminate causes of friction with the United States which was becoming recognized as a potential great power. Steps were also taken to reduce imperial rivalry with France. In 1902 the Salisbury government stunned public opinion by making an alliance with Japan, the rising power in East Asia. Directed against Russia, the Anglo-Japanese alliance was a clear recognition that, in that part of the world, Britain could no longer maintain her interests alone. By 1904 the Conservative government, now led by Balfour, had abandoned hope of good relations with Germany, finding the French exceptionally eager to be friendly. The result was an "entente" with France in 1904 which consisted of an agreement to resolve imperial conflicts and maintain friendly relations. Although the entente was not an alliance, and was not specifically directed against Germany or any other power, it led to Anglo-French military conversations concerning defense. The age of "splendid isolation" was drawing to its close.

Imperial Rivalries. Britain also faced new challenges in the imperial world as the major powers sought to improve their diplomatic leverage, military potential, and economic competitiveness by acquiring overseas colonies. France sought to balance the power of Germany by developing new sources of manpower and wealth in North Africa, West Africa, and Southeast Asia. Germany began building a navy and picking up whatever bits of colonial territory were available. As a result of the Spanish-American War, the United States acquired the Philippines and Puerto Rico. In 1895 Japan entered upon a career of imperialism by taking Korea from the moribund Chinese Empire. Rather suddenly Britain's imperial supremacy, unchallenged since the Congress of Vienna, was seriously threatened. Britain's industrial economy was predicated upon easy access to overseas sources of food, raw materials, and markets, and with profits declining at home, safe areas for overseas investment seemed more important than ever. To some extent the British were swept along by the imperialistic tide, but the British role in the age of "The New Imperialism" was different in two important respects. Britain was already an imperial power and some of her new imperialist ventures were designed to protect established positions. Furthermore, Britain was a free trade country; British acquisitions of territory kept them open to all comers, and thus were economically anti-imperialist.

In the 1880s the imperialistic fervor was at its height. After occupying Egypt in 1882 Britain consolidated her control of the Egyptian government and economy, and in 1898 the British occupied the Sudan, defeating the Sudanese at the decisive battle of Omdurman. In East Africa the navy had a base at Zanzibar which was used for patrolling the Indian Ocean, but Britain had not shown an interest in establishing colonies on the mainland. In 1885, however, the Germans claimed the East African territory of Tanganyika (now part of Tanzania). Salisbury reacted by asserting British control of Kenya. In 1888 the British East Africa Company was chartered to begin the development of Kenya, and in 1890 internal disorder in Uganda led the East Africa Company to establish its authority there. A year later conflicts with Arab slave traders led to British occupation of Nyasaland (now Malawi). Diplomatically, Salisbury's major concern was to establish good relations with Germany, and in 1890 another Anglo-German agreement further defined their respective territories in East Africa.

In West Africa France was the principal imperial rival. The British had maintained trading stations in West Africa since the later eighteenth century, but the abolition of the slave trade had made these stations of little value, and at times proposals were made to abandon them. By the 1880s, however, West African territories had become valuable for palm oil and rubber and intense economic competition began between the British and French for position in the region. In 1886 the Salisbury ministry gave a charter to the Royal Niger Company to develop trade in the area of the Niger River, and the Company extended its influence vigorously until 1900 when the British government took control of Nigeria. By that time the French were seeking British support against Germany in Europe, and disputes concerning the boundaries between French possessions and the British territories of Nigeria, Gambia, Sierra Leone, and the Gold Coast had been resolved. A somewhat similar situation developed in the Sudan, which the British viewed as vital to Egypt. In 1898 the British force sent from Egypt to establish control over the Sudan met at Fashoda a French force which travelled from French West Africa to stake a claim for France on the upper Nile River. For a time it appeared that an Anglo-French crisis would take place, but the French, much more concerned with Germany than the Sudan, gave way. The Fashoda incident resolved the imperial rivalry of Britain and France in Africa, and contributed to the improved relations which resulted in the Anglo-French entente of 1904.

Southern Africa. Southern Africa produced the most difficult problems for British imperial policy. In the Cape Colony tensions existed between the two principal white groups, the British and the Boers. The situation was further complicated by the black population who were laborers for the farms, mines, and factories. The colony of Natal, to the east of the Cape Colony, was dominated by British planters using African or East Indian laborers. The most pressing problems of the area grew out of the relationships between the two British colonies and the

Boer republics of the interior. These problems had been aggravated by Disraeli's annexation of the Boer republics in 1877 and Gladstone's withdrawal from the Transvaal in 1881.

The most remarkable figure of this period was Cecil Rhodes, a man of great leadership and ambition who rose to dominance of the diamond mines and political control of the Cape Colony. Rhodes was an imperialist who dreamed of a broad band of British territory linking southern Africa with the British possessions in East Africa, the Sudan, and Egypt. He was also a skilled propagandist who could play effectively upon imperialist sentiments in Britain. In 1888 he received a concession from Lobengula, king of the Matabele, to settle the territory which became Rhodesia, and in 1889 the Salisbury government chartered the British South Africa Company to develop the area. In 1893 Lobengula led a revolt of the Matabele, which was crushed, and thereafter the settlement of Rhodesia proceeded rapidly.

As a result of Rhodes's expansive policies, the Boer republics were trapped between the Cape Colony and Rhodesia. The Boers were led by the tough president of the Transvaal, Paul Kruger, who saw the Boer way of life jeopardized by the influx of outsiders (Uitlanders) who came into the Transvaal to develop the gold mines. Kruger resisted the claims of the Uitlanders for political rights and in 1895 the Uitlanders, supported by Rhodes, plotted to overthrow him. The plot was prematurely revealed when Rhodes's agent in Rhodesia, Dr. Jameson, led a party of men into the Transvaal before the Uitlanders were ready to rise. As a result of the Jameson Raid, as it was called, Rhodes was driven from office in the Cape Colony and Kruger began preparing for war, hoping to obtain German aid.

The prospect of German involvement in the Transvaal and the fall of Rhodes changed the views of the Salisbury government. The Colonial Secretary was Joseph Chamberlain, leader of the Liberal Unionists. He was a strong imperialist, but he had distrusted Rhodes and his highly personal form of imperial expansion. As the grievances of the Uitlanders mounted, the Salisbury government decided that war was inevitable and that it was necessary to overthrow Kruger to prevent the extension of German influence into the area. The Boer War began in 1899, and consisted of three phases: the Boer invasions of Natal and the Cape Colony, which were repulsed; the British invasion of the Orange Free State and the Transvaal, which led to the destruction of the Boer army; and a period of guerrilla warfare as British detachments hunted down Boer commandos. By the time the war ended in 1902 Rhodes was dead and Kruger died shortly thereafter.

In Britain the Boer War created a heated political controversy, especially within the Liberal Party, as patriots and imperialists supported the war while opponents of the war depicted it as the action of a swaggering bully. The efforts of a professional army to put down desperate guerrillas led inevitably to atrocities, and as reports reached the newspapers of British concentration camps in which large numbers of women and children had died, public opinion in Britain turned against the war. Although Britain won the war in southern Africa, the opponents won the war of words at home, and the Boer War discredited the imperialistic policies of the previous twenty years, as well as the Conservative government which had been responsible.

Chamberlain and Imperial Federation. During his years as Colonial Secretary, Joseph Chamberlain's major concern had been imperial federation. Threatened by the rise of international tensions and the declining competitiveness of the British economy, Chamberlain reacted by trying to bring Britain and her Empire closer together. His principal attention was given to relations between Britain and the self-governing colonies: Canada (united by the British North America Act in 1867), the six Australian colonies, New Zealand, the Cape Colony and Natal. The Golden Jubilee of Queen Victoria in 1887, and her Diamond Jubilee in 1897, brought the political leaders of the self-governing colonies to London and provided Chamberlain with an opportunity to discuss closer relationships. Chamberlain's proposals fell upon deaf ears. Having gained the right to manage their own affairs, the colonial leaders were unwilling to commit themselves to closer ties. One result of Chamberlain's search for imperial unity was the federation of the Australian colonies in 1901. Chamberlain also worked to improve the productivity of the dependent colonies — such as the British West Indies and the African colonies — through the development of new crops and the conquest of tropical diseases. In 1903 Chamberlain, still seeking the elusive goal of imperial unity, took a bold step. He defied accepted free trade doctrines and the political attractions of "cheap food" by proposing a protective tariff with preferential rates for the colonies. Having done so, Chamberlain discovered that the colonies were unenthusiastic, and that he had unleashed a disastrous political crisis at home.

"THE NEW LIBERALISM"

The Liberal Revival. Queen Victoria was succeeded in 1901 by her handsome and pleasure-loving son, Edward VII (1901-10), and a year later Lord Salisbury retired due to ill health. The leadership of the Conservative government passed to Salisbury's nephew, Arthur Balfour, but Joseph Chamberlain, who had acted almost as deputy premier in Salisbury's later years, had an equal claim to the position. In the Liberal Party Sir Henry Campbell-Bannerman, whose forthright opposition to the Boer War appealed to the idealism of many Liberals, was recognized as the spokesman for those elements in the Liberal Party who were committed to progressive ideas. In 1903 the Liberals and the Labour Representation Committee agreed to support each other's candidates against the Conservatives in the next election.

The Conservatives contributed significantly to their own downfall. Balfour's crumbling ministry was buffeted by controversy over social issues such as education and the licensing of pubs. The vital blow to the Conservatives, however, was dealt by Joseph Chamberlain, when he announced in 1903 his conversion to a protective tariff with imperial preference. Chamberlain's proposal attacked the twin principles of Victorian economic policy — free trade and cheap food. The Conservative government and party split on the issue, and in 1905 Balfour resigned and the Liberals formed a government. The long Conservative dominance had ended.

The Liberal government which took office in 1905 was exceptionally talented. As Prime Minister, Campbell-Bannerman displayed unexpected qualities of idealism and practical political sense and was capable of recruiting and leading a cabinet of remarkable individuals. When ill health forced Campbell-Bannerman to retire in 1908, he was succeeded as Prime Minister by Herbert Asquith, previously Chancellor of the Exchequer. Asquith brought to the office keen intelligence, a head for figures, and a Nonconformist background diluted by an Oxford education and a wealthy marriage. In some respects the most striking member of the ministry was the fiery young Welshman, David Lloyd George, whose intense personal ambition was fuelled by sympathy for the poor and antagonism toward aristocracy and privilege. The Liberal government also captured the imagination and support of Winston Churchill, who abandoned the Conservative Party on the issue of free trade. Early in 1906 the Liberals called an election, which was one of the most decisive of modern times. In the new Parliament the Liberals held 377 seats, the Conservatives 157, the Irish Nationalists 83, and there were 53 Labour members, some elected as Liberals and others under the auspices of the Labour Representation Committee. Although the issues were confused and the positions of the major parties far from clear, the election revealed an important shift in the mood of the electorate.

Social Legislation. One of the goals of the Liberal government was to come to grips with the major hazards of the industrial working class: old age, sickness, disability, and unemployment. The Old Age Pension Act (1908) provided modest assistance to the elderly in the form of five shillings per week for persons over seventy, a sum not so large as to reduce the inducement to save, but large enough to help those who had some personal or family resources to draw upon. In dealing with the problems of sickness, disability, and unemployment the Liberals faced problems which they traditionally had considered to be matters of individual responsibility. Liberal policy was much influenced by a young journalist named William Beveridge, who published in 1909 a book entitled *Unemployment: A Problem of Industry.* Beveridge pointed out that much unemployment was the result of economic forces for which the individual could not be held responsible, including cyclical fluctuations and technological change. Since this kind of employment was the result of industrial factors, the cost of coping with it should be born by industry. The proposals presented by the Liberal government, adopted in 1911 as the National Insurance Act, preserved the principles of individual responsibility and public economy by establishing a system of insurance against sickness, disability, and unemployment paid for by contributions from employers and workers. Provision for workers in occupations not covered by the act and for those suffering from long-term unemployment was still the responsibility of the poor relief system.

The liberal doctrines of economic individualism had always recognized the special claims of those who could not be considered free agents, such as women and children. As the Liberal ministers proceeded in their investigations of industrial problems they became aware of two kinds of workers who needed additional assistance — casual laborers and workers in "sweatshop" industries who were paid by the piece. These workers were protected neither by the factory acts nor trade unions. Their position in a competitive job market was weak, and they could scarcely be expected to bargain for themselves. Winston Churchill, who joined the Cabinet in 1908 as President of the Board of Trade, played an important part in dealing with both of these problems. Advised by Beveridge, Churchill obtained legislation establishing a system of labor exchanges which served a useful purpose in helping casual workers find employment. Churchill also responded to the needs of "sweated" workers by proposing the Trade Boards Act (1909) which was vigorously supported by the women's labor movement. Under the act, boards were established to set minimum wages in industries such as the making of clothing, lace, and paper boxes. Thus the Liberal government preserved the principle of individual responsibility where possible, while responding to those aspects of life in an industrial society where that premise could clearly be seen to be inoperative.

The Liberals and the Lords. As the Liberal government proceeded on its course, a major point of constitutional conflict emerged — the power of the House of Lords, in which the Conservatives were strongly entrenched. The Conservatives, who had a long tradition of social

David Lloyd George and Winston Churchill (Radio Times Hulton Picture Library).

concern, were not completely antagonistic to the Liberal social welfare legislation, but the Conservative majority in the Lords rejected Liberal measures dealing with voting, schools, licensing of pubs, and other schemes dear to the hearts of certain Liberal constituencies. It was clear that other Liberal goals which were even more controversial, such as Home Rule for Ireland or disestablishment of the Anglican Church in Wales, would encounter a fight to the death in the Lords. But the battle was fought on the question of the budget. In 1909 Lloyd George, who had succeeded Asquith as Chancellor of the Exchequer, was confronted with the need to raise more revenue, both for naval rearmament and to meet the costs of social legislation. His budget included taxation which fell principally on the wealthy: a progressive income tax, increased death duties, and new taxes on land. Stung to fury by Lloyd George's anti-aristocratic and "soak the rich" pronouncements, the House of Lords rejected the budget, thus challenging the long-established doctrine that public finance was the exclusive concern of the House of Commons.

The Liberals, led by Asquith and Lloyd George, now had a popular issue with which they hoped to defeat the Conservatives in the election of January 1910. They were disappointed. Lloyd George's attack on the House of Lords may have been of some electoral benefit, but the Liberals lost heavily and became dependent on the support of the Irish Nationalists and the forty Labour members. Although the peers agreed to pass the budget, the Liberals decided to seize the nettle and proposed a Parliament Bill which would curtail the powers of the upper House. In the midst of this controversy King Edward VII died, to be succeeded by his son, George V (1910-36). When attempts at a compromise failed, the second election of the year was called which was indecisive. When the Lords tried to amend the Parliament Bill Asquith came forward with the promise of the new King to create the number of peers needed for passage. In circumstances of high excitement, enough Conservative peers abstained or voted for the bill to permit it to pass. The Parliament Act of 1911 provided that the House of Lords could delay a bill for three years, but if passed in three consecutive years by the House of Commons a bill became law without consent of the Lords. Another provision of the act reduced the maximum term for elections from seven to five years. The inevitable effect of the Parliament Act was to reduce further the political power of birth and privilege. Although the delaying power of the House of Lords was still significant, essentially the hereditary aristocracy had followed the monarchy into a political role which was more ornamental than effective.

Home Rule. Having curbed the veto power of the House of Lords, the Liberal government, supported by the Labour members and the Irish Nationalists, moved forward with another controversial measure — Home Rule for Ireland. The Conservatives, who could no longer rely on the House of Lords, fought Home Rule by appealing to public opinion. The center of resistance to Home Rule was the Protestants of Northern Ireland, centered in Belfast. They formed a para-military body called the Ulster Volunteers and prepared to fight to keep from being engulfed in an Ireland dominated by Catholics. Using the slogan "Ulster

Mrs. Pankhurst arrested at Buckingham Palace, 1914 (Radio Times Hulton Picture Library).

will fight, and Ulster will be right," the Ulster Protestants were supported by many prominent Conservatives who attended mass meetings in Belfast and London. The Irish Nationalists also began preparing to fight, and attempts by the Liberal government to prevent civil war met with insubordination in the army. The Conservatives prepared for a last ditch stand in the House of Lords. The Home Rule Bill was passed by the Commons in 1912 and again in 1913, and each time it was rejected by the Lords, using the delaying powers reserved by the Parliament Act. The bill was passed for the third time in 1914, after which it would become law without consent of the Lords, but by then war had broken out in Europe and it was thought prudent to suspend the operation of the act. Thus the Irish question continued, to be further inflamed by the nationalist passions aroused during World War I.

Continued Unrest. The partisan conflict unleashed by the Parliament Act and Home Rule was matched by other forms of public unrest. A series of strikes by the large unions — such as the miners, railway workers, Lancashire cotton workers, London dockers, and the transport workers — disturbed national life. The women's suffrage movement also came to a climax. Although most of the suffragists sought to achieve their goals by the normal methods of political persuasion, a militant group, led by Mrs. Emmeline Pankhurst and her daughters, Sylvia and Christabel, adopted more extreme tactics. They heckled Liberal speakers, broke windows in main shopping streets, put acid in mailboxes, and set fire to empty houses. When imprisoned they went on hunger strikes, and their jailers resorted to forced feeding. Whether dealing with Ulster, strikers, or suffragists, the authorities made themselves look weak and foolish by an ineffectual mixture of conciliation and coercion. It appeared as if the political system was becoming less able to resolve political and social issues by the established methods of persuasion and voting.

THE ROAD TO WAR

Alliances. But the greatest failure of leadership was not at home. It was the failure of European diplomacy to resolve the international tensions which eventually led to war. The Salisbury ministry had sought to safeguard Britain through the entente with France which led to conversations between the two military staffs. The French, who had an alliance with Russia, worked zealously to resolve the differences between Britain and Russia, and after the Russian defeat in 1905 by Britain's ally, Japan, the Russians became more amenable. In 1907 Britain and Russia came to an agreement which resolved their imperial conflicts in Persia and Afghanistan, thus forming the Triple Entente of France, Russia, and Britain. The Germans, in turn, clung even more tightly to their alliance with Austria-Hungary which, since it nominally included Italy, was called the Triple Alliance.

From the British perspective, the greatest danger was the naval rivalry with Germany. It was a commonplace of the time that seapower was a vital factor in national power, and thus Germany, already the strongest land power in Europe, began building a powerful navy. The British could see only one reason for such a navy — to threaten the British position in the North Sea and the English Channel. The Liberal government responded with an ambitious naval building program, an undertaking made more necessary by changes in naval technology which made many of the British ships obsolete. The question of seapower which was vital to Britain but of secondary importance to Germany did more than anything else to poison relations between the two countries and keep Britain firmly in the camp of the Triple Entente.

The road to war was marked by a series of preliminary conflicts. In 1908 Austria-Hungary, supported by Germany, annexed the province of Bosnia, thus provoking violent reactions from Serbian nationalists who viewed Bosnia as an important part of the greater Serbia which they sought to achieve. In 1911 Britain and France stood together to protect the French position in Morocco against German threats. In 1912 and again in 1913 wars broke out in the Balkans, and finally another Balkan crisis led to the outbreak of general war. On June 28, 1914, the Archduke Franz Ferdinand, heir to the Austro-Hungarian monarchy, visited Sarajevo, capital of Bosnia, where he was assassinated by Serbian nationalists. The Austrians were determined to make an example of Serbia and issued an ultimatum which was tantamount to a declaration of war. The Serbians turned to their allies, the Russians, who decided that support of Serbia was essential to maintain their influence among the "little Slavic brothers" in the Balkans. The Germans felt it essential to support Austria-Hungary, their only reliable ally; the French felt it necessary to support the Russians, thus confronting Germany and Austria with a two-front war. The Austrians declared war on Serbia on July 28, and the Russians began mobilizing their forces. At this point the Germans became impatient, for their plan of battle was to strike hard at France, relying on the slow Russian mobilization to give them time to deal with the French. Thus, every day given the Russians to mobilize was a day lost on the western front. When the Russians refused to stop their mobilization, the Germans attacked France through Belgium. World War I had begun.

The Liberal government temporized in the face of the mounting European crisis. The ententes with France and Russia were not alliances, and the conversations between British and French military staffs had no official sanction. Britain had one clear commitment, a guarantee of Belgian neutrality made in 1839. However, as the crisis unfolded Britain had a larger concern — the possibility that the European continent might be dominated by one power, as in the days of Philip II, Louis XIV, or Napoleon, which might use the Channel coast as a springboard for invasion. Beyond these strategic considerations lay a Liberal belief in international law which appeared to be threatened more by Germany than by any other power. The German attack on neutral Belgium settled the matter and Britain declared war. When Sir Edward Grey, the Foreign Secretary, was called upon to explain the policy of his government, he resorted to such arguments as national honor, the sanctity of treaties, the balance of power, and international law. Although these noble words undoubtedly concealed a good deal of muddle, there is reason to believe that in his mind, and in the minds of his countrymen, these concepts were worth fighting for.

SUGGESTIONS FOR FURTHER READING

General works cited in the last chapter which continue to be useful are Webb, *Modern England*, Ensor, *England, 1870-1914*, G. M. Young, *Victorian England: Portrait of an Age*, and two works by George Kitson Clark, *The Making of Victorian England*, and *An Expanding Society*. Thompson, *England Landed Society* and Arnstein, "The Survival of the Victorian Aristocracy" also deal with the late Victorian period. A brief introduction to the period by Herman Ausubel, *The Late Victorians: A Short History* (1955) emphasizes the effects of "The Great Depression." William Ashworth, *An Economic History of England, 1870-1939* (1960) gives a more favorable view of the economic development of the period. Key biographies are Aubrey L. Kennedy, *Salisbury, 1830-1903: Portrait of a Statesman* (1953), Peter Fraser, *Joseph Chamberlain: Radicalism and Empire, 1868-1914* (1966), and J. G. Lockhart and C. M. Woodhouse, *Cecil Rhodes: The Colossus of South Africa* (1963). The development of the Conservative Party as the majority party may be followed in Robert Blake, *The Conservative Party from Peel to Churchill* (1970). The rise of working class problems to prominence may be seen in Herman Ausubel, *In Hard Times: Reformers among the Late Victorians* (1960) and three works by Henry Pelling: *A History of British Trade Unionism* (2nd ed., 1972), *The Origins of the Labour Party, 1880-1900* (2nd ed., 1965), and *Popular Politics and Society in Late Victorian Britain* (1968). Eric Midwinter has prepared two brief surveys of Victorian social legislation: *Victorian Social Reform* (1968) and *Nineteenth Century Education* (1970). See also David Roberts, *Victorian Origins of the British Welfare State* (1960). An interesting study of one aspect of the intellectual ferment of the time is William Irvine, *Apes, Angels, and Victorians* (1955). The changing roles of women are traced in Duncan Crow, *The Victorian Woman* (1971). Stimulating works concerning the imperial rivalries of the late Victorian period are C. J. Lowe, *The Reluctant Imperialists: British Foreign Policy, 1878-1902* (1967), and Ronald Robinson, John Gallagher, and Alice Denny, *Africa and the Victorians* (1961).

Entering the twentieth century the student still has the guidance of Webb and Ensor, as well as another general work, Alfred Havighurst, *Twentieth Century Britain* (2nd ed., 1966). Two books by Donald Read are also valuable: *Edwardian England, 1901-15: Society and Politics* (1972) and *Documents from Edwardian England, 1901-1915* (1973). Among the best biographies are John Wilson, *CB: A Life of Henry Campbell-Bannerman* (1973); Sidney Zebel, *Balfour: A Political Biography* (1973); Roy Jenkins, *Asquith: Portrait of a Man and an Era* (1964); Thomas Jones, *Lloyd George* (1951); and Lewis Broad, *Winston Churchill* (2 vols., 1958-63). The politics of social reform is followed in H. V. Emy, *Liberals, Radicals, and Social Politics, 1892-1914* (1973). Bentley Gilbert, *The Evolution of National Insurance in Great Britain: The Origins of the Welfare State* (1966) studies the key feature of the "New Liberalism." John F. Glaser, "English Nonconformity and the Decline of Liberalism," *American Historical Review,* LXIII (Jan. 1958) points out one of the reasons for the decline of the Liberal Party so quickly after its burst of power and energy. The rise of the Labour Party may be followed in Henry Pelling, *A Short History of the Labour Party* (4th ed., 1972) and Philip Poirier, *The Advent of the British Labour Party* (1958). A stimulating study of the breakup of Edwardian England is George Dangerfield, *The Strange Death of Liberal England* (1936).

There is an enormous literature on the coming of the First World War. A good overview is Laurence Lafore, *The Long Fuse: An Interpretation of the Origins of World War I* (1965). Britain's diplomatic involvements are examined by George M. Monger in *The End of Isolation: British Foreign Policy 1900-1907* (1963). For the naval questions which loomed so large in British foreign policy and domestic politics see Arthur Marder, *From the Dreadnought to Scapa Flow Vol. I: The Road to War, 1904-1914* (London, 1961).

15

War & Peace
Disappointments

1914-1931

During the First World War (1914-18), Britain created the largest army in her history and mobilized industry to produce unprecedented quantities of military supplies. The war scarred millions of lives. It also hurried the pace of change: these changes had started earlier, such as the decline of Britain as a Great Power, the movement of the self-governing dominions toward practical independence, extremism and violence in Irish politics, the disintegration of the Liberals, the rise of Labour, and the dominance of the Conservatives in British politics. Further intensified by the war were the sickness of the old export industries, the active role of the Government in the economy, the power of the large trade unions, the growth in state-provided social services, the partial blurring of class divisions, the improved job opportunities and political rights of women, and the decay of the Christian churches.

THE WAR OF ATTRITION

Britain was loosely bound to France by an entente or understanding; France and Russia were aligned against Germany and

British and French soldiers in the trenches (Radio Times Hulton Picture Library).

Austria-Hungary. The assassination of an Austrian prince in an obscure Balkan town triggered a crisis which led to general war. Britain sent her small army to the continent to support France against a German invasion. Public opinion warmly approved this decision after Germany violated the neutrality of little Belgium and endangered France. Though for the diplomats the war protected the balance of power, for the people it was a crusade against brutal German militarism.

Trench War. The British and the French stopped the German advance in a battle near the River Marne and afterwards the war on the western front became a defensive stalemate. Until the fighting ended in November 1918, fruitless attacks came one after another — deafening artillery barrages followed by infantry assaults through barbed wire and minefields, searchlights piercing the night, jagged shrapnel from mortar and artillery shells, rifle and machine gun bullets piercing bodies. Surviving attackers who leaped with bayonets into the enemy trenches rarely accomplished much — at the best the other army was pushed back a few miles into a new line of trenches. When the war ended the Germans and the western allies still occupied much the same territory that they had occupied four years earlier.

The western front devoured a generation. The British armed forces swallowed up nearly six million men, a third of the male population between their teens and mid-forties. The British Expeditionary Force endured 420,000 casualties in its greatest offensive; nearly 20,000 died on its first day alone, and many companies had nearly every man killed or badly wounded. The war cost the lives of nearly 750,000 British fighting men — more than had been killed in all her previous wars combined. The Empire sacrificed another 200,000 lives. Hundreds of thousands more were permanently crippled by wounds, gas, disease, or mental breakdown.

Military commanders, scientists, and diplomats looked vainly for alternatives to the slaughter. Few generals on either side emerged with reputations as strategists. Sir Douglas Haig, who from 1915 commanded the British Expeditionary Force, was a cavalryman like many British generals, and kept hundreds of thousands of horses grazing behind the front ready for the invasion of Germany which never happened. To open a new and supposedly easier front, the British tried to seize the Straits of Constantinople from the Turks. Despite the sacrifice of thousands of Australian and New Zealand soldiers on the beaches of Gallipoli the attack ended in utter failure. The only major battle between the high seas fleets, near Jutland in 1916, ended indecisively, in part because of the British admiral's caution. Both sides also used sea power in economic warfare — the Germans with submarines, the British with a less dramatic surface blockade. In hopes of a speedy victory scientists devised secret weapons: the Germans used poison gas first; the British, tanks. Britain and her allies persuaded Italy to enter the war in 1915, the United States with her vast economic resources and manpower in 1917. The Germans incited the Irish to rebel; the British incited the Arabs. Nothing, not even the collapse of the eastern front after the revolutions in Russia, broke the stalemate.

British soldiers who endured the terror and the tedium of the trenches respected the bravery of their German partners in suffering and distrusted the propaganda intended to arouse a hatred of the enemy and a confidence in early victory. A handful of soldier-poets gave voice to the mood of less articulate comrades — a weary scepticism about their leaders, a dull alienated anger at the fireside patriots who romanticized war, horror over its nightmare reality, and a sense of the brotherhood binding front line soldiers. The most brilliant of the war poets, Wilfred Owen, called war as "obscene as cancer." He was machine gunned to death a week before the Armistice which ended the killing.

War Socialism. Courage on the battle front was not enough. The home front had to be organized to manufacture enormous quantities of military supplies. Slowly and reluctantly the Government, with the cooperation of businessmen, created a kind of war socialism in which the Government controlled industry and trade. Military victory seemed more important than the peacetime principles which had guarded property rights and personal liberties. The Government acquired sweeping discretionary powers under the Defence of the Realm Act, personified as the meddlesome Aunt DORA. The success of war socialism helped undermine the old cult of laissez-faire and inspire a new faith in centralized planning, government by experts, and massive public expenditures to solve national problems.

The Government took over key industries and imposed indirect control over nearly all the others. Industry had to supply vast amounts of military equipment which it had not made before, such as gas masks, or had made only in small quantities, such as rifles. In a few days of heavy artillery fire the British army consumed more shells than in a nineteenth-century campaign. In 1914 the British army had only a little more than 1300 machine guns; over the next four years it acquired an additional 240,000. Established government arsenals and private contractors could produce only a fraction of the needed armaments. The Government set up a special Ministry of Munitions which created large new factories employing more than a million workers.

Manpower Shortage. In 1916 the Government ordered conscription of military-aged men when volunteers proved too few to satisfy the appetite of the western front. Even earlier the dwindling number of available men on the civilian front gave opportunities for women to enter jobs previously closed to them. Employers who hired them paid them about half the wages earned by men who did the same work. About 800,000 additional women worked in industry, 250,000 in farming, and 100,000 in transport. Offices and retail shops offered women more permanent gains. About 200,000 women took jobs in Government offices and more than twice this number worked in private offices; hundreds of thousands more became sales staff. The old stereotype of the male clerk was replaced by that of the business girl behind the typewriter or the counter. The role of women in the war helped reconcile former opponents of women's suffrage to their enfranchisement. Besides promises of political rights women gained new personal freedoms symbolized by shorter skirts and the disappearance of chaperones.

The scarcity of labor compelled the Government to court the working class. It included Labour politicians in wartime coalitions and created joint grievance boards on which trade unionists served with management. It encouraged new amenities in factories such as canteens which served inexpensive, hot food. Strikes took place despite these gestures of appeasement and appeals to patriotism. Senior trade union officials usually cooperated with the Government, but shop stewards, who combined ordinary employment with minor union offices, gave disgruntled workers militant leadership. The discontent of the workers was not ideological, but grew out of practical grievances such as high rents.

The scarcity of labor encouraged the use of machinery which required fewer highly skilled workers. Trade unions threatened to strike to keep out anyone who had not performed the normal apprenticeship and thus would have barred most available men and virtually all women. The Government persuaded the trade unions to accept the wartime dilution of skilled workers with the unskilled by promising that the practice would be temporary. In fact unskilled and semi-skilled workers who tended machines about which they knew little remained numerically dominant, and the differential between their wages and highly skilled craftsmen shrank.

Social Consequences of the War. During the war some of the old distinctions in the class structure became blurred. Before the war only the upper and middle classes had paid income tax but during it the working class paid, too. The scarcity of servants forced many middle-class families to do their own cleaning and cooking. To encourage productivity and to discourage absenteeism the Government attacked drunkenness, a traditional vice of working-class men. It watered the beer, increased taxes on alcohol — particularly whiskey, and reduced the hours of sale. The requirement that public houses close in midafternoon on weekdays began during the war. The Government also considered prohibition but feared that the people loved their beer more than they hated the Germans. The loss of ships which German submarines sank created shortages of imported food. Despite Government subsidies British shoppers faced inflated prices, long queues, and, in 1918, loosely enforced rationing for meat and the other scarce foods.

To stimulate cooperation with its war policies the Government combined propaganda with censorship. As radio did not yet exist, the mass circulation newspapers exerted the greatest influence. They depicted the Germans as a subhuman race that threatened western civilization, as cruel Huns who raped women and executed civilians in occupied territories and murdered wounded prisoners — actions which decent Tommies (British soldiers) never did. The Royal Family patriotically changed its German name to that of Windsor.

Public Opinion. A minority always rejected the official propaganda.

Even people who supported the war often disliked conscription, and sentiment in favor of an early compromise peace grew in the Labour Party after the revolutions in Russia. Despite the existence of vocal critics and a general war weariness, public opinion generally supported the Government's policies. Before conscription had been made law, young women tried to shame young men into volunteering by giving stay-at-home civilians white feathers which symbolized cowardice.

To justify the terrible military losses and the lesser civilian sacrifices the Government promised great rewards — national security, social justice, an enduring peace, and a better world. When peace came the Government lacked the ability and perhaps the will to honor its commitments; despite major social reforms during and after the war, the people considered themselves cheated. There was revulsion against war and a scepticism about politicians. Beneath the particular complaints lay numbing doubts about old beliefs in the basic goodness of man and a universe ruled with justice and compassion. After the war empty churches became common in middle-class districts as they long had been in working-class neighborhoods.

WARTIME POLITICAL LEADERSHIP

Asquith. In 1914 the Liberals and the Conservatives had an equal number of seats in the House of Commons, but with Irish and Labour support the Liberals controlled the Government. This encouraged national unity since the Liberals and the Labourites contained most of the minority who were uncertain about the rightness of the war, people whom a Liberal Government could convince or at least could quiet. The Conservatives, for two generations the war party, believed that they could win a wartime general election, but only at the risk of dividing the country.

As the war dragged on, dissatisfaction with its management forced the Liberals to admit the Conservatives and Labour to a coalition government in 1915. Unfortunately for the Liberal Party, the leadership of the Prime Minister, Herbert Asquith, failed to impress the press, the public, or his own colleagues. They complained about his dispassionate personal style almost as much as the lack of boldness in his policies. At the end of 1916 an intrigue between Asquith's principal Liberal lieutenant and the Conservative leader, encouraged by some newspapers, forced the Prime Minister to resign. Though the new Prime Minister, David Lloyd George, was also a Liberal, he had to depend on Conservative support. Most prominent Liberals refused to serve under him because of his apparent lack of fixed principles. Later he added enemies because of the brutality with which he discarded colleagues no longer useful to him.

Lloyd George. The new Prime Minister became one of Britain's greatest war leaders. The Conservatives who had hated Lloyd George as a radical supported the quick-witted Welshman when he identified himself with a military policy of decisive victory and a domestic policy of fighting socialism through social reform. Though Lloyd George lacked original ideas of his own, he was open to the ideas of others. He lacked personal administrative ability but recruited experienced businessmen to run Government departments. He had the self-confidence to surround himself with talented and independent-minded men and women. Lloyd George had great personal charm and a genius for arousing enthusiasm. He was a master of improvisation, a pragmatic solver of crises, a man of compromises who worried little about consistency.

Traditionally a large Cabinet composed of twenty-odd men — nearly all of them burdened with departmental administration — had controlled Government policy-making. In his major institutional reform Lloyd George replaced the traditional Cabinet with a War Cabinet of five or so men, most of them freed from departmental duties which would distract them from high policy. Though Lloyd George depended on Conservative votes he also had the support of a large number of less prominent Liberals. In 1917 he brought the controversial Liberal and ex-Conservative Winston Churchill into the Government. Lloyd George also recognized the importance of the Labour Party; he gave its leader, Arthur Henderson, a former iron worker, a seat in the War Cabinet.

Treaty of Versailles. Lloyd George spoke out in favor of a moderate peace settlement early in 1918 shortly before the American President Woodrow Wilson issued his similar, more famous Fourteen Points. The war had not yet been won and both leaders wanted to justify the purity of their motives in continuing the struggle. They promised that in redrawing the map of Europe they would consider the principle of national self-determination which would allow the transfer of some non-German-speaking border territories from German control, and also would imply the survival of a large, unified Germany. But the mood of the British public turned to revenge after the fighting ended. In the general election held later in 1918, politicians demanded that Germany be squeezed "until the pips squeak" in order to repay the victors for the cost of the war.

At the peace conference held in Paris in 1919 the British delegation resisted pressures to impose crippling reparations and to dismember Germany. Lloyd George and the other British leaders feared revolutionary Russia and wanted Germany strong enough to resist Bolshevism. The British Government considered the Treaty of Versailles a reasonable compromise. It forced Germany to accept the responsibility for the outbreak of the war, to pay large reparations, to restrict her armed forces, and to cede territories with non-German populations; yet it also left Germany as a large, united country with powerful industries. The British Government reluctantly accepted the American proposal for a League of Nations to help keep the peace, but trusted more in the strength of Britain's navy.

With Germany humbled Britain seemed to be more powerful than ever and could afford to be conciliatory. She had blocked any immediate threat of German supremacy in Europe, destroyed the German fleet, and made herself dominant in the Near East. In fact, Britain had passed the peak of her power. In contrast to the prewar two-power standard under which Britain had built a fleet equal to the combined strength of the next two largest navies, the British Government agreed in the early 1920s to restrict the number of its large warships to that of the American navy. Britain still had important imperial and commercial interests throughout the world but no longer commanded the military resources to defend them.

The Empire. The state of the British Empire illustrates the contrast between the illusion of renewed power and the reality of long-term decline. The white-dominated self-governing dominions — Canada, Australia, South Africa, and New Zealand — had supported the mother country during the war with men, money, and supplies. Some Britons expected that the wartime unity foreshadowed greater economic and political cooperation in peacetime. Instead, the dominions emerged as fully independent nations tied to Britain only by bonds of sentiment and self-interest. Britain accepted the new situation gracefully. In 1926 an imperial conference described the United Kingdom and the dominions as "autonomous communities within the British Empire, equal in status, in no way subordinate to one another," and in 1931 Parliament renounced its legislative authority over the dominions.

Britain showed less realism in adjusting her relations with the parts of the Empire without large European populations. In India a nationalist movement known as the Congress Party had developed before the war among the small, westernized middle class. After the war, under the leadership of the politican and holy man, Mohandas K. Gandhi, the Congress won the loyalty of the Hindu peasants who made up the bulk of the Indian people. In the agitation for self-government Gandhi urged the use of non-violent civil disobedience such as the boycott of British goods, violations of the Government salt monopoly, a refusal to pay taxes, and hunger strikes; however, violence did take place. In 1919 soldiers commanded by British officers massacred hundreds of demonstrators at Armritsar in the northwest. More important, the Hindu majority and the Muslim minority fought one another. The divisions within the Indian population of several hundred million enabled a few thousand British to remain the masters of the subcontinent.

As a result of the world war Britain won control over several Arab provinces of the old Turkish Empire; British domination over Egypt was continued. The British Government wanted control in the Near East because of its strategic location en route to India, especially because the Suez Canal through Egypt, connecting the Mediterranean and Red Seas, was vital in war. Between the world wars, the exploitation of oil added to the region's importance. Nominally Egypt and Iraq became independent kingdoms and Palestine a mandate supervised by the League of Nations, but Britain considered these states her possessions. Britain faced constant trouble, in part because of Arab nationalism, particularly in Egypt, and in part because of the conflicting wartime promises Britain had made to Arab leaders who wanted independence, to the French who wanted a colony in Syria, and to the Jews who wanted to fulfill the Zionist dream of a state in the land of their ancestors. The Balfour Declaration which offered the Jewish people a national home in the Holy Land encouraged Zionist immigration after the war.

THE IRISH CRISIS, 1912-22

Home Rule and Ulster. The problem of Ireland had long threatened to explode in civil war. In 1912 the Liberal Government introduced an Irish Home Rule Bill which became law in 1914. This legislation authorized an Irish Parliament and reserved for the British Parliament only a few powers such as foreign relations. The British public did not much care about the Home Rule Bill but in Ireland feelings ran high. The Roman Catholic majority insisted upon Home Rule and the Protestant minority strongly opposed it. In most of Ireland the Protestants were a scattered elite of landowners, clergymen, public officials, and professional men. In contrast, the northeastern counties in Ulster had a local Protestant majority dominated by Scottish-descended Presbyterians. The Ulster economy was built on the shipyards of industrial Belfast, not on peasant farms. If the rest of Ireland was to have Home Rule, Protestant Ulster wanted the country partitioned.

The Irish parties prepared to fight. The Ulstermen organized a military force, the Ulster Volunteers, and armed themselves in part with weapons smuggled from Germany, while the Irish Home Rule party reacted by forming the National Volunteers. The more adamant nationalists of the Sinn Fein Party preached economic, cultural, and political independence in order to purge Ireland of English influence. Friends of the Sinn Fein Party formed the Irish Volunteers. The most extreme nationalists belonged to the Irish Republican Brotherhood, a secret society which since the 1850s had made plots and bombs.

Ulster had powerful allies who might defy Parliament. Andrew Bonar Law, the Conservative leader, was of Ulster descent, and many army officers were Irish Protestants. The officers in a cavalry regiment stationed in Ireland submitted their resignations in what some people called a mutiny rather than risk being ordered to impose Government policy on Ulster.

The Easter Rebellion. The outbreak of the First World War quieted Ireland and postponed Home Rule. Ulster Volunteers and National Volunteers patriotically enlisted in the British army but the war encouraged the more extreme nationalists such as the Irish Republican Brotherhood to fight for a complete separation from Britain. In 1916 it organized a military uprising which began with the seizure of the General Post Office in Dublin on Easter Monday. The I.R.B. had infiltrated the Irish Volunteers in order to send them into battle against the orders of their commander. Evoking little sympathy among the Irish people, the Easter Rebellion failed to spread. The British unwisely executed most of the leaders; to appease American opinion they spared Eamon DeValera, the Brooklyn-born son of an Irish mother and Cuban father. The executions turned the defeated rebels into martyred folk heroes and radicalized the Sinn Fein into a party of violent revolution.

Guerilla War. In the elections for the British Parliament held in 1918 the Sinn Fein won almost every seat outside of Ulster. The Sinn Fein M.P.s convened in 1919 to declare themselves the legislature of an independent Irish republic. To defend it they created a military force called the Irish Republican Army. Fighting as guerillas without uniforms the I.R.A. depended on ambush, kidnappings, and assassinations and punished informers by shooting off their kneecaps. Michael Collins masterminded jail breaks and the murder of police detectives. Sympathetic Irish-Americans contributed funds to the I.R.A. for the fight against the British. When the British launched an indiscriminate counterterror, the Irish public accepted the I.R.A.'s brutality as justified. After many of the old Royal Irish Constabulary resigned, the British recruited a new police force from among demobilized soldiers. Called the Black and Tans because of their uniforms, they lacked the discipline of the army and committed atrocities which rivaled those of the I.R.A. The climax of terror came on Bloody Sunday in November 1920. In the morning the I.R.A. murdered a number of British officers in their homes while their families watched. In the afternoon the Black and Tans fired at random into a crowd at a football match.

The I.R.A. were no match for the British militarily but they had a powerful ally in the disgust and war-weariness which the British people felt. Late in 1921 the Irish insurgents negotiated with the British Government in London. Despite Conservative hostility to any compromise, the Coalition Government offered to concede virtual independence to Ireland as a free state within the British Empire — the same status as Canada — if the rebels would accept a nominal allegiance to the Crown and the partition of Ulster from the rest of Ireland.

Most of the I.R.A. negotiators, headed by Collins, accepted the terms as the best which they could get. When they returned to Ireland they faced strong opposition from republican and anti-partition forces led by DeValera. A majority in the Irish legislature endorsed the treaty and the voters supported the pro-treaty party in new elections. The adherents of the treaty set up a Free State with its capital in Dublin. The opponents of the treaty rebelled against the Free State in June 1922. Many leaders in the fight against the British lost their lives in battle with fellow Irishmen, including Collins who died in an ambush. In April 1923, most of the surviving anti-treaty leaders abandoned the war. A few diehards continued to resist, using the name of the I.R.A. for their secret terrorist organization.

FROM FLAPPERS TO FREUD

Women. Despite obtaining the vote, women exercised little political influence after the war. For young middle-class women social and economic changes mattered more. Though women failed to keep their wartime industrial jobs, they continued in large numbers in offices and retail services. Moreover, their social freedoms grew both in relatively superficial things such as smoking in public, and in more fundamental matters such as the sociological and economic consequences of smaller families. Most middle-class married women drastically limited their families through contraception and thus one- or two-child households became common. The open acceptance of contraception, at least among the comfortable classes, owed much to the efforts of Dr. Marie Stopes, the author of *Married Love* (1918) and founder in 1921 of Britain's first birth control clinic.

The press showed more excitement over something less important, the young women who defied old conventions about dress and behavior and who, it was suspected, violated the prohibition against premarital sex previously observed by middle-class females. The so-called flappers cultivated a boyish air, with breast-flattened, slender figures and short hair, but the message seemed sensual. Short skirts, flesh-colored stockings, high-heeled shoes, lipstick smiles, bare arms, and the abandonment of stiff, whalebone corsets shocked the older generation. Slenderness became an enduring feminine ideal which condemned to perpetual diets the full-figured women considered beauties in the Edwardian era.

London flappers, 1925 (Radio Times Hulton Picture Library).

Men shaved off their beards or trimmed their moustaches, exchanged their pocket watches for newfangled wristwatches, sometimes wore Oxford bags, the loose-fitting trousers favored for casual wear, but in general the masculine appearance had changed little since before the war. The men had little to match the youth cult of the flappers.

American Habits. American-style jazz bands became fashionable with the young for dancing, and the American habit of cigarette smoking also conquered the country, blurring the difference between the sexes — women would not smoke anything else — and the classes. In the past working men smoked pipes and the wealthy favored cigars. For the young the cinema became a classless form of entertainment. Perhaps a combination of Hollywood films and the new world importance of the United States had made American ways look modishly up-to-date. For instance, at parties sherry gave way to cocktails which mixed previously working-class gin with vermouth. Another American practice which took root in Britain was the newspaper gossip column which tyrannized the few to titillate the many.

The BBC and Betting. In contrast radio — the "wireless" — created a new, distinctively British institution. Radio was a Government monopoly operated by a semi-autonomous organization, the British Broadcasting Corporation. Though criticized as stuffy, puritanical, and paternalistic, the BBC established high standards in broadcasting, particularly for music and radio drama. The BBC acted as a middle-class schoolmaster by letting its audience have what was good for them rather than what ordinary people might have preferred.

The working class acquired new recreations more to their own taste — greyhounds racing after mechanical hares accompanied by wagering in a kind of poor man's horse race, and the enormously popular football pools. In a culture of poverty the possibility that a small bet might bring wealth or at least comfort made gambling appear a sensible effort at self-improvement.

Freud and Literature. In the 1920s the educated minority discovered Sigmund Freud, the Austrian father of psychoanalysis. Few Britons underwent analysis and not many read the books of Freud and his disciples, but many became familiar with some of the concepts and jargon of psychoanalysis and acknowledged the irrational side of human nature. Popular literature and cocktail party small talk began to puzzle over the meaning of dreams and childhood experiences and to play with such words as repression and inferiority complex.

In serious literature the American-born poet T. S. Eliot and the novelists James Joyce and Virginia Woolf challenged their readers and frequently defeated them with daring new structural techniques. Joyce also offended public opinion with his controversial erotic subject matter; his *Ulysses* was printed in France because it was banned in the English-speaking world.

POSTWAR POLITICS: COALITION, MEDIOCRITY, AND MUDDLE

Peacetime Coalition. When the war ended Lloyd George and the Conservative leader, Bonar Law, agreed to continue the Coalition Government, but aside from a few isolated individuals, the Labour Party withdrew. Lloyd George and Bonar Law issued a joint endorsement known as the coupon to Coalition candidates in the election held at the end of 1918. Aided by the prestige of military victory the Coalition supporters won a smashing majority. Ironically, the landslide left Lloyd George as a captive of his Conservative partners since they no longer needed the Coalition Liberals to have a majority in the House of Commons. The election shattered the Liberal Party by confirming its wartime division. The Asquith Liberals running without the coupon won only a handful of seats, while the Coalition Liberals won theirs largely through Conservative goodwill. Despite several brief-lived revivals the Liberal Party slowly declined into a minor party which lacked any hope of forming a Government.

Earlier the Labour Party had been a federation of socialist societies and trade unions loosely allied with the Liberals. By serving in the Coalition Government the Labour Party had gained experience and respectability; by withdrawing when the war ended it reunited the anti-war minority with the pro-war majority. It created local constituency party organizations and committed itself to a socialist program which advocated public ownership of industry. In 1918 the Labour Party elected only a few more M.P.s than the Asquith Liberals but it polled many more popular votes. The Labour Party benefitted from the sweeping suffrage reform which enfranchised all men over 21, though not from the extension of the vote to women. As the only serious alternative to a Conservative-dominated Government the Labour Party attracted disillusioned middle-class Liberals. It became the heir of the Liberal tradition as the party of peace and international cooperation and of the defense of civil liberties.

Not all Liberals joined the Labour camp. Lloyd George thrived in the hectic atmosphere of the years immediately after the war. Property owners, professional men, and managers relied on his energy, imagination, and popularity to save them from socialism at home and Bolshevism abroad. The end of the war did not mean the end of crisis: an influenza epidemic killed 150,000 people in Britain, the threat of mutiny forced the Government to scrap its complicated plans to delay demobilization until jobs existed for the soldiers, and half-hearted military intervention against the Bolsheviks angered working-class and radical opinion. Though the Labour Party and other British radicals disliked the undemocratic and brutal methods used by the Communist dictatorship, they welcomed the revolution as opening the way for a better life for ordinary Russians, and as a sign of the future collapse of the existing political and economic order throughout Europe.

The demand for consumer goods from a world starved by wartime austerities produced for a short time abundant jobs, high wages, and strikes. Skillfully mediating the industrial disputes, Lloyd George postponed the confrontation with the trade unions until unemployment weakened them. He pacified the coal miners with the appointment of a commission to study the problems of the industry, but when a majority of the commission recommended one form or another of nationalization, Lloyd George used the disagreement over specifics as an excuse not to act.

Lloyd George and his colleagues looked upon themselves as practical reformers. For a couple of years hopes remained high that a better world might come out of the war. In 1918 Parliament required secondary education through the age of fourteen and made the right to vote more democratic. In 1919 it created a Ministry of Health and in 1920 it extended unemployment insurance to millions of additional workers. To fulfill the promise of "homes fit for heroes" the Government paid local authorities and private contractors generous subsidies to build houses.

Then in 1921-22 the economy collapsed, spoiling Lloyd George's strategy for killing socialism with kindness. The old export industries such as textiles suffered the most. During the war American, Japanese, and other producers had invaded traditional British markets; after the war supply exceeded demand. By mid-1921 there were more than two million out of work in Britain and until the next war the unemployed never fell below a million. The Government provided them with money to survive, but it made little effort to create new jobs. Economy replaced reform as the official watchword. The Government drastically cut expenditures for education, housing, and other programs of social reconstruction.

Fall of Lloyd George. In the early 1920s rank-and-file Tory M.P.s rebelled against Lloyd George. They criticized the extravagance of the subsidies for working-class housing, complained that wartime controls restricting industry and business continued too long, and above all resented the appeasement of Irish gunmen. They worried that the Conservative leaders might accept a permanent merger of the Coalition parties. They saw Lloyd George as a corrupter of British politics. For instance, he both expanded the old practice of rewarding generous party contributors with titles of nobility and regarded the monies collected by the Coalition Liberals as his to use as he liked.

Lloyd George tried to save his position through a diplomatic triumph. He sought to conciliate Germany at the expense of France, but instead the Germans signed an ominous treaty of friendship with Russia. Next he threatened to fight when a Turkish army marched on the old capital of Constantinople which the world war allies occupied. The usually warlike Conservatives protested against Lloyd George's gamble that the Turks would back down.

In 1922, over the opposition of most of the Conservative members of the Cabinet, a caucus of Conservative M.P.s at the Carlton Club voted that the party should withdraw from the Coalition. The Government promptly resigned. Though only in his fifties, Lloyd George never held office again. The ailing Bonar Law came out of a brief retirement to head a purely Conservative Government composed of second-rank politicians. During the 1920s and the early 1930s the Conservatives, the Liberals, and Labour struggled to survive as major political parties. A fickle new electorate, a chronically depressed economy, and feuds within each party made for instability. Though the Conservatives won most of the elections, they twice sheltered behind a coalition headed by a Prime Minister from another party.

Baldwin and MacDonald. The Conservative Prime Minister who succeeded Lloyd George died within a few months of taking office. His successor, Stanley Baldwin, led the party from 1923 to 1937, and owed his selection to the unavailability of anybody else. As Prime Minister Baldwin lacked Lloyd George's energy and imagination, but he understood the ordinary voter. He practised the politics of conciliation — supporting moderate reforms more than right-wing conservatives liked — and through the new medium of radio he impressed the simplicity and honesty of his character on the public. Almost immediately Baldwin called for new elections to obtain approval for a protective tariff. In the short run his raising of the issue of protection united the pro-free trade Liberals and defeated the Conservatives. In the long run the protective tariff issue helped Baldwin because the Conservatives, who had favored the old Coalition, rallied to support protection. When no party won a majority in the election, the Liberals let Labour, which had defended free trade, form a minority Government.

Another personable, though mediocre politician, J. Ramsay MacDonald, headed the Labour Government of 1924. A sincere friend of international conciliation, he had opposed the First World War and worked to ease tensions between France and Germany after the war. In domestic policy, his socialism inspired vague, eloquent speeches but little action. For all of his limitations as a policy maker, MacDonald stood out as the ablest parliamentary tactician in his party. Despite being born the illegitimate son of a penniless maidservant, his good looks, elegant manners, and Scots accent — which bore no working-class taint — enabled him to enter the society of duchesses and millionaires. His career illustrates how the aristocratic embrace could tame humbly born radicals.

Despite MacDonald's desire to establish the respectability of the Labour Party, his Government fell during a Red scare. The Government was accused of leniency toward a Communist editor who supposedly had tried to subvert the loyalty of the army. During the election campaign which followed, a forged letter showed that a Russian official, Zinoviev, expected armed revolution in Britain. The Conservatives won the election with ease, and as usual, the Liberals turned out to be the biggest losers. Labour had increasingly replaced the Liberal Party as the progressive alternative to the Conservatives. An imaginative program for economic reform drafted in the middle and late 1920s under Lloyd George's leadership failed to revive the Liberals as a major party.

Food convoy, General Strike, 1926 (Radio Times Hulton Picture Library).

Baldwin was able to put together a much stronger Government in 1924-29 than for his first ministry. The Conservatives who had earlier supported Lloyd George joined Baldwin's new Government as did ex-Liberal Winston Churchill. As Chancellor of the Exchequer Churchill returned the British pound to the gold standard so that everyone could exchange paper currency for a fixed weight of the precious metal. Unfortunately the pound claimed an exaggerated value in gold, thereby handicapping British exports with high prices. Probably Neville Chamberlain, the son of the Liberal Unionist leader, did more constructive work than any other minister. He reformed local government finance and created a system of contributory pensions for the elderly, widows, and orphans.

The General Strike of 1926 dominated the second Baldwin Government. It grew out of a dispute in the coal industry: the owners wanted to reduce wages to compete with cheap foreign coal and the Government wanted to end its subsidy which had kept wages up. The miners refused to accept any cut in pay, even when a royal commission proposed to couple a reduction with a reorganization of the industry.

After the coal miners called a strike, the Trades Union Congress drifted into a sympathy strike. Despite rank-and-file solidarity in the unions which the T.U.C. called out, the Government maintained essential services with the help of middle-class volunteers who drove trucks, soldiers who unloaded ships, and sailors who shoveled coal at power stations. After nine days the Government maneuvered the T.U.C. into calling off its strike without obtaining anything in return. The coal strike continued until hunger broke it later in the year. Apparently some members of the Government had wanted to seize the opportunity of the General Strike to cripple the trade unions.

The trade union movement survived despite a drastic decline in its membership after the strike's failure and despite legislative restrictions on its political contributions. The Transport and General Workers' Union built a splendid headquarters building in 1928 which symbolized the continued power of the trade unions in the economy and in politics. Called Transport House, it was located near Parliament and also housed the T.U.C. and the Labour Party. Ernest Bevin, the tough, pragmatic leader of the transport workers, avoided strikes which he knew that he could not win. With the General Strike as the exception a spirit of compromise between trade unions and employers prevailed in the middle and late 1920s.

The Economy. The failure of the Conservatives to solve the problem of unemployment helped cost them the general election of 1929. On the eve of the American stock market crash MacDonald and the Labour Party formed a second minority Government. It soon staggered under the assault of the international depression which worsened the economic problems which had existed in Britain since the early 1920s. By the end of 1930 the number of the unemployed reached two and a half million.

The Government had difficulty in paying its own bills. It had to cut public expenditures to save money and, more important, to persuade bankers to advance new credits despite their fear of socialism. The Labour Chancellor of the Exchequer supported the traditional thinking that a Government must balance budgets even in a depression and that to abandon the gold standard would bring the ruin of the British economy. A minority in the Cabinet refused to accept the retrenchment which the experts demanded, particularly the drastic cuts proposed for the unemployed. Unable to agree on a policy, the Government resigned.

To the surprise of his old Labour colleagues MacDonald promptly agreed to head a non-party National Government to impose the economies and to save the gold standard. Although most Liberals and a few Labour M.P.s supported the new Government, the Conservative Party dominated it. A peaceful mutiny in the navy — really a strike —

persuaded the Government to limit the proposed cuts in the pay of the armed forces, the police, and the teachers. More important, the National Government abandoned the gold standard which it had been organized to protect, without the destruction of the economy which the bankers had predicted. Labour blamed the fall of its Government on a conspiracy of the bankers and the Tories and MacDonald's personal betrayal.

The National Government called a general election in 1931. Offering no program, it asked the people for a "doctor's mandate" of blind trust. It won a smashing victory over the disorganized Labour Party and remained in office to struggle with the disappointments of the interwar years until after the outbreak of the Second World War.

SUGGESTIONS FOR FURTHER READING

A recent bibliography for the twentieth century is Alfred F. Havighurst, *Modern England, 1901-1970* (1976). Havighurst also has written a reliable narrative history, *Twentieth-Century Britain* (2nd ed., 1966), for which a new edition has been promised. Trevor Lloyd, *Empire to Welfare State: English History, 1906-1967* (1970) is another dependable survey. The pioneering work by C. L. Mowat, *Britain between the Wars, 1918-1940* (1955) remains important for its sound judgment and detail. Two other general works, A. J. P. Taylor, *English History, 1914-1945* (1965), and L. C. B. Seaman, *Post-Victorian England, 1902-1951* (1966), stimulate with vivid, and sometimes controversial, interpretations of personalities and events. Sidney Pollard, *The Development of the British Economy, 1914-1967* (2nd ed., 1969), includes much social history. Though chatty and anecdotal, Robert Graves and Alan Hodge, *The Long Week-End: a Social History of Great Britain, 1918-1939* (1940), is well-informed. Sheila Rowbotham, *Hidden from History* (1973), offers a Marxist interpretation of the changing position of women in England from the seventeenth century to the 1930s. Horton Davies, *Worship and Theology in England*, vol. 5, *The Ecumenical Century, 1900-1965* (1965), provides a good introduction to religion, and Hubert J. Fyrth and Maurice Goldsmith, *Science, History and Technology*, Book 2, Part 2, *The Age of Uncertainty, the 1880s to the 1940s* (1969), to science.

For the First World War, see E. L. Woodward, *Great Britain and the War of 1914 1918* (1967); Arthur Marwick, *The Deluge: British Society and the First World War* (1965); Paul Johnson, *Land Fit for Heroes: the*

Planning of British Reconstruction (1968); and Victor H. Rothwell, *British War Aims and Peace Diplomacy, 1914-1918* (1971). Max Beloff, *Imperial Sunset,* vol. 1 *Britain's Liberal Empire, 1897-1921* (1970), also discusses Anglo-American disputes. The best biography of Lloyd George still is that by Thomas Jones (1951); probably the best of Baldwin is H. Montgomery Hyde's (1973). David Marquand has published the only scholarly life of MacDonald (1977). Bentley B. Gilbert, *British Social Policy, 1914-1939* (1970), analyzes the Government's response to mass unemployment. For Ireland see F. S. L. Lyons, *Ireland since the Famine* (1971).

16
Depression, War, & Welfare

1931 - 1951

The National Government, organized in 1931, was supposed to bring together the ablest individuals from all the parties in a brief suspension of partisanship to fight a financial and economic crisis. In fact it was led by mediocre persons — the increasingly fuzzy-minded MacDonald, the unheroic Baldwin, and the hardworking Neville Chamberlain. The two most dynamic men in public life, David Lloyd George and Winston Churchill, were not asked to join because lesser men feared their energy, persuasiveness, and ambition. Instead of a short life to deal with an emergency, the National Government survived in name for nearly ten years, but almost from the beginning it was really a Conservative Government. By the end of the first year the more independent-minded Liberal and Labour ministers withdrew because the Conservatives insisted on the creation of protective tariffs.

THE DEPRESSION

Government Policies. Retrenchment was the National Government's first priority. It balanced the budget in 1931 by cutting social programs, the pay of public employees, and unemployment benefits.

When domestic discontent frightened foreigners into exchanging British pounds for gold, the National Government was forced to abandon the gold standard which it had said was indispensable for economic survival. Ironically the failure to keep the gold standard helped the British economy. The value of the pound fell about a third in relation with other currencies which thus reduced the price of British exports and made it easier to find customers for them.

Though not committed to economic non-intervention, the National Government adopted no massive program of public works construction to create employment and stimulate demand as did most other industrial countries. A few innovative economists such as John Maynard Keynes and a few politicians scattered among the various parties demanded in vain that the Government organize, or plan, economic development. In 1934 the Government provided belated, token help for particularly distressed areas; it tried to persuade industrialists to locate factories in them and spent small amounts of money to subsidize training centers and other services. In addition the Government encouraged private schemes of "rationalization" to reduce production in the most afflicted industries, organized agricultural marketing boards, and kept interest rates low which made it easy for house buyers to get mortgages.

Human Consequences. For millions of men and women the depression of the 1930s meant no jobs, little money, great frustration, and crumbling self-respect. Even in good times working-class life was a grinding struggle to get by, often with the help of the neighborhood pawnshop and credit at the local shops. In 1932 nearly three million people lacked jobs, and even after the worst was over between one and a half and two million people remained unemployed. The North of England, South Wales, central Scotland, and Northern Ireland suffered the worst. They depended heavily on contracting industries — cotton textiles, shipbuilding, coal mining — which foreign competition and technological change had begun to choke even before the collapse of the world market. The young moved away or wasted their most productive years in poverty and idleness.

During the 1920s and the 1930s a jobless worker who had exhausted his unemployment insurance benefits received a small allowance paid out of national tax revenues, officially styled at various times as the uncovenanted, or extended, or transitional benefits, and unofficially known as the dole. Though preferred over poor law relief, the dole smacked of charity and the smallness of the payments forced the unemployed worker's family to make do with an unbalanced diet filled out with bread and margarine, tea and condensed milk. In 1931 as part of its economy drive, the National Government reduced the

Hunger marchers, 1936 (Radio Times Hulton Picture Library).

number of weeks for the insurance benefit, cut the amount of the dole, excluded most married women from it, and subjected it to the unpopular household means test which reduced payments when any member of a household enjoyed any income.

Despite the unemployment, extremist political movements failed to attract mass support. The aristocratic ex-Labour minister, Sir Oswald Mosley, organized the British Union of Fascists in 1932 but had few working-class followers. Within a few years the growing anti-semitism and brutality of his Blackshirts also repelled middle-class sympathizers. Working-class militants rallied behind the National Unemployed Workers' Movement in which Communists provided much of the leadership. Hunger marches from the distressed areas to London dramatized the plight of the unemployed, but they never reached a revolutionary size. Though bitter about the events of 1931, the Labour Party remained committed to democratic, parliamentary institutions. The trade unions which dominated the party avoided strikes and cooperated with management when the work force had to be reduced. The trade unions disliked radical intellectuals who talked about establishing socialism through a dictatorship and cooperation with the Communists. In 1935 a mild-mannered moderate, Clement Attlee, was chosen leader of the Labour Party.

Revival and Renewal. The thirties were not entirely negative in British economic and social development. The poverty, anguish, and waste inflicted by the worldwide depression obscured a basic shift in the British economy, away from the export-oriented heavy industries in the north to a variety of light manufacturing industries and service trades in metropolitan London and nearby counties. Unemployment in these sectors which served the domestic market was less, but most of the jobs paid low wages, and trade unions lacked the strength in them that they had in the older industries and among skilled men. The middle class grew in numbers, but as salaried employees of large companies rather than as independent businessmen.

The cheapness of the industrial raw materials and food which Britain imported contributed to an economic revival in the mid-1930s. The prices for meat, grain, and cotton fell even more than did those for the industrial goods which Britain sold. A relatively small volume of exports would pay for a large quantity of imports. Cheap building materials, low wages for construction workers, and low interest rates for mortgages created a housing boom. After 1932 the National Government stopped nearly all the subsidies which had enabled local councils to build houses for rental to working-class families. The construction industry became dominated by private contractors who built homes for sale to owner-occupiers. Before World War I the middle class had rented the homes in which they lived; in the 1930s they became home owners.

The middle class and the more fortunate of the working class enjoyed new comforts in the 1930s which contrasted with the poverty of those who subsisted on the dole. The industries which expanded in the 1930s produced everyday luxuries, from automobiles to small household appliances. In 1930 there were about a million motor vehicles in Britain and within the decade the figure doubled. Gas and electric cookers (stoves) replaced coal ranges for cooking. The radios, electric toasters, and vacuum cleaners used in millions of homes forced the electricity generating industry to expand enormously. Leisure became a profitable industry. Dance halls helped take courting outside the family parlor and make it both a more intimate and a more public relationship. In 1937 the first of the big seaside holiday camps was opened. By the end of the thirties paid annual vacations became common for working men. The unemployed had no holidays at the seashore but even they could escape in the dream world of the cinema. After the development of talking pictures in the late twenties, a quarter of the population went to film shows twice a week.

For popular reading the thirties was also a golden age. Beginning in 1935 Penguin Books attracted a large audience to quality books in cheap paper covers. Since the 1920s the middle class pursued a chaste love affair with the newspaper crossword puzzle. The detective story became an additional middle-class escape which appealed to the intellect as well as to the imagination. Whereas Hollywood provided most of the films which the British watched, British writers produced a wealth of detective novels read on both sides of the Atlantic. For instance, Dorothy L. Sayers created Lord Peter Wimsey, a monocle-wearing, aristocratic sleuth of broad culture and occasional eccentricity. In *The Nine Tailors* (1934) he solved an old jewel robbery and a new murder with the help of his knowledge of the art of church bell ringing.

Appeasement and the Road to War. After 1935 or 1936 the international dangers Britain faced outweighed her economic problems. Brutal and aggressive dictators trampled on the rights of militarily weaker states, on political democracy, and on personal freedoms. Britain tried to preserve peace by agreeing to what the warlike leaders of Germany, Italy, and Japan demanded, and this appeasement hurt the National Government's reputation in the long run even more than its lack of energy in fighting unemployment. The policy of appeasement enjoyed widespread support: some people hoped that the fascist dictatorships would block the expansion of Communism; some admired the vigor with which fascist states pursued economic development. The vindictiveness of France, the historians who attacked the allied claim that Germany bore the entire war guilt, and the economists who feared the practicality of large reparations persuaded many people that Germany had legitimate grievances.

In the 1930s Hitler appealed to the liberal principle of national self-determination, the right of German-speaking populations to live under the German flag, and the right of the German state to the means of self-defense exercised by its neighbors. It was possible to agree with the end if not the means when in 1936 the German army occupied the previously demilitarized Rhineland and again in 1938 when it united Austria to Germany. War memoirs and novels reminded the public of the mixture of stupidity and tragedy which World War I had been. To abandon appeasement meant to threaten Germany with war, and on the basis of the limited aerial bombardment in World War I it was expected that a new war would slaughter hundreds of thousands of civilians and shatter morale. The atrocity stories invented in the last war made it possible to dismiss the reports of Nazi brutality toward the Jews and political opponents as exaggerations.

Though the political Left hated Hitler, Mussolini, and the Japanese militarists, they disliked the idea of war and distrusted the National Government. In principle they favored strong action against an aggressor through the League of Nations or a collective security agreement in which Russia would take part. In practice the Labour Party opposed rearmament. In the first half of the decade pacifism was strong in the Labour Party. After the outbreak of the Spanish Civil War in 1936 the Left began to accept the necessity of fighting a war to stop the march of fascism.

On the political Right a few voices called for rearmament and for an end to the appeasement of Germany. Some of the Conservative opponents of appeasement had reputations as reactionary romantics who tilted at windmills. Winston Churchill in 1934-35 opposed legislation to give India partial self-government; he denounced the appeasement of Gandhi as strongly as he did the appeasement of Hitler. In 1936 he alone among well-known politicians urged Edward VIII (George V's son) not to abdicate when the Government insisted that the King must surrender his crown if he wanted to marry the twice-divorced American woman whom he loved. Edward did in fact abdicate, to be succeeded by his brother George VI (1936-52). Meanwhile, the young Foreign Secretary, Anthony Eden, resigned to protest the appeasement of Italy.

The last triumph of appeasement came at the Munich conference in 1938 when the British and French allowed the Germans to seize large parts of Czechoslovakia. Supposedly the lessons of history proved that war accomplished little, so why not have the peace conference before the war instead of after it, and let the other side have their minimum demands? The new Prime Minister, Neville Chamberlain, returned from a meeting with Hitler to a hero's welcome for having brought back "peace in our time." Trenches had been dug in the parks, sandbags were heaped everywhere, and millions of gas masks had been distributed. Though the public was relieved when it was told that the Prime Minister had prevented war, in fact he had only postponed it for a year.

When Hitler next turned his attention to Poland, Russia negotiated a non-aggression pact with Germany out of suspicion that Britain and France might make a deal with the Nazis at her expense. Without Russia as an ally the western countries could do nothing effective in Eastern Europe, but they pledged themselves to go to war if Germany attacked Poland. As a result when the Germans invaded Poland in September 1939, the Second World War began.

WORLD WAR II

The Phoney War and Norway. Despite their declarations of war the British and French did little fighting at first. After the Germans overran

Poland a "phoney war" replaced real war for more than eight months. Continuing the spirit of appeasement British bombers dropped propaganda leaflets. Serious fighting was confined to the high seas and the U-boats under them. The "phoney war" contrasted strangely with the prewar expectations of immediate massive bombing attacks. It had been feared that the Germans would drop gas bombs; even infants were equipped with gas masks. The hospitals grimly discharged ordinary patients to prepare for bomb casualties. In fact, the bombers did not strike until mid-1940, and the number of civilian fatalities from German bombs in Britain only slightly exceeded 60,000, a total less than half the number who died in the influenza epidemic which followed World War I.

In April 1940, the period of military inactivity ended when Germany seized nearby Denmark and invaded Norway. The British — who had plans to occupy strategic Norway themselves — sent troops to help the Norwegian army, but after a few weeks the Germans prevailed. Some Conservatives in the House of Commons agreed with the Labour Party that Britain needed new leadership and voted against Neville Chamberlain. Though Chamberlain carried this vote, his shrunken majority showed that he had become a source of disunity. He promptly resigned.

Winston Churchill headed the new Government. Less than a year ago he had been considered an aging has-been, his vigorous opposition to appeasement dismissed as a sign of his chronic aggressiveness. Churchill had no doubt that he was the right man to lead Britain. His bulldog-like chin, his ever present cigar, and his fingers raised in a V-for-victory salute made him a wartime caricature of John Bull. He came to symbolize his country's courage, stubbornness, and zest for life. In the crisis year of 1940 he offered only "blood, sweat, toil, and tears." His carefully prepared speeches, delivered with an aristocratic lisp, instilled an awareness of the gravity of the dangers confronting Britain together with confidence about eventual victory.

Churchill's was the most successful Coalition Government in British history. The Prime Minister spent most of his time on military and diplomatic affairs with the Labour Party ministers having a very large say in domestic matters. The leader of the Labour Party, Clement Attlee, became Deputy Prime Minister, and the head of the transport union, Ernest Bevin, Minister of Labour. Bevin acquired dictatorial control over the assignment of manpower; he forced industries with low wages and weak trade unions to improve pay and cooperate with the unions.

Dunkirk and the Battle of Britain. The day that Churchill became Prime Minister a disastrous stage of the war began. The French had prepared

Winston Churchill during the Blitz, 1941 (Radio Times Hulton Picture Library).

for a repetition of the kind of war they had fought in 1914-18 by constructing the massive fortifications known as the Maginot Line along the German border. Since they failed to extend these defenses along the Belgian frontier the German army outflanked the Maginot Line by attacking through Belgium. The French lacked a strong air force capable of supporting ground forces, and their generals used tanks poorly. In contrast the German *Blitzkrieg,* or lightning war, kept the western allies off balance with fast moving tanks supported by low flying aircraft. If the Germans had pressed their attack on the northern front they could have forced hundreds of thousands of allied soldiers to surrender but instead they saved their tanks for fighting further south. A motley armada of warships, channel steamers, and small civilian boats evacuated about 225,000 British troops and over 100,000 Frenchmen from the port of Dunkirk. It was a heroic effort to limit the scope of defeat. A few weeks later the French Government accepted an armistice which allowed the Germans to occupy most of the country.

The British, the Empire, and a few continental exiles continued to resist the Germans. Fearful that the French would turn their fleet over to the Germans, Churchill sadly ordered the British navy to sink any warships of her former ally which refused to surrender. Expecting a German invasion the British Government ordered street signs, railroad station names, and bus destination notices removed. It recruited over a million middle aged and elderly volunteers in a Home Guard. The British people rallied together in what has been called the Dunkirk spirit. Workers in war industries put in long hours of overtime and Sunday work. Production of vital aircraft soared dramatically, but eventually long hours meant fatigue and inefficiency.

Though the British army lacked trained men and heavy weapons to fight an invader, the British fleet could prevent the Germans from crossing the Channel unless the German air force won control of the skies. The British placed their hopes for survival on their Spitfire and Hurricane fighters. They also had the advantage of newly developed radar which detected the incoming planes and had broken the German secret codes; the Germans lacked fighter planes with adequate range to protect their bombers. Yet the RAF was hard pressed in the summer of 1940 during the aerial Battle of Britain as massive German raids followed without interruption. Fortunately for the British, the Germans turned their attention from the vital airfields, radar stations, and aircraft factories to London and other civilian targets in the hope of breaking morale. In mid-September the Germans realized that they had failed and abandoned their invasion plans.

New Allies. The British had fought alone in 1940 but their isolation ended with the German attack on Russia in June 1941. Before the Germans invaded Russia the British Communists had rejected the war as irrelevant to the working class and had embarrassed the Government with calls for deep shelters to protect the common people against bombing attacks. After the invasion they became loud-voiced patriots who urged higher production at armaments factories. Since the Russians became very popular a promise that the weapons would go to Russia guaranteed hard work at a war plant. The relations between the Governments lacked comparable warmth. The Russian dictator Joseph Stalin resented the slowness with which his remote western allies moved to open a second front on the European continent.

Britain gained a much more intimate ally when the Japanese attacked American and European possessions in Asia and the Pacific in December 1941. Previously, the Americans had sold the British substantial quantities of supplies, and after March 1941, under what was called Lend-Lease, had provided supplies without payment. Because British farmers had plowed up pastures to grow grain, the scanty British meat ration often consisted of Spam and other pressed meats from the United States. After the Japanese attack the United States became a full partner of the British in the war in Europe as well as in the East. The United States with its greater economic resources and manpower became the dominant partner. An American, General Dwight D. Eisenhower, eventually commanded the combined forces of the English-speaking countries in the West. According to wartime public opinion polls the Americans lacked the popularity of the distant Russians. Millions of GIs were, as the British said, "over-paid, over-sexed, and over here." In the long run the American entry into the war guaranteed victory. In the short run it strained British resources because the Americans took some of the supplies and the shipping which the British needed. The British also had to divert men and equipment to safeguard India against the Japanese and to satisfy the Austrialians and the New Zealanders.

In the first part of 1942, a variety of critics attacked Churchill's leadership. A few people advocated Sir Stafford Cripps as an alternative Prime Minister. In the 1930s he had been a left-wing member of the Labour Party until expelled for his advocacy of a popular front with the Communists; later he retreated from the Left. When Churchill became Prime Minister he sent Cripps to Moscow as ambassador. The public seemed to credit him with the Russian alliance though Hitler was the man responsible. When Cripps returned from Russia in January 1942, his popularity persuaded Churchill to make him a member of the small War Cabinet and Leader of the House of Commons.

Churchill's prestige was seriously undermined by military disasters in 1942 — the Japanese captured Singapore in February and the Germans took Tobruk in North Africa in June, with large, badly led garrisons surrendering in humiliating circumstances — and by inefficiency in industrial production. Though the critics of Churchill could not agree on what they wanted as a new policy, they all blamed him. This noisy sniping against Churchill's leadership was quieted by a series of military successes in North Africa beginning in November 1942, when a new commander, General Bernard Montgomery, won a major victory over the German Afrika Korps at El Alamein.

The Allied Offensive. It was time for an allied thrust. The Americans had hoped for an invasion of Western Europe as early as 1942. Fearing its cost Churchill favored attacking the enemy away from the center of his strength. To some extent Churchill's strategy prevailed. The victory at El Alamein was followed in a few days by American and British landings in French North Africa. In mid-1943 the allies crossed the narrow waist of the Mediterranean to invade first Sicily and then the Italian mainland. German resistance in Italy made the campaign there a slow war of attrition. Though Churchill got his way over North Africa and Italy he did not get the attack in the Balkans which he called the soft underbelly of Nazi-occupied Europe.

The western allies launched their major attack in June 1944, when they landed massive forces in Normandy in northern France. The artificial harbors, or "Mulberries," developed by British engineers allowed the allies to unload huge quantities of supplies without the control of a continental seaport. The allied armies quickly cut across northern France and liberated Paris, but stalled near the German border. Montgomery's scheme to shorten the war by dropping paratroopers into the Low Countries failed badly. During the last days of 1944 the Germans counterattacked in the so-called Battle of the Bulge.

Meanwhile heavy allied bombing slowly crippled Germany; in recent years this massive air attack has been criticized as inefficient and inhumane. In 1940-41 British bombing raids supposedly killed more RAF crewmen than German civilians. The British bomber command was committed to area bombing, mainly at night, with the object of breaking morale, rather than to attacks which pinpointed military targets. In a controversial raid near the end of the war, when the Germans had virtually no fighter plane defense, the allies killed over 100,000 persons at Dresden, a city with little military significance. Late in 1944 and early in 1945 the Germans struck back at British civilians with the so-called vengeance weapons. The V-1s, pilotless airplanes or buzz-bombs, caused terror as their approach could be seen and heard. The V-2s, which were rockets, were impossible to shoot down but their very speed meant that there was no time for fear. A considerable number of people were killed and large numbers of homes were destroyed before the allied armies captured the launching sites.

It was February 1945 before the allies began their invasion of western Germany. The Russians had already swept across Eastern Europe deep into German territory. Shortly before the Red Army captured Berlin Hitler committed suicide, and a few days later, early in May, the Nazi Reich surrendered unconditionally. The war in Asia continued for a few more months. The British contributed a brilliantly executed reconquest of Burma. Japan was near surrender when two atomic bombs hurried the capitulation. Though the Americans built and controlled the atomic weapons British scientists had played a major role in their development.

Evacuation of London children, 1940 (Radio Times Hulton Picture Library).

WARTIME BRITAIN

Dangers. Shortly after the war was declared considerably more than a million children, mothers of small children, pregnant women, and teachers were evacuated from London and other large cities likely to be bombed. When the bombs did not immediately fall, most of the refugees drifted back from the countryside and small towns where they had been sent. The middle-class families who took in working-class children had been shocked by lice, bed wetting, skin diseases, flimsy clothing, and cheap shoes. The conditions which the evacuation revealed and the sense of national solidarity which the war stimulated persuaded the Government to expand services for children such as subsidized school milk. During the war British children suffered from interrupted schooling and disrupted family life, but by the end of it they were physically healthier than at the beginning.

A sixth of the population moved soon after the outbreak of the war — soldiers, factory workers, and frightened adults, in addition to the children and mothers whom the Government had evacuated. The National Gallery stored its paintings in an abandoned Welsh quarry, and the London zoo killed its snakes. As a result of the blackout, to avoid showing German bombers their targets, the number of automobile fatalities during September 1939 doubled, and hundreds of thousands of pedestrians bumped into darkened lamp posts or tripped on stairs. Food rationing began early in 1940. The home front had begun to adjust to war.

Despite the abandonment of the plans to invade, the Germans continued to bomb British cities. During the war German bombs made one Londoner out of six homeless and the Government had to organize emergency shelter, clothing, and meals. Bombs tore up gas and electric lines and air raids and false alarms disrupted industrial production. Hundreds of thousands of people had to be recruited to work as air raid wardens, fire fighters, and other emergency workers. The easily frightened had left, which perhaps helps explain why morale did not break. In fact suicides and drunk arrests decreased. The Government manufactured a variety of personal and family-sized shelters. Thousands of Londoners huddled in the underground railroad stations where they avoided the terrifying sound of the bombs as well as the bombs themselves. The East End slums near the London docks were hit particularly hard, but no place was safe. Even Buckingham Palace was bombed.

Bombing raids smashed entire medium-sized cities. The destruction had surprisingly little lasting effect on industry. Production of tanks in Coventry returned to normal within six weeks of a devastating attack. The Germans also bombed places without military importance such as the cathedral town of Canterbury. The bombing raids blurred the distinction between civilian and soldiers. Most British troops were in training camps and in less danger than civilians in the big cities.

Shortages. As the war grew longer reserves of manpower and supplies grew shorter, so by 1943 there was virtually full employment. Large military forces, eventually five-million strong, competed for manpower with huge armaments industries. The airplane industry, for example, employed 1,700,000 people by 1944, the majority of whom were women. Nine out of ten single women, and eight out of ten married women did some kind of work during the war; women aged 19 to 30 could be conscripted, with a choice of industrial work or enlistment in the uniformed services, and women were assigned combat duties in anti-aircraft batteries. To avoid antagonizing Irish nationalists there was no conscription in Northern Ireland, not even for military-aged men. Elsewhere men who were not conscripted were directed into essential jobs by the threat of losing their exemptions. Compulsion could go only so far. There were strikes, ordinarily short and local, and extensive absenteeism.

The shortage of shipping, aggravated by German U-boats, and the diversion of supplies to the war effort, created frustrating scarcities. British housewives stood in long queues, made meals without favorite foods, and constantly repaired irreplacable clothes. Meat was particularly scarce as were semitropical commodities such as cane sugar and chocolate, sad news for a people who liked their beef and sweets. The Ministry of Food coaxed people to abandon the old rule in brewing tea of adding an extra teaspoon "for the pot." The fillers, bread and potatoes, were not rationed, and for morale beer and tobacco also were unrationed. On the other hand, a nutritious, but unpopular gray National Loaf replaced white bread, beer was watery, and both beer and tobacco frequently scarce. Clothing was both rationed and standardized so that a woman could have only so many pleats in her skirt.

Planning for Reform. As the military situation improved the British people could think about more than survival. In December 1942, the Beveridge Report on social insurance was published and 600,000 copies, or summaries, were sold. Sir William Beveridge proposed a moderate, consensus program, guarantees of an adequate income during illness, industrial injury, unemployment, and old age — all to be funded by compulsory, universal insurance. He emphasized that his scheme made three assumptions — that the Government would provide a public system of medical care, subsidies for families with children, and a high level of employment. Public enthusiasm forced the Government to pledge its support despite fear that the reforms might exceed the economic resources of a war-weakened country.

During the war the Coalition Government began plans for a public medical service and in 1944 it enacted legislation providing free, universal secondary education. The caretaker Government which ruled between the end of the Coalition and the postwar election enacted family allowances paid to mothers with more than one child. The Second World War generated more social reform than the First World War.

AUSTERITY AND SOCIALISM, 1945-51

The Labour Party rejected Churchill's offer to prolong the Coalition until victory over Japan, because like most people the Party had expected that the war in the East would last another year. Elections were held in July 1945; experts had predicted a Conservative victory but instead Labour won a landslide. The public believed that Labour was the best party to enact postwar reforms and remembered the unemployment of the interwar years. Suddenly Churchill and his party were out of office despite the glory of military victory. Churchill had not helped his cause by warning that his former Coalition partners might rule through a Gestapo-style police state. Despite intrigue to replace him as party leader Clement Attlee became Prime Minister. As so often, the greatest electoral loser turned out to be the Liberals who were almost wiped out.

Austerity. A multitude of financial and economic crises confronted the new Government. When the Japanese war ended suddenly, the Americans promptly stopped Lend-Lease and required the British to pay for everything they imported from the United States. With difficulty the British negotiated a large American loan at a low rate of interest only to see the borrowed money shrink rapidly because of postwar inflation. It was not until the Cold War convinced the American public that it needed strong European allies that the United States offered substantial reconstruction aid. In 1947, the American Secretary of State, George Marshall, proposed that aid be given and in 1948 the Marshall Plan began to pump its billions of dollars of assistance into war-ravaged Europe.

Britain had enormous material needs. German bombs had destroyed or damaged hundreds of thousands of homes and ordinary construction and repair had been suspended. British industry had been distorted by the war; the peacetime aircraft industry, for example, would not need a capacity to produce more than 20,000 planes a year. Britain had lost many of her vital markets to competitors and other old customers had no way of paying. Only the United States could supply much of the manufactured goods, raw materials, and food which Britain needed. To pay for them she exported automobiles wanted by the home market.

The British people had fought in hope of a better life, not merely for a return to prewar conditions. Perhaps only a party identified with the working class could have obtained acceptance for the peacetime sacrifices which in fact followed the war. Because Britain had to worry about food supplies for the continent, bread and potatoes were briefly rationed which had never happened during the fighting. Meat was rationed until the mid-1950s. In the late 1940s declining productivity in the mines, a shortage of railroad cars to move the coal, and an exceptionally severe winter combined to create a desperate fuel shortage. Factories had to be closed in 1947 for want of fuel, idling millions of workers and undercutting the effort to export goods overseas. The use of electricity at home was prohibited between nine and noon and between two and four in the afternoon. In a new kind of blackout street lights were turned off and the BBC suspended its new television service.

In November 1947 Sir Stafford Cripps became Chancellor of the Exchequer. This intense, austere man preached self-denial with religious fervor. Not only did he keep rationing but he also let prices rise. In 1949 he devalued the pound by about 30 percent which made exports cheaper and imports dearer. Cripps considered the sterling area vital for British economic stability. Britain benefited from the dollar sales of the sterling countries — the dominions, former protectorates, and colonies which had currencies based on the British pound and dependent on the great London banks for credit. Consequently Cripps downplayed any British role in European economic cooperation which might weaken the sterling bloc.

Nationalization and Welfare. The socialism of the Labour Government took two main forms, public ownership of selected basic industries and the combination of compulsory insurance and free services known as the welfare state. Many of the industries which were nationalized needed massive capital investment. Government ownership also permitted the reorganization of the fragmented coal industry and raised the hope that its bad labor-management relations might improve. The Bank of England, also nationalized, had functioned as a quasi-government body; the decision to nationalize probably was revenge for 1931 when the bankers allegedly had conspired to bring down a Labour Government. Electricity, gas, railroads, scheduled airlines, overseas cables, buses, and most long distance trucking also were brought under national ownership. The old owners were compensated. Some of them, such as the gas companies, had been municipal authorities.

Nationalization produced little change in the operation of the firms. Semi-autonomous public boards, largely recruited from the old managers, ran the public industries and workers and consumers had little influence. The work force was not incorporated in the civil service so that strikes to enforce wage demands were legal. Morale did not improve because the workers were employed by the nation and the problem of absenteeism continued. One argument for nationalization had been to provide funds for modernization, but the Government often starved the nationalized industries of capital. In general the Conservatives had little complaint about the industries which the Labour Government selected to be nationalized in the mid-1940s. Most industry remained privately owned and the Labour Government had no plans to end capitalism in Britain.

The major controversy over nationalization arose when the Government attempted to nationalize the iron and steel industry. Labour wanted at least one industry under public control which had a chance for economic success. Iron and steel was a basic industry and it needed Government help for expansion and modernization. As it took the Labour Government several years to develop a specific plan, it feared that the House of Lords might use its powers to postpone the nationalization bill beyond the next general election. Therefore the Government passed legislation reducing the powers of the Lords to delay bills passed by the Commons to a single year.

The social legislation which the Labour Party enacted in the mid-forties affected the lives of ordinary people more than did the nationalization of a few industries. As the reforms grew out of a national consensus the Conservative Party did not oppose the Labour proposals in principle. Improved insurance schemes offered incomes for the elderly, the unemployed, the sick, and the victims of industrial accidents. For those inadequately provided for by the insurance system there was a catch-all program of national assistance. The cost of these welfare services exceeded that of previous social programs far less than generally taken for granted. In the 1930s massive unemployment had compelled public authorities to pay out immense sums which could be spent on other services after the war.

The creation of a free National Health Service turned out to be the most popular of the new social programs with the ordinary public, the most controversial because of the opposition of the general practitioners, and in the long run the most difficult to finance. Beginning in 1948 British residents became entitled to free medical, dental, and hospital care as well as free drugs, eye glasses, and dentures. The Minister of Health, Aneurin Bevan, the eloquent, hot-tempered leader of the Labour left wing, had difficulty persuading the British Medical Association to cooperate. Though the specific disputes concerned how doctors would be compensated, the physicians disliked any lay control over the practice of medicine. In later years the hospitals provided the greatest problem for the National Health Service. Most were old but expensive to replace and their staff complained of low pay, long hours, and poor conditions.

Labour's Foreign Policy. The foreign policy of the Labour Government differed little from what a Conservative Government would have advocated. For reasons of national security Britain had always opposed any country which tried to control all of Europe. The limitations on personal freedoms in Russia added an ideological quarrel. Ernest Bevin, the trade unionist turned Foreign Secretary, was strongly anti-Russian and anti-Communist. As an indispensable ally of Attlee, he exercised great discretionary authority. The British joined the Americans and the French in resisting a Russian blockade of the allied enclave in Berlin through an airlift of vital supplies. In 1949 Britain became a charter member of the North Atlantic Treaty Organization, the military alliance which opposed the Russians in the Cold War in Europe. The Labour Government maintained the country's Great Power status by developing its own nuclear weapons. In 1950 Britain sent a small military force to support her American ally in the Korean war.

Palestine was Bevin's bitter failure. He followed Britain's traditional pro-Arab policy despite the Jewish sympathies of the American Government. He attempted to restrict postwar Jewish immigration to the British-controlled territory even when that meant herding refugees from Hitler into new concentration camps. Serving as a buffer between the Arabs and the Jews in Palestine cost the British money that they could ill-afford to spend, and lives as well. Unable to work out a settlement Britain withdrew in 1948. In the war which followed the new State of Israel established its control over most of Palestine.

India provided the Labour Government with its great moral triumph. For years successive British Governments had promised some kind of self-government to the Indians. The divisions in India, particularly between the Muslims and the predominantly Hindu Congress Party, made it difficult for the British to withdraw without condemning the subcontinent to civil war. The leaders of the Congress Party, Jawaharlal Nehru and Mohandas K. Gandhi, had refused to cooperate with the British during World War II. By the threat of unilateral withdrawal the British persuaded the Congress Party and the Muslim League to agree to a partition, the Muslims to control the new state of Pakistan, the Congress the remainder of India. As a result, full-scale religious warfare was avoided, but hundreds of thousands died in communal riots, and millions more fled to the part of the subcontinent assigned to their religion.

The Labour Party won another general election victory in 1950. The margin was very narrow and a weary, aging Government found it difficult to proceed. Cripps died and Ernest Bevin retired. Aneurin Bevan resigned to protest the imposition of small charges on eye glasses and dentures and the decision to rearm the West Germans as an ally against the Russians. The Labour Government forced a new election in 1951 in an effort to get a clear mandate to rule, but instead it lost a close election to the Conservatives. Unfortunately for the Labour Party, rising prices for the materials which Britain imported had weakened the economy.

The fall of the Labour Government in 1951 marked the end of the immediate postwar era. As an appropriate symbol the Government had organized a national celebration called the Festival of Britain to show the revival of the country from the destruction and deprivation of World War II. Modernistic buildings arose on the site of a bombed-out dock district on the South Thames to house a series of exhibits on the centenary of the Crystal Palace Exhibition of 1851. Britain was still threadbare, her streets still pockmarked with bomb craters, and the sausages had little meat in them, but the road to recovery and prosperity seemed open.

SUGGESTIONS FOR FURTHER READING

Most of the books recommended for the previous chapter also are useful for this one. A number of biographies have valuable selections on 1931-51 including that by Henry Pelling on Winston Churchill (1974), Alan Bullock on Ernest Bevin (1960-67, third volume to come), Michael Foot on Aneurin Bevan (1962-73), and Bernard Donoughue and G.W. Jones on the Labour politician, Herbert Morrison (1973), and the memoirs of another Labour politician, Hugh Dalton, particularly his concluding volume for 1945-60, *High Tide and After* (1962).

The novelist J. B. Priestley gives an impressionistic, contemporary view of the mid-1930s in *English Journey* (1934). Noreen Branson and Margot Heinemann, *Britain in the Nineteen Thirties* (1973), presents social history as seen from the Left. On Mosley the best book is Robert Benewick, *The Fascist Movement in Britain* (2nd ed., 1972). In 1974 Frances Donaldson published a new study of the fascinating abdication crisis, *Edward VIII*. There is a large literature on appeasement, for instance, W. N. Medlicott, *British Foreign Policy since Versailles, 1919-1963* (2nd ed., 1968), Martin Gilbert, *The Roots of Appeasement* (1967), Donald Lammers, *Explaining Munich: The Search for Motive in British Policy* (1966), Keith Robbins, *Munich* (1968), William R. Rock, *British Appeasement in the 1930s* (1977), and, of course, Winston Churchill, *The Gathering Storm* (1948).

For the war the best introductions are Henry Pelling, *Britain and the Second World War* (1970), and Angus Calder, *The People's War: Britain, 1939-45* (1969). M. A. Fitzsimons has analyzed Bevin's diplomacy in *The Foreign Policy of the British Labour Government, 1945 1951* (1953). For the domestic policies of the postwar Labour Government see Pauline Gregg, *The Welfare State: an Economic and Social History of Great Britain from 1945* (1967); the important study by Harry Eckstein, *The English Health Service* (1958); and the lively book by Harry Hopkins, *The New Look: a Social History of the Forties and Fifties in Britain* (1963). Michael Sissons and Philip French have edited *The Age of Austerity, 1945-1951* (1963) which includes essays on both the significant and the trivial.

17

Recovery & Crises

1951 to the Silver Jubilee

In the last quarter century, Britain has lost an Empire and entered into a union with her Western European neighbors which may lead to the creation of a powerful United States of Europe. She has shared in a revolution in social behavior symbolized by the international popularity of the singing group, the Beatles, and has felt the strains of regional nationalisms and urban guerilla warfare in Northern Ireland.

Despite the importance of these events, economic problems dominate recent British history. In the 1950s Britain completed her recovery from her wartime ordeal. Before the decade ended, well-stocked meat counters and shop windows left only a memory of the long years of rationing, shortages, and drabness. In the 1960s ordinary people took for granted that they could afford expensive luxuries such as color televisions, automobiles, and Mediterranean holidays. Underneath this blush of prosperity the British economy was basically, and increasingly, unhealthy. Compared with North America, Western Europe, and Japan, Britain had stagnated; in price, quality, and reliability her industrial products often could not compete in international markets. A huge foreign debt, a currency which lost value in relation to other currencies, and a high rate of domestic inflation

Shopping center in Croyden, Surrey.

marked the difference between the standard of living Britain tried to acquire and the much lower one her industrial production could support. The grim facts became painfully clear in the mid-1970s when a sharp rise in the price of oil strained the economies of all the major industrial countries. The weak suffered the most, and the country which had started the Industrial Revolution had stumbled into the ranks of the weakest.

AFFLUENCE AND FREEDOM

Despite the underlying economic problems, the 1950s, 1960s, and 1970s brought most people new material comforts and new social freedoms. At moments of crisis newspaper headlines screamed about economic disaster, and sometimes Government policies intended to strengthen the national economy pinched the average person — such as by making credit purchases difficult; but ordinarily the problems of the economy troubled only the experts. Life was much more comfortable than before the war, an age of affluence for the fortunate majority with the guarantee of the comprehensive services and subsidies of the welfare state for everyone. Virtually full employment and improved wages struck hard blows at the prewar culture of poverty. By the middle 1950s a third of all the pawnshops which had flourished a generation earlier closed for lack of customers.

The Mass Market. British businessmen courted the increasingly prosperous mass market with intensive advertising and with installment credit for the purchase of large consumer durables such as refrigerators and washing machines. Multiple-branch retail chains such as the Marks and Spencer clothing stores standardized quality at a high level and kept prices down. Large self-service grocery stores replaced the small shops in which clerks had collected goods for customers. New technologies created frozen foods, easy to clean synthetic fabrics, cheap plastics, and television.

The new products and the new stores eased the household burdens of women, and aside from the young no other group underwent more dramatic changes. The rising proportion of women who married, usually at a young age, forced the civil service and the schools to abandon in the early 1950s the old rule that women retire when they married. Popular women's magazines reflected and reinforced the forces for change. In the early 1950s one of them, *Woman,* added a million sales with a how-to-do-it format ranging from cookery to child rearing, cosmetics to sex.

Leisure. Leisure changed greatly — there was more of it, more money was spent on it, and more of it was enjoyed at home or in cars which were extensions of home. The television set quickly changed from its status as a luxury of the well-off to a necessity of the working class. Television viewing took many men out of the public house, as the increase in the sale of bottled beer showed. At first the state-owned British Broadcasting Corporation, financed by license fees, enjoyed a monopoly. Beginning in 1955, the Independent Television Authority offered an advertising-financed alternative. ITV attracted many working-class and lower-middle-class households away from the BBC with a schedule of light entertainment and American adventure stories. Competition from television forced many cinemas to close, and the diversion of advertising revenues drove many newspapers out of business.

Some people feared the changes which transformed British society. They complained about Britain becoming Americanized, or losing its own national character because of a restless enthusiasm for novelty and an indifference toward traditional standards, which in turn undermined social stability. In the late 1950s and the early 1960s church memberships declined substantially. The special English vice of gambling grew more conspicuous when Parliament legalized off-track horse race betting and gambling casinos in 1960. The Queen's sister married a photographer with a Bohemian reputation. The Profumo scandal of 1963 hinted at a self-destructive dimension of the new permissive society. John Profumo, the Secretary of State for War, had an affair with a young model, Christine Keeler, who also had been involved with a Russian naval officer. Profumo at first told the House of Commons that the charges were false, then admitted them and resigned. Investigations by the courts and the press revealed an unsavory world of expensive prostitutes, drugs, and violence, as well as a possible security risk.

The young, who had the most time and the most discretionary income to devote to leisure, developed a kind of subculture in which recorded music played a prominent part. Helped by improved record players and cheap plastic recording discs the record industry sold four times as many records as before the war. A climax of the frenetic years of social and cultural rebellion came in the middle and late 1960s. A young group of musicians and singers, the Beatles, represented the explosion of talent and defiance. Beginning in 1964 their vigorous music and working-class Liverpool accents sold millions of records on both sides of the Atlantic. In 1965 the Queen honored them for their contribution to exports by granting them membership in the Order of the British Empire.

Swinging London replaced the staid image of the British as old-fashioned and almost Victorian. Although reality lay somewhere

The Beatles (Dezo Hoffmann, Ltd.).

between the old and new images, gaudy boutiques on Carnaby Street and Kings Road, unisex clothing, and long-haired males provided outward signs of a new cult of revolt and material gratification in which the young acted as leaders. In 1966 the mini-skirt — its hemline often no more than mid-thigh — became modish among long-legged, boot-wearing "dolly birds." Pornographic books, magazines, and films, and live sex shows grew commonplace. Though street solicitation remained illegal, prostitution itself was legal, and many brothels thinly disguised as saunas advertised in the newspapers. By the mid-1960s two out of three children born to mothers under twenty had been conceived out of wedlock. Before the decade ended homosexual acts and abortion were legalized and capital punishment was abolished. The respect for law and order declined; as recently as 1965 only 79 policemen were victims of assault in Britain, but ten years later the number had grown to 2835. The old rules often seemed forgotten.

Other social changes which developed more quietly had greater significance than pop singers and short skirts. In 1901 only a quarter of women aged twenty to twenty-four were married; by 1966, a majority. In 1911 only 14 percent of women who worked were married; in 1966, 55 percent. Between 1911 and 1966 the number of blue collar workers barely grew despite an increase in population, while white collar workers increased by 176 percent. In 1948 there were fewer than two million private cars; in 1968, nearly eleven million. Though the proliferation of the automobile gave a new mobility to individual drivers it forced a reduction in railroad service and threatened the countryside with road traffic and road builders. In 1970 eighteen-year-olds received the right to vote, and another statute required employers, beginning in 1975, to pay women equal pay for the same work.

Education changed more slowly. By the standards of virtually every other industrial country it remained strikingly non-egalitarian. Many boys from well-off families attended fee-charging private schools, misleadingly called public schools, and the students in the state system were sorted out, on the basis of an examination taken at age eleven, between university-oriented grammar schools and other less prestigious ones. In the 1960s and 1970s comprehensive schools which offered both grammar school and other curricula were created in some towns. Despite a rapid expansion in higher education — the number of full-time students doubled during 1963-70 — few working-class children continued their studies beyond their mid-teens.

Racial Tensions. There was also a growth in racial hostility. During the 1950s and 1960s hundreds of thousands of blacks from the West Indies and Asians from the Indian subcontinent emigrated to Britain. In the late 1950s there were ugly anti-colored riots in the Notting Hill section of London. In 1963 Parliament passed the first of a series of Commonwealth Immigration bills which made it difficult for non-whites from the Commonwealth to emigrate to Britain, yet allowed the people of the white Commonwealth to emigrate with relative ease. The non-white immigration which continued aroused hostility in working-class neighborhoods where the blacks and Asians settled. A right wing Tory, Enoch Powell, called for the compulsory repatriation of non-whites to their native countries. The Labour Government appeased the opponents of immigration with new restrictions, but also enacted a Race Relations Act to protect the non-whites who had already settled in Britain and their children from discrimination.

By the middle 1970s one in every thirty-three inhabitants of the United Kingdom was non-white. The non-whites were concentrated in London and other large industrial cities. Often they had conspicuous jobs as, for instance, in public transport. Assaults on colored people

West Indian immigrant at Victoria Station, London (Radio Times Hulton Picture Library).

became so common that a new word, Pakibashing, was coined to describe the beating of a Pakistani or other non-white.

THE LAST DAYS OF THE OLD ORDER

In the early 1950s there was a strong sense of a new era beginning, which the accession of the young Queen Elizabeth II in 1952 and her impressive coronation ceremonies in the following year strengthened, but the reality was different. Elderly veterans of past political battles still led the major parties. Clement Attlee and Winston Churchill did not retire until 1955, shortly before the stubborn illusions about Britain as a Great Power in her second Elizabethan Age were rudely shaken.

Butskellism. After struggling to a narrow victory in the general election of 1951 the Conservatives remained in office under four Prime Ministers until 1964. The aging Churchill headed the first Conservative Government. Out of a mixture of practical politics and principle the Conservatives accepted most of what the Labourites had done. The term Butskellism, from the names of the last Labour Chancellor of the Exchequer, Hugh Gaitskell, and his Conservative successor, R. A. Butler, was invented to describe this continuity of moderate economic and social policies. In a non-ideological age when almost everyone accepted Keynesian economics, moderate Labourites and moderate Conservatives alike supported a mixed economy which combined capitalism in most industries with an active Government role to encourage growth and stability.

The Conservative Government intervened in the economy to restrain the rise in prices or to expand the number of jobs, a kind of "stop, go" balancing act. The Conservatives kept many wartime restrictions such as meat rationing until 1954 and retained rent control for most working-class housing. They differed from Labour by enlarging the proportion of homes built for owner-occupiers. Though the Conservatives created small fees for dentistry and medical prescriptions, they accepted in principle that general taxation should finance the National Health Service. Of the nationalized industries only iron and steel and long distance trucking were sold back to private businessmen. The coal mines, the railroads, the canals, the docks, the electric power stations, and the Bank of England remained under public ownership.

Suez and the Illusions of World Power. Regardless of party, the British still saw their country as a world power. They took pride in the ill-fated Comet, supposedly the best passenger jet in the skies and proof that the

Coronation of Queen Elizabeth II, 1953 (Radio Times Hulton Picture Library).

British could thrive in the world of modern technology. The tragic crashes which forced its grounding foreshadowed more serious shocks to national self-confidence. For a time the Conservative Government acted as if it had the economic resources to support Great Power status. The first British atomic bomb was detonated in 1952. British soldiers crushed the Mau Mau terrorists in the East African colony of Kenya and the Chinese Communist guerillas in Malaya, and held their own against the Greeks anxious to drive them out of Cyprus. Though the British Government gave most colonies extensive home rule, none got full independence between the late 1940s and the late 1950s; particularly in tropical Africa the British Empire still looked impressive.

The Suez crisis of 1956 shattered the myth of British power. Though Egypt had been an independent state since the First World War, Britain considered it part of the Empire and British troops garrisoned the Canal Zone. After an Arab nationalist, Colonel Gamal Abdel Nasser, seized power in Egypt, the British reluctantly withdrew their troops. When Nasser failed to get an American loan for a dam to exploit the waters of the Nile, he asked the Soviet Union for help and nationalized the Suez Canal. Then war broke out between Egypt and her old enemy Israel. After the Israelis had routed the Egyptian army, the British and the French sent troops into the former Canal Zone on the excuse that the war endangered the operation of the waterway. Anthony Eden, who had recently become Prime Minister, saw Nasser as a kind of Hitler, someone to be crushed before he became too dangerous. The United Nations and the United States denounced the Suez intervention as an act of aggression, and the British and the French turned out to be too weak to act in defiance of their American ally. At the beginning of 1957 Eden resigned on the grounds of ill health.

Macmillan. Eden's successor Harold Macmillan restored Conservative morale. Shrewd, tough-minded, skillful at presenting the right public image and more than a little lucky, Macmillan always seemed in control of the situation. A newspaper cartoonist pictured him as Supermac, a kind of Superman with a moustache and drooping eyelids. Though a member of the publishing Macmillan family, he had turned into a kind of aristocrat with the help of a marriage to the daughter of a duke; at one time six of nineteen members of the Cabinet were related to him, a record which an eighteenth-century Whig might have admired. Before the war Macmillan had built a reputation as a social reformer and as a strong opponent of appeasement of Nazi Germany. Since 1951 he had done well in a succession of Cabinet posts. In the struggle for power in 1957 he shouldered aside his more liberal rival, R. A. Butler, whose enemies rememberd him as a supporter of appeasement in the 1930s, and who lacked Macmillan's ruthless ambition.

Under Macmillan's leadership the Conservative Party again presented itself as the natural ruling party, practical men unbothered by doctrinaire ideology. In contrast, the Labour Party squabbled, Left against Right, over abstract ideas about which it then had little power to do anything, such as the further nationalization of industry. During the late 1950s Hugh Gaitskell, the moderate who succeeded Attlee as party leader, and Aneurin Bevan, the perennial leader of the party's rebellious Left, quarrelled almost continually. The divided Labour Party was badly beaten in the general election of 1959. Macmillan skillfully used television and national prosperity in his campaign. With vulgar effectiveness he reminded the voters that they had "never had it so good." It was the third consecutive general election in which the Conservatives had increased their majority. The future of the Labour Party appeared bleak.

End of Empire. Macmillan cheerfully presided over the dissolution of the British Empire, recognizing the "wind of change" bringing black self-government to Africa. After Ghana in West Africa became independent in 1957, the British Government arranged the transfer of power in its other colonies and protectorates in almost indecent haste. In Africa, in Southeast Asia, and in the Caribbean imperial possessions became independent states. In nearly all cases there had been no violent opposition to British rule. Only on the Mediterranean island of Cyprus did the majority of the population sympathize with the guerillas who fought the British garrison. The old white dominions became outnumbered by the new non-white states which had acquired their independence since the Second World War. The white minority regime in South Africa found the new Commonwealth uncongenial and left it.

Britain took pride in her role as leader of a multi-racial family of nations, a bridge between the rich and the poor. The existence of the Commonwealth disguised the disintegration of the Empire and made it easier for the British to accept the new reality or to ignore it. In practice the Commonwealth became little more than periodic conferences of Prime Ministers. The British hoped that they had firmly planted their own political institutions: a representative legislature, a non-political judiciary and civil service, a military subordinate to civilian authority, and freedom of the press — in short, constitutional government. The shallowness of the British heritage quickly became clear. One-party states, charismatic dictatorships, military coups, and communal violence among religious, language, ethnic, and tribal groups became the norm. About all that survived of the old Empire was English as the language of the ruling elite — sustained by linguistic divisions in the local populations and the influence of the United States. Perhaps white-ruled Rhodesia provides the most telling example of British failure and British decline. In 1965 the white settlers in the small southern African colony unilaterally declared it an independent state to prevent Britain from imposing black majority rule; supposedly Britain's democratic heritage was irrelevant. Britain proved too weak to force little Rhodesia to change its racial policies. In 1977 India made itself a heartening exception to this discouraging pattern. By democratic elections the Indian people peacefully replaced a government which earlier had suspended civil liberties. India reclaimed its status as the world's most populous democracy.

The Decline of Military Power. In military affairs as well, common sense was mixed with an unrealistic ambition for a new kind of greatness. The Government drastically reduced the number of men in uniform and of overseas bases. In 1957 it announced that in three years conscription would end. There were painful rows when historic regiments were amalgamated. The Government intended to apply the financial savings to create a force of nuclear-armed missiles. In 1957 it detonated Britain's first hydrogen bomb. The lesson of Suez had been only incompletely learned.

A large section of British public opinion rejected nuclear weapons as immoral and demanded that Britain set an example by renouncing them. Thousands of men and women, radicals and non-political people, devout Christians and Marxists, joined in the protest marches of the Campaign for Nuclear Disarmament. The annual conference of the Labour Party briefly endorsed unilateral nuclear disarmament despite Hugh Gaitskell's objections. Both the proponents and the opponents of British nuclear bombs assumed that what Britain decided had a world-wide significance. Though the supporters believed that Britain could maintain an independent role in international affairs, in fact she no longer had the industrial and financial resources. In 1962 when the United States cancelled the development of a missile which Britain had contracted to buy to carry her nuclear bombs, the fact of dependence could not be avoided. The opponents of nuclear weapons assumed that moral leadership would earn Britain a position of world influence, but it is impossible to know whether her nuclear disarmament would have dissuaded other countries from developing their own atomic weapons.

The EEC. Despite the relative prosperity of the Macmillan years the British economy failed to grow as rapidly as that of its neighbors. Property speculators and retail-chain entrepreneurs sometimes accumulated large fortunes. The lower middle and working classes bought second-hand cars and travelled on package tours to Spanish seaside resorts. But the standard of living in other countries grew faster. The Common Market — officially the European Economic Community — successfully combined the West European countries such as France and West Germany into a single economic system without barriers to trade among members. Jolted by the prosperity of the EEC which she had refused to join as a charter member, Britain first organized a loosely-knit trade organization of smaller countries and then in 1960 belatedly applied for membership in the Common Market.

The British Government wanted to join the Common Market for political as well as economic reasons. Many people expected that economic unity would lay the basis for political unification. In an age of continental superpowers Britain could hope to count for something as part of a united Europe, but not alone. The Commonwealth lacked substance, and the "special relationship" with the United States did not provide much real influence with this other English-speaking power. A former American Secretary of State brutally complained that Britain had lost an empire without finding a new role. The British Government hoped to recover that sense of national purpose and power within the Common Market, but early in 1962 President Charles de Gaulle of France vetoed Britain's application for membership.

The Tory Fall. For Macmillan 1963 was the year of reckoning. The Prime Minister's magic was wearing thin. In the preceding year he purged a third of his colleagues from his Cabinet in search of a fresh image. In 1963 itself the Profumo scandal broke, as well as new revelations in the spy cases which had rocked Britain repeatedly since the war. Kim Philby, a retired intelligence agent, fled to the Soviet Union where he joined his partners in treason, the diplomats Burgess and MacLean who had defected in the early 1950s. The combined effect left a general impression of decadence and incompetence in high places.

Later in the year a serious medical operation convinced Macmillan that he must resign as Prime Minister and as leader of the Conservative Party. By chance, when Macmillan announced his retirement, the annual party conference was in session which added to the drama of the struggle for the succession. The Conservatives had no procedure for electing a leader. Traditionally he had emerged out of a consensus of the party leadership. Most of the Cabinet probably favored R.A. Butler who had long been considered well-qualified to become Prime Minister. To everyone's surprise Macmillan and the party officials preferred the Foreign Secretary, the Earl of Home, even though he was a member of the House of Lords. A recent change in the law enabled him to renounce his title, and as a commoner, Sir Alec Douglas-Home, he could stand for election to the House of Commons. Butler declined to fight, but a couple of younger men retired to the backbenches in anger. One ex-Cabinet member published an attack on the party bosses — whom he derided as the "magic circle" — for ignoring the will of the party.

Macmillan's triumph in imposing Douglas-Home as his successor was a short-lived one. Though Douglas-Home was a decent, likable man and a competent diplomat he understood little about Britain's economic problems. As Prime Minister he made the Conservative Party appear out-of-date and out-of-touch. By comparison, Labour began to look like the party with the modern ideas and business-like leaders. Hugh Gaitskell had died late in 1962 and Aneurin Bevan a couple of years earlier. The new leader of the Labour Party was Harold Wilson.

THE RISE OF THE GRAMMAR SCHOOL BOYS

Labour and a Faltering Economy. Wilson was a grammar school boy,

EUROPE IN 1977

FINLAND

NORWAY
Oslo

Stockholm

SWEDEN

BALTIC SEA

SCOTLAND

Edinburgh

NORTH

SEA

DENMARK

Copenhagen

Dublin

IRELAND

WALES

ENGLAND

The Hague

ATLANTIC

London

NETHERLANDS

Brussels

BELGIUM

Berlin

GERMAN
DEMOCRATIC
REPUBLIC

Warsaw

P O L A N D

Bonn

FEDERAL

Prague

BRITISH TERRITORIAL LIMIT

LUX.

REPUBLIC

CZECHOSLOVAKIA

OCEAN

Paris

OF GERMANY

Vienna

Budapest

△   GAS FIELDS

▲   OIL FIELDS

COMMON MARKET

F R A N C E

Bern

SWITZERLAND

AUSTRIA

HUNGARY

Zagreb

YUGOSLAVIA

I T A L Y

Rome

P
O
R
T
U
G
A
L

Madrid

S P A I N

Lisbon

MEDITERRANEAN   SEA

educated in a state secondary school rather than in a fee-charging public school. Unlike Attlee and Gaitskell and nearly all the Conservative leaders who were part of the old elite of public school boys, Wilson represented the new meritocracy of men and women who climbed the scholarship route from grammar school to university. The son of a Yorkshire pharmacist, Wilson had studied at Oxford, taught economics there, spent the war as a civil servant, and been elected to Parliament in the Labour landslide of 1945. A few years later he became the youngest member of Attlee's Cabinet and still later was one of the ministers who resigned in the company of Aneurin Bevan. When Gaitskell's death made the leadership available, he had been the candidate of the Left. Nevertheless, he was a pragmatist who cared little about abstract ideas or consistency. Supremely confident, he dominated his colleagues, few of whom had any ministerial experience.

In the general election held in 1964 Labour barely defeated the Conservatives, but Wilson governed as if his tiny majority had been ten times as large. For instance, he boldly renationalized the iron and steel industry. In a new general election in 1966 Wilson was rewarded with a comfortable majority. Unfortunately votes could not reinvigorate the economy. Even after a freeze in wages and prices and a huge international loan, the Government was forced to devalue the pound in 1967 — a tacit admission that Britain had become poorer and that her industrial productivity was lower than that of most other industrial countries. To fight inflation the Wilson Government used its control over the nationalized industries to order management to cut back capital investment, to hold down prices, and to resist wage demands. To save money the Government also supported drastic reduction in train service, despite its unpopularity with the public and the unions. The Government hoped to reform Britain's reputation for numerous strikes by proposing legislation to encourage negotiation and mediation and discourage local strikes begun without the authorization of the national union officers. The anger of the powerful trade unions forced the Government to abandon this industrial relations bill.

Economics largely dictated the decision to cut back Britain's military commitments outside of NATO. In 1967 the Government announced that by the mid-1970s Britain would withdraw virtually all her servicemen stationed east of Suez. In 1968 Britain further acknowledged that she was merely a European power when she abandoned her protectorate in Aden which had guarded the Red Sea approaches to the Suez Canal.

The Conservatives and the Common Market. In 1970 Wilson called a general election which he had expected to win, but surprisingly the Labour Party lost. The new Conservative Prime Minister, Edward

Heath, resembled his Labour predecessor in some ways more than he did any previous Conservative leader. The method of selecting a Conservative leader had been reformed. Like Wilson, Heath had been elected by his parliamentary colleagues. He too was a grammar school boy from an ordinary home, whose carpenter father had prospered to become a small building contractor. Heath had attended Oxford on a scholarship and then had strengthened his new middle-class status during the war by rising to the rank of colonel. In politics he lacked popular appeal, but his administrative ability and personal integrity won respect.

Heath's Government recorded one great accomplishment, the successful negotiation of entry into the Common Market. Britain officially joined the European Economic Community on New Year's Day, 1973. It was a controversial decision. Many people worried about the effect on national sovereignty and blamed rising food prices on the tariffs which as a member of the Common Market Britain had to erect against non-members. Other changes loosely associated with the entry into Europe — a decimal currency, metric weights and measures, and celsius scale temperatures — also provoked grumbling from people who disliked interference with their everyday lives.

Heath began his ministry strongly committed to economic competition as a solution to Britain's problems. While a Cabinet minister in the middle 1960s, he had pushed through a bill which prohibited manufacturers from requiring minimum resale prices, and as Prime Minister his Government authorized the creation of commercial radio to compete with the BBC. Heath broke with Butskellism, the bipartisan consensus which provided for Government intervention in a largely capitalist economy to appease the working class. Heath attempted to reduce the number of strikes with an Industrial Relations Act. It had little practical effect other than angering the unions. In 1972 low productivity and a drastic price increase in oil imports forced the Heath Government to allow the pound to float to its natural market level. In effect the float began a continuing devaluation of the pound; the floating pound sank.

By the end of his ministry Heath had retreated from his doctrinaire support for a free market economy. His Government gave public funds to keep the bankrupt Rolls-Royce motor car and airplane engine company and the Upper Clyde shipbuilders in operation. Inflation broke out of control, in part because the Government had allowed the supply of paper money to increase by 270 percent in less than four years to encourage industrial growth. To combat this inflation Heath imposed mandatory controls on wages and prices and tried to set an example of wage restraint in the nationalized industries.

As a result slowdowns and strikes on the railroads, at the electric power stations, and in the coal mines — all nationalized industries — crippled the country. The Government ordered a drastic reduction in fuel consumption when the miners refused to work overtime. At the beginning of 1974 business and industry were restricted to a three-day week. Street lights were ordered turned off and television broadcasting was reduced. When the miners called a strike, Heath responded by ordering a general election to appeal for public support.

Northern Ireland. One of the most serious problems to face any Government in the late 1960s and 1970s, Conservative or Labour, was the wave of violence and terrorism which racked Northern Ireland. When the rest of Ireland became a separate state early in the 1920s, the six northeastern counties of Ulster remained united with Britain. The local Protestant majority clung to union with Britain as a guarantee against union with a largely Roman Catholic Ireland. Northern Ireland had its own Parliament and ministry, dominated by the Protestant Unionist Party, and also elected M.P.s to the British Parliament.

Influenced by the struggle for equal rights for blacks in the United States, a civil rights movement sprang up in Northern Ireland in the late 1960s. Instead of asking for the incorporation of Ulster in the Irish Republic, the civil rights movement demanded equal rights for Catholics within the existing political structure. Catholics had been discriminated against in government jobs and tax-subsidized housing; gerrymandering and property qualifications often deprived them of votes in local elections. The civil rights marches provoked violent clashes with the police.

Soon the civil rights movement faded away, and a revived Irish Republican Army stood in its place with its traditional weapons of the bomb and the revolver. The I.R.A. was divided into two factions, the Marxist-leaning Officials and the larger and more violent Provisionals. I.R.A. shootings and bombings and the unpopularity of the Ulster police with the Catholic community forced the British Government to send the army into Northern Ireland in 1969. The introduction of internment without trial in 1971 and incidents such as the new Bloody Sunday, in which paratroopers killed thirteen Catholics in a riot at Londonderry early in 1972, further alienated the Catholic minority. At the same time the Protestants complained that the British had failed to support the loyalists. In 1972 a Conservative Government suspended the Protestant-controlled provincial administration. Angry at the failure of the authorities to suppress the I.R.A., Protestant paramilitary organizations began a counterterror.

Wearily, the British Government searched for a way in which the peoples of Northern Ireland could live together. In 1974 the British introduced a new provincial government in which the two religious communities would share power. Working-class Protestants organized a widespread strike which forced the collapse of this experiment. A convention was elected in 1975 to draw up a new constitution, but it could agree on nothing.

Meanwhile sectarian murders struck down hundreds on crowded Belfast streets and lonely rural roads, in homes darkened for sleep and in noisy bars. The I.R.A. extended the terror into Britain. Seven died and 120 were injured when two Birmingham pubs were bombed in 1974. Late that year the I.R.A. called a holiday truce which was extended in return for the gradual release of interned suspects. The truce slowed but did not stop terrorism. In 1975 London was struck by a series of bombings at the Tower of London, Harrods' department store, the Hilton hotel, and underground railroad stations, and there were dozens of frightening hoaxes as well.

Few Ulstermen claimed to favor violence, and neither Protestants nor Catholics comprised a cohesive party, but the prospects for an early solution to the Ulster troubles looked dismal. The best faint hope came in the mid-1970s when women of both religious communities organized a peace movement. As part of their campaign Ulsterwomen travelled to the United States to discourage Irish-Americans from contributing money to the I.R.A. and its charitable "front" organizations.

Devolution. Even in Britain disunifying tendencies threatened to unravel the proud Union Jack. In the middle 1970s most of Labour and some Conservatives reluctantly accepted the nationalist demands for elected assemblies in Scotland and Wales. As these two countries had been Labour strongholds, the Labour Party had to blunt the appeal of the nationalist parties. The lack of national institutions other than a language which only a minority spoke and the poverty which made financial autonomy unlikely hampered Welsh nationalism. In Scotland the distinctive legal and religious institutions, the history of a kingdom which was united with England's as recently as the eighteenth century, and the possibility of economic self-reliance — most of Britain's offshore oil and gas lies off the coasts of Scotland — combined to strengthen the nationalist movement. Though few Scottish nationalists and fewer Welshmen wanted independence, all the nationalists demanded more self-government than the assemblies thus far proposed by the Labour Government would provide.

Wilson Again. Harold Wilson returned to power in 1974. Labour won only a plurality of seats in the Commons, but formed a majority with the support of the minor parties. Wilson ended the coal strike that had forced Edward Heath into the election, and in a second election late in the same year Labour won a paper-thin majority. The Labour left wing wanted to take advantage of the widespread financial difficulties which business suffered. Anthony Wedgwood Benn, the controversial Minister of Industry, advocated a kind of nationalization by investing public monies in private firms. After its bankruptcy, the huge motor car company, British Leyland, came under Government control. The Labour Government committed itself to nationalize shipbuilding and aircraft manufacturing.

In the elections of 1974 the Labour Party had pledged itself to leave the Common Market unless it could negotiate better terms than had the Conservatives. Many left-wing Labour supporters disliked the European Economic Community out of fear that membership would prevent them from building socialism in Britain. Other moderate and right-wing Labour M.P.s strongly favored British participation in a united Europe. To keep his party together Wilson shifted his position frequently. He escaped his dilemma by holding a national referendum in 1975. Members of the Cabinet campaigned on opposite sides. Though some right-wing Tories supported the Labour left-wing in opposition to the Common Market, the public voted for continued membership by a large majority. People no longer expected that the Common Market would solve Britain's economic problems, but they feared that Britain would be worse off outside than inside.

A STOCKTAKING: THE STATE OF BRITAIN

Unresolved Economic Problems. Britain's continued status as a permanent member of the United Nations Security Council, despite her economic and military decline, underscores how recently her power and prestige have faded. Compared with all but a handful of states Britain remains an industrial giant, rich in human skills, in manufacturing plants, and in transportation infrastructures. The British people live far better than in the recent past. Compared with the other leading industrial countries, unfortunately, Britain lags in capital investment, technological and entrepreneurial training, and harmony between labor and management. It lacks the natural resources of continental-sized states such as the United States. Britain has to import half of its food and four-fifths of its raw materials. West Germany, which Britain helped defeat in World War II, maintains a higher standard of living with less unemployment and little inflation. In Britain the central government consumes 60 percent of the gross national product, and the central and local governments continue to increase their spending more rapidly than the gross national product increases. Taxation is as high as anywhere, as much as a 92 percent personal income tax in the highest brackets.

Other countries have economic problems too, but most have done better than Britain. British industry has become uncompetitive. It fails to adjust to changes in the market, has not taken advantage of improved technology, lacks aggressive salesmanship, and often charges higher prices than its competitors. It has acquired a reputation for strikes which have interrupted deliveries to customers. Some Conservatives complain that the welfare state has sapped the will to work, but countries such as Sweden with even more generous public services compete in the world market successfully. In recent years Japan and Scandinavia took shipbuilding orders away from British yards; Japanese and German cars sped ahead of British ones in the important American market and also invaded the British market. In many instances — as for example, electric typewriters — British manufacturers abandoned a growing industry altogether.

Signs of crisis have multiplied. At one point the annual rate of inflation exceeded 25 percent. In the final two years in which Wilson served as Prime Minister the value of the pound fell more than 40 percent. To cut back public spending the Labour Government abandoned two expensive projects, a tunnel under the English Channel and a new London airport. It kept a third prestige venture, the Concorde, a supersonic jet passenger plane built in cooperation with the French. The Chancellor of the Exchequer, Denis Healey, slashed ordinary expenditures, including those for social welfare. Wilson tried to slow inflation through voluntary wage restraint, a "social contract" with the trade unions which limited wage increases while protecting the worst paid workers from the full force of inflation.

Some politicians have pinned their hopes for economic recovery on the huge, recently discovered fields of gas and oil offshore in the North Sea. The first oil from under these stormy waters was delivered in 1975. It is expected that in the 1980s Britain will become a major oil exporter. Unfortunately, Britain's gas and oil deposits are already heavily mortgaged, in effect being the security for the huge debts which Britain owes to foreign banks and governments.

Changing Political Leadership. In 1976, Harold Wilson unexpectedly resigned at age 60 on the ground that he should give other men of his generation a chance to lead the Labour Party and the country. Though he failed to solve Britain's economic problems, Wilson had directed the revival of his party. Before he became leader Labour had lost three consecutive general elections; under his leadership it had won four out of five elections.

James Callaghan succeeded Wilson as party leader and Prime Minister. In contrast to his predecessor, a former university teacher, Callaghan had left school at age 14. He was a popular figure, "Sunny Jim," a party veteran who had held all the major Cabinet offices — the

Exchequer, the Home Office (which then included responsibility for Northern Ireland) and the Foreign Office. Callaghan narrowly defeated Michael Foot, the leader of the Left, who then became deputy leader. Both Callaghan and Foot were older than Wilson. Roy Jenkins, the leader of the party's Right, retired from Parliament to become Secretary General of the European Economic Community. Early in 1977 Anthony Crosland, the Foreign Secretary, died and his successor, David Owen, is one of the youngest Cabinet Ministers ever. Within a few years a new generation probably will run the Labour Party. As a result of resignations, deaths, and by-elections Labour has lost its slim parliamentary majority. In 1977 Callaghan, in order to stay in office, had to enter into a loose arrangement with the small Liberal Party, which angered the Labour left-wing.

By the time that Wilson retired, Edward Heath no longer led the Conservative Party. Tainted with defeat and criticized by the Right for drifting leftward, he was ousted in 1975. As he was still relatively young some Conservatives feared that he might be tempted to join a Labour-dominated coalition. Margaret Thatcher, the first woman to head a major party in a large industrial country, succeeded Heath. Her father was a grocer and small-town mayor. She had been educated at the local grammar school, studied science at Oxford, and later qualified as a lawyer. In elections in May, 1979, British voters chose Margaret Thatcher England's first woman Prime Minister.

Callaghan as Prime Minister continued Wilson's economic policies. He too tried to persuade trade unions to limit their wage demands, restricted public spending, and accepted a high rate of unemployment as the price of the fight against inflation. The immediate situation remained very discouraging. Even nature failed to cooperate: in the summer of 1976 the country suffered the worst drought in recorded history. Though inflation fell to a rate of about 15 percent, it stayed higher than in most other industrial countries. Unemployment exceeded the worst figures since the Second World War. The Government avoided a seamen's strike in September 1976, only by allowing a large wage increase which undermined confidence in its determination to fight inflation. As a result the pound fell to a record low, about $1.60, a loss of over half of its value since 1974 and a far cry from its worth of over $4.00 in 1949. Since the dollar too had declined in value this comparison understated the fall of the pound. As proof that it would resist inflation the Government increased the interest rate for home mortgages and cut public spending still more. In return the International Monetary Fund provided a standby credit of almost four billion dollars. Though this gave the country some breathing room, and the profits of offshore oil and gas offer a basis for hope, economic recovery remained sadly distant.

A HERITAGE OF LIBERTY AND ORDER

Britain's greatness does not rise and fall with the value of the pound. It rests on a way of life which most other countries can only envy. For centuries foreigners have puzzled over the happy knack the British show in combining liberty with order. Political democracy, civil liberties, and the rule of law are fragile miracles and should not be taken for granted, but in Britain their future seems more secure than almost anywhere, rooted as they are in universal acceptance, a spirit of compromise, and a rejection of violence as a legitimate way of settling political disputes. Anyone who reads the uncensored British press, observes the police who maintain the peace without firearms, hears a Hyde Park orator speaking in behalf of his cause, or watches a protest demonstration at Trafalgar Square appreciates the British achievement, living as a free people in a largely authoritarian world.

Political restraint grows out of qualities deep in the British character, as for instance, the celebrated British respect for personal privacy. A society in which eccentrics can flourish is also one in which rebels can find tolerance and learn it too. Fair play insists on the right of others to be different, to be wrong, even to be hateful. This restraint is not indifference or coldness. No people has created a more vigorous humanitarian tradition, from the abolition of the slave trade to the Oxfam relief organization today. Rather it reflects a common-sense, practical frame of mind which distrusts abstract doctrines and respects the dignity of the individual. In the silver jubilee year of Queen Elizabeth II Britain remains a country easy to love because of the decency and maturity of her people, the most precious heritage of all.

SUGGESTIONS FOR FURTHER READING

Many of the books mentioned for the two previous chapters also are useful for the years since 1951. The *Annual Register* provides a detailed contemporary narrative. For statistics, see *Britain: an Official Handbook* (published annually), A. H. Halsey, ed., *Trends in British Society since 1900* (1972), and Judith Ryder and Harold Silver, *Modern English Society: History and Structure, 1850-1970* (1970).

Historians are only beginning to study recent British history. Politicians have written numerous memoirs, such as the multi-volume works of Anthony Eden (1960-65) and Harold Macmillan (1966-73), the short, elegant account by R. A. Butler (1971), and Harold Wilson, *A Personal Record: The Labour Government, 1967-1970* (1971). One of the members of Wilson's Cabinet, Richard H. S. Crossman, has published his diaries, (1975-1977). Political scientists have supplied numerous interpretive books and "instant histories," including R. T. McKenzie, *British Political Parties* (2nd ed., 1963), Richard Rose, *Politics in England* (2nd ed., 1974), David Butler and Donald Stokes, *Political Change in Britain* (2nd ed., 1974), and the series of books written by Butler with collaborators on the various general elections and the Common Market referendum. Hugh Thomas, *The Suez Affair* (1967) is a solid study, and Richard Rose, *Northern Ireland* (1976), a useful introduction into the complexities and passions of Ulster.

Anthony Sampson, *New Anatomy of Britain* (1971), and its earlier editions, afford a mainly anecdotal look at the holders of power. Other useful, but essentially journalistic, books include Vernon Bogdanor and Robert Skidelsky, eds., *The Age of Affluence, 1951-1964* (1970); Christopher Booker, *The Neophiliacs: A Study of the Revolution in British Life in the Fifties and Sixties* (1969); and Bernard Levin, *The Pendulum Years: Britain and the Sixties* (1970). Daniel Snowman, *Britain and America: an Interpretation of their Culture, 1945-1975* (1977) provides a comparative perspective. For the study of recent British history the monthly magazine *Encounter* is important to read. For a recent survey, see C. J. Bartlett, *History of Postwar Britain, 1945-1974* (1977).

A number of bibliographies exist which list scores of books and articles, usually arranged by subject headings such as Political History, Cultural and Intellectual History, Religion, and the like. The most comprehensive bibliographies are those jointly produced by the American Historical Association and the Royal Historical Society, of which the following have appeared: Edgar B. Graves, *A Bibliography of English History to 1485* (1975), Conyers Read, *Bibliography of British History. Tudor Period* (2nd edition, 1959), Mary Frear Keeler, *Bibliography of British History. Stuart Period* (2nd edition, 1970), Stanley Pargellis and D. J. Medley, *Bibliography of British History. The Eighteenth Century, 1714-1789* (1951), L. M. Brown and I. R. Christie, *Bibliography of British History, 1789-1851* (1977), H. J. Hanham, *Bibliography of British History, 1851-1914* (1976). A series of bibliographic handbooks prepared under the auspices of the Conference on British Studies is shorter but particularly valuable for citations to articles in scholarly periodicals. The following have appeared: Michael Altschul, *Anglo-Norman England, 1066-1154* (1969), DeLloyd J. Guth, *Late-Medieval England, 1377-1485* (1974), Mortimer Levine, *Tudor England, 1485-1603* (1968), William L. Sachse, *Restoration England, 1660-1689* (1971), Josef L. Altholz, *Victorian England, 1837-1901*

(1970), and Alfred Havighurst, *Modern England, 1901-1970* (1976).

A good series of historical maps is in Martin Gilbert, *British History Atlas* (1969) and in Chris Cook and John Stevensen, *Longman Atlas of Modern British History* (1977). Useful guides to the types of records which exist, and the limitations on understanding the past which result, are to be found in the series "The Sources of History: Studies in the Uses of Historical Evidence" of which the following which deal with England in whole or part have appeared: G. R. Elton, *England, 1200-1640* (1969), T. H. Hollingsworth, *Historical Demography* (1969), and C. L. Mowat, *Great Britain Since 1914* (2nd edition, 1977). A bibliography of articles recently published in historical journals appears three times a year, including a section on "British Commonwealth and Ireland" edited by Frederic A. Youngs, Jr., and Michael E. Moody, in *Recently Published Articles* (published by the American Historical Association). A critique of historical writings since World War II is in G. R. Elton's *Modern Historians on British History, 1485-1945. A Critical Bibliography, 1945-1969* (1970). W. B. Stephens' *Sources for English Local History* (1973) can help develop a fuller understanding of English communities. The principal historical journals which deal particularly in English history are *English Historical Review, Historical Journal* (formerly *Cambridge Historical Journal*), *Bulletin of the Institute of Historical Research, Past & Present, Economic History Review, History, Journal of British Studies,* and *Albion*, the last two published in the United States.

Appendix

KINGS AND QUEENS OF ENGLAND

Important Kings Before the Norman Conquest

Bretwealdas
c.   477–491   Aelle, King of the West Saxons
c.   560–584   Caelwin, King of the West Saxons
     584–616   Aethelbert, King of Kent
c.   600–616   Raedwald, King of East Anglia
     616–632   Edwin, King of Northumbria
     633–641   Oswald, King of Northumbria
     654–670   Oswiu, King of Northumbria

King of Mercia
     758–796   Offa

Kings of the West Saxons
     802–839   Egbert
     866–871   Aethelraed
     871–899   Alfred
     899–925   Edward the Elder

Rulers of England
     959–975   Edgar the Peaceable
     979–1016   Aethelraed the Redeless
    1016–1035   Cnut
    1042–1066   Edward the Confessor
    1066   Harold Godwinson

Normans
    1066–1087   William I
    1087–1100   William II
    1100–1135   Henry I
    1135–1154   Stephen

Angevins-Plantagenets
    1154–1189   Henry II
    1189–1199   Richard I
    1199–1216   John
    1216–1272   Henry III
    1272–1307   Edward I
    1307–1327   Edward II
    1327–1377   Edward III
    1377–1399   Richard II

Lancastrians

1399—1413	Henry IV
1413—1422	Henry V
1422—1461	Henry VI

Yorkists

1461—1483	Edward IV
1483	Edward V
1483—1485	Richard III

Tudors

1485—1509	Henry VII
1509—1547	Henry VIII
1547—1553	Edward VI
1553—1558	Mary (I)
1558—1603	Elizabeth I

Stuarts

1603—1625	James I
1625—1649	Charles I
1649—1660	Commonwealth and Protectorate
1660—1685	Charles II
1685—1688	James II
1688—1702	William III and Mary (II)
1702—1714	Anne

Hanoverians

1714—1727	George I
1727—1760	George II
1760—1820	George III
1820—1830	George IV
1830—1837	William IV
1837—1901	Victoria
1901—1910	Edward VII
1910—1936	George V (House of Windsor)
1936	Edward VIII
1936—1952	George VI
1952—	Elizabeth II

PRIME MINISTERS OF ENGLAND

1721-1742	Sir Robert Walpole	
1742-1744	John Carteret	
1744-1754	Henry Pelham	
1754-1756	Duke of Newcastle	
1756-1757	William Pitt, the Elder	
1757-1761	Pitt the Elder and the Duke of Newcastle	
1761-1762	Duke of Newcastle and Lord Bute	
1762-1763	Lord Bute	
1763-1765	George Grenville	
1765-1766	Lord Rockingham	
1766-1768	William Pitt, Lord Chatham	
1768-1770	Duke of Grafton	
1770-1782	Lord North	
1782	Lord Rockingham	
1782-1783	Lord Shelburne	
1783	Charles James Fox and Lord North	
1783-1801	William Pitt, the Younger	
1801-1804	Henry Addington	
1804-1806	William Pitt, the Younger	*Party*
1806-1807	Charles James Fox	*Distinctions*
1807-1809	Duke of Portland	*Begin*
1809-1812	Spencer Perceval	
1812-1827	Lord Liverpool	Tory
1827	George Canning	Tory
1827	Lord Goderich	Tory
1828-1830	Duke of Wellington	Tory
1830-1834	Earl Grey	Whig
1834	Lord Melbourne	Whig
1834-1835	Sir Robert Peel	Tory
1835-1841	Lord Melbourne	Whig
1841-1846	Sir Robert Peel	Tory
1846-1852	Lord John Russell	Whig
1852	Lord Derby and Benjamin Disraeli	Tory
1852-1855	Lord Aberdeen	Coalition
1855-1858	Lord Palmerston	Whig
1858-1859	Lord Derby and Benjamin Disraeli	Tory
1859-1865	Lord Palmerston	Whig
1865-1866	Lord John Russell	Whig
1866-1868	Lord Derby and Benjamin Disraeli	Tory
1868-1874	William E. Gladstone	Whig-Liberal
1874-1880	Benjamin Disraeli	Tory-Conservative
1880-1885	William Gladstone	Whig-Liberal
1885-1886	Lord Salisbury	Tory-Conservative
1886	William Gladstone	Liberal

1886-1892	Lord Salisbury	Tory-Conservative
1892-1894	William Gladstone	Liberal
1894-1895	Lord Rosebery	Liberal
1895-1902	Lord Salisbury	Conservative-Unionist
1902-1905	Arthur Balfour	Conservative-Unionist
1905-1908	Sir Henry Campbell-Bannerman	Liberal
1908-1916	Herbert A. Asquith	Liberal
1916-1922	David Lloyd George	Coalition
1922-1923	Andrew Bonar Law	Conservative-Unionist
1923-1924	Stanley Baldwin	Conservative
1924	J. Ramsay MacDonald	Labor
1924-1929	Stanley Baldwin	Conservative
1929-1931	Ramsay MacDonald	Labor
1931-1935	Ramsay MacDonald	National Government
1935-1937	Stanley Baldwin	Conservative
1937-1940	Neville Chamberlain	Conservative
1940-1945	Winston Churchill	Conservative
1945-1951	Clement Attlee	Labor
1951-1955	Winston Churchill	Conservative
1955-1957	Sir Anthony Eden	Conservative
1957-1963	Sir Harold Macmillan	Conservative
1963-1964	Sir Alec Douglas-Home	Conservative
1964-1970	Harold Wilson	Labor
1970-1974	Edward Heath	Conservative
1974-1976	Harold Wilson	Labor
1976-1979	James Callaghan	Labor
1979-	Margaret Thatcher	Conservative

Index